READING HOMER'S *ODYSSEY*

READING HOMER'S *ODYSSEY*

Kostas Myrsiades

Bucknell University | University Press
Lewisburg, Pennsylvania

Library of Congress Cataloging-in-Publication Data

Names: Myrsiades, Kostas, author.
Title: Reading Homer's Odyssey / by Kostas Myrsiades.
Description: Lewisburg, PA : Bucknell University Press, 2019. | Includes bibliographical references and index.
Identifiers: LCCN 2018058895 | ISBN 9781684481361 (pbk. : alk. paper) | ISBN 9781684481316 (hc-plc : alk. paper)
Subjects: LCSH: Homer. Odyssey.
Classification: LCC PA4167 .M97 2019 | DDC 883/.01—dc23
LC record available at http://lccn.loc.gov/2018058895

A British Cataloging-in-Publication record for this book is available from the British Library.

∞ The paper used in this publication meets the requirements of the American National Standard for Information Sciences—Permanence of Paper for Printed Library Materials, ANSI Z39.48-1992.

www.bucknell.edu/UniversityPress

Distributed worldwide by Rutgers University Press

Manufactured in the United States of America

To Linda,

who has shared my own odyssey for over a half century,
and to my children and grandchildren,
who would like to know what I do now that I have retired

CONTENTS

PREFACE

Reading Homer's "Odyssey" is a book-by-book commentary on the epic based on forty-two years of reading and teaching the *Odyssey* to both graduate and undergraduate students in a variety of courses and seminars. Among the many essays and books written on the *Odyssey* that inform this reading, a selection for further reading for each of the twenty-four books of the epic is included at the end of each book's commentary. The reading is intended primarily for comparative and general literature courses on Homer's epics taught in translation, but not merely as a written aid to be referred to in simplifying a complex work. Rather, it attempts to present the *Odyssey* as a unified and coherent work of literature (with lapses due to its beginnings in an oral tradition).

However, the reading is neither a critical study nor a study on the epic's authorship or the nature of its orality. Analysts, a movement given birth by A. F. Wolf in 1795, still argue that both the *Iliad* and *Odyssey* were composed by many hands, while Unitarians, dominant in the twentieth century, argue for a single authorship. In the 1930s, Milman Parry added to the debate by suggesting the epic's oral nature, which gave rise to a group called the Oralists. In the mid-twentieth century, Ioannis Kakrides proposed yet another group, the Neoanalysts, a kind of Unitarian movement arguing that a single author had used earlier poems to create his own. Since then, various approaches to reading the *Odyssey* have appeared using narratology, structuralism, ecocriticism, feminism, psychoanalysis, and poststructuralism, among other literary movements. The present commentary assumes the *Odyssey* was written by a single author (named Homer) who might also be the author of the *Iliad*, or at least one familiar with that epic, and who considered his work a continuation of and a response to the *Iliad*. The many inconsistencies and lapses throughout the *Odyssey* further point to a Homer who built his work on previous oral versions of the narrative, which he integrated into a unique whole and set to writing between 620 and 600 B.C.E.

Although the *Odyssey* continues the Trojan War myth long after the *Iliad* narrative ends (with Hector's death) and shares many of the same themes and values of that epic, it is also a response to the *Iliad*'s warrior culture to which it is compared and which it finds inadequate in a post-Trojan world. After Achilles' death and the defeat of Troy by using Odysseus' ploy of the wooden horse (neither of these two events is part of the *Iliad*), Odysseus, among other surviving heroes, prepares his return home. It is at that point that Homer's Odysseus enters a world in which survival depends on one's ingenuity and agility (*mētis*)[1] rather than strength alone (*biē*). Although the post-Iliadic warrior still seeks fame (*kleos*) and gifts (*gerā*) with which to measure his worth, he must now acquire them not through prowess in battle alone but also through intelligence if his *nostos* (homecoming) is to be realized.

This reading of the *Odyssey* addresses a number of themes repeated throughout the epic. Among the epic's most prevalent, hospitality (*xenia*) is the most defining for a warrior's successful return, since in Homer's seventh-century B.C.E. world the returning veteran's only option for food and lodgings, besides thievery, depends on the generosity of those who welcome him on the way. The importance of offering hospitality to strangers, respected by both hosts and guests, is under the jurisdiction of the Greeks' premier god, Zeus Xenios, the god of strangers and travelers. Those who obey Zeus's sacred law are rewarded and those who break it are punished, as numerous episodes illustrate. In addition, hospitality makes possible the accumulation of additional wealth. Since in the preliterate world of Homer's heroes one's worth is measured in tangible objects, gifts received and treasure amassed through raids increase one's worth. The greater the number of gifts and goods stockpiled, the greater the fame, which in turn secures one's reputation and immortality. Mortality is ephemeral; the only immortality available to humans is to be remembered and honored for their deeds and wealth in the memories of present and future generations. For mortals, who operate in a world of struggle, action, and endurance, the immortality of the gods is undesirable, a living death of inaction and stagnation, which conceals humankind's achievements and causes them to go unnoticed and unsung.

However, force and agility of mind alone are insufficient if one lacks the assistance of the Olympian gods. Honoring and sacrificing to the gods is yet another theme, which if neglected ends in negative outcomes but if observed yields positive ones. Although the Olympians demand their due of every human action, Zeus early in the epic also stresses self-reliance. The gods help only those who listen to their advice and do not allow their instincts to override their reason.

In the Odyssean journey, mortals seek experience and knowledge to aid them in bringing order and peace to a chaotic world lacking the guidance of god and king. Humans look beyond the interests of self to the interests of the community. Unlike the *Iliad*, which emphasizes the individual achievement, the *Odyssey* praises the virtues of home and family. Family unity and cooperation, illustrated by Odysseus' and Alcinous' families, achieve more positive results, whereas a disconnected family like Agamemnon's ends in grief. A family unit dominates when each family member works for the good of the whole and each family member knows his or her place within the group. Men govern the state (*polis*), while women's domain is the home (*oikos*). Allegiance and honest service to one's master and to his or her possessions are rewarded, as exemplified by the faithful servants in Odysseus' household. Homer's epic values the civilized, proper behavior, and etiquette over the uncivilized, a life of ease, inactivity, and stagnation. The *Odyssey* is an epic based on principles that reveal the disasters that befall men's unlawful ways and their disrespect of the gods.

Reading Homer's "Odyssey," which begins and ends in Ithaca, is presented in two equal parts: an external homecoming (*Od.* 1–12) consisting of three tetrads and an internal homecoming (*Od.* 13–24) composed of three tetrads.

I. External homecoming
   A. Telemachus' Journey (*Od.* 1–4): The present situation in Ithaca is outlined and Telemachus' journey, which provides the prince with the experience and knowledge needed to rule effectively, is described.
   B. Odysseus from Calypso to the Phaeacians (*Od.* 5–8): The captive hero, Odysseus, is released by the nymph Calypso to reach the Phaeacians, who entertain him and ferry him home.
   C. Odysseus' Wanderings (*Od.* 9–12): Odysseus narrates his ten years of wandering to the Phaeacians.

II. Internal homecoming
   A. Odysseus and Telemachus at Eumaeus' Hut (*Od.* 13–16): Odysseus arrives at the swineherd's (Eumaeus') hut to reveal himself to his son and to plot the suitors' demise.
   B. Odysseus and Telemachus Strategize at the Palace (*Od.* 17–20): Odysseus, in disguise, returns with his son and Eumaeus to his palace to battle the suitors.
   C. Revenge, Reunion, and Reconciliation (*Od.* 21–24): Odysseus, his son, and his faithful herdsmen defeat the suitors, and the hero is reunited with his wife and father and reconciled with the Ithacans.

The discussion of each of the epic's twenty-four books is further partitioned into sections (and subsections when deemed necessary) wherever Homer's text permits in order to stress the length and the importance placed on specific topics and episodes. Percentages of a book's total size are provided for each of these sections to further demonstrate the significance Homer places on various topics and episodes, enabling the reader to evaluate the emphasis given to certain themes and topics (e.g., the Cyclops' episode occupies 81% of *Od.*9, whereas the Cicones' and Lotus Eaters' episodes in the same book occupy 8% and 4%, respectively). Endnotes are provided throughout to clarify and complete myths that Homer leaves unfinished, to explain certain terms and phrases, and to furnish background information whenever necessary. Finally, an exhaustive general bibliography on the *Odyssey* completes the reading of the epic.

The reading further calls attention to Homer's narrative techniques—digressions, similes, irony, symbolism, inconsistencies, repetitions, prophecies, and divine forecasts. Throughout his narrative, Homer often digresses to provide backstories of characters introduced for the first time in order to enhance their standing as people with families and backgrounds rather than presenting them merely as positive or negative figures. The same holds true for objects (e.g., Odysseus' scar and bow), which play a major role in the epic. The many elaborate similes used compare the author's characters to everyday local events and to animals to further reveal their psychology and to contrast the differences between instinct and reason, the monstrous and the civilized, order and chaos, the rational and the irrational, and mortals and immortals. Irony is used to illustrate the unpredictability of life and how wishes and hopes often turn bitter. Prophecies and divine forecasts constantly inform the reader of the epic's inevitable end. Inconsistencies and repetitions are noted in the discussion to explain the epic's oral beginnings and inform the reader of possible earlier versions of the *Odyssey* used to stitch together Homer's narrative.

Throughout the text, commentary is integrated with Homer's text to provide a seamless telling of the *Odyssey* narrative. Special significance is given to the early recognition of the beggar/Odysseus by Penelope and his household staff, since this is an area of controversy in *Odyssey* scholarship.

Other major topics and themes of interest commented on include the purpose of Telemachus' journey, Odysseus' rejection of Calypso's offer of immortality, the cinematic qualities of the epic's structure, the nature and purpose of Odysseus' many lies, Homer's use of various myths to comment on the larger homecoming narrative, the use of the Atreus myth to contrast Odysseus' family unit to that of Agamemnon's, women's role in the epic, the oral singer's function in preserving in memory great deeds, and a discussion of the *Odyssey*'s true ending.

The manuscript is keyed to Richmond Lattimore's 1967 translation of the *Odyssey* (Harper and Row), from which the quotations used are taken. It is the author's contention that Lattimore's English verse translation comes closer than any other available to approximating the Greek of Homer's *Odyssey* line by line. The Greek text utilized is A. T. Murray's two-volume set in the Loeb Classical Library series (Homer, *The Odyssey*, trans. A. T. Murray, rev. George E. Dimock, 2 vols. [Cambridge, MA: Harvard University Press, 1995]).

READING HOMER'S *ODYSSEY*

PART I

FROM ITHACA TO WONDERLAND

CHAPTER 1

TELEMACHUS' JOURNEY (*OD.* 1–4)

Book 1

The *Odyssey* of Homer (seventh-century B.C.E.) is a long oral narrative poem of 12,109 lines that emerges out of the *Iliad*'s warrior society (patriarchal, polytheistic, monarchical, and slaveholding), in which losing one's honor is tantamount to losing one's worth as a warrior. Once its hero, Odysseus, leaves Troy, however, he enters a different world with different moral values.

The epic begins with a unit of four books usually referred to as the *Telemachia*, or the books of Telamachus, Odysseus' son. In these books, the young prince matures and learns the lessons of kingship in order to aid his father upon his return to regain his kingdom from his mother's suitors. The poem, like the *Iliad*, opens with an invocation (the proem) in which the poet seeks inspiration from the Muse, a goddess,[1] to assist him in reciting his tale, but it is not narrated chronologically. It begins with Telemachus in Ithaca at the same time that Odysseus prepares to leave Calypso's island (in *Od.* 5; his eleventh of twelve adventures), where he spends seven years. From Calypso, he sails to his twelfth adventure on Scheria (*Od.* 6–8), where he recites his earlier adventures (*Od.* 9–12), and from there is conveyed to Ithaca after an absence of twenty years (*Od.* 13–24). Thus, Homer begins his narrative in Ithaca (*Od.* 1–4) and ends it in Ithaca (*Od.* 13–24), using this geographically real locale to frame a mythic one (*Od.* 5–12).

Od. 1 covers the first day of the *Odyssey* narrative (de Jong, *Narratological*, 588), which for the present reading is divided as follows:[2]

- I. Introduction (21%)[3]
  - A. Proem
  - B. Odysseus' aborted homecoming
  - C. Council of the gods
- II. Ithaca (79%)
  - A. Athena visits Telemachus in Ithaca
  - B. Telemachus with the suitors

I. Introduction

I.A. Proem, 1–10. By invoking the Muse to tell the story through him, Homer alerts his audience that he cannot recite his tale uninspired. The oral tradition from which the *Odyssey* emerged concretizes the abstract (inspiration/Muse). The author becomes an intermediary between the goddess and the audience, a special individual through whom the tale is told. The epic's first word, *andra* (man), highlights the epic's overall theme,[4] the story of a warrior returning home after a twenty-year absence. Homer does not say, "Tell me, Muse, of Odysseus," but rather, "Tell me, Muse, of the man," implying a more inclusive journey of man in general, one who through endurance, courage, and an agile mind weathers life's storms to reach his destination. Odysseus is such a man, "the man of many ways" (*polytropos*), a term that stresses the hero's ability to change with the changing times, and one who considers all options before choosing the best one. Versatility (*polytropia*) enables him to return home, whereas his companions and other returning veterans who lack it perish.

Homer first inquires how Odysseus' homecoming was detained after he sacked Troy's sacred citadel (1.1–2).[5] In other words, Odysseus is punished for plundering a god's temple. The killings he committed in Troy during the ten-year-long siege are not mentioned, nor are his affairs with Circe and Calypso. Like Jehovah, who does not tolerate disobedience in the Old Testament, the Homeric gods punish those who trespass against them, but Odysseus' trespass is not as heinous as that of his companions, who devoured the oxen of Helius.[6] The hero's suffering then lasts until his debt to the gods is paid, whereas his companions die for their greater crime. Thus, it is not Odysseus' fault that he returns without his companions to Ithaca; rather, his companions' fate is the result of their own "wild recklessness" (1.7). Odysseus tries to prevent their deadly action but cannot, although he tries, and thus Zeus takes away their day of homecoming. It is at this point that Homer's Muse begins the tale of Odysseus' *nostos* (1.9–10).

One wonders why Homer refers only to the companions who devoured the sun's oxen, since most of Odysseus' men are lost in the Laestrygonian episode (eleven of his twelve ships; see *Od.* 10); another seventy-two men die in the Cicones episode (*Od.* 9), and six men are devoured by the Cyclops (*Od.* 9). By the time Odysseus reaches Thrinacia, the sun's island (*Od.* 12), only one ship remains. Perhaps Homer isolates that adventure in the proem because Odysseus finally finds himself completely alone to make his way to Calypso's island, from where his homecoming is assured, as tradition requires. Further, the Thrinacia adventure stresses death to those who transgress against the gods, whereas Odysseus' other mythic adventures do not.

I.B. Odysseus' Aborted Homecoming, 11–26. The invocation over, three questions are posed:

1. Where is Odysseus?
2. Why was his homecoming aborted?
3. How is his homecoming to be achieved?

First, Odysseus is the last warrior to reach his destination alive and is detained by Calypso, who wants to make him her husband. Second, his aborted homecoming is due to his archenemy, Poseidon (the sea), who refuses to give him the necessary weather. Third, Poseidon, away visiting the Ethiopians, gives the other Olympians the opportunity to force him to abort his anger; alone and against the will of all the gods, Poseidon cannot utterly destroy Odysseus.

In his absence, the Olympians meet at the insistence of Athena. But why is Odysseus to be released now? Why did the goddess not ask for his release earlier? There are two possible answers. First, Athena's wrath against the Greek warriors has only now run its course. Homer never quite explains what caused Athena's anger other than to suggest that Hermes made it clear to Calypso that, on their voyage home, the Greeks offended her, and she let loose an evil tempest against them (5.108–109). Her anger finally abated, Athena requests Odysseus' release from captivity. Second, her request coincides with the visit by Odysseus' archenemy, Poseidon, to the Ethiopians, an opportune moment to end the hero's wanderings, which, out of respect for her uncle, the sea, who hampers Odysseus' return, she was unable to achieve earlier.

I.C. Council of the Gods, 27–95. At the council, Zeus questions why mortals blame the gods for their ills when it is their own recklessness that is responsible for the evils they suffer (1.32–34). The gods, then, are not completely responsible for mortals' actions. Mortals are not mere puppets; fate alone is not responsible for their actions, but rather their "own recklessness" earns them sorrow beyond what fate grants. As illustration, Zeus turns to the House of Atreus.[7] In Homer's version, Aegisthus marries the wife of his first cousin Agamemnon once he leaves for Troy and then has Agamemnon and his men killed at a banquet honoring their return. Although Aegisthus is warned not to kill him or court his wife (1.39), he ignores the gods' warning, and Orestes, Agamemnon's son, later kills him in turn. This myth, referenced in six of the epic's twenty-four books (*Od.* 1, 3, 4, 11, 13, and 24),[8] serves as an example to those who fail to heed the gods' advice. Although the gods point out the right path, ultimately the decision rests with the individual. Second, the myth sets up parallels between Odysseus' family (Odysseus, Penelope, and Telemachus) and Agamemnon's (Agamemnon, Clytemnestra, and Orestes). In Homer's view, agreement and like-mindedness (*homophrosunē*) between husband and wife lead to prosperity and unity, whereas disagreement between a couple leads to disaster, not only for the couple but for the entire nuclear family. Clytemnestra's infidelity, which leads to her husband's murder, also affects their son Orestes, who, according to custom, is required to avenge his father's death. The Atreus myth not only contrasts positive and negative family units but serves as a warning for Penelope and Telemachus, whose situation could lead to disaster for Odysseus. Will Penelope remain faithful to her husband and resist pressure to marry one of the suitors? Will Telemachus assist his father upon his return and, like Orestes, avenge him should his mother falter?

Athena agrees that Aegisthus' death was merited; anyone acting as he did should suffer the same fate. But she feels sorry for Odysseus because he is still languishing at Calypso's, who is using her feminine charms to hold him against his will (although he shares her bed for seven years). Calypso is identified as the daughter of Atlas, the "malignant" (*oloōphron*) who, tradition says, led the Titans (rulers of the universe before the Olympians) in a rebellion against Zeus. *Oloōphron* is used for two other characters in the epic: Aietes (10.137), Medea's father and Circe's brother, and Minos (11.322), a Cretan king and Zeus's son who judges the dead in the underworld. Perhaps the association of *oloōphron* with three dangerous characters with ties to Circe and Calypso underscores the quandary Odysseus finds himself in, which requires divine intervention.

Athena queries Zeus (1.62) concerning Odysseus' delayed homecoming, which surprises the father of the gods, since he admires both Odysseus' intelligence and his devotion to the gods (1.65–67). He points to Poseidon as the cause of his delayed homecoming, citing his grudge against Odysseus for blinding the Cyclops, his son (a brief digression intervenes again to identify the Cyclops' father and mother and the circumstances of his birth [1.70–73]). However, Odysseus was pursued by Poseidon even before the Cyclops' blinding (9.67–69, 80–81). It would seem Homer prefers to blame Poseidon rather than Athena's wrath for the delayed homecoming. The choice of Poseidon, the sea, not only is a more realistic one but also negates a lengthy explanation for Athena's change of heart. Nevertheless, the gods' council (1.27–95) clarifies four points:

1. Odysseus is held captive, and his relationship with Calypso is forced.
2. Zeus's fondness for Odysseus is due to his intellect and his respect for the gods (emphasizing *mētis* [mind] over *biē* [strength]).
3. Odysseus' homecoming is deterred because he plundered Troy's citadel and incurred the gods' anger.
4. Odysseus' *nostos* is due to Olympian unity, which overrides Poseidon's single objection.

Once Odysseus' release is enabled, Athena turns to Telemachus. She will go to Ithaca to bring about his journey to seek news of his father, which will give him the confidence he lacks as a prince and enable him to gain some standing (*kleos*) as Odysseus' son. She also proposes that Hermes, the messenger god, be sent to Calypso to announce Odysseus' release. These two actions occur concurrently—Athena's journey to Ithaca (*Od.* 1) and Hermes' journey to Calypso (*Od.* 5).

Two characteristics of Homer's narrative technique are by now apparent. First, most of *Od.* 1 is presented in direct speech, a practice accounting for about 50 percent of the entire epic, which molds the *Odyssey* into a dramatic piece with a multitude of contributing voices, a format allowing Homer to delve into the psychology of his characters. This is especially explicit in the Helen-Menelaus exchange (*Od.* 4) and later in Odysseus' narration of his adventures (*Od.* 9–12). Second, it is Homer's modus operandi to provide brief biographical sketches of characters who have key roles in the epic. He momentarily retards the main narrative to introduce such personages, as in the case of Polyphemus (1.70–74) and Eurycleia

(1.428–433). These character introductions are given a brief synopsis, which includes the names of their parents and even grandparents, as well as their place of residence. Each character becomes part of a family unit and is loved and mourned by someone; each individual life is precious (seen more insistently in the *Iliad*, where most of the hundreds of warriors who are slaughtered on the battlefield are given an identity of at least a line or two, presenting him or her as a life that matters rather than as a nameless annihilated soul). The emphasis on family unity is a major *Odyssey* theme, which is contrasted in the families of Odysseus and Agamemnon and in the idealized family of Alcinous (*Od.* 6–8), where all its members work for the benefit and happiness of each other.

II. Ithaca

II.A. Athena Visits Telemachus in Ithaca, 96–323. When Athena alights on Ithaca disguised as Mentes (gods, except in rare cases, appear to mortals only in disguise; in this case, a family friend who never appears in propria persona), she encounters the "haughty" (1.106; *agēnor*) suitors, a word that describes them again later, in 1.144. From the reader's first encounter with these men seeking Penelope's hand, they are characterized as haughty, lofty, insolent, and prideful. Telemachus, noticing Mentes/Athena is neglected by the suitors, is scandalized that the hospitality due a stranger is not observed. He welcomes the stranger, promises entertainment and dinner, and only then inquires about the guest's purpose. The lengthy passage that follows (fifty-nine lines) provides the reader with some first impressions of the young prince and the situation in Ithaca.

1. By contrasting the ways in which the two groups are served, the passage emphasizes the importance of hospitality and the distinction between proper and improper behavior, a civilized decorum versus the "haughty" suitors' uncivilized manners. For Mentes/Athena and Telemachus, water is poured from a "golden pitcher" held in a "silver basin"; they eat on a "polished table" and drink from "golden

goblets." For the suitors, only the food and drink are emphasized—they are served bread "heaped up in baskets," and they drink from "mixing bowls." For the civilized Mentes/Athena, quality is stressed over quantity; for the less civilized suitors, content takes precedence.

2. The passage introduces Telemachus as a courteous, intelligent, and cautious young man but at the same time helpless and inexperienced as he sits among the suitors grieving and watching his inheritance depleted. He first relieves Mentes/Athena of his spear and places it next to Odysseus' spear rack, honoring him while at the same time demonstrating caution in disarming a guest before carefully seating him apart from the suitors, fearing the uproar might affect the guest's appetite. At the same time, he provides the privacy needed to question him out of earshot of the suitors.
3. The passage introduces the first of two bards in the *Odyssey*, Phemius (the other is Demodocus in *Od.* 8), who entertains the suitors because they force him (1.154), implying his discomfort in performing for the suitors (which saves him from slaughter at the end of the epic).

Finding the opportunity to confide in his guest, Telemachus muses about a father he believes dead, who would send the suitors scurrying from the palace, a feat he is unable to carry out himself. Telemachus hungers for male companionship, a father figure he can turn to for help. After all, Telemachus has been brought up by women since birth. His grandfather Laertes no longer resides in the palace but instead lives in the country, cared for by an old woman ever since Odysseus left for Troy. Eumaeus, the swineherd, who later presents himself as a father figure, by his own account hardly comes to Ithaca but instead stays on his farm. The prince has no one to guide him and teach him the ways of a ruler. Thus, Mentes/Athena suggests a journey to Pylos and Sparta, where he will be exposed to the way of kings.

Mentes/Athena identifies himself as a merchant, a guest-friend of Odysseus in search of bronze in exchange for iron. However, iron, available in

Homer's seventh-century B.C.E. world, was not available during the period of the Trojan War (ca. 1184 B.C.E.), the Age of Bronze. Such inconsistencies, which become more pronounced in the *Odyssey*, are due perhaps to the existence of multiple versions of the *Odyssey* (and many Homers?), parts of which were edited into the version we possess today. Seeing the prince besieged by suitors seeking to marry his mother and deprive him of his inheritance, and in desperate need of a mentor who could help him gain confidence and experience to deal with his enemies, Mentes/Athena offers him that confidence. He alerts Telemachus that his father is alive and held captive somewhere. In even stronger terms, the goddess offers him a prophecy. Although at present a captive, Odysseus will soon be home. The goddess then asks whether he is Odysseus' son (1.207). Posing this question has a double purpose. First, she reminds him that he is of an age to be in charge. Second, she is giving him the confidence he needs by reminding him of his lineage. Telemachus' ambivalent statement that only his mother knows whose son he is (1.215–216) emphasizes his confusion about his own identity and the role he should play.

This important exchange also contrasts Penelope, the good wife, with Clytemnestra, the bad wife. Penelope waits faithfully for twenty years for her husband's return. In Homer's patriarchal society, a man must know his legitimate heirs, who will inherit his property and wealth, which is possible only if a wife is above reproach. A man's sexual encounters, on the other hand, like Odysseus' affairs with Circe and Calypso, do not affect the continuation of his legitimate line and are not cause for condemnation. Athena's inquiry calls attention to the fact that Telemachus does not know the father who left him as an infant and relies on his mother's word that he is indeed his father's son. In a society in which one's identity is so tied up with one's lineage, Telemachus takes his on faith. By questioning his birth, Mentes/Athena assures him that the gods have not given him a birth that will go nameless (1.222).

The goddess next questions the purpose for the ongoing festivities in the palace (1.225–226). She asks Telemachus what occasion (such as a wedding, a public festival, or a communal dinner) necessitates such a gathering. In other words, if it is not a holiday or an important event, such revels are inappropriate. It is one thing to offer hospitality to a guest and another to party without purpose. Hospitality is protected by divine law, by Zeus Xenios,[9] for good reason. Without it, travel becomes impossible. To move from one place to another in Homer's Greek world requires the goodwill of strangers to provide food and lodgings. However, the cooperation of both guest and host is needed. A traveler depends on the goodwill of the host as much as the host depends on the good behavior of the guest. To ensure a guest-host relationship, identification is not required until the guest is fed and cared for, and by the same token a guest cannot abuse a host's kindness (by abducting one's wife, for example, as Paris did by running away with his host Menelaus' wife, Helen, causing the Trojan War). The emphasis on hospitality in the epic distinguishes the civilized from the barbarous (the Cyclops and the suitors). It is for this reason that Mentes/Athena questions the banquet's purpose in Odysseus' *megaron* (great hall). Not only do the suitors behave arrogantly and disgracefully, but they are doing so at an illegitimate function (1.227–229).

The goddess' concerns empower Telemachus to voice his own personal worries: his inheritance and his honor. First, a once-prosperous house has fallen in disrepair for lack of a man to turn the tide, which diminishes his fortune. Second, the way he supposes his father died at sea lessens his own fame and honor (*kleos* and *timē*). An ignoble end (dying unsung and unmourned) stigmatizes his father and taints his own fame and honor. Immortality for mortals is to have one's deeds live on in the memory of others and not disappear into oblivion. Had Odysseus died a hero in Troy, he would have won great fame for both of them, stressing the importance of one's genealogy to one's identity. Telemachus is also unhappy about his powerlessness against the suitors, which is complicated by his mother's indecisiveness regarding whether to refuse or accept a hateful marriage and make an end of the matter. Telemachus seems to harbor a feeling of resentment toward his mother, who is not in a hurry to marry, thus preventing him from his inheritance (although, as we discover later, the suitors have other ideas concerning his fortune).

To improve how both he and his father will be remembered, Telemachus needs the physical grave that the Achaeans would have heaped over his father had he died in battle, for without a physical marker, a hero's fame does not exist. One needs news (another meaning of *kleos*) to keep Odysseus' memory alive, as Athena indicated at the gods' council, the reason for sending Telemachus to Sparta and Pylos to ask after his father's homecoming. Fame and glory can only be disseminated through hearsay, eyewitness accounts, personal testimony, and any other form of oral news. In this respect fame, glory and honor become synonymous with news, reports, and rumors, all legitimate meanings of *kleos*. Telemachus' other concern, his inheritance, needs a person possessing rhetorical and intellectual prowess, along with physical strength, to safeguard it, but these qualities, which further define the Homeric hero, are still lacking in the youthful prince.

Full of indignation at Telemachus' situation, Mentes/Athena reminds him of the necessity for Odysseus' presence and relates the myth of Odysseus in search of poison arrows (1.259–265).[10] Homer periodically incorporates myths in the epic to create a quilt of mythology that serves as commentary on the larger narrative of Odysseus' *nostos* and the hero's psychology. In presenting Odysseus as a destroyer of men who is in search of poison, Mentes/Athena portrays a character to be feared, one who will show little mercy upon his return. In the *Odyssey*, wishes and predictions made by gods and prophets are realized. Through such predictions, Homer assures the reader that his tale will eventually return to its established course, regardless of the narrative's many digressions. Mentes/Athena must convince Telemachus of the plausibility of his father's return (1.197, 200, 203) so he will do her bidding, since he believes his father dead (1.166–168), but Telemachus is not persuaded. It will take Menelaus in *Od.* 4 to at least sway him to entertain the possibility of his return. Athena, nevertheless, must prepare Telemachus for his father's eventual homecoming, and some 168 lines after her arrival, the goddess reveals the real purpose for her presence—to convince him of the following:

1. Telemachus should call an assembly to request that the suitors return to their homes.
2. Telemachus should send his mother to her father, Icarius, for marriage preparations.
3. Telemachus should avail himself of Athena's services.

In other words, the goddess stands ready to assist, but, as Zeus warns in lines 33–34, the choice is his. He must now take the initiative to act on his father's behalf (as Orestes did for Agamemnon):

1. Travel to Pylos and Sparta to seek news of Odysseus.
2. Wait one year before taking any action should he discover his father alive.
3. Should he discover his father has died, return and build a tomb in his father's honor, give his mother in marriage, and kill the suitors by treachery or openly (1.296; signaling the suitors' deaths are sanctioned by the gods).

He is now of an age to take matters into his own hands, and he should not continue clinging to his childhood. Turning to the Atreus myth again, the goddess compares Telemachus to Orestes, who avenged his father's death by killing both his mother (Clytemnestra) and his father's cousin (Aegisthus), winning great glory for himself. A son must avenge the father and inherit the father's wealth. The mother, a possession herself, claims no rights to her husband's property; in his absence, she is under male control (her son or father). Unlike Aegisthus, the "thoughtful"[11] Telemachus heeds the goddess' advice and in the end prevails. Upon departing, Mentes/Athena reminds Telemachus to do her bidding (1.305).

Telemachus, again eager to demonstrate his good breeding, invites the disguised goddess to bathe, rest, and receive a gift, the duty of a host to his guest. The value of tangible gifts (*gerā*) not only bestows honor on an individual but also increases one's fame. It is for that reason that Odysseus cannot return empty-handed; to do so would be to return without honor. Eager to leave, the goddess asks Telemachus to hold the intended gift until her return; the quality of the gift offered determines the quality received. In other words, he will be repaid in kind for observing the laws of hospitality. Full of determination and courage, his morale boosted by Mentes/Athena and aware of a god's presence (1.323), Telemachus returns to the suitors' feast rejuvenated.

Athena leaves without her spear, which played a prominent role when she first alighted on Ithaca. That Athena leaves without it is either an oversight (epic inconsistency) or intentional. Perhaps, it signals her eventual return and symbolically predicts the conflict to come.

II.B. Telemachus with the Suitors, 324–444. At the feast, Phemius sings of the Greeks' homecoming, "which Pallas Athene had inflicted upon them" (1.327), a song that reinforces the idea that Athena, and not Poseidon, was the cause of the Greeks' delayed, and in many cases unrealized, homecomings. Penelope modestly appears for the first time in the epic (her sense of decorum marked by two attendants and the veil in front of her face) to beg Phemius for a happier tune (the present one makes her long for Odysseus). Telemachus, perhaps emboldened by Mentes/Athena, resents his mother's interference and wants to show that he is in control. Athena assumes that household authority is his when she later tells him to give his mother to a husband (1.292). As it turns out, his enthusiasm is only bluster, as the reader realizes at the Ithacan assembly of *Od.* 2. Nevertheless, he takes offense at his mother's request and chides her that the bard should not be faulted for his choice. An audience always prefers the latest songs. She should not interfere in what he considers a man's responsibility. He boldly chastises her by reminding her that Odysseus was not the only one denied a homecoming and orders her back to her quarters, claiming sole authority in his household (1.359). Penelope, amazed at her son's tone, returns to her rooms hurt by his manner but thankful for his sudden maturity. Telemachus' outburst, however, serves a second and perhaps a more important purpose. In defending Phemius' right to sing the latest circulating song, he is defending *kleos*, the most recent news to reach him from the war. Like a messenger, Phemius (from the word *phemizo* [prophecy], which conjures up *kleos*) incorporates into songs the latest reports. Telemachus wants to hear the latest songs, for it is such news that confers glory on those sung.

The prince, euphoric with his newfound sense of authority, harshly addresses the suitors, who are also surprised by his tenacity. He announces he will call an assembly (at Athena's recommendation) to demand they vacate the palace and hold their feasts elsewhere using their own resources. If, however, they decide to waste his fortune, they can continue to do so, but he will pray to the gods that Zeus reverse their fortunes (1.379). The suitors bite their lips in amazement at the daring way Telemachus has spoken to them. Athena, having put her plan in effect, forecasts what will eventually occur, another example of Homer's recurrent reminders that the *Odyssey* narrative will return to its customary path and conclude with the suitors' deaths.

The suitors are obviously troubled by Telemachus' new posture. Antinous, the suitors' leader, intimates that some god must have prompted him to speak so daringly, a troublesome notion, as it would indicate that the gods favor Telemachus. Perhaps to placate him, Antinous agrees the kingship of Ithaca belongs to Telemachus by birthright, although he secretly hopes it will be denied him. Eurymachus, the second-in-command, grants Telemachus' right to his possessions but not necessarily the kingship. However, as the reader will soon learn, Eurymachus is duplicitous (16.435–447). He admits his love for the prince openly while at the same time he plans his murder. The naïve Telemachus, delighted, is not opposed to the kingship if Zeus wills it but is aware of the competition now that Odysseus is gone. However, he insists on his claim over his household and the servants his father won by force. Of major concern to the suitors, however, is the gods' involvement in the prince's newfound voice. Eurymachus suspects the stranger, who by the look of him seems notable, and asks if he brought a message from Odysseus, who is on his way back to Ithaca. Although the suitors believe Odysseus dead and are confident that, even if he is alive, he will be no match for so many of them, they still harbor fears of his unexpected appearance. The "thoughtful" Telemachus, exhibiting one of his father's main traits, *polytropīa*—cunningness, thoughtfulness, and carefulness in considering his next step—is quick to remind Eurymachus and the suitors that his father is dead, keeping his suspicions about him to himself. He affirms he no longer expects his father's return, has little regard for messages to the contrary, and pays little heed to prophecies or to the diviners his mother often summons. He assures them the stranger is a friend of his father, but in his heart the prince has recognized Athena (1.420). For the reader, Telemachus has already answered Athena's earlier question regarding his birth in the affirmative. As the suitors and Telemachus exit, Homer, as is his practice, digresses to introduce Eurycleia, Telemachus' nurse, who will recognize Odysseus' scar upon his return. She is the daughter of Ops, son of Pisenor (rarely in the epic does memory extend beyond the third generation), and Laertes bought her at a young age for twenty oxen and favored her as much as his own wife but, fearing his wife's anger, never slept with her. Her short biography informs us of a woman's worth in the patriarchal and slaveholding society of the *Odyssey*, a society in which even a faithful slave is part of a family unit. It is perhaps a clever touch on Homer's part that the final lines of the *Odyssey*'s first book are given to Eurycleia as she tucks Telemachus in bed (1.436–44) after Athena's efforts to initiate his adulthood.

Selected Bibliography: *Od.* 1

Ahl and Roisman, "*Odyssey*," 27–42.
Amory, "Gates."

Bassett, "Proems."

Clark, "Telemachus."

Clarke, *Art*, 5–29.

Clay, "Beginning."

Combellack, "Blameless."

D'Arms and Hulley, "Orestia-Story."

Floyd, "Homer's."

Frazer, "Eurymachus'."

Jacobson, "Homer, *Odyssey* 1.132–3."

Jones, "KLEOS."

Jones, *"Odyssey" Books 1 & 2.*

Kahane, "First Word."

Katz, *Penelope's*, 63–72.

Louden, *The "Odyssey,"* 69–103.

Marks, *Zeus*, 17–35.

Nagler, "Odysseus."

Nieto Hernández, "Odysseus."

Olson, "Stories of Agamemnon."

Pedrick, "Muse."

Pucci, "Proem."

Reece, *Stranger's*, 47–58.

Rijksbaron, "Why?"

Scott, John A., "First Book."

Scott, William C., "Repeated."

Walsh, "*Odyssey* 1.6–9."

Further commentary on *Od.* 1 in General Bibliography I.

Telemachia

Alden, "Role."

Apthorp, "Obstacles."

Austin, "Telemachos."

Beck, Deborah, "Speech."

Belmont, "Athena."

Clarke, *Art*, 30–44.

Eckert, "Initiatory."

Finley, John H., Jr., *Homer's*, 139–158.

Heath, "Telemachus."

Heitman, *Taking*, 50–62.

Katz, *Penelope's*, 29–48, 120–128.

Klingner, "Fight."

Martin, Richard M., "Telemachus."

Millar and Carmichael, "Growth."

Murnaghan, "Trials."

Nieto Hernández, "*Odyssey*."

Olson, *Blood and Iron*, 65–90

Petropoulos, J.C.B., *Kleos*.

Reinhardt, "Homer."

Roisman, "Like Father."

Rose, Gilbert P., "Quest."

Said, *Homer*, 132–149.

Scott, John A., "Journey."

Scott, William C. "Teaching."

Thalmann, "*Odyssey*," 31–46.

Wehrli, "Penelope."

Wissmann, "Athena's."

Penelope

Armstrong, "Penelope's."

Armstrong, "Picture."

Buchan, *Limits*, 206–236.

Clayton, *Penelopean*, 83–122.

Combelleck, "Why Does."

Crooke, "Wooing."

Devereux, "Penelope's."

Doherty, "Athena."

Doherty, *Siren*, 31–63.

Felson-Rubin, "Penelope's."

Felson-Rubin, *Regarding*.

Finley, John H., Jr., *Homer's*, 1–24.

Foley, "Penelope."

Foley, "Virgins."

Gregory, "Unravelling."

Heitman, *Taking*.

Hellelman, "Homer's."

Hellelman, "Penelope."

Ingalls, "Nausikaa."

Jamison, "Penelope."

Kurtz, "Mind."

Levaniouk, "Penelope and the *Pênelops*."

Mackail, "Penelope."

Marquardt, "Penelope."

Mueller, "Penelope."

Murnaghan, *Disguise*.

Murnaghan, "Penelope's."

Murnaghan, "Reading."

Nagler, "Penelope's."

Nieto Hernández, "Penelope's."

Perysinakis, "Penelope's."

Thomas, "Penelope's."

Watrous, "Artemis."

Whallon, "Name."

Yamagata, "Clothing."

Zerba, "What."

Suitors

Allen, "Theme."

Bassett, "Suitors."

Dilworth, "Fall."
Dimock, "Crime."
Lateiner, "Suitors'."
Levine, "Homeric."
Levy, "Odyssean."
Louden, *Homer's*," 244–257.
Murnaghan, "Odysseus."
Ritoók, "Homeric."
Scodel, "Suitors'."
Sternruck, *Suitors*.

Book 2

The present book can be read in two parts: the assembly called by Telemachus and the assembly's aftermath. The first part, a dramatic exchange between seven speakers,[12] is presented primarily in direct speech (76% of the section), while the second part of the book focuses on Telemachus' forthcoming journey.

I. The assembly (60%)
II. The assembly: aftermath (40%)

I. The Assembly, 1–259

Telemachus wakes to the same line (in a slightly altered form) that appears each time a new day begins: "Now when the young Dawn showed again with her rosy fingers" (2.1). Normally, this line is followed by a stock scene (eating, dressing, praying), which appears in the same or slightly altered form. In the present case, Telemachus' dressing scene (3–5) is identical to Menelaus' in 4.308–310, ironically contrasting the inexperienced prince with a seasoned warrior. In appearance, Telemachus acts the part of a warrior, but in reality, he is still an adolescent. In full regalia, the prince enters the appointed assembly holding a spear and accompanied by two dogs, causing stares from those awaiting his presence. As he takes his father's seat, he displays confidence and poise but is at the same time unprepared for leadership, as the reader soon discovers. To contrast Telemachus' inexperience in presiding over an assembly, Homer begins with a brief biographical sketch of the first character to confront him, the elder Aegyptius, the father of four sons, among them Antiphus and the suitor Eurynomus. The elder Ithacan is still mourning and waiting for Antiphus, who sailed with Odysseus to Troy twenty years earlier. Unbeknownst to him but known to the reader, Antiphus was the last of Odysseus' six companions to be devoured by the Cyclops, and Eurynomus will be killed by Odysseus in 22.241–246. Aegyptius, anxious for news of his son, questions the assembly's purpose, since none has taken place during Odysseus' absence. He is impatient to know whether it signals Antiphus and the army's return. The juxtaposition of Aegyptius' sorrow and anxiety to Telemachus' selfish reasons for calling the assembly (he wants the Ithacans to drive the suitors out of his palace) adds to the prince's appearance of immaturity, as it shows that he has not considered how an assembly at this time might affect the populace. Since assemblies are called for public and not private events, and since one has not been held since Odysseus left Ithaca, calling one now raises false alarms for those Ithacans waiting for the return of relatives who accompanied Odysseus to Troy.

Aegyptius offers his blessing to the one responsible for the assembly (hoping for good news), which Telemachus mistakenly interprets as a compliment. With scepter (*skeptron*)[13] in hand and possessing the emblems of a seasoned warrior, spear (*ekhos*) and sword (*ksiphos*), Telemachus admits he called the assembly for purely personal reasons: the loss of his father and more importantly his inheritance, which the suitors are consuming daily. Standing before the Ithacans in his royal trappings, the prince creates an ironic figure—a warrior who suddenly reverts to the timid youth of *Od.* 1 (58–59, 60–61, 62). Unheedful of his earlier boast to his mother that the power in the household is his (1.359), he now dodges a leader's responsibilities and cries for help by blaming the Ithacans for not acting on his behalf:

1. The suitors should seek Penelope's hand not from him but from her father, Icarius.
2. The Ithacans should right an unendurable and lawless situation, and all of them should be ashamed for allowing the abuse of his estate.
3. The suitors' actions bring shame to the assembly and are an affront to Ithacan honor.
4. The suitors' actions are an insult to justice, to Zeus, and to Themis,[14] the goddess of what is right and proper and the embodiment of divine order, law, and custom.
5. The Ithacans should not punish him in revenge for some evil his father might have committed.

Telemachus concludes by further playing on Ithacan sympathy and a sense of justice, stating he would be better off if those at the assembly, rather than the suitors, consumed his goods, for then he could use the law to regain his losses, but in his present situation, he has no recourse. Frustrated, he dashes the scepter to the ground and ends his statement in tears (2.81), presenting a picture of an angry child unable to have his way. Although Telemachus shows some daring in consenting to address the assembly, he still lacks the rhetorical and intellectual prowess, as well as the physical strength, required of a prince. The "thoughtful" Telemachus, in his haste to take charge, has not clearly stated his opinions, as his father would have in a similar situation.

Antinous accuses Telemachus of shaming the suitors and trying to turn Ithacan opinion against them, and he blames his mother's trickery in delaying her marriage as the source of the prince's problems. He then launches into an account (a speech within a speech) of her weaving trick (presented on three different occasions in the *Odyssey*: 2.94–110, 19.138–156, and 24.128–150), which, along with the bed trick in *Od.* 23, establishes her as Odysseus' equal, earning the couple the term *homophrosunē*. Homer's Muse enumerates Penelope's many special gifts and compares her to three ancient queens, Tyro,[15] Alcmene,[16] and Mycene,[17] whose myths are narrated in *Od.* 11. These women mistook gods for their husbands and bore them sons, whereas Penelope remains cautious and faithful throughout the *Odyssey*. Even at the end, after Odysseus has slaughtered the suitors and revealed himself to her, her concern that he might be a god in disguise puts him to a final test (23.183–204).

Antinous, confining his observations to Penelope's weaving trick, insinuates unclear thinking on her part, even though her actions won her a great reputation for faithfulness. Aware of Telemachus' performance before the assembly, he warns the prince that his livelihood and possessions will continue to diminish as long as his mother resists marriage, and he cautions him that the suitors have no intention of vacating the palace. The prince, showing his defenselessness and his youth, admits he cannot force his mother out of the house against her will:

1. He fears his grandfather Icarius.
2. He fears his mother's curses should he force her out.
3. He fears damage to his public image.

With little effect, he again makes a feeble attempt to drive the suitors from his home by appealing to a higher authority, Zeus, to right the injustice. He prays that the god might somehow do for him what the Ithacans will not—get rid of them without recompense (2.145). Using the same threatening words used against them earlier (asking that Zeus reverse their fortunes [1.379]), Telemachus shows that his maturity thus far amounts to little more than a few emotional outbursts and reveals a lack of discipline in his inability to hold his temper (in contrast to his father, who must hold his for the greater part of his return [*Od.* 13–22]).

Nevertheless, the gods do not abandon the young prince. The assembly was part of Athena's plan all along to give the prince confidence, cause him to admit his immaturity, and convince him to consent to the journey prepared for him. For the present, Zeus hears his prayer; offers a positive sign, a black and a white eagle flying over the assembly; and gives voice to

Halitherses, an aged prophet, to foretell the suitors' destruction at the hands of Odysseus. Halitherses has all the qualities necessary to predict the future truthfully: age and a reputation for reading the meaning of birds. This is a reminder for the epic's external audience that prophecies in the *Odyssey* come true, since what Halitherses predicted twenty years earlier will soon occur (Odysseus will return without his companions after years of suffering ([2.174–176]). As is to be expected, the suitors neglect the warning, and Eurymachus, a nonbeliever, bids Halitherses to go babble his prophecies to his own children, who are young enough to put up with his foolishness. Eurymachus, in a hubristic tone, lays bare the qualities that will spell the suitors' end:

1. He mocks and belittles prophets and prophecies
2. He falsely accuses Halitherses of prophesying for personal gain.
3. He refuses to consider the possibility of Odysseus' return.
4. He intimates punishment for anyone inciting Telemachus' anger.
5. He insists on continuing to squander Telemachus' possessions with no thought of reparation.
6. He resents wasting time waiting for Penelope's decision when he could court other women.

Telemachus, admitting defeat, realizes that the Ithacans' general reluctance to act on his behalf implies that, although they do not sanction the suitors' behavior, they fear retaliation, since many of the suitors are foreigners from neighboring islands. Further, he realizes the suitors control Ithaca. Thus, his appeals to the public conscience and the suitors' fair-mindedness will not produce positive results. He decides on another strategy—to follow Athena's advice. Leaving matters in the gods' hands, he petitions the suitors for a ship and twenty men to sail to Pylos and Sparta to seek news of his father. If, after a year, his efforts have not uncovered information concerning his father's whereabouts, he will return, build a tomb in his father's honor, and give his mother in marriage (previously, he wanted his maternal grandfather to assume this responsibility). Although his proposal shows he is finally ready to take matters into his own hands, he still finds himself deficient in the elements needed to govern: *epea* (words), *euboulia* (good counsel), and *erga* (deeds).

Mentor, to whom Odysseus entrusted the safekeeping of his estate, tries to persuade the assembly to act, reminding the Ithacans of Odysseus' past kindness. More concerned with the public's silence than with the suitors' violent deeds, Mentor blames the Ithacans for their inaction, since they outnumber the suitors. The suitor Leocritus rebukes Mentor, accusing him of recklessness and of trying to incite the Ithacans to rise up against them. He claims that even should Odysseus return, he would be greatly outnumbered. He advises the crowd to disperse but consents to allow Mentor and Halitherses to assist Telemachus on his journey, which he doubts will ever take place. Fearful and unwilling to involve themselves in Telemachus' private matters, the crowd scatters to their homes, while the suitors return to the palace.

Besides casting light on Ithacan society, the assembly scene develops Telemachus' character and clarifies a number of recurrent issues:

1. Assemblies, rarely called, are held for major public events, not private ones.
2. Unschooled in *euboulia*, Telemachus has not yet reached the maturity needed to rule.
3. Many Ithacans (represented by Aegyptius) resent Odysseus for having taken their sons to war.
4. Men in Ithacan society dominate women, who are managed by their fathers, husbands, or sons.
5. The suitors want to force Penelope's marriage by diminishing Telemachus' wealth, since property is associated with status and power.
6. Divine signs (the two eagles sent by Zeus) interpreted by prophets are fulfilled.

7. Unbelievers (the suitors) and breakers of the laws of hospitality are punished.
8. Prophecies and omens assure that Odysseus' *nostos* will follow its universally accepted pattern, regardless of the misdirections and retardations the *nostos* narrative often takes.
9. Repetition of phrases is common in oral composition.
10. The scepter in Homeric epic is a symbol of power that gives authority to the one who wields it.
11. That an assembly has not convened during Odysseus' absence raises the question of Ithaca's rule. Since Laertes retired to his country estate, and Telemachus was too young to assume his father's role, anarchy rules in Ithaca, a main reason for the suitors' behavior.

II. The Assembly: Aftermath, 260–434

After the negative reception received from both Ithacans and suitors, Telemachus prays to Athena, conflicted by his decision to journey to Pylos and Sparta. Sensing the need for further motivation, Athena appears as Mentor (not the earlier Mentes) to encourage him. The goddess notes that the sons who can match their fathers are few, since the greatness of the past in Homer is rarely equaled by the present. Still confident that Telemachus, neither thoughtless nor a coward, will rise to the occasion and, like Orestes, assist his father on his return, Mentor/Athena advises him to neglect the suitors, who will one day perish (another glimpse of the *Odyssey*'s outcome from Athena herself). Mentor/Athena promises continuing support to accompany him on his journey and pledges to fit out a ship and provide volunteers to go with him. Although Telemachus is still reluctant, the goddess has carried out her mission—to encourage him and give him confidence (2.89).

Back at the palace, a smiling and confident Antinous approaches Telemachus and invites him to eat and drink as they once did, suggesting that in the past Telemachus dined with Antinous. It is not clear, however, whether Antinous' reference to a past time (2.305) refers to earlier suitor feasts or perhaps to a time before the courting of Penelope when the two men were on better terms. Antinous vouches that the suitors will provide Telemachus with a ship and companions for his journey, but Telemachus sees through the suitor's hollow words and wonders how he can dine with someone who has ravaged his home since childhood (2.313), a comment that raises the issue of the length of time the suitors have pursued Penelope. In describing Penelope's weaving trick, Antinous suggested she fooled them for three years. If the courting began early in Odysseus' absence, some of the suitors were children themselves. If, on the other hand, Telemachus is only now approaching adulthood, he could have been considered in "childhood" three years earlier. Perceiving Antinous' cunning, Telemachus draws his hand from the suitor's and foolishly threatens to cause him harm whether he stays in Ithaca or goes abroad as a passenger. Although Telemachus, throughout this scene, exhibits some Odyssean qualities (seeing through Antinous and the suitors' ulterior motives), he still lacks the discipline to deal with them (he threatens when he should secretly plot against them, as his father does in the latter books of the epic).

Once he leaves, the suitors, considering him a threat, mock him and begin to plot against him. A few of the younger, more arrogant men allege the prince will hire cutthroats to murder them and will travel as far as Ephyre for medicines to poison their drinks, an ironic reference to Athena's earlier comment that Odysseus was in search of a poison to kill men (1.259–261). Others hope Telemachus drowns or becomes a drifter like his father, so they can divide his possessions and offer the palace to the man who marries his mother.

Telemachus' preparations for his journey give Homer the opportunity to describe Odysseus' wealth and confirm that his *kleos* remains intact. Telemachus, already halfway through the *Telemachia*, has yet to manage his affairs without Athena's constant presence. Operating on his own, he both irritates the suitors and the Ithacans and displays an inability to deal with matters of state. The goddess, having procured a ship, gathers volunteer sailors, puts the suitors to sleep, and readies the ship for the journey. Telemachus' only chore is to inform his nurse, Eurycleia, of his trip and demand her silence. Under way, the crew fill their bowls with wine and, in contrast to the suitors, pour libations to the gods, who demand respect and assist those who offer it.

Selected Bibliography: *Od.* 2

Haft, "*Ta de nun.*"
Heitman, "Stakes."
Jones, *"Odyssey" Books 1 & 2.*
Klingner, "Fight."
Lowenstam, "Shroud."
Shapiro, "*Odyssey.*"
Whallon, "How."
Yamagata, "Clothing."
Further commentary on *Od.* 2 in General Bibliography I.

Book 3

Od. 3 covers three days and two nights (days three, four, and five) of the forty-one-day narrative, dividing this book into three parts, each representing a full day:

I. Day three (81%)
II. Day four (17%)
III. Day five (2%)

The first two days in Pylos emphasize sacrifices to the gods and Nestor's lessons on piety. Each of these two long days begins with a sacrifice—day three devoted to Poseidon and day four to Athena. During these devotions, Telemachus experiences both fear of and admiration for the gods. The fifth day has Telemachus traveling by chariot to Sparta.

I. Day Three, 1–403

Day three finds Telemachus on his way to his own odyssey. He leaves Ithaca to establish his own identity, in contrast to his father, who is returning to Ithaca to establish his. From this point onward, the epic parallels Telemachus' *nostos* with that of his father. The experiences gained will change him from the youth of the first two books to the man he becomes when he returns to Ithaca in *Od.* 15. His journey prepares him to represent the third generation of the house of the Arcesiads.[18] In contrast to the past, when his source of role models was a household of women, for the present, his role model is Mentor/Athena, who leads him to Nestor's peacetime world, where for the first time he encounters veterans of the Trojan War. Through Nestor's reminiscences, he enters a world where gods are honored, the pious rewarded, and the rights of strangers acknowledged.

Sacrifice and hospitality (activities the suitors neglect) are the main activities of this book. Telemachus arrives during a colossal sacrifice to Poseidon—4,500 people are sacrificing eighty-one black bulls (nine divisions of 500 people, with each division sacrificing nine bulls), feasting on entrails, and burning thighbones to the gods. Mentor/Athena's education begins with his urging Telemachus to put aside modesty and approach Nestor for news of his father. Young, inexperienced, and perhaps recalling his abortive attempt at the Ithacan assembly, the prince falters. How should he approach a king with Nestor's reputation? How close should he get to him? How should he address him, lacking experience in close discourse? Nevertheless, he exhibits good manners even in his distressfulness that a young man should question an elder. In the presence of the oldest and wisest warrior from Troy and one of the two most respected rhetoricians (the other is Odysseus), Telemachus, for the first time, comes face to face with the attributes of heroic stature: *biē* (physical strength) and *boulē* (deliberate discussion). Mentor/Athena urges him to overcome his shyness and embarrassment and address Nestor. Proper etiquette must be coupled with an inquisitive mind if the prince is to fulfill his mission.

Promising he will find the appropriate words in his heart, the goddess grants him courage and reminds him of his good breeding. Encouraged, Telemachus, along with Mentor/Athena, approaches the Pylians and is first greeted by Pisistratus, Nestor's youngest son, who, exhibiting the proper behavior of a prince, seats them between his brother Thrasymedes and his father, serves them animal innards, and pours wine in a golden cup. He then offers the cup first to Mentor/Athena (the oldest of the two men), asking him to pray to Poseidon, in whose honor the festival is dedicated, and then to pass the cup to the young stranger so that he too can offer a prayer to the immortals, in keeping with custom. The goddess, delighted with the protocol, is quick to acknowledge Pisistratus' proper etiquette and thoughtfulness, because he gave her the goblet first (3.53).

Telemachus observes with interest the prayers and libations to the celebrated god, a ritual in which protocol demands the eldest pray before the youngest (an act neglected at the suitors' feasts). Such consideration given to the immortals so impresses Athena that, in her own prayer to Poseidon, she asks for a safe passage home for herself and her ward once their mission is completed, glory for Nestor and his sons (denoting health and fame), and a blessing on all the Pylians present. Athena, mindful that the sacrifices in progress are dedicated to Poseidon, shows respect to him by ironically including him in her prayer when in fact it is she who is bringing it all about (3.62). It is interesting to note that the goddess, a woman herself, does not include Nestor's wife and daughters in her prayers. Judging from those present at the sacrifice and considering the patriarchal world in which Homer's characters operate, it appears that the 4,500-strong crowd consists of men only. Women participate by staying home to weave and occupy themselves with household chores.

Telemachus follows with a prayer of his own, after which both he and Mentor/Athena are invited to join the communal feast. Nestor does not attempt to determine the guests' identities (whether those of pirates or law-abiding citizens) until after the meal. Without bias, Nestor is curious to know whether they come on business or are recklessly roving the seas as pirates. Whatever their mission—business or piracy, common activities of the period—both are due the hospitality offered to all strangers as long as that kindness is not abused. Hospitality demands that the host, out of courtesy, not ask his guests' identities until after they are welcomed and fed. The contrast here with the suitors in the earlier books is again made apparent—although treated hospitably by Telemachus, they abuse the privilege.

Encouraged by the hospitality offered him, Telemachus breaks his silence to ask about his father and to win a good reputation for himself. Just as his father needs to identify himself to the Cyclops after blinding him, Telemachus needs to let his hosts know his identity. *Kleos*, news of who he is, is also reputation, a sense of belonging and not operating in a vacuum. He identifies himself as one on a private, and not a public, mission seeking news of his father, whom he believes dead, and hopes Nestor can enlighten him regarding whether his father died on land or in the billows of Amphitrite.[19] It is apparent Telemachus still believes his father is dead, as he indicates on a number of occasions throughout *Od.* 1 (166, 354, and 413). Even on his return voyage home, he tells the prophet accompanying him, Theoclymenus, that Odysseus must have died a mournful death (15.267–269). Until he is reunited with his father in *Od.* 16, Telemachus holds little hope for Odysseus' survival. From Nestor, he seeks assurance so he can return to Ithaca and build a tomb in his father's honor.

Nestor, always eager to talk about the past, a trait held over from the *Iliad*, warns that the evils suffered by the Achaeans in Troy are too many to relate. They are so many, in fact, that it would take him six years to relate them if his audience did not tire and run away. He, nevertheless, begins his long-winded reminiscences, which occupy half of the third day (3.102–328), providing Telemachus with the first news of his father as a hero. Nestor identifies four Greek heroes killed in Troy—Ajax (Aias), Achilles, Patroclus, and his own son Antilochus. Confirming his reputation for long tales (see *Il.* 11.667–761),[20] he begins with the nine years the Greeks fought the Trojans unsuccessfully, which culminated in Zeus's ending the war through Odysseus' cunning (the wooden horse). He interrupts himself to compliment Telemachus, a young man who speaks like his father—encouragement for the self-esteem of the prince, who might still doubt his identity.

Returning to his narrative, Nestor shares that in all his years in Troy, he never had an argument with Odysseus but was forever one with him in mind (*Od.* 3.128–129), crediting himself equally for ending the war with the wooden horse ploy. After the sack of Troy, many encountered difficulties on their return, instigated by Athena's anger (3.135), which caused Agamemnon and Menelaus to quarrel. For Nestor, the brothers' quarrel and the Achaeans' troublesome homecomings were willed by Zeus and caused by Athena in her anger over the Greeks' lack of righteousness. Nothing more is mentioned of the goddess' anger either by Nestor or Homer.[21] Nestor's reminiscences provide the background for the Achaeans' homecomings:

1. At the end of the war, Agamemnon and Menelaus call an assembly to harangue their intoxicated men about a supposed crisis.
2. The two brothers quarrel: Menelaus wants the Achaeans to withdraw from Troy immediately, while Agamemnon wants to sacrifice to Athena to soften her anger, but she would not listen to him.
3. The brothers' disagreement splits the army: Menelaus, Nestor, Odysseus, and half of the army decide to leave Troy, while the other half remains with Agamemnon.
4. Those following Menelaus have another quarrel when his contingent reaches Tenedos (a small Aegean island not far from Troy), and they reconsider their leaving.
5. Odysseus' faction decides to return to support Agamemnon.
6. Nestor's faction continues with his flotilla toward home. His comment that he realized the gods were devising trouble (3.166) is further praise for his clear-sightedness. Not only does he anticipate trouble and take action, but he also compliments himself for being a great rhetorician and takes half credit for the wooden horse.

7. Diomedes also leaves and is joined later by Menelaus and his troops, who meet each other in Lesbos (an island in the northeastern Aegean not far from Troy). The gods provide them with a sign to sail across the middle of the sea for Euboea (a large Greek island separated from mainland Greece by the narrow Euripus Strait).
8. By nightfall, those traveling with Nestor arrive at Geraistos, a harbor in Euboea, where they sacrifice to Poseidon, thanking him for their safe passage—another bit of swagger for Nestor for arriving home unhampered, favored by Poseidon's seas.
9. Four days later, Diomedes arrives at Argos and Nestor continues to Pylos unencumbered.
10. Nestor is in total ignorance of what happened to those who remained behind but has some news through hearsay: Achilles' men, Philoctetes, and Idomeneus had a good voyage home.

Throughout his monologue, Nestor presents himself as the wisest and most astute of the survivors, for he chose well in both Atridae quarrels[22] by sailing away with Menelaus and not turning back with Odysseus. When he and his crew decide on the best route, they choose one that takes them directly and without delay to their destination. Thus, in narrating his *nostos*, Nestor does not neglect to boast that his advice alone offered a safe voyage home before he turns to the Atreus myth (3.193–200), which makes its third appearance in the *Odyssey*, offered here as an example of a son's duty to his father, as well as a panegyric for sons in general. An alternate title for the *Odyssey* could well be "Fathers and Sons." Throughout the epic, a man's fortune rests in the hands of his son. A son inherits the family wealth and *kleos* and perpetuates one's line, the only immortality possible for a mortal. Without an Orestes, Agamemnon could not be avenged. Laertes retires from life once he thinks his son Odysseus will never return to Ithaca. In *Od.* 4 the reader senses melancholy at the double wedding of Menelaus' daughter and illegitimate son, who is appropriately named

Great Sorrow (Megapenthes), for Helen had no other children after her only daughter (4.12). Menelaus, a man whom Telemachus marvels at as one who rivals Zeus in wealth, will not leave behind a legitimate heir. In *Od.* 3 old Aegyptius' ignorance of his sons' fate becomes more piteous to the reader with the knowledge that one son is dead and another is soon to die. Even Eumaeus, a slave, mourns the lack of a wife (14.64), which leaves him without a son to perpetuate his name.

Nestor advises Telemachus to use Orestes' example for his own *kleos* by killing the suitors so that in the future men can speak well of him (3.200). The prince agrees that Orestes' glory will be immortalized and hopes the gods will grant him strength to take revenge on the suitors. The story of Orestes provides the prince with another step to manhood: he must have the physical strength to overcome the suitors. For Homer, the justice of Orestes' actions is beyond question, for by avenging his father he wins glory and honor, exactly what society expects of Odysseus' son.[23] Nestor, however, makes no mention of Clytemnestra, Orestes' mother, who takes center stage in Greek tragedy (fifth-century B.C.E.) in the murder of her husband. In Nestor's patriarchal world, the guilt is placed solely on the male, Aegisthus.

The unlawfulness of the suitors' actions in faraway Ithaca has reached Pylos, which prompts Nestor's observation that the prince has yet to attain the maturity needed to face his enemies, since he either is universally hated or allows his bad treatment (3.214–215). In other words, unless everyone in Ithaca, as well as the gods, is against him because his cause is unjust (which is not the case, since Athena supports him), why is he not taking the initiative to act? Orestes' example is proof that a man does not behave that way. Nestor recalls Athena's love for Odysseus and hopes he will return to avenge his honor. However, if the goddess should lavish the same love on Telemachus that she did on his father, the prince has nothing to worry about and the suitors can forget marriage. Nestor's remarks become prophetic, and his hope that Athena treat Telemachus as she treated his father is already a reality. He is reminding the prince to take action as Orestes did to avenge his father and that his growth to manhood is certain under Athena's tutelage.

Telemachus' doubts of his father's return (3.228) surprise Mentor/Athena. How can he question the gods' power? Turning to the Atreus myth again, the goddess cautions Telemachus: it is better to suffer hardships and return home safely than to return unburdened and be killed by one's own wife and cousin. Better to have a life of struggle and survive than have one of ease and perish, another of Homer's themes in the epic, illustrated both in Calypso's offer of immortality in *Od.* 5 and in Achilles' remarks to Odysseus in *Od.* 11. Athena's linking for the first time of Aegisthus with Clytemnestra as an accomplice to their crime is a warning Odysseus must heed; nothing can be taken for granted, not even Penelope's long-standing reputation as a faithful wife. With Athena's backing, the cautious and cunning Odysseus will not suffer Agamemnon's fate. There is only one thing the gods cannot grant: immortality for mortals. Death, a major theme in the *Odyssey*, comes to all alike. It is death that separates humans from the gods.

Still apprehensive of his own ability to follow Orestes' example, Telemachus cannot envisage his father's return. He needs to know more about Aegisthus' plot against his brother. Praising Nestor for his wisdom, he asks permission to query him on Agamemnon's *nostos*: (1) How did Agamemnon die? (2) Where was his brother Menelaus when the king was killed? and (3) What scheme had Aegisthus devised to kill Agamemnon? Telemachus' inquisitiveness allows the poet to digress to relate through Nestor Menelaus' *nostos* (3.254–312). As elsewhere in the epic, Homer momentarily retards the progress of the main narrative to relate background information about characters (Eumaeus, Eurycleia, Phemius, and Demodocus), events, or objects that play a major role in Odysseus' *nostos* (e.g., Odysseus' scar and bow). Nestor responds first to Telemachus' concern about Menelaus' whereabouts. If Menelaus was in Argos, how was Aegisthus able to commit the crime? It seems Homer here wants not only to justify Menelaus' absence but also to account for the years necessary for Orestes' coming of age. Nestor's failure to account for Menelaus' absence leaves the reader wondering why a warrior of his status shirked his familial duties; Menelaus' exegesis of his own *nostos* in the Proteus episode (*Od.* 4) clarifies this absence. The story of Menelaus' *nostos* also draws a parallel between these two families, a contrast that protects Menelaus' reputation as a responsible Homeric warrior while at the same time laying stress on the importance of the son's coming of age to avenge his father.

Before continuing with Menelaus' *nostos*, Nestor digresses to contrast the coward Aegisthus with the Greek warriors in Troy. While the Achaeans were in Troy accomplishing many hard tasks, Aegisthus remained in Argos to seduce another man's wife. Given Nestor's patriarchal society, he believes Clytemnestra would not have committed adultery if Aegisthus had not forced her (in Athena's earlier version of these events, Clytemnestra and Aegisthus are equally culpable [3.234–235]). Since women are weak, Agamemnon left her in the charge of a singer, whom Aegisthus subsequently exiled on a desert island. Only then was Aegisthus able to seduce the queen. Unlike Penelope, Clytemnestra needed moral supervision to remain faithful, a comparison that underlines the difference between these two women—morally strong Penelope does not need the external support that Agamemnon's wife required. Once the bard guarding Clytemnestra was removed, she proved too weak to resist Aegisthus' advances. The choice of a singer to guard Clytemnestra is also convincing, since, throughout the *Odyssey*, songs are used by Phemius and Demodocus to keep alive heroic deeds. Such a bodyguard could remind Clytemnestra of her husband's heroism, preserving his memory and reminding her of her marriage vows and duties. In the absence of such prompting, Clytemnestra's moral weakness leaves her susceptible to predators like Aegisthus. To further emphasize Aegisthus' guilt, Nestor points out the insult of his sacrificing to the gods *after* eliminating the singer.

Nestor picks up Menelaus' *nostos* again (3.276–277) where he left off ninety-four lines earlier. This technique of delaying a scene to be picked up later, common in the *Odyssey*, is used for dramatic effect and creates anticipation. After *Od.* 4 Telemachus does not appear in the epic again until *Od.* 15. At Sounion (a promontory at the southernmost tip of Greece), Menelaus is delayed by his steersman's mysterious death by Apollo. Later a storm splits his fleet in two—half of the ships are driven to Crete and destroyed (although the men survive); the other five ships, led by Menelaus, are swept to Egypt. While sailing in foreign lands for seven years, Menelaus amasses wealth, allowing time for Aegisthus to perform his vicious crime. Thus, Menelaus' seven-year *nostos*, as recited by Nestor, accomplishes a number of purposes:

1. It provides Menelaus an alibi for not avenging his brother.
2. It provides time for the Aegisthus-Clytemnestra dictatorship to progress and for them to plot against Agamemnon.
3. It provides time for Orestes to come of age to avenge his father.
4. It provides the time to accumulate the wealth needed for Menelaus' *kleos*. Since reputation is directly proportional to accumulated wealth, he cannot return home empty-handed, no matter how treacherous the journey. Odysseus reaches Scheria having lost all the wealth he accumulated in Troy but returns to Ithaca a wealthy man. Menelaus, too, returns wealthy, his fame intact.

In the eighth year, Orestes returns, kills, and buries his uncle and his hateful (3.310) mother. Nowhere, however, does Homer implicate Orestes in his mother's death, as later tradition does, although her own role in her husband's death is mentioned on four different occasions (11.410–411, 11.453, 24.97, and 24.199–202); her death is left unexplained. Not having Orestes openly implicated in his mother's death serves as an example for Telemachus that shows he is not obligated to kill his own mother even if she is unfaithful to Odysseus. Penelope, of course, remains faithful, and so emphasis is placed on the son's duty to avenge the father. Nestor's words are a further reminder and a warning to Telemachus not to linger long away from home while his possessions are depleted, for the suitors might divide up his property and render his journey profitless (3.315–316).

Often Homer interjects a scene to lighten the more serious mood of another. Having reached the end of the third day, Nestor now encourages the prince to visit Menelaus, the last warrior to arrive from Troy, and provides him with a chariot, horses, and his sons as escorts. Mentor/Athena, tired by his long-windedness since he has occupied most of the conversation of *Od.* 3, suggests retiring for the evening, but Nestor will not hear of it before another sacrifice to Poseidon and the other gods. The sacrifice over, Mentor/Athena and Telemachus rise to leave for their vessel but are again detained by another of Nestor's speeches as he urges them to sleep in the comfort of his home; not to do so would be an insult to his hospitality and an offense to his sense of generosity. Mentor/Athena hunts for excuses to decline the invitation:

1. As the eldest among the crew, he must return to the ship to keep an eye on the young sailors.
2. He announces a long-overdue visit to the Caucones on the following day, which necessitates rest.

However, he volunteers Telemachus and urges Nestor to speed the prince to Menelaus. He then returns to the ship in the likeness of a vulture (3.371–372). Convinced that he is in the presence of Athena Tritogeneia (3.378),[24] the god who prizes Odysseus more than any other among the Greek warriors, Nestor again calls for prayers and promises to sacrifice an unbroken yearling cow and gild her horns with gold if Athena bestows health on his family and himself. Once Nestor and his company reach the palace, he again showcases his devotion and offers more prayers to Athena. Finally, after the daylong prayers and libations are finished, Telemachus has little choice but to occupy a special bed in the palace. However, this light-hearted scene, which emphasizes Nestor's excessiveness and causes even the goddess to run away, serves a number of purposes:

1. Athena allows herself to be identified, albeit as a vulture (not an apt image for a goddess), further testament to Nestor's hospitality and devotion to the gods and the reason Athena answers his prayer (often mortal prayers are refused).
2. Nestor recognizes Telemachus' special qualities for, even though young, he is accompanied by a god.
3. One's immortality rests on one's reputation and the regard in which people hold a just, god-fearing, and hospitable person.
4. The prince, still aware of his inexperience, is encouraged by Athena to speak from the heart.
5. Success requires effort, coupled with the gods' willingness to assist those they favor.
6. The gods' love and assistance are bestowed on those mortals whose piety and devotion are shown through sacrifices.
7. A son's duty to his father and family is emphasized through the examples of Orestes and Nestor's sons, especially Pisistratus.
8. Successful and peaceful rule requires hospitality, order, rational behavior, and a united family unit.
9. Telemachus' earlier doubts concerning his paternity are laid to rest by Nestor, who likens him to Odysseus in words and appearance.

II. Day Four, 404–486

Day four begins as day three ends, with prayer—Nestor's preparations for his promised devotions to Athena. The introduction of his six living sons[25] (present at the festivities), along with a seventh, the great warrior Antilochus, fallen in Troy, serve as a testament to his good fortune and the gods' appreciation for his piety. Continuing with Nestor's unceasing sacrifices, Homer now digresses to describe meticulously not only the execution of a proper sacrifice but also Nestor's (the exemplar of the just and righteous man) final sacrifice (3.421–463), whose complexity and richness can be summarized as follows:

1. The sacrificial animal is brought to Nestor.
2. Telemachus' crew (except for two sailors left behind to guard the ship) is invited to the sacrifice.
3. The goldsmith Laerkes is called to gild the cow's horns in gold.
4. Servingwomen prepare the feast to follow.
5. Athena's presence is required in spirit only (she left as Mentor to visit the Caucones).
6. Nestor's sons Stratius and Echephron lead the sacrificial cow to the altar.
7. A third son, Aretus, brings water and scatters barley from a basket.
8. A fourth son, Thrasymedes, stands ready to strike the cow with a sharp ax.
9. A fifth son, Perseus, holds a dish to collect the animal's blood.
10. Nestor begins the rites: he pours purified water, scatters barley, prays to Athena, and flings hairs cut from the victim's head into the fire.
11. Nestor's daughters, daughters-in-law, and wife, Eurydice, raise their shrill cries, the climax of the ritual. At this point Thrasymedes strikes the cow.
12. Nestor's sixth son, Pisistratus, slaughters the cow, letting the blood drain in a basin.
13. Men carve the animal into pieces, wrap the thighbones in a double fold of fat, and top them with shreds of flesh.
14. Nestor burns the thighbones and pours wine over them while the young men around him hold five-pronged forks (*pempobola*) to taste the animal's entrails.
15. The remainder of the meat is cut into small pieces and roasted.
16. Nestor's youngest daughter, Polycaste (one of two daughters mentioned by name), bathes Telemachus, anoints him, dresses him, and seats him beside Nestor.
17. All dine on the roasted meat.

Once the feast is over, Nestor calls for preparations to be made for Telemachus' journey to Sparta and, escorted by Pisistratus, the two travel all day long, arriving at sunset at Diocles' house in Phera, where they spend the night.

III. Day Five, 487–497

Early the next morning, the third day since the prince arrived in Pylos (the narrative's fifth), Telemachus and Pisistratus again journey all day and arrive in Lacedaemon (Sparta) at Menelaus' palace in the evening. *Od.* 3, full of rituals, prayers, and the rewards that grace the person who observes them, instructed the prince in right behavior toward the gods and contrasted the godless suitors with the devoted Nestor. Telemachus' schooling in the ways of the just and righteous man continues in *Od.* 4, where *xenia* (hospitality) takes center stage as devotion to the gods does in *Od.* 3.

Selected Bibliography: *Od.* 3

Andersen, "Agamemnon's."
Cook, "Note."
Grethlein, "How Old?"
Marks, *Zeus*, 112–31.
Minchin, "Homer on."
Panchenko, "Aoidos."
Reece, *Stranger's*, 59–70.
Roisman, "Nestor."
Sammons, "Quarrel."
Further commentary on *Od.* 3 in General Bibliography I.

Book 4

Telemachus spends the remainder of the evening with Menelaus and Helen, who recount what they remember and admire most about Odysseus. *Od.* 4

divides into two sections; in the first, Sparta dominates three-quarters of the book, and the second, the last quarter of the book, returns the reader to events taking place in Ithaca.

I. Telemachus in Sparta (74%)
   A. The evening of day five
   B. Day six
II. The situation in Ithaca (26%)

I. Telemachus in Sparta

I.A. The Evening of Day Five, 1–305. In Lacedaemon, the princes find the king engaged in a double wedding. Hermione, his daughter by Helen, is being sent to Achilles' son, Neoptolemus, while his illegitimate son Megapenthes, born of a slave woman, is marrying Alector's unnamed daughter. Although a double wedding is in progress (entailing singer, acrobats, feasting, and so on), the mood seems solemn. Menelaus and Helen are not part of the festivities, although their neighbors and the townspeople are celebrating within. The father-son relationships of Odysseus and Telemachus and Agamemnon and Orestes hint at Menelaus' disappointment that his only son is illegitimate. Even the name Megapenthes ("great sorrow") suggests Menelaus' regret in lacking a legitimate heir. Further, Homer's comment that the gods gave no more children to Helen (4.12) adds to the somberness of the scene.

Telemachus and Pisistratus are welcomed by Eteoneus, Menelaus' right-hand man, who is given Homer's customary brief background. Eteoneus fails to greet the strangers properly (perhaps out of concern for their untimely presence) by detaining them while he seeks his master's permission. The servant's insult in not offering the strangers immediate hospitality angers Menelaus (4.32–33), for he acknowledges that his survival during his seven-year sojourn depended on the goodwill of strangers and must be returned in kind. Hospitality for him equates to survival, as it must have for those from Homer's era in general. In the expanding world of

Homer's time, travel and economic expansion depended on safe accommodations. Lacking commercial accommodations, it was up to the general public to host strangers, whoever they may be; in order to enable such an exchange, guests must behave properly. In Homer's world, to violate this guest-host bond is to suffer the gods' anger. Thus *xenia* becomes the jurisdiction of Zeus Xenios, the father of gods and travelers (strangers); to break this bond becomes a punishable act. Perhaps, then, the Trojan War was fought not merely to retrieve a wayward wife but in fact to avenge the violation of a sacred trust—hospitality.

Menelaus' legendary hospitality is established through descriptions of the opulence of his palace's wealth and the lavishness of the feast he sets before the two princes. After all, much of his wealth is due to the generosity offered him during his travels. Thus, once bathed, anointed with oil, and dressed in cloaks, the two young men are seated next to the king for a lavish feast, which Homer describes in detail. First, a maid pours water from a golden pitcher for the guests to wash their hands (4.52–53) and collects it in a silver basin (4.53). Next, a polished table (4.54) is placed before them on which a housekeeper sets generous amounts of bread and appetizers. A carver then serves platters of meat and places beside them golden wine glasses (4.58). Such attention to detail (also in Nestor's sacrifices in *Od.* 3) shows the importance such rituals have in a civilized society and the reason why those who degrade them are taken to be undisciplined and uncivilized. The care used to serve the meal in the ritual highlights not only the bounty of the food but also the richness of the implements, accentuating Menelaus' hospitality. As a wealthy man, his hospitality must match his station if it is to be taken as genuine, as later, in *Od.* 14, the swineherd's generosity exceeds his meager possessions. Serving the meal conveys a sense of sophistication and civilization on the part of Menelaus' household, in contrast to the suitors' feasts, where the quantity of food (their greed) is given priority over utensils. Nor are Menelaus' guests questioned until they have eaten. Telemachus' exposure to such behavior provides the yardstick with which the reader can measure him and judge the actions of the suitors and the mythic hosts Odysseus encounters on his journey home.

Throughout *Od.* 3 and *Od.* 4 (as well as in the Phaeacian episodes in *Od.* 6–8 and 12–13), proper behavior, and its opposite, is overemphasized. Menelaus and Nestor are overly hospitable because they experienced hunger firsthand. Menelaus not only feeds his guests but even offers them his own choice portion (4.65–66). Proper behavior earns fame, externalized and concretized in one's wealth just as appearance displays character in Homer's world, where the good are handsome and the bad ugly. Menelaus is aware of his guests' identity at once, for their outer appearance exposes their pedigree (4.62–63).

Impressed by the bronze and gold surrounding him, Telemachus whispers to Pisistratus that Menelaus' palace must be like Zeus's own. The king, overhearing the conversation, quickly responds, lest Zeus be offended by Telemachus' comparing a mortal to him. Although Menelaus possesses much, he quickly makes clear the high price he had to pay. Wealth affords Menelaus little pleasure, since he wandered for years in strange places to amass it at great personal loss—his brother killed by his cousin and by his wife's treachery (4.91–92). He feels responsible not only for his brother's death but also for those lost defending his cause in Troy, and he concedes that his wealth provides neither happiness nor relief. Given a choice, he would give a third of his wealth in exchange for his comrades' lives. The mention of Clytemnestra again as an accomplice to her husband's murder is a further reminder of the caution required of Odysseus in approaching Penelope. As Odysseus tells Nausicaa in 6.181–184, a united family where man and wife live in harmony is the only true happiness.

Menelaus' memories of his fallen comrades recall Odysseus, whose absence troubles his sleep, and he expresses compassion and sympathy for Odysseus' family. Hearing his father's name, Telemachus weeps. Menelaus, noticing his guest's grief, wonders whether he should wait for the prince to provide his identity or break etiquette and ask for it himself, but at that moment Helen, in her first appearance, enters like Artemis (4.122).

Comparing Helen to Artemis rather than to Aphrodite (the cause of her abduction by Paris) is perhaps a way of stressing Helen's preferred state. Now reunited with her husband, she presents herself as the proper hostess and queen. Being likened to Artemis gives her a more dignified air, since Artemis was not only one of the most independent goddesses but also the one who most guarded her virginity. Helen relegates Aphrodite, the cause of her fractured marriage, to the past. Later Helen admits it was the madness Aphrodite bestowed that caused her to forsake her home, exonerating herself of willful wrongdoing. Homer nowhere directly accuses Helen of running away with Paris. He allows her to speak in her own voice, as he does in the story she offers Telemachus, in which she claims repentance not long after her madness. Before the princes, she enters with the demeanor of the proper housewife, accompanied by three maids, which is a sign of modesty when in public, a practice Penelope follows throughout the epic. As befits a queen, the basket the maid Phylo carries was presented to Helen by Alcandre, the wife of King Polybos of Egyptian Thebes (legendary in Homer's time for its wealth). The cultivated always honor guests through a hospitality measured in gifts. Phylo places the symbols of a woman's occupation (a basket full of yarn and a spindle) next to her seated mistress. Helen then inquires about the strangers' identity, amazed that the appearance of one of the princes reminds her of Odysseus' son, whose father went to Troy for her sake (4.145; disclosing her guilt for causing the war). Menelaus agrees with Helen's assessment that the stranger must be Telemachus, for he too sees similarities in the prince's features, and then weeps, recalling Odysseus. The fact that three such formidable people (Menelaus, Helen, and earlier Nestor) who know Odysseus well recognize Telemachus as his son is a sign of his breeding and good character. It allays Telemachus' fears, if he still harbors any doubts, that he may not be Odysseus' son. Pisistratus, whose proper behavior serves as an example to Telemachus, divulges Telemachus' identity, states the purpose of their visit, and adds that without a father, a son is defenseless against his enemies, indicating not only the need for experience and authority to maintain peace but also the importance of the father-son bond.

Pisistratus' comments hasten Menelaus' expression of love for Odysseus; he would empty an entire city merely to keep him and his family by his side. Such devotion reveals the depth of his obligation to Odysseus and the power he exercises over his kingdom. At this tribute all shed tears, even Pisistratus, who is reminded of Antilochus, the fallen brother he never met. His tears allow Homer to comment on one of his major themes: humans must embrace death, for they are helpless to do otherwise. Menelaus congratulates Pisistratus on his thoughtfulness and sensitivity, which reveals the son in the father. Zeus values good breeding in men like Nestor, which weaves for them and their sons good fortune: *biē* (force) and *boulē* (counsel), which are needed for manhood.

During dinner, Helen slips a drug so powerful into the mixing bowl of wine that whoever drinks it eases all pain:

> not if his mother died and his father died, not if men
> murdered a brother or a beloved son in his presence.
> (4.224–225)

Since the drug has a role in the couple's relationship, a brief historical sketch is offered. Where did it come from? How did Helen acquire it? The reader is offered little else beyond the names of the characters involved (the Egyptian Polydamna, wife of Thon, and the healing god Paieon, later associated with Apollo), as is customary with those holding minor roles in the *Odyssey*. However, the names given are all from Paieon's race. The drug is a medicine of tranquility, a medicine that allows one to forget the past that seems to plague both Menelaus and Helen. At the beginning of *Od.* 4, Helen laments giving birth to a single child and Menelaus regrets not having produced a legitimate son. Both feel guilty for the Trojan War and the human deaths it caused. Menelaus would give up part of his kingdom if Odysseus were to return safely home. The drug's potency suggests the degree to which the past torments them; only with the help of drugs can they face it. Since Helen casts the medicine into the wine they are drinking, her purpose could also be to ease her own guilt for having abandoned her husband, or perhaps to ease the pain of having to live with him again.

The story of the procurement of this poison and other myths collected throughout the epic were inherited from multiple Homers before they were woven into a single narrative by the Homer of our *Odyssey* (M. L. West, *Making*), many with their roots in Near Eastern tales (Louden, *Homer's*). Homer's art is not one that creates or invents all the different tales and myths found in the epic (since they already existed in a variety of forms); rather, the author borrows these to create Odysseus' story, utilizing the parts of the myths needed to make his point. He can either add to the original or eliminate material not relevant to his purpose. He then juxtaposes these myths to reveal character psychology or to comment on the themes of Odysseus' *nostos*. We are to assume either that the original audience was familiar with the myths associated with these characters or that further information was unnecessary for Homer's immediate purposes. For the modern reader, many of the names and myths referenced are familiar only from later mythology or remain obscure Homeric creations.

One of the best examples of Homer's approach to myth is the anecdotes Helen and Menelaus offer their young guests. In prefacing their reminiscences of Odysseus, both admit that his heroic feats revealing the nature of his character were so many that Helen could not begin to name them all (4.240–241). Why, then, do they each choose to narrate the specific accounts they do from the many available to them, and why are their stories presented in the order they appear in the text—Helen's followed by Menelaus'? Further, it should be noted that these stories are told in Helen's and Menelaus' own voices. Their direct discourse reveals more about them than about Odysseus: what each perceives about her or his own present situation; what each is thinking while delivering the story; what each considers valuable in the story. Are these selected reminiscences then told for Telemachus' benefit or for their own? Are Helen and Menelaus providing the news Telemachus seeks concerning his father, or are they more interested in justifying their private feelings to each other?

Once Helen mixes her drug in the wine bowl and orders the glasses filled, she invites her husband and the princes to eat while she entertains them with one of Odysseus' many exploits. She selects an undertaking he carried out during the Trojan War, which for her stood out from his other exploits (4.244–264). There is no way, of course, for the reader to know exactly what Homer adds to or omits from the myth Helen relates. What is obvious is that Helen's version of Odysseus' feat expresses personal thoughts and feelings, just as Menelaus' tale does. But first Helen's story:

1. Odysseus, as a beggar, enters Troy to spy and is recognized only by Helen.
2. Helen questions Odysseus, but he initially reveals nothing.
3. Helen bathes Odysseus, anoints him with oil, and gives him clothes, even though he is a threat to the Trojans.
4. Helen swears not to reveal Odysseus' identity, betraying her allegiance to her husband (Paris) and the Trojans.
5. Odysseus confides in Helen and reveals to her the Greeks' plans for Troy.
6. Unrestrained by Helen, Odysseus returns to his camp unnoticed, but only after killing many Trojans.
7. The Trojan women lament the carnage Odysseus leaves behind, except for Helen, whose allegiance has changed and who is ready to return to Menelaus.
8. Helen is repentant in abandoning her country, husband, and daughter and blames Aphrodite for her madness.
9. Helen regrets leaving Menelaus, a husband she now claims to be both intelligent and handsome.

These nine observations leave the reader with a number of unanswered questions and provide little news about Odysseus' whereabouts. First, why does Helen focus on herself rather than on Odysseus? Why does she bathe a foreign spy and swear not to reveal his identity to the Trojans, who are fighting for her sake? More importantly, why does Odysseus, the cleverest of Greek heroes, reveal the Greeks' plans to Helen? Last, what does Helen tell Telemachus about his father that will help him in his quest to discover whether he is alive or dead? Helen's story informs us that early in or midway through the war (we cannot precisely tell when, but certainly long before the end of the war), she had a change of heart about abandoning her home and family, a realization she comes to earlier in the book (4.145–146). She will have us believe that Odysseus accepts her repentance, places his trust in her, and completes his secret mission with her assistance. Throughout her tale, Helen is careful to make clear that she is no longer loyal to the Trojans (she does not cry at the Trojan deaths like the other women) and realizes her mistake in abandoning Menelaus for Paris, an error on her part that she attributes to Aphrodite.

Menelaus politely agrees with everything his wife says (4.266) but immediately launches into his own memory of Odysseus, in which he praises the hero's fearlessness and cunning (4.271–289). For Menelaus, Odysseus' most memorable feat occurred at the end of the war when the Greeks in the wooden horse were ready to exit and set Troy on fire. He recalls Helen approaching the wooden horse with her second Trojan lover, Deiphobos,[26] Paris' brother, to expose the Greeks hiding inside. She mimicked the voices of the men's wives, hoping one of them would cry out and expose the others. Anticlus would have succumbed had Odysseus not clasped his mouth, preventing him from screaming. Menelaus' story, then, is less about Odysseus' feat in preserving a Greek victory and more about Helen trying to sabotage the Greeks up to the very end of the war. In this way, he refutes Helen's earlier comments that she repented long before the war was over and was ready to return to Menelaus. He disavows her helping Odysseus spy when, up to the end, she was still an enemy to the Greeks. How could she still desire Menelaus when she was with her second Trojan lover after Paris' death?

Helen seems compelled to justify herself to Menelaus in order to assuage her guilt for the countless deaths caused by her abandoning him. She wants the reader to believe she rescinded on her mistake early during the war when she helped Odysseus spy on Troy. Menelaus' tale accuses her of lying. How can she claim repentance when she was actively engaged in helping the Trojans up to the very end? By now Telemachus is aware of the animosity and mistrust that exist between Helen and Menelaus. Realizing that news of his father is not forthcoming, he suggests retiring for the evening. The long evening ends as Helen and Menelaus go off to bed, portrayed in a rather cold and impersonal light, given what has occurred (4.305).

I.B. Day Six, 306–624. Menelaus rises and goes directly to Telemachus to ask whether a public or private need brought him to Sparta (4.312–314). It is the third time in *Od.* 4 (20, 302, and 312) that Menelaus uses *heros* to address the prince, signaling the prince's maturation since Ithaca. Telemachus explains he seeks news of his father and, in frustration, discloses conditions in Ithaca: his goods devoured, his lands destroyed, his palace full of enemies, his cattle and sheep slaughtered, and his mother plagued by suitors. The king, deeply angered at what he hears, responds with a typical Homeric simile (4.335–340), which fulfills a number of objectives. First, it shows the difference between Odysseus (the lion) and the suitors (the doe), who are no match for him. Second, the suitors are not only unrealistic but in fact blind to think that they can occupy a lion's den without retribution. Third, the simile foreshadows what will eventually occur. The lion will return to his den, and the doe and fawns (the suitors' associates) occupying it will be destroyed.

The Homeric simile (a basic simile reversed: A is like or as B reversed to B is like or as A) is one of Homer's most powerful compositional elements. In the simile, A's (Odysseus) being compared to B (the lion) is reversed so the object of comparison, B (the lion), comes before the object to be compared, A (Odysseus). This reversal allows the poet to elaborate on the object of comparison before revealing what is being compared. Further, it focuses and expands on familiar objects and incidents to clarify a situation (e.g., dead and dying suitors compared to recently caught fish twitching in the sun in 22.384–389), or it focuses on the state of mind of the object to be compared (e.g., Odysseus, about to be conveyed home by the Phaeacians, compared to a farmer aching for supper after a day's work in 13.31–35). It also serves to contrast the mythic with the real world (e.g., blinding the Cyclops with a stake compared to a shipwright's boring a hole with his drill in 13.31–35).

Menelaus invokes the gods to grant Odysseus' return with the strength he exhibited over Philomelides of Lesbos,[27] for then the suitors would find a quick death and marriage a painful business. As in other cases, here Homer does not elaborate on the myths he employs but briefly cites the parts needed to make his point. Menelaus now turns to the tale of Proteus, the old man of the sea (4.351–547), a digression occupying almost two-thirds of Telemachus' full day in Lacedaemon. In relating his own *nostos*, the king makes us aware of the requisites for Odysseus' own homecoming. He begins where Nestor stopped when narrating Menelaus' *nostos* (3.302), when the winds drive Menelaus and his crew to Egypt for neglecting to render a complete hecatomb (a sacrifice of one hundred oxen) to the gods before their journey, an analogue to Odysseus' own detainment. Both warriors are exiled on an island: Menelaus on Pharos and Odysseus on Ogygia. Both islands are inaccessible: Menelaus' was as far as a ship can sail in a day (4.355–456), and Odysseus is so far removed from civilization that even Hermes questions the distance (5.100–101). Both islands are ruled by divinities: Proteus (a sea god) in Pharos and Calypso (a nymph) in Ogygia. Additionally, in each case a divine force intercedes to gain each man's release: Eidothea for Menelaus and Hermes for Odysseus.

Throughout the Proteus episode, Menelaus uses first-person narration (as Odysseus does in his wanderings [*Od.* 9–12]), describing events as he wants to remember them. Is the reader then to question the events he reports? Are Menelaus' memories real or the truth as he wants it represented? Such technique allows for multiple psychological insights and interpretations. Marooned for twenty windless days on Pharos, unable to sail and with his supplies depleted, Menelaus is greeted by Proteus' daughter, Eidothea, who asks why he procrastinates on the island while his men go hungry. Explaining he is detained against his will (for perhaps offending the gods), he begs for the name of the god who imprisons him. Eidothea informs him that only her father can help. However, Proteus, a shapeshifter, reveals knowledge only when forced after being captured while asleep and held tight while he metamorphoses through his many shapes—lion, serpent, leopard, boar, water, and tree. Exhausted and returned to his original shape, he can then reveal one's future. The lesson for Odysseus in the Proteus tale is to embrace life's obstacles, to weather the changing times, and to be flexible (*polytropos*, one of Odysseus' epithets), the only way to complete one's *nostos*. Menelaus must hold the shapeshifter Proteus tight in his embrace until he reveals his way home. This tale then underscores Odysseus' own challenge: to endure all obstacles encountered and never to accept defeat but rather to embrace life until he is released by the gods.

Eidothea explains her father's devious ways and agrees to help Menelaus capture him when he emerges at high noon from the sea. On the following day, Menelaus and three companions don four newly skinned seal skins offered them by Eidothea and wait (the source of these skins is not disclosed). At high noon Proteus emerges, counts his seals (he counts his seals in fives [4.412]), and falls asleep. Menelaus and his men rush the god and hold him tight until he submits (462–463). Why is Proteus satisfied enough with his seal count to permit him to return to sleep, since there are four extra seals among his group? Had he noticed seals missing, he would not have been such an easy target for Menelaus and his men. One plausible answer is that since Proteus counts by fives, he and the four new seals (Menelaus and his three men) make a group of five, and since only groups of five appear among his flock, he does not bother with the total—one group of five too many. If, on the other hand, Eidothea killed four of her father's seals for their skins, those four would account for the total, but Homer has no interest in such details.

Menelaus asks for release from the island and the name of the god preventing it. Proteus instructs that the gods will grant his wish only if he returns to the Nile and sacrifices to the gods he neglected earlier. Thus, the theme of neglected sacrifice (offering the gods their due), of which the suitors are guilty in the *Telemachia* and Odysseus' crew in the *Cyclopeia*[28] (*Od.* 9), sends Menelaus back to Egypt, a long and painful journey. Accepting his fate, Menelaus inquires how many of his comrades-in-arms arrived home safely from Troy. Proteus cautions that the answer will cause him great sorrow, since many were killed on their return. Of three returning Achaean leaders, two were lost at sea, while one survived but remains captive somewhere in the vast ocean. Of the lost leaders, Ajax (the Lesser, son of Oileus), hated by Athena (4.502),[29] was driven against rocks by Poseidon but saved from drowning by clinging to a rock. However, he defied the gods (he boasted that despite the gods, he escaped the sea [4.504–505]), and Poseidon split the rock in anger and drowned him for his hubris, a sin the Homeric gods do not tolerate. The second lost leader eventually made land at the edge of Thyestes' estate, which his son Aegisthus occupied, and was spotted by his spy, who was paid to watch for Agamemnon's arrival for an entire year.[30] At an elaborate feast in the king's honor, twenty of Aegisthus' men ambushed and killed Agamemnon and his companions. Proteus' version of the Agamemnon story is a warning for both Odysseus and Telemachus, for the suitors have the same fate in mind for both. Odysseus, unlike Agamemnon, will, however, use his guile to foil the suitors and live. Proteus' lesson is one of caution and mistrust, two of the qualities that define Odysseus. Proteus urges Menelaus to hurry home in hopes of finding Aegisthus alive so he can avenge his brother, but if Orestes has already carried out the deed, Menelaus will arrive in time for the burial, reiterating for the reader a brother's responsibility to his family. The reader, however, is already aware that Orestes killed his uncle, which reinforces the duty the son owes the father, a duty Telemachus must bear in mind.

Although saddened at the news of his brother, Menelaus asks Proteus about the third lost leader, Odysseus. Now, 205 lines after Menelaus promised Telemachus to tell all and hold nothing back, he addresses Odysseus' *nostos* in 6 lines (4.555–560): in a vision, Proteus sees Odysseus on an island, weeping in his captor Calypso's cavern, where he remains without men or ships to convey him home. Except for these 6 lines and the 13 on Ajax, the Proteus tale treats Menelaus' homecoming and Agamemnon's death. Yet through this myth, the reader is made aware of the conditions for Odysseus' return and Telemachus' success—guile and agility for Odysseus, and Orestes' example for Telemachus. The mention of Odysseus on Calypso's island serves also as a transition from the *Telemachia* to Odysseus' sojourn on her island in *Od.* 5 and gives Telemachus his first concrete news of what happened to his father.

Menelaus again returns to his own homecoming and Proteus' prophecy. His fate is not to die in Argos, for the gods will convey him to the Elysian Field (4.563–564). The king's idyllic destiny, mentioned only once in the epic, does not follow the usual Homeric eschatology, in which those who die (including Achilles and Agamemnon) are destined for Hades. Proteus explains Menelaus' exception—his marriage to Helen and status as son-in-law to Zeus—before he dives into the sea, never to be heard from again. Menelaus will be rewarded with a place in the Elysian Field, a less heroic fate than that of his fellow warriors, who died in Troy without the expectation of an afterlife. Although Menelaus' powerlessness to avenge his brother represents a blight on his honor, he alone among the Achaean heroes will achieve immortality. Homer's single mention of the Elysian Field must be seen in contrast to Odysseus' situation: when offered immortality by Calypso in the next book, he refuses to accept it. The inevitability of death gives mortality its edge over immortality, since what is achieved through struggle is inevitably lost in death, a struggle illustrated in Hades by Sisyphus, who, as punishment for his craftiness and deceitfulness, rolls a rock up a hill only to have it roll back down in a constantly repeated process. It is the struggle without recompense, endurance against all odds, and the awareness of one's end that give humans dignity in Homer.

His Proteus tale over, Menelaus invites Telemachus to remain with him in Lacedaemon for twelve more days, promising gifts: three horses, a chariot, and a goblet to use in offering libations to the gods. Exhibiting signs of his maturity, Telemachus, though moved by Menelaus' hospitality, begs to return to his companions waiting for him at Pylos (like his father, he chooses the everyday struggles of Ithaca over Menelaus' idyllic existence). Showing practicality and thoughtfulness, he begs Menelaus to exchange the gift of three horses for one more appropriate to Ithaca's rough terrain, preferring to leave the horses for Menelaus' enjoyment, for Ithaca is a rugged land suited only to raising goats. Menelaus, impressed with the prince's reasoning (4.611), exchanges the horses for the most esteemed item in his home: a solid silver mixing bowl with gold rims, the work of the god Hephaestus, a compliment to Telemachus' growth and the esteem he is held in by his father's equal. As Menelaus is exchanging Telemachus' gift, banqueters arrive at the palace, bringing their own sheep and wine, in stark contrast with the suitors in Ithaca. In Menelaus' civilized society, guests contribute to the household of a king who is among the wealthiest of mortals. The suitors, from the most prosperous households of Ithaca and the surrounding islands, feast on Odysseus' goods, offering nothing in return. The order in Lacedaemon, which brings prosperity and peace, is contrasted with the chaos in Ithaca, which brings disaster.

II. The Situation in Ithaca, 625–847

We return to the unruly suitors, whose ringleaders, Antinous and Eurymachus, sitting apart from the others, are approached by Noemon, who inquires about Telemachus' return, anxious to retrieve his ship. Unaware of Telemachus' absence, Antinous demands to know when Telemachus left, who and how many men accompanied him, and whether they are servants or Ithacans. He insists on knowing whether the ship was commandeered against Noemon's will or whether it was offered voluntarily. It is obvious that Antinous and the suitors must now take Telemachus seriously. He is no longer the young man who they thought would never leave Ithaca but rather a threat to be reckoned with. He might even have gathered a force against them. Noemon admits loaning his vessel willingly and adds that some of the finest young men of Ithaca accompany him. He suspects Mentor is among them, or perhaps a god, since only yesterday he saw Mentor in Ithaca, but Antinous is too blind to realize the gods are assisting the Arcesiads. His refusal to consider the possibility of the gods' presence in Telemachus' affairs and his defiance of them put him on the level of Ajax, whom Poseidon drowned for the same kind of arrogance (4.500–511). Raging with anger, Antinous and Eurymachus muster the suitors to take measures against this new threat posed by the prince. In disbelief that a young boy (4.665) could outwit the suitors, Antinous turns to Zeus for Telemachus' destruction before he reaches full manhood (4.667–668). In an ironic twist, his wish will be fulfilled, but it will be his life and not Telemachus' that will not come to full measure. He requests a ship and twenty men to lie in wait for the prince, hoping to murder him as he nears Ithaca.

Throughout this section, Homer crosscuts in true cinematic fashion between scenes of the suitors in the banquet hall and those of Penelope in her quarters. A technique common in the *Odyssey*, it stops the reader short of a scene's climax before jumping to another. One must then wait, sometimes for many books, before Homer picks up the delayed scene (the suitors' ambush suggested in *Od.* 4 will not occur until *Od.* 15). In the scenes that follow, a sense of urgency is created as Penelope learns of her son's absence, the plot to murder him, and the renewed chaos created by the suitors.

1. Cut to the herald Medon,[31] who, overhearing the suitors' plot, rushes to inform Penelope.
2. Cut to Penelope, who thinks Medon has been sent to have the maids prepare the suitors' dinner, which she hopes will be their last. Her

resentment contrasts the justice of Odysseus' past kindness to his people with the suitors' present unruly behavior and calls attention to the effect the king's absence has on Ithaca.

3. Return to Medon, who now informs Penelope that the worst is yet to come; he overheard the suitors plotting to murder Telemachus on his return, the first time the queen has heard of her son's absence and his impending murder. Regaining her composure, she wonders why Telemachus considered such a journey. Medon suggests that perhaps a god inspired Telemachus to investigate his father's homecoming (sanctioning the journey as an authorized undertaking), or perhaps his own impulse led him to Pylos and Sparta.
4. Return to Penelope, who is bewailing the loss of her husband and the threat against her son. The gravity of the prince's journey now preoccupies Penelope, along with Odysseus' absence.
5. Penelope summons her old male servant, Dolius, to call on Laertes to intervene in the suitors' plan to murder Telemachus. If this is the Dolius in *Od.* 24, who manages Laertes' estate, one wonders what he is doing in Ithaca, since later (*Od.* 24) we learn he is unaware of what is happening at the palace.
6. Turn to Eurycleia, who confesses her knowledge of Telemachus' absence, which she took an oath not to reveal. She urges Penelope not to embitter old Laertes but to place her fate in the hands of the gods.
7. Back again to Penelope, who returns to her private quarters and prays to Athena, who hears her prayer (4.767). That Athena hears the queen's prayer is prophetic, for such foreshadowing, common in the *Odyssey*, reminds the audience of the suitors' fate.
8. Cut to the suitors, who are raising a tumult in the halls.
9. Zero in on Antinous, who reprimands the suitors to be discreet, fearing someone might report them to the queen (Medon has already done so). Antinous' fear is not of informing Penelope of the suitors' intentions but rather of the possibility that the public may

turn against them, since at the assembly (*Od.* 2) Telemachus had some support.

10. Return to pick up the thread of the last suitor scene, in which Antinous and twenty of his companions prepare to ambush the prince.
11. Cut to Penelope in her chambers, pondering whether her son will live or die at the suitors' hands. Here she is compared to a lion surrounded by hunters closing in for the kill, the only lion simile devoted to Penelope of the seven in the *Odyssey* (five refer to Odysseus and one to the Cyclops). The image of the lion, which alludes primarily to Odysseus, represents strength, and thus Penelope is associated both with strength and with Odysseus; like Odysseus, she will eventually prevail over the suitors. The lion simile used for both husband and wife further bears witness to their like-mindedness (*homophrosunē*).
12. Return to Penelope, who is troubled in her sleep. Iphthime, Penelope's sister, is sent by Athena in a dream to allay the queen's fears and assure her of Telemachus' safety. The dream informs her that her grief is due less to her husband's absence than to the possibility of losing her son. When Penelope asks Iphthime about Odysseus, the specter drifts away, refusing to answer. It seems that, for the moment, Penelope is preoccupied with her son, which supersedes her thoughts of Odysseus. However, it is not clear why in the dream her sister refuses when asked to provide any information on Odysseus' whereabouts. Since Athena sends the dream, her refusal to even say whether he lives or has died is stranger still, as all along the goddess has made known his imminent return. Perhaps she wants that to remain a secret so as not to jeopardize the element of surprise he will need to eliminate the suitors.
13. Cut to the suitors, who set sail on the open sea, plotting Telemachus' demise. The *Telemachia* ends with the suitors lurking in the harbor of a rocky island, Asteris, which lies halfway between Ithaca and

Samos (later Cephallenia). At the end of the *Telemachia*, both Odysseus' return and Telemachus' fate remain in suspense. Although Telemachus will not return until *Od.* 15, the reader is reminded of him three times before then (5.18–27, 13.411–428, and 14.171–184).

Selected Bibliography: *Od.* 4

Ahl and Roisman, *"Odyssey,"* 27–42.
Athanassakis, "Proteus."
Belmont, "Menelaus."
Bergren, "Helen's."
Buchan, *Limits*, 50–71.
Griffith, "Sailing."
Harris, John, "Proteus."
Lonsdale, "Protean."
Louden, *Homer's*, 105–123.
Olson, "Stories of Helen."
Plass, "Menelaus."
Powell, "Narrative."
Reece, *Stranger's*, 71–100.
Schmiel, "Telemachus."
Shewan, "Telemachus."
Further commentary on *Od.* 4 in General Bibliography I.

CHAPTER 2

ODYSSEUS FROM CALYPSO TO THE PHAEACIANS (*OD.* 5–8)

Book 5

Odysseus' *nostos* begins in *Od.* 5, read in four sections:

I. The gods' second council (9%)
II. Hermes' visit to Calypso (21%)
III. Odysseus' decision to leave Calypso (23%)
IV. Odysseus' voyage to Scheria (47%)

The first third of *Od.* 5 (I and II) narrates Odysseus' first appearance in the epic and Athena's efforts to obtain his release from Poseidon. The remainder of the book centers on Odysseus' preparations to leave Ogygia and his struggles to escape Poseidon's wrath (III and IV). Preparations to leave Ogygia (III) are in two parts: day one, Calypso's efforts to detain Odysseus; day 2, Odysseus builds a raft. In section IV, almost half of *Od.* 5, Odysseus battles Poseidon's storm to reach Scheria, represented by four massive waves, each framed by a simile; two large ones, which almost drown the hero, and two quelled by Athena, which surface after Poseidon leaves the scene and drive the hero ashore. The first two compare the hero's raft to thistle and dry chaff scattered indiscriminately back and forth by the four winds; the third compares the hero sighting land to children welcoming a father back to life after a long illness; and the fourth compares the hero's bleeding hands being pulled forcefully from a rock to an octopus' tendrils being detached from his shelter. A fifth simile compares the hero's exhaustion to a buried burning log—five similes in 231 lines, the largest concentration of similes in the epic.

I. The Gods' Second Council, 1–42

In the gods' first council (*Od.* 1), Athena pleads with Zeus for Odysseus' release from Calypso, and Hermes is sent to inform her of the gods' decision, while Athena goes to Ithaca to assist Telemachus (1.84–89). On the seventh day of the *Odyssey* narrative, we return to the gods on Olympus to follow Athena's second request for Odysseus' release—Hermes trip to Calypso's island. Although the second council is a continuation of the first, Telemachus is almost at the end of his journey (4.620–624), since the first four *Odyssey* books narrate Athena's visit. Telemachus' story continues when we return to him in *Od.* 15 on the dawn of the thirty-sixth day (15.1–300). Homer's confusing method of narrating simultaneous events as if occurring consecutively has Athena leaving Ithaca and Telemachus in *Od.* 1, while Hermes at the same time leaves for Ogygia in *Od.* 5. Thus, the *Telemachia* and the first three hundred lines of *Od.* 15 occur at the same time as Odysseus' journey from Ogygia (*Od.* 5) to Ithaca (*Od.* 13.70). Father and son will finally meet at Eumaeus' hut in *Od.* 16 and be reunited at 16.188. The present book opens with Dawn rising, as she does on five previous occasions (*Od.* 2.1, 3.1, 3.404, 3.491, and 4.306), but in a new way: "Now Dawn rose from her bed, where she lay by haughty Tithonos" (5.1).[1] Mention of Dawn's lover contrasts his situation with Odysseus'. Calypso, like Dawn, offers her lover immortality, adding youth to keep him ageless, but Odysseus still refuses her offer, whereas Tithonos accepted without being offered eternal youth. Odysseus accepts mortality's struggles in order to remain vital and alert; Tithonos settles for an immortality of inertia due to Dawn's error.

At the gods' council, Athena pleads for Odysseus' plight, reminds the gods of the deteriorating conditions in Ithaca, and accuses them of neglecting the hero. Zeus, taken aback by Athena's comments, reminds her that the plan for Odysseus and Telemachus' return is hers, as is fated. Not even the Olympians can change fate, for fate is beyond their control. Zeus then summarizes the remaining events of the narrative, as he does on several other occasions. Perhaps these summaries emphasize the need to remind an audience in oral presentations what has already occurred and what is yet to come, since the entire narrative would be too long to recite in a single performance:

1. Odysseus is to begin his return on a raft.
2. Suffering hardships, he will sight land on the twentieth day and land in Scheria, home of the Phaeacians.
3. In Scheria he will be honored like a god and sent home on a ship loaded down with gifts.
4. Having survived Poseidon's anger, Odysseus will arrive in Ithaca to punish the suitors.
5. Telemachus will return home safely.

II. Hermes' Visit to Calypso, 43–148

Argeiphontes[2] (43; Hermes) departs for Ogygia, Calypso's island, taking the guise of a "shearwater" (51; a medium-size, long-winged seabird). Calypso is introduced singing at her loom and weaving, an occupation that defines both mortal and immortal women in Homer's epics. The lush landscape of black poplar and cypress trees around her cave evokes both a Garden of Eden and a place of death. In our first glimpse of the epic's hero, he is crying on the beach. He no longer finds the nymph pleasing, suggesting that initially he did. Lying with her out of necessity (5.154) and against his will (5.155) for seven years, Odysseus realizes that a life of inactivity is not one suitable for mortals. Hermes explains his purpose: Zeus demands the release of Odysseus, who, along with other Troy veterans, was detained by Athena's storms. The goddess is again made responsible for delaying the Greeks, although the final storm that lands Odysseus alone on Ogygia and kills his remaining companions is due to Zeus at Helius' prompting, which is essential for the Thrinacia episode (*Od.* 12). Athena's repeated implication in the Greeks' aborted homecomings is perhaps the standard version in the myths of Odysseus' *nostos*. Homer, however, does not dwell on this version, preferring to implicate the sea (Poseidon), which all returning heroes must contend with. It also provides justification for the majority of Odysseus' wanderings, which result from the Cyclops' blinding, an expansion of the father-son theme, in this case the father coming to his son's aid. In this way Homer is able to extend his epic with the number of adventures necessary to fill the hero's ten-year absence. This makes Athena's absence as the Arcesiads' patron goddess all the more plausible, as she had to remain incognito out of respect for her uncle Poseidon's anger.

Hermes' complaint about the immense distance of Calypso's home from anywhere else (5.100–101) adds to the depiction of Ogygia's detachment. This isolation, along with the nymph's cavern (the minor goddess Circe lives in a house) and the derivation of Calypso's name (*kaluptein*: to hide, to conceal), gives greater credence to Ogygia as a place of concealment—and death. Odysseus remains hidden from mortal life until Athena intercedes for his release from Poseidon's anger. Calypso, however, protests the hero's freedom, claiming she is being treated unfairly for loving a mortal she saved from death, whom she wants to immortalize. She cites Dawn and Demeter, whose mortal lovers Orion and Iasion were killed by Artemis and Zeus, respectively, implying a double standard between male deities and female gods. However, since Zeus must be obeyed, she will release the hero, but she has neither ship nor companions for him; she can only offer advice.

III. Odysseus' Decision to Leave Calypso, 149–262

Calypso approaches Odysseus, who is longing for home by the seashore.[3] He receives the news with caution, as is his nature and the reason for his eventual success. Calypso vouches for her good intentions and holds a banquet in his honor, underscoring the incompatibility between the two: Odysseus is served mortal food while the minor deity feasts on nectar and ambrosia. After the meal, Calypso tries to discourage Odysseus from abandoning her by pointing out the difficulties ahead. If he stays, she will offer him immortality, but Odysseus declines, careful not to offend her. Diplomatically agreeing that Penelope can never match Calypso's beauty and stature, he nevertheless desires home and mortality and is willing to endure the hardships. This pivotal passage highlights the type of man needed to survive in Homer's world. Odysseus endures no matter what the situation; denying struggle is denying life itself. Immortality, the lack of struggle and endurance, is, in short, a living death in which nothing ever changes. Ogygia, in the middle of Ocean, far from civilization, is at a distance that even Hermes is reluctant to traverse. In Ogygia, Odysseus' exploits and fame remain unknown, hidden from the world of men who struggle to win fame. Without struggle, there is no fame. Life is precious because it is short, whereas immortality lacks challenge and thus meaning. Even the name of her island, Ogygia, in Hesiod's *Theogony* (86), is the name given to Styx, the river in Greek mythology that forms the boundary between Earth and the underworld. Odysseus has chosen life (mortality) over death (immortality) to preserve his identity. As Nikos Kazantzakis has his Odysseus exclaim in *The Odyssey: A Modern Sequel* (1938), "Salt like death gives spice to life."[4]

Preparations are under way for Odysseus' journey the day after Hermes' arrival. Odysseus escapes eternal stagnation only because he is civilized and has the knowledge to build a craft. Unlike the Cyclops, Odysseus' skills both as a carpenter and as a sailor enable his survival, the difference between civilization and barbarism. His expertise in building a craft is explicit in a simile that compares his raft to the bottom of a cargo ship built by someone skilled in carpentry (5.249–251).

IV. Odysseus' Voyage to Scheria, 263–493

His work completed in four days (days eight through eleven), Odysseus is ready on the fifth (day twelve) for his most harrowing experience: the confrontation with Poseidon's fury before he is released from his wrath. For the next seventeen days (days twelve through twenty-eight), he makes good headway under optimal conditions, but on the eighteenth day (day twenty-nine), within sight of Scheria,[5] Poseidon spots him while returning from the Ethiopians (1.22). Realizing the gods' change of heart on further delaying Odysseus, Poseidon nevertheless threatens to vent his anger. He gathers the clouds, churns the waves, and covers the earth and sea in thunderbolts and darkness. Fearful of drowning, which he deems unheroic, Odysseus reflects on his fallen comrades, who died honorably as warriors. Had he died in Troy, he too would have had his rites and glory (5.311). Death at sea is a blight on his *kleos* (fame). In Troy deeds brought honor; at sea his trials leave him without a monument to mark his passing. As Odysseus contemplates his imminent unheroic death, Poseidon's first massive wave crashes on him, throwing him overboard. The wave's power, expressed in the first simile, tosses the raft about as dry thistle blown by a strong wind (5.328–329), an image that stresses the helplessness of man against the forces of nature. Lunging for his raft, he crawls aboard, and relying on his resourcefulness, he holds on to it as tightly as Menelaus held on to Proteus.

A sea goddess, Ino, called Leucothea,[6] once mortal, comes to his rescue and advises him to remove his clothing, abandon his raft, and swim for land. Before she disappears in the likeness of a gannet, she offers him her immortal veil for safety (*kredemnon*, mentioned four times in this section [5.346, 351, 373, and 459]), which she instructs him to fasten under his chest and return to the sea once on land. Odysseus, always cautious, weighs his options (some god could be weaving a trick against him) and deliberates on two available courses: to abandon the raft, as the goddess urged, or to hang on. Opting for the second choice, he stays on the raft, since the shore is too far to swim, but abandons it once the raft is dashed to pieces. Odysseus relies on his own resourcefulness even before he acts on a god's advice. Unlike his companions, he survives because he uses his mind. In the world of the *Odyssey*, unlike that of the *Iliad*, the mind, and not just one's prowess in battle, defines one's *aretē* (excellence). The second wave shatters Odysseus' raft and tosses it about uncontrollably like a piece of dry seed husk (5.368–369). The hero, astride a single beam, strips off his clothes, ties Ino's veil around his chest, and throws himself into the raging sea. Seeing Odysseus adrift, Poseidon abandons him and turns his horses toward his palace at Aegae.

Athena now enters to calm the storm winds and arouse the North Wind so Odysseus can eventually reach land. Still fearing death, he continues to battle the heaving swells for two more days and nights (days twenty-nine and thirty). On the third morning (day thirty-one), the winds cease, the sea calms, and Odysseus, lifted high on a third wave, sights land. A third simile at this critical moment compares him both to a father and to his children (5.394–398). Odysseus, who is "dead" in Ogygia and nearly drowned at sea, is restored to life like the simile's father, who is wasting away from an illness. The gods set him free of his sickness, and his children welcome him back from a near-death experience, as Odysseus welcomes the sight of land. That Odysseus' absence is associated with a disease, something harmful, is also a comment on Poseidon, whose hatred and jealousy have kept Odysseus from Ithaca for the past ten years.

Odysseus' joy at sighting land is short lived, for not far offshore, he hears the crash of heavy surf. As he sees no other way to reach dry land, Odysseus' heart sinks once more. If he approaches the shore, a wave can toss him against the rocks. If he tries to swim in the hope of finding a beach, a gale can carry him back to open sea. Again, he is at the mercy of Poseidon, who might at any moment rear some monster out of the waves. As he ponders available options, a fourth and final wave sweeps him toward the rocks, but Athena indicates a way to avoid his being flayed alive and having his bones crushed. Relying on his mind for the right strategy, he clings to a reef until the giant wave passes, but the backwash tosses him out to sea again. The fourth simile underscores his helplessness (5.432–435). He leaves torn skin from his hands glued to the rock, just as pebbles are left stuck in the octopus' suckers as it is dragged away from its shelter. Only his wit and agility save him now, illustrating the chasm existing between the warrior world of the *Iliad*, where strength is paramount, and the world of the *Odyssey*, where mere strength is useless against the forces of nature. With the goddess' help (Athena gives him foresight [5.437]), Odysseus swims clear of the surf and scans the shore for a sheltered spot from which he can safely reach land. Arriving at the river's mouth, free of rocks and sheltered from the winds, he makes for shore. Realizing his helplessness against nature, Odysseus prays, showing his humility, and begs for pity as he approaches the river god as a suppliant. The river stems its current, for the gods assist only those who truly acknowledge their existence and divine superiority. Admitting his inferiority before the gods, beaten by the sea, his body swollen, salt water gushing from his mouth and nostrils, unable to speak and hardly able to breathe from weakness, Odysseus finally finds himself on land.

Exhausted, Odysseus gathers his strength, unties the veil still around his waist, and returns it to the sea. His body torn by his twenty-day ordeal since leaving Calypso, he again considers the possibilities open to him. If he remains where he is through the night, the chill and dew will kill him. If he crawls in the woods beyond the shore, he will be left defenseless, too tired to resist wild beasts. Such careful weighing of all possible scenarios exhibits Odysseus' agility as he ponders his best course of action. Settling for the second option, Odysseus crawls to the woods and collapses under two olive trees—one cultivated, the other wild. The mention of wild olive is significant, given the role olive wood plays throughout the *Odyssey*. The olive tree is not only sacred to Athena but also an instrument of Odysseus' intelligence, for an olive log was used to blind the Cyclops, and an olive trunk (a symbol of his marriage's firmness) bolsters his marriage bed. Here he lies between a wild and a cultivated olive—his past and future. He is at a crossroads between death and life, which the olive trees, Athena herself, will preserve.

In a fifth simile, Athena envelops the exhausted Odysseus in sleep as he lies buried in a pile of leaves, cradled within the two olive trees (5.488–491). Like the embers, kept buried so the fire they harbor will not extinguish, Odysseus, barely alive when he lands on Scheria, is buried under the leaves of the two olive trees. He is reborn by Athena's rekindling the life in him as one revives the dying embers of a log, preventing it from being extinguished. All four previous waves and their accompanying similes feature Odysseus as an insignificant piece of matter tossed about indiscriminately by forces of nature until he is revived from a near-death experience and promised renewed life by Athena in a mortal world, having survived the wilderness of a mythic realm. On the following morning, the thirty-first day of his *nostos*, he, like rekindled embers, is reborn to abandon his Iliadic past for his Odyssean present. Of the forty-one days of the *Odyssey* narrative, twenty-five are described in this book, more than in any of the other twenty-three books of the epic.

Selected Bibliography: *Od.* 5

Anderson, "Calypso."
Apthorp, "Language."
Casson, "Odysseus'."
Clarke, *Art*, 45–66.
Crane, *Calypso.*
Dyson, "Second."
Hogan, "Temptation."
Holtsmark, "Spiritual."
Kardulias, "Odysseus."
Louden, *Homer's*, 124–34.
Louden, *The "Odyssey,"* 104–129.

Mark, "*Odyssey* 5.234–53 . . . Reappraisal."
Mark, "*Odyssey* 5.234–53 . . . Clarification."
Marks, *Zeus*, 36–61.
Reece, *Stranger's*, 101–122.
Reinhardt, "Adventures."
Said, *Homer*, 150–188.
Scott, William C., *Artistry*, 118–126.
Thalmann, "*Odyssey*," 47–63.
Vernant, "Refusal."
Further commentary on *Od.* 5 in General Bibliography I.

Book 6

Od. 6 continues the thirty-first day of the *Odyssey* narrative before turning to day thirty-two, which occupies the remainder of *Od.* 6 and *Od.* 7. In the first section, Athena arrives in Scheria to introduce its people and prepare Nausicaa's trip to the shore. The second and longest section deals with Nausicaa's encounter with Odysseus at the shore. The third section returns the princess and Odysseus to the Phaeacian court.

I. From Scheria's palace to the shore (26%)
II. Meeting at the shore (50%)
III. From the shore to Scheria's palace (24%)

I. From Scheria's Palace to the Shore, 1–84

As Odysseus lies exhausted in a heap of leaves, Athena arrives at the Phaeacians, who formerly lived in Hyperia, a land next to that of the Cyclopes. Because of the Cyclopes' superior strength and their animosity toward the Phaeacians, Nausithous, their leader, migrated to Scheria, a place far from other mortals. There he settled his people, isolating them from outside influence by building a wall around their new city. Thus, the first impression given of the Phaeacians is of their isolation and distance from the rest of the mortal world, reminding us of Calypso and her isolation on Ogygia. Each occupies a no-man's-land, keeping mortals like Odysseus hidden from life while in their company.

Athena, disguised as Nausicaa's friend, comes to her in a dream to remind her not to neglect her household duties, luring her to the shore, where she will accidentally wake Odysseus. As a young girl of marriageable age already courted by the best Phaeacians, Nausicaa must concern herself with her appearance, as well as the well-being of her entire family. In the present instance, the family laundry needs washing. The goddess advises her to ask her father for the mules and cart so she can travel to the washing places far from the city to attend to her responsibilities. There is a protocol for right behavior, whether it is in marriage, praying to the gods, receiving a stranger, or caring for one's family. Nausicaa's dream informs us of a citizen's station within a nuclear family, whose values are contrasted with those held by the suitors in Ithaca. Furthermore, Nausicaa's courtship is contrasted with Penelope's, in which the suitors occupying her home pressure her to marry. In Scheria, Nausicaa is oblivious to suitors yet unknown to her, who will follow an orderly procedure in courting her.

On the following morning (day thirty-two), Nausicaa approaches her parents, who are pursuing their duties. The home (*oikos*) and its care are the responsibility of women, while men's duty is the city's governance (*polis*), a division of labor that becomes a major theme in the Greek tragic dramas of the fifth century B.C.E. Requesting the wagon, Nausicaa uses her maiden charms to get her way (6.57) and supports her request by emphasizing the duties expected of her. Women in Homer's epics represent a powerful force, which both deters and enables males in achieving their goals. Calypso and Circe become both obstacles and facilitators in Odysseus' *nostos*. Feminine charm can also be a powerful and often negative force for mortals. The Trojan War was due to the abduction of a woman, Helen, while the ongoing disorder in Ithaca is due to Penelope's refusal to select a husband.

Nausicaa's first justification for her request is her concern that her father must look his best in performing his civic duties. Second, she mentions her five brothers, three still bachelors, and the need that they be seen in public in clean clothing. Third, embarrassed to speak with her father of her future marriage (although he understands her request [6.67]), she considers her own appearance. We here become aware of what Peter Green calls the "individual, original activity [which moves] the [*Odyssey* narrative] forward" (*Green*, 13). Nausicaa, who seeks conveyance for personal reasons, lies to her father, who understands what she is concealing, though she does not think so. In a rather modern, realistic scene, Nausicaa uses indirect communication (as in 6.276–284) to veil her true purpose, and her father accommodates her to spare her feelings.

Nausicaa's appeal to her duties in a household of men is a comment on the entire family and Nausicaa's part in it. Negative comments against family stain the reputation of all, the strongest family being a united one, capable of weathering the evils that befall it. We are again reminded of Agamemnon and Clytemnestra, a weak family, as opposed to Odysseus and Penelope, a strong one in which like-mindedness (*homophrosunē*) triumphs. The ideal family is singularized once more when Alcinous orders his servingmen to harness the wagon while the queen, Arete, prepares a picnic basket for her daughter and her attendant women. The queen herself prepares the foodstuff, just as the princess takes care of her own laundry. The duties of individual family members remain the same for rich and poor alike. These values stand in contrast to those of the gods, who are often depicted as frivolous. Mortality's brevity demands cooperation for a happier existence, whereas immortality, free of death and life's struggles, gives little meaning to such values.

II. Meeting at the Shore, 85–250

While the laundry is drying in the sun, Nausicaa and her friends bathe, anoint themselves with oil, eat their dinner, and play a game of ball. A simile (6.102–109) compares Nausicaa to the goddess Artemis, a comparison

Odysseus also makes later in the book, significant in both instances for depicting the girl's character. A huntress associated with the life of nubile girls and the youngest among the three virgin goddesses (the other two are Athena and Hestia), Artemis is the ideal comparison for Nausicaa. Like Artemis, Nausicaa displays courage; she is a strong, unwavering girl in the presence of danger (she stands firm before a naked Odysseus, while her handmaidens run away). Not only is Artemis a virgin goddess (6.109), but her virginity is associated with honor and purity, one not to be defiled (see the myth of Actaeon).[7] Further, the goddess' beauty and youthful, free-ranging spirit are further qualities that bear comparison to Nausicaa. Just as Artemis towers over her companion nymphs in stature, so, too, does Nausicaa outshine and tower over her maids.

While waiting for the laundry to dry, Nausicaa throws a ball to a handmaiden, who misses it, eliciting screams from the girls and waking Odysseus. The hero, always cautious and suspicious of his surroundings, wonders where he has landed. Is he again among violent and savage people, or is he now among hospitable and just strangers? Since chronologically the Phaeacian episode is Odysseus' last adventure, it is not surprising that he is confused about his whereabouts. For the past ten years, he has gone from one harrowing adventure to another, most involving savages and violence, thus his legitimate concern in wondering what he is about to face. The voices of young girls could be human, bestial, or divine. Nevertheless, Odysseus rises from the thicket in which he is sleeping to face this new challenge, as he has done many times before.

His first act before facing the girls is to hide his private parts with a leafy branch. A simile (6.130–135) compares him to a mountain lion whose hunger drives it to raid fenced-in domestic flocks, a telling comparison illuminating the difference between the man who weighs his options before acting and the beast that acts on instinct alone. Odysseus, hungry and grubby after a twenty-day battering at sea, waits for the opportunity to satisfy his hunger, but unlike the lion, he uses his mind to control his instincts. Not knowing whom he is facing, he first examines the situation before deciding on a course of action. His good breeding makes him hide his private parts instinctively, and only then does he advance cautiously toward the girls, to whom he appears terrifying. They flee, except Nausicaa, for like the goddess Artemis, she stands firm and unafraid.

Odysseus next debates how to approach Nausicaa without frightening her. If she is an immortal, custom demands he kneel and clasp her knees, but if he is facing a mortal, such a gesture would send the wrong signal, given his nakedness. Whatever course he decides to take must satisfy both mortal and immortal. Favoring mind over instinct, he decides the best approach to addressing the young girl is to keep his distance and use language (intellect) to win favor rather than clasping the girl's knees and thus face anger should she turn out to be mortal. He begins with an appeal (6.149–185) displaying the agility of his mind to convince the girl that he is both civilized and trustworthy.

Odysseus' four-part entreaty to Nausicaa (appeal [6.149–161], self-identification [6.162–169], supplication [6.170–179], and reward [6.180–185]) begins with his asking her on his knees whether she is mortal or a goddess (6.149). He first addresses her as a god, comparing her to Artemis in beauty, figure, and stature (6.150–152), emphasizing her beauty as his reason for not supplicating her as custom demands by clasping her knees, a beauty that mesmerizes him and makes him afraid of provoking her anger. On the other hand, if she is not a god, likening her to Artemis signals that he respects her virginity and privacy, the reason for keeping his distance in his naked and wild appearance. Having explained his reluctance to approach her, Odysseus compliments her as a maiden of good breeding whose behavior honors her family and her future husband: "Three times blessed are your father and the lady your mother, / and . . . your brothers too" (6.154–155), but most of all the one who, after conferring gifts on her, leads her home as his bride (6.159–160). Her beauty and behavior will lead to the husband whose gifts will be a testament to the reputation she deserves. The reader is reminded of the behavior of the suitors, who instead of rewarding Penelope's beauty, waste her fortune.

Odysseus, without revealing his name, identifies himself in such a way that she can ascertain his character. Her beauty, the wonder that keeps him immobilized, reminds him of a tree he saw in Delos by Apollo's altar. By comparing her to the palm tree, he introduces clues that he wants her to notice. The tree was in Delos[8] (a familiar holy site) by Apollo's altar (the god of prophecy and Artemis' brother) when he visited there with a following of many people. That Odysseus was there with many people signals that he is not only a believer visiting the tree under which both gods were born but also a man of rank who went there with many followers. Having established his credentials, Odysseus adds that the journey meant hard suffering for him (6.165) so he can more easily explain his twenty-day ordeal. Still ignorant of his host's ideology, Odysseus is reluctant to mention Troy. Thus, he not only explains his hesitancy to touch her but also identifies himself as both a religious man who has no designs on her person and a man of reputation and importance.

Odysseus continues to explain his presence on the shore; after twenty days at sea, he landed on Scheria. He reveals his ordeal at sea but cleverly avoids mentioning Poseidon, which serves him well later when he discovers he is among a seafaring people who revere the god. To malign Poseidon as an enemy would have risked Nausicaa's questioning his credibility. Instead, Odysseus presents himself as a mere mortal seeking assistance. Holding his hunger at bay and asking for clothing and directions to the city, he shows self-control and good breeding. The future blessings he confers on Nausicaa—a husband, a home, and agreement between husband and wife—are the very qualities that make Odysseus' homecoming possible. It is the like-mindedness that exists between him and his wife that will prove unassailable to the forces trying to divide them.

Nausicaa is persuaded by Odysseus, since he seems like a thoughtful man. She accepts that his troubles are due to fate and thus worthy of assistance, for fate does not determine one's degree of goodness or evil, since Zeus dispenses justice as he wishes. As a suppliant in her country, he is due hospitality, and she will provide clothing and anything else he needs.

Claiming Scheria is loved by the immortals, she identifies herself as King Alcinous' daughter and warns that Odysseus' safe return home rests in her mother's hands, leaving open the question of Arete's power. Turning to her maids, Nausicaa reprimands them for running away, reminding them that, loved as they are by the gods and removed from the world of men, they have nothing to fear but are obligated to receive Odysseus, since all strangers and wanderers are sacred to Zeus. Nausicaa's trust in the gods, however, will be shattered by the end of Odysseus' stay. Poseidon, the Phaeacians' patron god, will petrify the ship and the crew that convey Odysseus home and threaten the Phaeacians with an encircling mountain range, cutting them off forever from foreign visitors.

Before leading Odysseus to the city, Nausicaa orders her attendants to feed and bathe him, but out of modesty, she does not offer to bathe him herself. The task is left to her maids, who lead the stranger to a place sheltered from the wind, lay out clothes, and supply olive oil for his skin, keeping their distance. Since slaves never hesitate to bathe guests once ordered (8.449–455, 10.357–365, 23.153–155), the girls' refusal to bathe the stranger can be taken as an inhospitable act, although their reluctance is justified, for often in Greek myths both human and divine maidens are abducted and raped.[9] Fearful of approaching a naked man who initially appeared terrifying to them, Nausicaa's young companions scatter in panic. Odysseus, sensing the maids' reluctance to carry out the princess's orders, again shows his good breeding and modesty by asking them to stand aside so he can bathe alone. The maids, relieved at his consideration, report his words to their young mistress, endearing Odysseus to the princess, whose infatuation with the stranger leads her later to imagine a husband like him. Odysseus' civility in protecting the maids from Nausicaa's reprimands is later used in support for the princess in response to her father's admonition for not bathing the stranger (7.295–296).

Once Odysseus has bathed, anointed, and clothed himself, Athena enters unseen to make him taller, a transformation compared to a masterpiece of silver overlaid in gold and fashioned by a master craftsman trained by Hephaestus and Athena (6.232–235). Odysseus, reborn from his past exploits, is ready to face life again. No longer will he undergo the torments of the past nine years but in four days will arrive home a rich man. Nausicaa informs her companions that the stranger looks like a deity visiting their island, musing that her future husband should be like him if he were willing to remain in Scheria (6.244).

III. From the Shore to Scheria's Palace, 251–311

Although Nausicaa is not an obstacle to Odysseus' *nostos* as Circe and Calypso were, it is notable that in her youthful musings of Odysseus as a good husband, she singles out one stipulation—only if he is willing to remain in Scheria, the same condition both Circe and Calypso require of Odysseus were he to accept their offers and the main reason for his refusal. He does not want to remain a Nobody in a no-man's-land. Preparing to direct him to the palace, Nausicaa offers some observations on her ideal society—it abounds in temples and is not interested in war. A seafaring people, they excel in ships and sailing, in which Poseidon plays a major role. Her main concern is not being seen with the stranger and facing gossip. She worries about causing a scandal among the Phaeacians, which might shame her and her family's reputation; she deems such behavior improper. In order to avoid gossip, she instructs Odysseus to separate from her entourage when they near the town and wait unseen in a grove of poplars sacred to Athena near the palace until she and her friends arrive first. Only then is Odysseus to ask for directions, which any Phaeacian can provide. Once at the palace, Odysseus is instructed to bypass Nausicaa's father and go directly to her mother and embrace her knees. Although Alcinous is presented as the head of both his family and kingdom, we have a hint in Nausicaa's request of a matriarchal rather than a patriarchal society (the norm in Homer's epics). However, this turns out not to be the case. Scheria's values are analogous to those in Ithaca, but a distinction is made here between the surreal world of Scheria and the real world of Ithaca. Odysseus has ascended slowly from a mythical landscape to

Scheria's less mythical one, but he is still far from the mortal world he is trying to reach.

Having provided directions, Nausicaa whips the mules to a steady trot in consideration for the stranger and the maids following on foot. As the sun sets on day thirty-two at Athena's sacred grove, Odysseus stops until Nausicaa's party reaches the palace, and prays to Athena for Phaeacian pity (6.325–326). Although the reader is aware of Athena's constant presence in *Od.* 5 (she asks for his release from Calypso, plans his landing on Scheria [5.382–387], assists him in reaching shore [5.425–429 and 437], and protects him once on shore [5.491–493]), Odysseus feels neglected and believes the goddess has not offered him assistance since he left Troy. Now, as he prays, she acknowledges his prayer, but out of respect for her uncle Poseidon, who still rages against the hero, she decides not to interfere openly until Odysseus reaches Ithaca.

Selected Bibliography: *Od.* 6

Ahl and Roisman, *"Odyssey,"* 43–70.
Austin, "Nausikaa."
Austin, "Wedding."
Belmont, "Telemachus."
Bolmarcich, "Homophrosune."
Buchan, *Limits*, 36–49, 181–205.
Cairns, "Mixing."
Clarke, *Art*, 45–66.
De Vries, "Difficulties."
Garvie, *Homer*.
Glenn, "Odysseus."
Griffith, "Temple."
Gross, "Nausikaa."
Gutglueck, "Detestable."
Ingalls, "Nausikaa."
Irwin, "Odysseus'."

Jones, "*Odyssey* 6.209–223."

Lattimore, "Nausikaa's."

Louden, *Homer's*, 135–163.

Pache, "Odysseus."

Reece, *Stranger's*, 101–122.

Rose, Gilbert P., "Unfriendly."

Said, *Homer*, 150–188.

Shapiro, "Coming."

Vallillee, "Nausikaa."

Van Nortwick, "Penelope and Nausicaa."

Watrous, "Artemis."

Further commentary on *Od.* 6 in General Bibliography I.

Book 7

The three sections of *Od.* 7 take place at the Phaeacian palace on the evening of day thirty-two. The first thirteen lines describe Nausicaa's arrival (I), followed by Odysseus' (II). The remainder of the book is devoted to Odysseus' time in the presence of the Phaeacian king and queen (III).

I. Nausicaa's arrival at the palace (4%)
II. Odysseus' arrival at the palace (34%)
III. Odysseus in Alcinous' palace (62%)

I. Nausicaa's Arrival at the Palace, 1–13

Once the princess enters the palace courtyard, her brothers help unload the cart, showing her the same consideration that she had earlier shown them. Nausicaa retires to her chambers, attended by her nurse, Eurymedusa. A brief biographical sketch of the nanny follows: she arrived by ship from Apiraea (perhaps brought by merchants involved in the slave trade), was given as a prize to Alcinous, and nursed Nausicaa. Her fate is indicative of servants' fates in the *Odyssey*—most come from royalty, are abducted at an early age, and are sold to a wealthy benefactor, in whose household they serve for the remainder of their lives. Once Nausicaa enters her chambers, Eurymedusa lights a fire and prepares her supper, rounding out an image of familial cooperation, warmth, and safety. The princess will not appear again except for a brief farewell to Odysseus when he leaves Scheria (8.457–462).

II. Odysseus' Arrival at the Palace, 14–133

Until Odysseus arrives in Scheria, Athena is careful not to encroach on Poseidon's territory, but once there, she remains at Odysseus' side for the remainder of the epic, revealing herself to him on numerous occasions. Here disguised as a young girl, the goddess drifts a mist about him as he sets out for the palace in order to shield him from passersby who might ask questions. Isolated, the Phaeacians are suspicious of strangers, perhaps the reason Athena needs to hide Odysseus in a fog. Her caution prepares us for the ambivalences and contradictions that become apparent in Scheria: the Phaeacians are neither divine nor mortal but *anchitheoi* (5.35; close to the gods). They live in a distant land isolated from other people where war is unfamiliar. Their fields produce all types of fruit year-round and remain lush through all four seasons (7.128). The gods themselves are free to visit and feast among them (7.203). This is a magical place, a utopia, where people constantly feast and dance and live in peace and prosperity. Nausicaa calls her people *hyperphialoi* (6.274; insolent men), a word used often to describe Penelope's suitors, equating the Phaeacians to the suitors. Perhaps what is being suggested is that the hassle-free life on Scheria is not much different from the life practiced by the suitors in Ithaca during Odysseus' absence. However, the unhampered lifestyle of Scheria is unsuited to the real world of strife, reason enough for Odysseus' unwillingness to remain there any more than he is willing to stay with Calypso.

The young girl points the way for Odysseus and warns him to proceed silently and avoid eye contact. He is not to ask directions from the locals, since they are suspicious of strangers. On the other hand, the hospitality he gets in Scheria is equal to (if not greater than) that received by Telemachus from Nestor and Menelaus. Such mixed Phaeacian signals serve to differentiate the fantasy world of Scheria from the real world of Ithaca. Scheria is a semimythical world of men interested in ships, which move swift as thought or like birds, a world in sharp contrast to Ithaca. It is a dangerous place, for everything the Phaeacians possess comes from the Earthshaker, Odysseus' enemy Poseidon.

As Odysseus makes his way to Alcinous' palace, he is aware of Poseidon's influence, which accounts for his caution not to identify the god as his enemy. At the palace, the girl/Athena advises Odysseus to enter without fear, for the bold man, even though a stranger, always comes off best. Odysseus is aware he is in the company of no ordinary child, given the girl's knowledge of Phaeacian culture, but he does not recognize the goddess, who describes for him and the reader the Phaeacians' background.

1. Queen Arete is related to her husband's family.
2. The first king, Nausithous, son of Poseidon and Periboea (the youngest daughter of Eurymedon, king of the giants),[10] ruled the Phaeacians. He bore two sons, Alcinous and Rhexenor. Rhexenor married and produced a daughter, Arete, but he was killed by Apollo for reasons unknown. Alcinous, Rhexenor's brother, then married his niece.
3. Arete is honored and loved by the king, her children, and her subjects, who look on her as a god. Her intelligence and judgment resolve quarrels among those she favors.

Odysseus is to approach Arete cautiously, for if she befriends him there is hope he will reach home. Again, the reader is reminded that Odysseus' homecoming rests with Arete's goodwill. The importance placed on Arete's opinion is more likely due to her intelligence, her perceptiveness, and the trust she inspires in the general public. In the meantime, Athena leaves for Athens and the house of Erechtheus (7.81),[11] but no indication is given that Odysseus suspects the girl to be the goddess, since in *Od.* 13.314–319 he complains of not having seen Athena since leaving Troy.

Odysseus' reaction to Alcinous' palace and its surroundings bears comparison to Telemachus' admiration of Menelaus' (*Od.* 4) and points to the differences between the semidivine world of Scheria and the mortal world of Sparta and Ithaca:

1. The palace walls are of bronze with a frieze of blue lapis; the palace doors are gold with silver pillars.
2. Immortal guard dogs of gold and silver constructed by Hephaestus keep watch over the palace. (It is interesting to note that arrivals in the *Odyssey* are often greeted by dogs. See 2.11, 7.91–94, 14.30–37, 16.4–10, 16.162–163., 17.62, and 17.291–327.)
3. Drinking and feasting sessions are held before golden torch-bearing statues of boys set on pedestals to light the night.
4. Fifty servingwomen, experts like Athena herself in the art of weaving, carry out the household tasks with an opulence that overwhelms Odysseus.
5. In a magnificent four-acre orchard flourish all kinds of luxuriant fruit trees always in their prime whose yield never flags or dies.
6. The vineyards are never in short supply, so that while new grapes ripen for harvest, others lie in open fields baking into raisins and others are crushed for wine vats.
7. Beds of vegetables of every kind remain green year in and year out.
8. Two springs dispense water; one irrigates the garden, and the other is reserved for drinking.

Unlike Menelaus' palace, whose splendors captivated Telemachus, Alcinous' palace contains both qualities of the surreal (dogs and boys of gold) and those of the real, a bounty that captures Odysseus' admiration, in whose own storeroom lie piles of gold and bronze, bins full of clothing, and jars of olive oil and wine (*Od.* 2.338–340). Odysseus, whose own wealth is legendary, remains speechless before the opulence of Alcinous' home, a reaction that sets it and Scheria in the realm of the gods.

III. Odysseus in Alcinous' Palace, 134–347

The Phaeacian leaders are pouring libations to Argeiphontes (Hermes), who, like Poseidon, is one of their major gods. Odysseus goes straight to Arete and clasps her knees as the mist engulfing him dissipates; all present fall silent to see a stranger beseeching the queen, the king, and the feasters for conveyance home. He prays the gods grant the king's heirs his property and the rights the people have given him (7.149–150), a prayer remindful of Telemachus' dispute at the Ithacan assembly (*Od.* 2) and the suitors' refusal to comply. Echeneus, the oldest Phaeacian, finally breaks the silence. In both Homeric epics, advanced age is equated with wisdom, for in Homer's oral society (one that has not developed literacy), longevity provides the longest memory of things past. Such societies rely on those who can recall past events in order to judge and resolve present ones. Echeneus, like Nestor in *Od.* 3, objects that the stranger is sitting on the ground and asks Alcinous to offer him a chair and supper and to pour libations to Zeus, who upholds the sacred rights of suppliants. Echeneus' unease contrasts with the suitors' contrary behavior in denying hospitality to Mentes/Athena in *Od.* 1 and to the beggar/Odysseus when he arrives in Ithaca.

To be reminded of the laws of hospitality due to strangers when such laws seem familiar to them further exposes the ambiguity of the Phaeacian world. Indeed, earlier, in *Od.* 6, Nausicaa orders her maids to care for the stranger, since all strangers are sacred in the sight of Zeus (6.207–208). At the same time, however, we learn from both Nausicaa (6.274) and Athena (7.32) that the Phaeacians are suspicious of strangers. Their isolation, their history with the giants, and the prophecy concerning their future (8.564–571) make them cautious in accepting strangers and explain

Alcinous' reticence in accepting Odysseus until alerted by the elder. Embarrassed, Alcinous unseats his favorite son, Laodamas, and sits Odysseus next to him. Odysseus is then served on a polished table (7.174) and washes his hands from water poured from a golden pitcher held above a silver basin (7.172–173), which is described in a repetition of the same passage used for Athena in *Od.* 1.136–138 and for Telemachus in *Od.* 4.52–58. The works of art humankind is capable of are a testament to its capacity to rise above the instinctive and mundane. In all three instances (*Od.* 1, 4, and 7), when serving Odysseus, Athena, and Telemachus, quality takes precedence over quantity, in contrast to the suitors' treatment. The dinner ends with Alcinous calling for more wine and acknowledging the hospitality due to strangers by repeating verbatim the lines (7.180–181) quoted by Echeneus earlier (7.164–165).

Alcinous suggests retiring for the evening, promising to call the Phaeacian elders at dawn to further entertain their guest, sacrifice to the immortals, and announce the stranger's safe passage home (without asking his identity). Either Alcinous is anxious to rid himself of a potential problem, or he is compensating for his earlier lapse in hospitality. For Odysseus, Scheria remains a strange place, which accounts for his not revealing his identity. Both Athena's earlier warnings and his own observations caution him to tread carefully. Strangely, Arete, whom he first embraced upon entering the palace as both Nausicaa and Athena advised him, has yet to speak. Perhaps she is carefully taking stock of his character before inquiring about the clothes he is wearing (7.238). For now, it is the king who welcomes him and promises to return him safely home.

To see his guest safely home, Alcinous is aware that he must endure whatever the heavy Spinners[12] spun for him at birth, suggesting humans are controlled by fate (*aisa, moira*), which encompasses the time appointed for death and the events following birth. Poseidon can punish Odysseus, but he cannot destroy him if his appointed time is not due. Nevertheless, the gods are to be feared, and since they often visit Scheria, the stranger could be a god deserving their hospitality. This close relationship between the Phaeacians and the Olympians further sets them apart from the inhabitants of Odysseus' Ithaca. Also, the Phaeacians' relationship to the Cyclopes and the giants, previously mentioned, further separates them from the real world and links them to the mythic world from which Odysseus has just escaped. Scheria is not only a land halfway between the divine and mortal worlds but also part of the wonderland through which Odysseus journeys.

Odysseus, grasping Alcinous' concern that he might be a visiting immortal, assures his hosts he is not a god but rather a mortal and begs the king to allow him to finish his dinner as he launches into a tirade on hunger (7.216–217). This diversion is not the first time the epic references the power of the belly.[13] Recognition that the belly's needs can overpower reason and must be controlled is a further sign of Odysseus' intelligence and an excuse to avoid dealing with any other issue until that need is met. The attention given the belly perhaps also reflects the poet's period, since it is constantly mentioned.[14] But there is no hard evidence for this view other than that Homer's seventh-century B.C.E. world was one of relative poverty and limited achievements, a condition that did not abate until the second half of the eighth century when the Greek world underwent a renaissance. Following the reference to hunger, Odysseus again reminds the king of his promise to send him home on the following day. His appeals are received with approval by those present, who urge his passage home.

Arete finally breaks her silence when she recognizes the clothes Nausicaa has loaned him. Curious to know how Odysseus obtained them, she poses three questions: (1) Who are you? (2) Who gave you your clothing? and (3) Where did you come from? (7.238–239). Odysseus responds to Arete's questions in reverse order, as is Homer's custom, but tactfully avoids her first question. Mindful of Athena's and Nausicaa's advice that his journey home depends on the queen, he must first win her loyalty before he can reveal his identity. He begins with his stay at Calypso's, for he anticipates what Arete wants to know: Why did Nausicaa offer him her sons' clothing, and did anything transpire between them? He is careful to point out that his presence on Calypso's Ogygia was an event beyond his control, but one that saved him from drowning. Even though Calypso promised to make him immortal, she never won him over, though he spent seven years resisting her advances. Once released, he coped with Poseidon's waves (but does not say why) for seventeen days and landed naked and exhausted on Scheria. Tactfully, he neglects to mention the nightly lovemaking he engaged in for the greater part of his stay in Ogygia. Thus, he indirectly assures Arete that his only interest in Nausicaa was for her ability to procure clothes to hide his nakedness. Once he responds to Arete's main concern (her daughter's treatment), Odysseus turns to his own agenda: acquiring safe passage to Ithaca. He points out that after seven years in Ogygia, Calypso herself urged him to leave, hinting that Arete should do likewise. Moreover, he points out that the goddess provided him with provisions needed for his trip, hoping for similar treatment from the Phaeacians.

Odysseus lives up to his reputation by omitting another crucial feature of his tale, the fact that he alone reached Ogygia because his companions sinned against Helius (the sun god) by devouring the sacred cattle. Aware that Poseidon is a Phaeacian god, he further omits the god's role in his suffering, attributing his being washed ashore on Scheria to luck and his determination to survive. Disregarding the queen's first question, he compliments Nausicaa's beauty and good manners, pointing out that having been supplicated as if she were a goddess, she responded as a mature, intelligent woman and offered him food, wine, a bath, and clothing. Odysseus is careful not to include details that might reflect negatively on the princess (e.g., she ordered her maids, who refused to obey her, to bathe him). He praises Nausicaa as a person of reason, and one who weighs her options before reaching a decision. He characterizes her as a young girl beyond her years in intelligence, praise calculated to solidify himself in her parents' favor. His comments also reveal why Odysseus confers such praise on Nausicaa: she is a younger version of Penelope, bold, cunning, and calculating, a female version of himself and a mortal copy of the immortal Calypso.

Persuaded by Odysseus' tale and his compliments to his daughter, Alcinous reprimands her for not following protocol to lead the stranger to the palace herself. Odysseus again defends her, absorbing the blame for not following her to the palace. Fabricating an excuse, he lies that although she urged him to follow her, he refused out of embarrassment, fearing for her reputation and for what her parents might think of her. With this lie, one of many Odysseus tells to win the loyalty of those he tests, he both defends Nausicaa and presents himself as a discerning man of good breeding.

Impressed, the king pays the stranger a compliment, praying to Zeus, Athena, and Apollo that he stay in Phaeacia to be called his son-in-law (7.313), but he will not force him (7.315–316). Odysseus can leave as early as the following day, nor should he be concerned about the distance, even if it is farther away than Euboea. If Euboea is the farthest point known to the Phaeacians (7.322–323), they might not be familiar with the location of Troy, which is much farther north. However, in *Od.* 8 Demodocus sings of the Trojan horse, indicating their familiarity with Troy as a legend. Homer notes that Alcinous' sailors traveled only once to Euboea, when they transported Rhadamanthys there on the way to Tityos and returned home on the same day, emphasizing the surreal speed of their ships. Although Rhadamanthys is mentioned earlier, in 4.564, and Tityos later, in 11.576–581, no mention of the journey's purpose to Euboea appears anywhere in the epic. Happy for the offer to be conveyed home the next day, Odysseus prays that Zeus grant Alcinous unceasing glory (7.332; *kleos esthlon*), the fame every Homeric hero seeks. Arete in the meantime orders her attendant women to prepare a bed for Odysseus, accepting the stranger as someone worthy of her trust.

Selected Bibliography: *Od.* 7

Ahl and Roisman, "*Odyssey*," 43–70.

Buchan, *Limits*, 36–49, 181–205.

Carnes, "With Friends."

Clarke, *Art*, 45–66.
Cook, "Ferrymen."
De Vries, "Phaeacian."
Dolin, "Odysseus."
Faraone, "Hephaestus."
Finley, John H., Jr., *Homer's*, 74–92.
Garvie, *Homer.*
Karp, "Need."
Louden, "Eumaios."
Newton, "Rebirth."
Olson, "Women's."
Peek, "Propriety."
Reece, *Stranger's*, 101–122.
Reinhardt, "Adventures."
Reinhardt, "Homer."
Said, *Homer*, 150–188.
Segal, "Phaeacians."
Tebben, "Alkinoös."
Webber, "Hero."
Whittaker, "Status."
Further commentary on *Od.* 7 in General Bibliography I.

Book 8

Od. 8 opens on the morning of the thirty-third day, the longest day and night of the epic, lasting until 13.17. The book divides into four parts—a lengthy introduction, followed by Demodocus' three songs.

I. Introduction (12%)
II. Demodocus' first song (31%)
III. Demodocus' second song (37%)
IV. Demodocus' third song (20%)

I. Introduction, 1–71

Odysseus (referred to for the first time as *ptoliporthos Odusseus* [8.3; spoiler of cities]) wakes up early on his third day in Scheria to attend a Phaeacian assembly and later the games, where his physical strength is questioned. Although *mētis* (cunning, intelligence) has predominated his adventures, *biē* (force) is still required for survival but with restraint, a restrain he exhibits when asked to participate in the Phaeacian games. For the present, Athena, disguised as Alcinous' herald, urges the people to attend the assembly. For the occasion, the goddess transforms the hero for two reasons: first, to ensure for Odysseus the Phaeacians' love and respect necessary to carry out his homecoming; second, to prepare him for the trials of strength, which will earn him great esteem for physical ability, a skill the Phaeacians consider the greatest glory that a man can achieve (8.147). Still ignorant of the stranger's identity, which plagues him, Alcinous announces his intention to send the stranger home. No Phaeacian visitor was ever held against his will—a kindness that will cost the king dearly. Once the fifty-two-man crew is selected to convey Odysseus home, all are invited to honor their guest with a final feast.

Following the feast sacrifices, the herald Pontonous enters with Demodocus, who is introduced as one loved by the gods to whom the Muse has given the power of song even though he is blind (8.64). Homer here expands his homage to oral singers, which began with Phemius, whose performance tamed the unruly suitors, who sat listening in silence (1.325–326). Homer draws a loving portrait of Demodocus as one greatly respected (perhaps a tribute to himself, who tradition says was also blind). Although blind to the physical world, Demodocus possesses internal sight, which views people as they really are. The worlds created by his art not only entertain but in fact transport their audiences to a higher reality—hence Pontonous' care to seat him on a special chair (8.65), hang his lyre on a peg over his head, and show him how to retrieve it, before he sets food and drink beside him.

II. Demodocus' First Song, 72–255

Demodocus sings of the quarrel that took place between Odysseus and Achilles before the Achaeans set off for Troy. Little is known of this quarrel other than the information given in the few lines devoted to it here (8.75–82). It stands in contrast to the famous quarrel between Achilles and Agamemnon (the wrath of Achilles), which is the raison d'être for Homer's *Iliad.* All we are told of the Odysseus-Achilles quarrel is that it was prophesied to Agamemnon by Apollo when he visited his sacred shrine, which made him happy that the conflict between the Greeks and Trojans was about to begin (8.81–82). There are several possible reasons why Homer chose this lesser-known quarrel for Demodocus to sing of rather than the more familiar one. First, the song sets in opposition two themes that permeate the *Iliad* and the *Odyssey*—*biē* in the *Iliad* and *mētis* in the *Odyssey.* Homer sees the Odysseus-Achilles quarrel as one contrasting the world views of the two epics. Achilles' emphasis on force fails at the end to bring the war to completion, whereas Odysseus' emphasis on intelligence (the wooden horse) succeeds. Indeed, all three of Demodocus' songs stress intelligence over force as the best way of achieving heroic fame (*klea andrōn*), intelligence and cunning being essential for survival in the *Odyssey* (the tales of *Od.* 9–12). The Odysseus-Achilles quarrel also prepares the audience for Odysseus' encounter with the suitors, who rely on their prowess to get their way. Odysseus, who in the end succeeds mostly through cunning, would be helpless against 108 men if he relied on force alone.

Demodocus' song moves Odysseus to tears; each time Demodocus pauses, Odysseus wipes his eyes with his cape and pours a libation to the gods. When the singer resumes at Alcinous' request, Odysseus' tears again begin to flow. A possible reason for the song's effect is Odysseus' awareness that the Trojan War and the part he played in it have become legend, immortalized. Perhaps he feels vindicated that, after ten years of fighting and another ten of wandering, his fame is secure. Alcinous, aware of his guest's distress, suspects he is no ordinary individual. He interrupts the singer and invites everyone to take part in athletic games, so the stranger, once home, can brag to his friends about how the Phaeacians excel in boxing, wrestling, jumping, and running (everyone longs for *kleos*).

Fourteen athletes are identified to take part in the games, in addition to Alcinous' three sons. The athletes' names, all associated with the sea,[15] reinforce the Phaeacians' preoccupation with the sea and their expertise as sailors. Two of the contests, those in running and boxing, are won by Alcinous' sons, Clytoneus and Laodamas, respectively. This double honor for the king's family confirms the gods' regard for his sacrifices and hospitality. Among the peace-loving Phaeacians, fame takes the form of athletic contests, whereas in the *Iliad*'s warrior society, it is expressed in military prowess.

Laodamas, noticing Odysseus' physique, politely invites him to participate but offends him without intending to (8.146), punctuating the significance placed on physical ability. Odysseus, disregarding the affront of his host's son, declines the offer, claiming that the worries he harbors take precedence over games. But the athlete Euryalus, who won the wrestling match, insults Odysseus by roughly and insensitively alleging that he resembles a merchant more than an athlete and is more concerned with his cargo and profits than athletics. Odysseus is offended at being called a merchant, one who travels for profits (8.163), rather than an athlete. He interprets Euryalus' comment as identifying him as a bad person, perhaps even a pirate. After all, merchants throughout the *Odyssey* and the *Iliad* are responsible for abducting upper-class youths and selling them into slavery. Eumaeus' story (*Od.* 15) serves as a prime example of this practice, and Odysseus, in his lie to Eumaeus, himself claims to have been abducted by a Phoenician man (the main occupation of Phoenicians in the *Odyssey* is trade), who sells him in Libya (14.295–297). He warns Euryalus not to judge a book by its cover (8.167–168). In other words, some people are granted beauty but lack brains, while those with brains sometimes lack beauty (appearance vs. reality). Euryalus has the physique but lacks the mind (8.177). Angered at the affront to his honor (his enhanced appearance does not expose his inner strength), Odysseus further reprimands Euryalus, observing that when he still had trust in youth and strength, he could be counted among the best (8.180–181). Fuming at the insult, he jumps up, seizes a discus that is bigger and heavier than the one the Phaeacians used, and throws it farther than anyone else. Athena, in the guise of a local man, measures Odysseus' throw and reports that none of the Phaeacians could come close to Odysseus' mark, let alone surpass it. Rejoicing, Odysseus is now ready to compete in any of the contests if challenged but refuses to compete against Laodamas, his host, for fear of abusing the host-guest relationship, pointing out the value placed on hospitality and proper etiquette.

Odysseus' anger, however, is not appeased; he needs to prove his physicality even at the cost of his homecoming. Once shamed by Euryalus into proving his manhood, he can no longer withhold his identity and lowers his guard, willing to take on any contender, acknowledging he can stand out in any mortal contest. He demonstrates his skill with the bow, revealing all but his name and admitting that only Philoctetes surpasses him in archery. Odysseus' need for praise is part of his identity, his *kleos*. Failure to inform the Cyclops of his triumph over him is not to have triumphed at all. Accepting Calypso's immortality is not to have his deeds acknowledged and his fame sung for generations to come. However, Odysseus is careful not to set himself above experts of old like Heracles (Hercules) and Eurytus, claiming to be better only among those of his generation. For Odysseus, as for all Homeric heroes, the present can never measure up to the past; each new generation seems weaker than the one before it. Odysseus cannot claim to equal the greatness of Heracles or Eurytus without being arrogant or dangerously overconfident; nor can one compete with the gods. Eurytus' expertise with the bow, for example, led him to challenge Apollo, which angered the god and led to his death (8.227–228); defying the norms of behavior or challenging the gods risks hubris. Odysseus defends his manhood by claiming he can throw a spear farther than anyone else can cast an arrow. His only weakness is running, a skill he could not practice on the high seas.

Alcinous, sensing the hero's irritation, flatters him, pointing to his excellence, and agrees that no one who knows how to speak sensibly would act as Euryalus. He invites Odysseus to participate, amending the major Phaeacian activities mentioned earlier by eliminating boxing and wrestling as areas in which they excel and adding instead feasts, lyre and dances, changes of clothing, baths, and beds (8.248–249). He paints a people at peace with limited war skills whose days are filled with feasts, entertainment, and leisure. Alcinous admits songs are tales to be enjoyed. Thus, when Demodocus sings and Odysseus cries, the Phaeacians express no emotion at all; what they hear is mere entertainment. Alcinous interrupts Demodocus in order not to upset his guest. Having had enough of eating and being entertained, they can move to the next activity. Although in its approximation to the real world of humankind Scheria is a step above Odysseus' earlier mythic worlds, it still remains a mythic realm, albeit halfway between the sites of his earlier mythical wanderings and Ithaca. To distract Odysseus from Euryalus' insult, Alcinous now calls for a dance, one of five activities (seamanship, running, dancing, and singing are the other four) in which his people excel. Requesting a second song from Demodocus, the king invites his best dancers to entertain his guest, hoping Odysseus might praise Phaeacians' skills once home and gain *kleos* for them.

III. Demodocus' Second Song, 256–469

Demodocus' second song, the longest of the three, treats Ares and Aphrodite's affair (8.266–366). In it Ares makes love to Aphrodite in her husband's absence. Helius, the sun god, spying the couple, alerts Hephaestus, who returns to set an intricate snare around his wife's bed. When Ares comes back for more lovemaking, the couple is entrapped in the spiderlike chain. Hephaestus then calls on Zeus and all the other Olympians to witness his wife's infidelity, refusing to release them until Zeus forfeits the dowry for his unfaithful daughter (8.319). The Olympians present (not the female gods, who absent themselves out of modesty), amused by Hephaestus' handiwork, marvel at the lame god's success in overtaking the powerful Ares through cunning. In a lighthearted scene that follows, Apollo asks Hermes whether he would make love to the shackle-bound Aphrodite had he the chance. Hermes, delighted, replies he would bed the golden goddess even if the chains were tripled. The immortals laugh at Hermes' boldness, but Poseidon asks for the couple's release and vouches that Ares will pay what the blacksmith god demands. Hephaestus, fearing that once Ares is freed he will void his debt, has Poseidon agree to act as surety. Hephaestus then releases the couple, who leave for their respective homes.

Demodocus' song serves to contrast the differences existing between the mortal and immortal worlds and gives expression to Odysseus' present and future circumstances.

1. It prefigures on a divine level Odysseus' situation with the suitors. Hephaestus uses his intellect, traps Ares seducing his wife, and demands retribution. In like manner, Odysseus will vanquish the suitors using his intellect to win back his wife.
2. The song contrasts the world of the gods with the world of men. Ares and Aphrodite's lovemaking is amusing to the gods—an elaborate joke played on lovers by an absent husband, as Hermes' comments to Apollo illustrate. Nothing tragic results from the affair; on the other hand, the suitors will die. In the mortal world, struggle and impermanence reign, whereas nothing ever changes in the immortal world; there are no consequences to the gods' meaningless acts. The gods' laughter (8.343) directed at Hermes' desire to mate with Aphrodite underscores this point. They either are amused at the pair caught in the sexual act or are laughing at Hermes' remark that he does not mind

being laughed at as long as he can bed Aphrodite. More likely, however, the laughter is a condemnation of the act. Earlier, when Hephaestus invites the gods to gaze at the couple, he refers to the act as *erga gelasta* (8.307; laughable deeds). This phrase, still common in modern Greek, refers to acts that cannot be taken seriously and deserve ridicule.

3. Demodocus' song also looks back to the misunderstanding between Odysseus and Euryalus, who, like Ares in the song, misconstrues the difference between reality and appearance, another *Odyssey* theme. Just as the powerful and handsome Ares falsely feels superior to the lame and ugly Hephaestus, so does the youthful Euryalus misjudge the older Odysseus, as the suitors will misjudge the beggar Odysseus.
4. The song further comments on force (*biē*) versus intellect (*mētis*), a theme that surfaced in Demodocus' first song regarding the Odysseus (*mētis*)/Achilles (*biē*) quarrel, whose outcome is clarified in the bard's third song. Ares and Aphrodite's lovemaking features the same theme, which unites all three songs. Intellect (Hephaestus' trick) triumphs over force (the war god). That Ares is the god implicated with Aphrodite is also telling and comments on Demodocus' first song. Military prowess, represented by Ares and the *Iliad*, is insufficient for Troy's destruction. In the end, it is the artisan Hephaestus' cunning, the intellect represented by Odysseus, that destroys the city.
5. Further, Demodocus' lay contains elements of Odysseus' *nostos* in miniature. Like Hephaestus, the disguised Odysseus returns to Ithaca an ugly, old man (17.201–203 and 17.336–338). And, like Hephaestus, Odysseus relies on *mētis* (once he lands on Ithaca) and *technē* (skill with hands, craftsmanship—e.g., building a raft [5.249–251]).
6. Another connection between Hephaestus and Odysseus is the bed as a test of fidelity. Hephaestus entraps Aphrodite in their marriage bed, just as Penelope uses the bed Odysseus built to test his fidelity.
7. A final comment is made on the power of Homer's art itself, which, like Demodocus' lays, not only elicits pleasure and captivates

audiences but also educates men and preserves their great feats (*klea andrōn*). While the lame Hephaestus' art overpowers the stronger Ares, blind Demodocus' songs look beyond the physical world of the sighted Phaeacians.

Homer congratulates the singer (and by extension himself) for bringing joy to the court, and Odysseus congratulates Alcinous for his two sons' dance. His cunning praise is especially valuable in ensuring him continued hospitality and more gifts to follow, which Alcinous wastes little time in requesting the twelve Phaeacian kings to contribute. He then implores Euryalus to apologize for his rudeness and offer Odysseus a gift as well. Euryalus wishes Odysseus a safe voyage and graciously offers him a bronze sword with a silver handle, addressing him as "father" and asking forgiveness for any impropriety. The gesture pleases Odysseus, who wishes Euryalus prosperity, presenting an example of proper behavior among those present. Once differences are rationally considered, the two reach a peaceful consensus, in contrast to the suitors, who refuse to listen to points of view other than their own.

The twelve Phaeacian kings' gifts are added to Arete and Alcinous' contributions, which Arete places in a chest and warns her guest to bind with a tight knot so that no one robs him should he fall asleep during the voyage. Odysseus obeys, securing the chest with a knot Circe taught him. Arete's warning is puzzling, since it is hard to imagine who among the Phaeacians would steal the gifts. The sailors magically deliver the sleeping Odysseus to Ithaca, pile his gifts on the shore, and return to Scheria before he wakes. Perhaps Arete's warning recalls an earlier version of the narrative, like the bag of winds Odysseus' companions opened while he slept, thinking it full of gold (10.46–49).

Nausicaa gazes at Odysseus as he passes her to join the nobles before taking his leave of Scheria. Given only two lines and relinquishing any hope of Odysseus' staying behind as her husband, she hopes to be remembered:

> Goodbye, stranger, and think of me sometimes when you are
> back at home, how I was the first you owed your life to.
> (8.461–462)

Odysseus vouches to pray to her as to a goddess for saving his life (8.467–468), a nice sentiment on Odysseus' part, although he will not refer to her again, not even when he relates his adventures to Penelope (23.310–343). What is especially interesting in this episode of Demodocus' second song (and throughout the entire *Odyssey*) is the psychological insight shown in the exchanges of the characters involved, and the realism with which they are presented. Anger, kindness, suspicions, fears, misspoken words, hurt feelings, and a variety of slices of life are dealt with minimally and with emotion.

IV. Demodocus' Third Song, 470–586

At the banquet Odysseus offers Demodocus a choice piece of meat. This unusual gesture from a guest, preempting the host's responsibility, shows the high esteem in which Odysseus holds the singer. Unlike the Phaeacians, for whom Demodocus' songs are mere entertainment, Odysseus views these songs as preserving the past, and as such, bards, sanctioned by the gods (8.479), are entitled to respect. Odysseus preempts his host again by praising Demodocus for the accuracy of his material and the realism with which he delivers it, as one who himself witnessed the incident being sung about. Breaking protocol for a third time, he requests a third song, one of the wooden horse that Odysseus filled with warriors (8.494). Referencing his name for the first time but not identifying himself, he vows to announce the singer's divine gift to all humankind, further praise for both Demodocus and Homer. Odysseus is at last prepared to reveal himself but prefers that Alcinous discover his identity on his own. He realizes the Trojan War and his part in it have entered history and is anxious to hear himself immortalized in song, perhaps the reason for breaking protocol and addressing Demodocus before his host does.

Demodocus' third song (8.499–520) begins at the point the Greek forces set fire to Troy and board their ships. Odysseus and his chosen group of men are left behind, crouched in the wooden horse's belly, while the Trojans debate its fate. Demodocus sings how the warriors under Odysseus' command stream out of the wooden horse at night to ravage the city and how, accompanied by Menelaus, Odysseus goes to Deiphobus'[16] house to fight his grimmest battle and retrieve Helen. But before Demodocus begins, the stranger points out that it was Odysseus who filled the horse with men and who sacked Troy. Assigning the responsibility for Troy's destruction to himself provides Odysseus a rationale for the quarrel between himself and Achilles in Demodocus' first song—the war was won by mind, not might—and establishes Odysseus, and not Achilles, as the true hero of the Trojan conflict, a conclusion prepared for as early as 4.271–289 when Menelaus mentions Odysseus' role in the wooden horse. In *Od.* 11 Odysseus again emphasizes his role in Troy's defeat when he claims the command was his (11.523–525). Demodocus' song establishes Odysseus as the true hero of Troy and the *Odyssey* as a continuation of the *Iliad.* The *Iliad* concluded with Troy still intact after Hector's death. The song resumes the unfinished war and ends it with Odysseus' wanderings. This episode, along with the homecomings and two other episodes in the *Odyssey* (Neoptolemus' part in Troy [11.508–537] and Achilles' funeral [24.36–94]), makes a good case for single authorship of the *Iliad* and *Odyssey.* First, none of the incidents reported in the *Iliad* are repeated in the *Odyssey.* Second, the episodes mentioned in the *Odyssey* complement the *Iliad* and round off the story of the Trojan War. However, there are other considerations (linguistic, for example) that support multiple authorship for the two epics.

Demodocus' song moves Odysseus to tears again, an emotional state expressed in one of the strongest similes in the *Odyssey* (8.523–532). Odysseus is compared to a Trojan woman who, beaten and driven into slavery, witnesses her husband's fall. Homer counterpoints Odysseus' pride in the part he plays in the man's death to the destruction and loss of life for which he is responsible. Drawing a comparison between a warrior and a woman is atypical unless a negative comment is intended on the warrior's *aristeia*[17] (see Agamemnon's wounding in *Il.* 11.269–72). However, Odysseus' tears are not tears of joy at seeing his feats pass into memory; they are tears of sorrow for the war's human destruction. Perhaps Homer is acknowledging the horrors of war and conveying Odysseus' remorse for his role. The simile makes an even stronger statement—both the victor and the vanquished suffer the same fate. The defeated lose their homes and loved ones, but so do the victors, among whom Odysseus is the prime example. He sheds tears not only for the widow but also for his ten-year-long wanderings and the future that awaits him in Ithaca. The widow who laments her dead husband is also Penelope crying for her own lost husband.

Alcinous alone notices Odysseus' distress and calls an end to the festivities, declaring that the song, intended for enjoyment, has brought sorrow to his guest. No longer able to keep himself from inquiring the stranger's identity, Alcinous asks for his name and his city (8.550–555), softening his inquisitiveness by seeking information to convey him home. Alcinous' great humanity becomes apparent when we consider his father's prophecy (8.564–569): the Phaeacians, in conveying a stranger home, will anger Poseidon, who will petrify the ship and pile a mountain around the city. Alcinous does not question fate; he observes hospitality's rules whatever the consequences. He appeals again for his guest's identity, asking for the lands he visited and the men he saw, whether wild, savage, or lawless. Out of compassion, he wants to know why his guest weeps. But before Odysseus answers, the book ends, with Alcinous still waiting for a reply.

Selected Bibliography: *Od.* 8

Ahl and Roisman, "*Odyssey*," 71–121.

Alden, "Resonances."

Andersen, "Odysseus."

Aronen, "Genealogy."
Beck, Deborah, "Ecphrasis."
Bliss, "Homer."
Braswell, "*Odyssey*."
Braswell, "Song."
Broeniman, "Demodocus."
Brown, Christopher G., "Ares."
Buchan, *Limits*, 72–106, 181–205.
Burkert, "Song."
Clarke, *Art*, 45–66.
Cook, "Ferrymen."
Davies, "Climax."
De Vries, "Phaeacian"
Edinger, "Lay."
Finkelberg, "First Song."
Finley, John H., Jr., *Homer's*, 74–92.
Garvie, *Homer.*
Gottesman, "Pragmatics."
Harrison, "Odysseus."
Holmberg, "Hephaistos."
Nelis, "Demodocus."
Newton, "Odysseus and Hephaestus."
Olson, "*Odyssey* 8."
Paton, "Book VIII."
Peek, "Propriety."
Reece, *Stranger's*, 101–122.
Reinhardt, "Adventures."
Rinon, "*Mise en abyme*."
Rinon, "Tragic."
Said, *Homer*, 150–188.
Sano, "Story."

Segal, "Phaeacians."

Tebben, "Alkinoös."

Whittaker, "Status."

Wilson, "Demodokos'."

Zerba, "Penelope."

Further commentary on *Od.* 8 in General Bibliography I.

CHAPTER 3

ODYSSEUS' WANDERINGS (*OD.* 9–12)

Odysseus' *Apologoi*

In the *apologoi*[1] Odysseus assumes the bard's role to recite his adventures in his own words, which end with his arrival in Scheria (*Od.* 6). Once the *apologoi* are over at the end of *Od.* 12, Odysseus is ready for the final lap of his journey (*Od.* 13–24).

Several points should be kept in mind in approaching the *apologoi*:

1. Odysseus is reciting these tales to the Phaeacians, on whom his return to Ithaca depends. He knows that what he says and how he says it make a difference in how he is perceived.
2. Odysseus is reciting these tales long after they occur. He is thus looking at them both from the outside as a spectator and from the inside as one who experienced them.
3. Odysseus is speaking both to an internal audience (the Phaeacians) who know only what they hear and to an external audience (the readers) who are privy to what he says (direct speech) and to the author's third-person narration.

The *apologoi*, the longest story-within-a-story in Homer's works, covers a ten-year period and occupies 2,140 lines (a little over one-sixth of the entire epic), with a single intermission at 11.328–384, where Odysseus stops but is persuaded by Alcinous to continue. The tales are performed on the evening of the thirty-third day of the *Odyssey* narrative, which begins in *Od.* 8 and continues through *Od.* 13.17. Recited in flashback, the *apologoi* can be grouped in a variety of ways to emphasize their unique structure:

1. Ciconians, 9.39–83
2. Lotus-Eaters, 9.83–104
3. Cyclops, 9.105–566
4. Aeolus, 10.1–79
5. Laestrygonians, 10.80–132

6a. Circe, 10.133–574

7. Underworld, 11.1–327 and 11.385–640

6b. Circe, 12.1–143

8. Sirens, 12.144–200

9a. Scylla (and Charybdis), 12.201–259

10. Thrinacia, 12.260–425

9b. (Scylla and) Charybdis, 12.426–446

11. Calypso, 12.447–450

Even a simple scheme such as this one shows a definite pattern in the arrangement of the stories. The visit to Hades (7) is the midpoint of the *apologoi*, with six tales preceding it (1–6a) and six following it (6b–11). Furthermore, the Hades episode (7) is encompassed by the Circe episode—the last 439 lines of *Od.* 10 and the first 143 lines of *Od.* 12 (6a and 6b). Similarly, the Thrinacia episode splits the Scylla and Charybdis episode into two parts (9a and 9b). Once Odysseus begins the Calypso episode (11), which we know from *Od.* 5, he breaks off his narration after four lines, since he recited his arrival from Ogygia to Scheria the night before (7.241–286).

Each of the *apologoi* books (except *Od.* 11) contains three tales, the third larger than the two preceding ones—the Cyclops episode of *Od.* 9 (466 lines) is larger than the Cicones and Lotus-Eaters episodes combined

(66 lines). Circe's tale in *Od.* 10 (583 lines) is larger than the Aeolus and Laestrygonians episodes combined (131 lines). The same holds true for *Od.* 12; the Thrinacia episode (165 lines) is larger than the Sirens and Scylla and Charybdis episodes combined (137 lines). Unlike *Od.* 5 (Calypso) and *Od.* 11 (underworld), each of which occupies its entire book, *Od.* 9, 10, and 12 contain two short (s) episodes followed by a third long (l) one. Further, in each of the three books (9, 10, and 12), the episodes alternate between mild violence (m) and violent adventures (v):

Od. 9: Cicones (sv); Lotus-Eaters (sm); Cyclops (lv).
Od. 10: Aeolus (sm); Laistrygones (sv); Circe (lm).
Od. 12: Sirens (sm); Scylla and Charybdis (sv); Thrinacia (lm).

A more elaborate scheme (Most, "Structure"), illustrated here, divides the *apologoi* in two groups of five tales each set in a symmetrical ring composition around the central underworld episode (the *Nekyia*):

TROY
    (two-day storm)
    Cicones
        Lotus-Eaters [a]
            Cyclopes [b]
                Aeolus [c]
            Laestrygonians [b]
        Circe [a]
    NEKYIA
        Sirens [a]
            Scylla (and Charybdis) [b]
                Thrinacia [c]
            Charybdis (and Scylla) [b]
        Calypso [a]
    (two-day storm)
    Scheria
ITHACA

Odysseus' journey begins in Troy and ends in Ithaca. A two-day storm occurs before the first adventure (the Cicones), paralleling the two-day storm before the hero's last episode (Phaeacians); both events take place in less mythic worlds than the others. The adventures indicated by [a] attempt to deprive the hero of his homecoming—the Lotus-Eaters and Circe through drugs, the Sirens and Calypso through their erotic powers. The [b] adventures delay Odysseus' *nostos* through cannibalism (Cyclops, Laestrygonians, Scylla and Charybdis); in the [c] episodes, which are physically nonthreatening, the hero sleeps, jeopardizing his *nostos*.

A third scheme (Tracy, *Story*) divides the adventures into two parallel sets of four in which nonviolent adventures alternate with violent ones, separated by the *Nekyia*, which is preceded and followed by the Circe episode:

1. Lotus-Eaters	Circe	1. Sirens
2. Polyphemus	*Nekyia*	2. Scylla (and Charybdis)
3. Aiolus	Circe	3. Thrinacia
4. Laestrygonians		4. Charybdis (and Scylla)

Chronologically, the *apologoi* precede *Od.* 5–8, arranging Odysseus' journey in the following order: *Od.* 9–12, 5–8, 13–24. Beginning the homecoming with *Od.* 5 places the mythic and mostly folkloric material between the semireal mortal world of Scheria and the real world of Ithaca, downplaying the mythic and emphasizing the real, thus making the journey more plausible. The same argument can be made for the entire epic—the narrative is enclosed between Ithaca in the first four books (*Telemachia*) and Ithaca in the final twelve books (*Od.* 13–24); the *Odyssey* begins where it ends, giving it a circular and tightly knit structure.

Given Odysseus' nature as a man who uses trickery and lies to achieve his aims, one has to at least consider whether he has an ulterior motive in reciting these tales; to what degree, if any, does he embellish them for his listeners? For example, one might consider several reasons why Odysseus wants to personalize and even exaggerate his adventures. First, he desires to reach Ithaca as soon as possible. He can use these tales to create the pity and admiration he deems necessary to ensure his safe passage home. Second, he holds great admiration for singers and for his own recitation. Is he reciting his adventures as facts, or is he interested in how they are perceived? Third, Homeric warriors want their feats to bring fame. To what extent, then, is he manipulating them to present himself in a more favorable light?

Book 9

Once Odysseus discloses his identity, he narrates his first three adventures.

I. Odysseus revealed (7%)
II. Cicones (8%)
III. Lotus-Eaters (4%)
IV. Cyclops (*Cyclopeia*) (81%)

I. Odysseus Revealed, 1–38

Odysseus is finally ready to answer the four questions put to him by Alcinous at the end of *Od.* 8:

1. What is your name? (8.550)
2. Where do you come from? (8.555)
3. Where were you driven off your course? (8.573)
4. Why do you weep? (8.577)

Odysseus answers the fourth question first by paying tribute to Demodocus, who brings enjoyment to a feast. In praising Homer's art, he also makes a distinction between the suitors' revels and Alcinous' banquets. In Ithaca the unruly suitors hardly pay attention to Phemius, whereas in Scheria, where order prevails, everyone is attentive to Demodocus—the difference between a world of chaos and one at peace. The emphasis on family and civilized life, which Homer stresses throughout *Od.* 8, reintroduces Odysseus to the world he is striving to attain. Once among the Phaeacians, he enters a land created by the ingenuity of humankind's tools and technology. Although Circe's and Calypso's homes were rich and prosperous, they are still part of raw nature, wild and untamed. In Scheria Odysseus finds order and an appreciation of what humans can achieve with their own hands and minds.

Odysseus comes to better understand the importance of a unified family in achieving harmony. Arete and Alcinous are a team—he covers matters of state, while she controls the home. While Alcinous welcomes Odysseus into his home, Arete holds back, noticing that Odysseus' clothes are her son's. Only a woman in charge of a home notices such details. Until she can satisfy her curiosity about the garments, she waits to welcome the stranger, a precaution her husband does not consider. Although Alcinous and Arete complement each other, they are independent of each other, whereas Odysseus and Penelope are more even-tempered—the opposite sides of the same coin. Nevertheless, it is this solidarity within the family unit that rouses Odysseus and convinces him that Penelope, although lacking Calypso's beauty and grace, is still a better choice for him.

Odysseus turns next to Alcinous' first and second questions: he identifies himself as Odysseus, son of Laertes (9.19), and continues with the geographical location of Ithaca. A few lines later he comments on another *Odyssey* theme, the virtues of home and family (9.34). It is Odysseus' love of home and family that makes it possible for him to refuse Alcinous' offer to remain in Scheria as the king's son-in-law. Not to offend Alcinous, he claims his longing for Ithaca is such that not even Calypso (or Circe), who desired him, could persuade him. He then addresses Alcinous' third question and begins his tales of endurance (in contrast to Demodocus' songs of action), marking the distinction between the hero as doer in the *Iliad* and the hero as sufferer in the *Odyssey.*

II. Cicones, 39–83

Odysseus begins with the word *Iliothen* (9.39; from Ilion), relocating from the real to the mythic world, from which he will shift slowly back again in his final adventure. Leaving Troy, he is driven ashore on Ismarus, a Ciconian city,[2] which he sacks, but when he urges his men to leave, they mutiny. The delay allows the Ciconians to call for reinforcements, killing seventy-two of Odysseus' troops (six men from each of his twelve ships). The remainder escape, along with their enemies' wives and children, who are never mentioned again. Such oversights as this omission of the fate of the captured wives and children could be the result of the *Odyssey* author's inheritance of multiple versions of Odysseus' adventures, which he edits for his own narrative needs. Thus, the tale used here could contain details from the original source that were either not redacted or merely ignored.

Odysseus' first adventure occurs not far from Troy, and his character and actions are still that of an Iliadic warrior who sacks cities, kills his enemies, and enslaves women and children. But at the same time, changes in his behavior are surfacing. For example, when he orders his men to flee the Ciconians, they do not obey his commands. In the *Iliad*, he alone rounds up the fleeing Greek soldiers after Agamemnon's dream sends them scurrying to their ships (*Il.*2.185–208); in Ismarus he seems unable to control his drunken men, allowing the Ciconians to slaughter many of his companions. Although this change marks the beginning of Odysseus' transition from an Iliadic past to an Odyssean present, the change is also necessitated by his *nostos*, which has him returning home alone. His adventures then serve to gradually eliminate his twelve ships and the men in his command, who are destroyed by their wild recklessness (*Od.* 1.7). As a hero of note, Odysseus cannot be held responsible for their loss. Fortunate to have escaped with most of his men, he encounters bad weather, forcing him to seek land.

Early in the epic (2.174–176), eighteen years of the hero's twenty-year absence are accounted for, including the ten-year-long war, the seven years spent with Calypso (7.259), and the one year with Circe (10.469). The two years that are unaccounted for correspond to the remaining ten of twelve destinations (see note 1 of the present chapter), but the time spent in each, as well as the time elapsed between each, is not always provided. Leaving Ismarus, Odysseus encounters a storm and spends two nights and days on land. On the third day, he leaves but encounters more bad weather, which sweeps his ships south for nine days, reaching the Lotus-Eaters on the tenth. We know neither the length of the trip from Troy to Ismarus nor how long it takes to travel from Ismarus to land. If the days provided by the epic for the nine adventures are totaled, they would not equal two years. Such detailed chronology, then, is not in Homer's interest other than to give plausibility to his narrative. Further, the storm that takes Odysseus and his crew to the Lotus-Eaters effectively separates him from the known world. From this point of his wanderings until he reaches Ithaca in *Od.* 13, he is in Neverland, the mythical realm.

III. Lotus-Eaters, 83–104

Odysseus' stay with the Lotus-Eaters is short. Once the crew disembarks, Odysseus sends a detail of two men and a herald to scout the area. Again, the three men neglect their orders and, instead of scouting the land and reporting back to their commander, they, without coercion, taste the lotus flower, which robs them of their desire to act on their commitments or to return home. Odysseus rescues them by force and sets sail, fearing that others might also taste the flower and forget their homecoming. The episode stresses a number of concerns for a successful homecoming for both Odysseus and his men:

1. It supports Odysseus' guiltlessness in his men's own destruction. He is a leader who strives not just for his own safety but also for that of his men.
2. It illustrates that if Odysseus' men are left to their own devices, they will act on instinct rather than reason.

3. It emphasizes the importance of and the need for Odysseus' leadership if the journey is to be successful. The companions are followers. On their own, they err. The journey requires initiative, self-control, and willpower.
4. The constant preoccupation for Odysseus and his men must always be home. To neglect that goal implies havoc.
5. Strength (*biē*) alone, used in the first adventure (Cicones), is inadequate if not bound with mental capacity (*mētis*).

IV. Cyclops (Cyclopeia), 105–566

Odysseus and crew sail next to the Cyclopes' land, one of Odysseus' longest tales, which covers the remainder of *Od.* 9. The episode is presented in a ring structure in which the opening and closing can be viewed as completing a circle:

1. Sail to Cyclopes' island (9.103–104)
    2. At nearby island (9.105–176)
        3. On Cyclopes' island: cave exterior (9.177–215)
            4. Cyclopes' island: cave interior (9.216–460)
        3. On Cyclopes' island: cave exterior (9.461–542)
    2. At nearby island (9.543–559)
1. Sail away from Cyclopes' island (9.560–566)

Odysseus first describes and contrasts the Cyclopes with his own kind:

1. They neither plow nor plant anything but rather gather whatever nature allows.
2. They lack institutions.
3. They have no councils.
4. They live in caves.
5. They have no laws. Each Cyclops is the law for his own family and cares nothing about the others.

These observations are made long after Odysseus has had time to reflect on them (he is narrating his adventures to the Phaeacians many years after their occurrence). Thus, they characterize him more than they do the Cyclopes. In Scheria, where he tells the tale, he is not the same man he was in the giant's cave. His interests have turned from engaging in the heroic feats described in his wanderings to taking a greater stake in civil life—marital loyalty, hospitality, and civic order. At the end of the eleven episodes, he sees the paradisiacal existence of the Cyclopes in the same way he saw Calypso's offer of immortality: as a living death. Mortals need an active mind to survive in the world of humankind with its struggles; the stupefied and lethargic worlds of the Lotus-Eaters and the Cyclopes are places where one exists as a "nobody."

After an indeterminate period of sailing, Odysseus reaches Goat Island, a flat, uninhabited, wooded land populated by hundreds of goats directly across from the Cyclopes' land. He is puzzled as to why such a rich, fertile land with fresh water remains unplowed and unsown, feeding droves of goats rather than humans. He notices that the Cyclopes, whose island is easily reached by ship, could take advantage of Goat Island's wealth but also notes that the Cyclopes have neither ships nor shipwrights to build them craft and thus are unable either to take advantage of the island's resources or to trade with others. Technical knowledge and cultivation of crops, then, could make this island inhabitable. Civilization, for Odysseus, is the ability of humans to control and improve nature, but above all, civilized humans need technology to build ships in order to expand their world. In its present state, Goat Island is merely another Ogygia or Aeaea, a virgin paradise, stagnant, isolated, and forever unchanging, alien to mortality and civilized humans.

In its isolation, Goat Island resembles Scheria. Although the Phaeacians are technologically advanced, they have little to do with the outside world and become completely isolated once Odysseus is gone. One wonders why they did not settle Goat Island once they were driven out by the Cyclopes from the land they once shared. Since the Cyclopes' lack of technology did not pose a threat, the Phaeacians did not have to journey as far as Scheria (6.4–10). Homer does not provide an answer except to say that civilized humans use their minds to control their surroundings and thus rely on their initiative, which in turn frees them from the gods' control, whereas the uncivilized remain slaves to their environment and to god's generosity. To be free, mortals must control the world they live in, which can only be accomplished through intellect and not by force alone.

In the evening, Odysseus arrives on Goat Island in a fog, unaware of his whereabouts. After spending the night and the whole of the following day feasting on goat meat, Odysseus, on the third day, crosses over to probe the nearby island, where voices and bleating goats are heard. Always "roaming with a hungry heart"[3] (another reason why Odysseus wanted to escape Calypso's insulated island), he wants to learn about the natives. Are they violent without justice or hospitable to strangers? On the island, he spots a cave organized to stable large flocks of goats and sheep, the home of a lawless giant who is herding his animals some distance from his den. Leaving his ship behind, Odysseus, with twelve chosen companions, explores the cave, carrying with them Maron's goatskin of wine (9.196). Since the wine plays a major role in subduing Polyphemus, Odysseus digresses in his tale to introduce it.

1. The proprietor of this special wine is Maron, a Ciconian priest of Apollo.
2. Maron's gift was offered to Odysseus for saving his wife and son from harm. In addition to twelve jars of wine, Maron offered Odysseus seven talents of gold and a mixing bowl of silver, emphasizing his hospitality, in contrast to the Cyclops'. Odysseus' mention of the gifts is his sly nudge to his Phaeacian hosts, since he is relating this tale to them.
3. The secret recipe of this potent, unmixed wine is known only to Maron, his wife, and a servant, a fact that increases its value.
4. The wine is so powerful that whoever drinks it must mix one cup with twenty measures of water.

This digression (like those describing the olive pole that blinds Polyphemus and the bow used to defeat the suitors) introduces us to one of the ploys Odysseus uses to survive. Leaving nothing to chance, Odysseus explains why he decides to bring the wine along; he has the good sense to anticipate that whoever lives in the cave might not have knowledge of law and hospitality. The wine backstory, then, not only identifies one of the means to subdue the giant but presents Odysseus as a man of forethought, one whose experience has taught him to be cautious and to always expect the worst.

Entering Polyphemus' cave unannounced, his companions beg him to steal whatever provisions are needed and leave (baskets of cheese, pens with lambs and kids, and pails of milk). In retrospect Odysseus realizes he should have left, but at the time he wanted to see whether Polyphemus would give him presents. Unlike his companions, not only does Odysseus have the curiosity to question and experience life, but as a warrior he is also interested in reaping the rewards of hospitality. It is interesting that although Odysseus is a guest himself in the Cyclops' cave, he does not question his right to remove another's goods without having them offered to him. Perhaps Odysseus feels entitled, since he considers the Cyclopes uncivilized. Raiding seems to be an acceptable practice for warriors, as we see time and again in the *Iliad* and in the Cicones episode. But why then expect a gift from Polyphemus? If he is uncivilized, without laws or customs, he would not be expected to abide by Odysseus' rules. This is not a problem that concerns Homer, but given the emphasis on Odysseus' ingenuity and perceptiveness, it is a question one could pose. Odysseus and his men simply enter the cave, build a fire, and help themselves to the cheeses while waiting for their host.

Polyphemus' cave is not unlike that of a mortal shepherd or farmer. He arrives carrying wood to make a fire and prepares his flocks for milking. The disparity in his size and his strength compared to those of his guests becomes apparent when he lifts a rock to block the opening of the cave that would require more that twenty-two four-wheeled wagons for humans to move (9.241–242). Having completed his chores, he spots the strangers and asks their identity, their destination, and their business, in contrast to Alcinous, who delayed questioning Odysseus until the end of his stay. The Cyclops, dispensing with hospitality, makes his queries the first order of business. Frightened by his enormous size and booming voice, Odysseus identifies himself and his crew as lost Achaeans returning from Troy who request the hospitality due to strangers, imploring him to honor and respect Zeus Xenios. The impious giant considers Odysseus foolish but will later depend on his father, Poseidon, for revenge once blinded. By making the giant Poseidon's son, Homer clarifies why Odysseus suffers the sea's wrath. In stressing his brute size, strength, and uncouthness, Homer explains his lack of civilization and the reason he does not fear the gods. On the other hand, the giant has a Greek name (Polyphemus) and the duties of a mortal shepherd, which both Hellenizes and demythologizes the episode. When Odysseus escapes the giant's cave by hanging underneath the giant's prize ram, Polyphemus addresses it with pathos and affection (9.447–454) like any mortal shepherd devoted to his flocks. Softening the tale's folkloric qualities and pitying a cannibal who devours six men is Homer's way of creating a monster capable of human feelings. Of the episode's 245 lines, only nine (9.289–293, 311, 344, and 373–374) deal with cannibalistic acts.

Once the Cyclops falls asleep, Odysseus deliberates how he and his company might escape the cave. Since the exit is blocked with the immovable boulder, he and his men are trapped in the cave until the Cyclops releases them. Killing the giant would keep them imprisoned in the cave without means of escape. Thus, Odysseus abandons killing Polyphemus and waits for dawn, when the Cyclops again snatches two men for his breakfast and leads his sheep to pasture, slipping the huge rock in place behind him. Odysseus and his men could escape once the boulder is removed, but the giant would catch sight of them. Spotting an olive trunk large enough to serve as a mast, Odysseus devises a plan. His men cut a six-foot piece, plane it smooth, sharpen one end to a point, and place the still-green log in the fire to harden until it glows (9.379). Such details might again be remnants of a tale Homer inherited; perhaps the device used to blind the Cyclops was not originally olive wood but something else (iron?) that glowed when heated without disintegrating. For Homer, however, olive wood (a symbol of endurance and stability associated with Athena and wisdom) suggests not only Odysseus' *mētis* but also an act sanctioned by the goddess. Hiding the stake under the dung lining the cave, the men draw lots to choose four among them who will help Odysseus drive it into the Cyclops' eye. As luck would have it, the four men Odysseus would have chosen for the task are the very four who draw the lots (luck or divine agency?).

When the giant returns and reseals the opening, he snatches another two men for his dinner. Odysseus now offers the giant the undiluted wine. He drinks it, asks for more, and promises the stranger a guest gift if he reveals his name. Odysseus offers him the magic wine three more times, and when the inebriated Cyclops can drink no more, he reveals his name: Nobody (*outis*) (9.366). Some forty-nine lines later (9.414), Odysseus uses *mētis* in referring to his "nobody" ploy instead of *outis*, which points to the hero's craftiness and intelligence (*mētis* read as *mē tis* means "no one").[4] Hearing the stranger's name, the Cyclops honors his promise of a guest gift—to eat Odysseus last, after he devours the remaining companions, one of several perversions of hospitality Polyphemus commits:

1. He feasts on his own guests.
2. He demands to drink alone, ignoring gods and guests.
3. He asks Odysseus' identity before offering him a bath, food, and rest.

When the intoxicated giant is asleep, Odysseus and his chosen companions pierce the giant's single eye with the glowing beam of olive wood, an act compared in two similes to the art of shipbuilding and blacksmithing. In the first simile, Odysseus and his men force the beam into the Cyclops' eye as someone with a brace and bit bores into timber (9.384–385).

In the second, the blinding is described as resembling a blacksmith's plunging a glowing ax into cold water, the steaming noise of the water being associated with the crackling and sizzling of the burning eye. The uncivilized Cyclops is bested by a civilized race using intelligence (technology) rather than brawn. Polyphemus' distressing screams that Nobody is killing him (9.408) attract the other Cyclopes, who think him insane, an illness sent by Zeus, and advise him to pray to his father, Poseidon, to alleviate it. Using the word *mētis* instead of *outis* to identify himself as Nobody, Odysseus makes it clear that force (*biē*) alone, so admired in the *Iliad*, is no longer viable in a post-Trojan world unless craft (*mētis*) accompanies it.

The blind Polyphemus removes the boulder blocking the cave's entrance and sits in front of it, hoping to grab Odysseus and his companions, but Odysseus puts another scheme into action. Lashing six sets of three rams side by side, he ties each of his remaining companions to a middle ram's underbelly. For himself, he picks the finest and largest ram and holds on to its underbelly, waiting for dawn, when the giant releases his flock from the cave.[5] Early on the fifth day since their arrival, Odysseus and his men make their escape as Polyphemus searches each sheep lumbering out to pasture, missing the men underneath. Freed, Odysseus releases his men and orders them to their ship with many of the Cyclops' sheep. Out at sea, he taunts the Cyclops, who tosses a huge rock in front of the ship, driving it back toward the shore. Once the ship has traveled twice the distance as before, Odysseus, still the Iliadic warrior, taunts the Cyclops again; his men plead with him to stop, but Odysseus remains unappeased. Undying fame (*kleos aphthiton*) requires that his deeds be known if they are to live in memory and song. Thus, he identifies himself as the one who blinded Polyphemus, Odysseus, sacker of cities (9.504; *Odussea ptoliporthion*). Knowing his action will not go unheeded by Poseidon, he is willing to take the chance rather than live unacknowledged and remain Outis/Mētis.

The name Odysseus recalls for Polyphemus the prophecy of Telemus, a once preeminent prophet among the Cyclopes who predicted Polyphemus' loss of an eye to a man named Odysseus. However, the Cyclops expected someone handsome with great strength, not a little niddering and feeble man (appearance versus reality). Although the loss of his eye was fated, Polyphemus was warned by the gods (as Aegisthus was in *Od.* 1), a warning he mistakenly interpreted as referring to a man with strength and size. He tries one more time to entice Odysseus to return to shore, promising Poseidon's protection, but Odysseus taunts him for a third time. In a final speech, contrary to the expectations for a departing guest, Odysseus curses Polyphemus and wishes him dead (rather than wishing him well), boasting that not even Poseidon can heal his eye (9.525). But a mortal is not in a position to predict what the gods will bequeath; Odysseus will suffer for his reckless arrogance. Polyphemus entreats Poseidon to prevent the hero's return, but if his *nostos* is fated, Polyphemus prays that he be delayed and lose his companions. The Cyclops again tosses a large boulder behind the ship, almost grazing the rudder, but the tidal wave created forces the ship to beach on Goat Island. There Odysseus distributes the confiscated animals equally among all his men and sacrifices the large ram to Zeus, who refuses his prayer. The gods receive humans' offerings but do not always accept their prayers. The following day, the sixth since reaching the island, Odysseus and his men leave, glad to have escaped the Cyclops.

Selected Bibliography: *Od.* 9

Aasved, "Sirens."
Ahl and Roisman, "*Odyssey*," 92–121.
Atchity, *Critical*, 181–186.
Austin, "Odysseus."
Awine, "Non-Homeric."
Bakker, "Polyphemos."
Beck, Deborah, "Odysseus."
Bremmer, "Homeric."
Bremmer, "Odysseus."
Brown, Calvin S., "Odysseus."

Brown, Christopher G., "In the Cyclops'."

Buchan, *Limits*, 18–35, 72–88, 133–180.

Byre, "On the Description."

Calame, "Myth."

Clarke, *Art*, 45–66.

Clay, "Goat Island."

Clayton, "Polyphemus."

Cook, *"Odyssey,"* 93–110.

Davidson, "Arrival."

De Jong, "Subjective Style."

Ford, "Odysseus."

Friedrich, "Heroic."

Garrison, "Great."

Glenn, "Mezentius."

Glenn, "Polyphemus Folktale."

Glenn, "Polyphemus Myth."

Hall, "No Man's."

Hershbell, "Parmenides."

Jacobson, "Cacus."

Katsouris, "Euripides'."

Levine, "Sophocles'."

Mondi, "Homeric."

Most, "Structure."

Newton, "Ciconians."

Newton, "Aristotelian."

Newton, "Assembly."

Newton, "Poor Polyphemus."

Newton, "Rebirth."

Nieto Hernández, "Back."

Niles, "Patterning."

Olson, *Blood and Iron*, 43–64.

O'Sullivan, James, "Nature."

O'Sullivan, James, "Observations."

Page, *Folktales*, 1–22.

Parry, Hugh, "*Apologos.*"

Pazdernik, "Odysseus."

Podlecki, "Guest-Gifts."

Reece, "Phaeacians."

Reece, "Polyphemus."

Reinhardt, "Adventures."

Rinon, "Pivotal."

Said, *Homer*, 150–288.

Schein, "Odysseus."

Schroeder, "Cyclopean."

Scully, "Doubling."

Segal, "Divine."

Simpson, "*Odyssey* 9."

Stewart, "Odysseus"

Thalmann, *Odyssey*, 65–93.

Webber, "Hero."

Zoidis, "Odusseus."

Further commentary on *Od.* 9 in General Bibliography I.

Book 10

In *Od.* 10 Odysseus again narrates three adventures. In *Od.* 9 he defeated a giant, representing anti-institutional man, hostile to the male world of law and order (*polis*). In *Od.* 10 he defeats Circe, representing antimoral woman, hostile to the domestic female world of the family (*oikos*).

I. Aeolus (14%)
II. Laestrygonians (9%)
III. Circe (79%)

I. Aeolus, 1–79

Odysseus' fourth adventure lands him on a floating island. There Aeolus,[6] a human in charge of the winds, tranquilly resides with his family (six sons married to six daughters). Little else is known about Aeolus' homeland, for by the time Odysseus arrives, he is fully ensconced in a folktale world that lacks geographic specificity. Aeolus offers Odysseus hospitality for a month, and in return, he is entertained by tales of Achaean exploits. At the end of the month, the king provides Odysseus conveyance to Ithaca, presenting him with a bagful of all the winds except the West Wind, which is set free to gently blow his ships safely home. After ten days, in sight of Ithaca, Odysseus falls asleep, and his men, suspicious the bag is full of silver and gold, open it (how Odysseus knows what his men say or think while he is asleep is not considered). The winds, set free, create a tempest, driving the ships back to Aeolus. Humankind's own folly, this time greed, once more brings suffering on Odysseus and his companions. Odysseus wakes to find his ships on the open sea and, for the first time in the epic, contemplates suicide. He decides to endure (*etlēn*), another word that defines the Odyssean hero. Odysseus' endurance against all odds and careful weighing of all available options enable his return, but homecoming is denied to his companions, who lack his qualities. Back on the island, Odysseus again seeks Aeolus' assistance, admitting his men's folly. Aeolus, realizing the gods' unwillingness to see Odysseus safely home, orders him to leave.

II. Laestrygonians, 80–132

After sailing for six days and nights, Odysseus arrives on the seventh at Lamus' citadel (named after its founder) in the Laestrygonian city of Telepylus, a land so far north that the sun never sets on it, suggesting that Telepylus is a fairyland far from the world of mortals. In the deadliest of Odysseus' adventures, he loses eleven of his twelve ships, along with their crew, leaving only his own ship. The Laestrygonians, like the Cyclopes, are cannibals, but unlike the one-eyed giants, they possess civilization and technology, as evidenced by the lethal weapons used to spear Odysseus' men.

Odysseus' entourage arrives at the harbor, which is surrounded by a cliff with a narrow entrance. Sensing a trap, Odysseus alone anchors his ship outside this entrance while the other eleven ships sail through. One wonders why Odysseus does not warn the others to follow suit, but the point here is that he is careful and anticipatory (as he is in the Cyclops' cave), whereas his men forge ahead without giving thought to possible impediments. It is more convenient for them to sail straight into the calm harbor (10.93) than to berth outside and be inconvenienced to climb a cliff (10.96). Telemachus will show the same good sense as Odysseus when in *Od.* 15.547–557 he sends his ship with his companions ahead to Ithaca while he goes on foot to Eumaeus' hut.

The three men Odysseus sends to scout the town meet the unnamed daughter of Antiphates (the Laestrygonian king) drawing water from Artakiē.[7] The young maiden, comparable to Nausicaa, points the way to her father's palace. Not only is the girl's background Hellenized, but its fairy qualities are deemphasized: her father has a Greek name, lives in a palace, has a family, and attends the assembly. However, once Odysseus' men enter the palace, they meet a colossal woman who immediately summons her husband. As in the Cyclops episode, once the king arrives, he snatches and prepares one of Odysseus' three companions for dinner. Antiphates calls on his fellow Laestrygonians, who pelt Odysseus' ships with boulders and spear the men for their dinner. Odysseus, anchored outside the harbor entrance, escapes, but the other eleven ships are destroyed. Thus, within seventeen lines (10.116–132), Odysseus loses all his ships and men, with the sole exception of his own ship and the men on it. Both the previous and present adventures emphasize thoughtlessness and greed, downplaying the mythic and attributing loss of life to shortsightedness in not considering possible dangers.

III. Circe, 133–574

The next episode begins with a brief background on Circe, sister of Aeetes,[8] both children of Helius and the Oceanid Perse. Homer provides little else on Circe's genealogy, and he does not mention Aeetes' part in the tale of Jason and the Argonauts, although two lines in *Od.* 12.69–70 imply acquaintance with the myth. It is possible that since the voyage of Jason predates that of Odysseus', some of Odysseus' adventures could be based on that journey (see the discussion of *Od.* 12, I. Return to Aeaea, later in the present chapter).

On the morning of the third day, his longest period of inactivity, Odysseus scouts for possible life. Spotting smoke, he ponders whether to investigate first or return to provide food for his companions. Placing his men's welfare before all else, he kills a large stag, since food supplies are running low. This act presents Odysseus still struggling for his companions' welfare after having lost eleven of the twelve ships under his command. On his fourth day on Aeaea, Odysseus is disoriented and unaware of his whereabouts, unable to determine where the sun rises or sets. Since, as a sailor, he is familiar with navigation, this statement must be interpreted metaphorically as indicating a loss of identity, direction, and purpose. At this point of the journey (halfway through his wanderings), Odysseus and company have lost their way, and it will take the sorceress Circe and the trip to the underworld to lead them home.[9] Unrelenting, he divides his crew into two, appointing a relative, Eurylochus, and himself as leaders in order to determine which of the two groups will explore the island. The lot falls on Eurylochus and the twenty-two weeping men in his command. Throughout the Circe episode, the companions are presented as being weary and hungry. Fearful of what lies ahead after having already faced the cannibal Laestrygonians and Cyclopes, they are reluctant to follow orders and do so unenthusiastically. Odysseus, on the other hand, insists on forging on to meet any challenge set before him. In the first of three expeditions to Circe's palace, Eurylochus' division comes upon lions and wolves, which fawn on them like household pets. Fearful of the animals, the men dread knocking on Circe's door but stand transfixed at the sounds of singing and weaving. Although Circe is a goddess and a witch possessing potent drugs, she is nevertheless portrayed as a woman much like Penelope. These attributes not only humanize the magical aspects of her tale but also present her as a sensual woman who threatens the *nostos* of Odysseus as Calypso does.

Polites (Odysseus' dearest friend, who appears only here), a member of Eurylochus' division, suggests they inquire about the sounds. Circe welcomes them, but the faint-hearted Eurylochus, suspecting treachery, stays outside. Once in Circe's home, the men are offered hospitality, drugged, turned into pigs, and driven into pigpens, but their minds remain intact. The confused Eurylochus returns to the ship to explain what transpired. Leaving Eurylochus behind, Odysseus is driven (10.273; *anankē*) to confront the situation. As in the Cyclops episode, he would rather risk his life than leave the cave unexplored, as his men urge him to do. *Anankē* (necessity) is his character's fate to know and understand. On the way, he encounters Hermes, in the guise of a young man, who warns him of Circe's dangers.

1. He recounts Circe's guiles and offers him moly, a medicine that makes one immune to drugs.
2. Odysseus must approach her with drawn sword; she will invite him to her bed, which he cannot refuse.
3. After swearing not to weaken or unman him, she will free his companions and care for him.

Odysseus is welcomed by the goddess, who prepares a potion for him to drink, but she is unsuccessful in changing him into a pig. As Odysseus rushes her with his drawn sword, she clasps his knees and begs for mercy, realizing he is the Odysseus Hermes spoke of, the one on whom her magic will not work (10.329). Odysseus' mind is agile, active, and unwilling to surrender to anyone, as his encounters with the Cyclopes, the Laestrygonians, and the Lotus-Eaters exemplify. He even ponders Ino's advice (see 5.339–362) before rejecting it and devising his own plan. His companions, on the other hand, are docile, easily manipulated (as seen in the Lotus-Eaters episode), and ruled by instinct.

Once Circe releases Odysseus' men, he goes back for the remainder of his companions, whom he finds grieving and weeping. Their joy in seeing him is illustrated in a simile expressing both their complete dependence on him and their weakness and reckless behavior when he is not present. The men are compared to young calves rushing to their mothers (Odysseus) as they return from a day of grazing. The calves, like Odysseus' crew, miss their mothers' milk and become agitated and reckless (10.412–413). Eurylochus, mistrustful, resists following Odysseus and encourages his companions to do the same, reminding them of Odysseus' recklessness in the Cyclops' cave. Odysseus ponders decapitating him for insubordination, but his anger is checked by his companions, who promise to accompany him and to leave Eurylochus behind to guard the ship. Fearing Odysseus' reproaches, Eurylochus decides to tag along (his only other role in the *Odyssey* is a brief appearance in 11.23). Eurylochus' nearly mutinous action contributes to Odysseus' loss of control over his men, a process that began in the Cicones episode and reaches a crisis in the cattle of the sun episode. His companions' insubordination shows the extent to which Odysseus' world has changed since Troy. As an Iliadic warrior, he was unique among his peers in his ability to control the Greek troops (see *Il.*2.188-206) but in a post-Troy world, he can no longer manage his men by force alone. Like the calves in the simile, they need a guide to lead and nurture them.

Aeaea is a kind of Lotus Land where, instead of ingesting the lotus to erase the past, Odysseus loses sight of his homecoming by abandoning himself to satisfying his physical needs for an entire year. Circe, like Penelope, uses her charms and tricks to make pigs of the suitors who court her for three years, as she weaves and unravels her father-in-law's shroud. But unlike Penelope, Circe is not family oriented, which is crucial for a woman in the *Odyssey*. In Aeaea the family unit is negated. Like Calypso's island, Aeaea is a faraway mythical land where, once again, Odysseus is caught in an eternal stagnation in which *kleos* and *timē* hold little meaning. Circe, unlike Calypso, makes no mention of marriage, and there is no son to continue Odysseus' line.[10] The Circe-Odysseus union, like his union with Calypso, is a sterile one, a continuous, unvarying life of ease devoid of challenges. After a year of oblivious bliss, Odysseus is awakened by his companions to resume life and struggle.

Odysseus' transition from warrior to peacemaker is not yet complete, as he learns from Circe, who informs him that he must make yet another journey: to Hades (10.491–492). He must descend to the deepest level of the mythic world before he can ascend into the world of mortals; he will visit death and be reborn as the new, post-Troy hero of the *Odyssey*. The goddess's directions to Tiresias parallel those Eidothea gives Menelaus in approaching Proteus (4.365–430). In both episodes, a semidivine woman instructs a hero on how to complete his *nostos*. Eidothea informs Menelaus that Proteus alone can show him the way home; Circe informs Odysseus that only the seer Tiresias can tell him how to reach Ithaca. In each instance, a specific approach to the seer is demanded before a response can be obtained. Eidothea advises Menelaus to hold on to Proteus until he speaks; Tiresias must first drink lamb's blood before he answers. In both cases the instructions must be followed verbatim.

Odysseus, terrified that he must visit mortality's end and return, breaks down and weeps, but, a man of endurance, he relents and inquires who will be his guide. Circe informs him the undertaking is one he must perform on his own and provides directions and the sacrifices needed to fulfill it. She directs Odysseus to Persephone, the wife of Hades and queen of the underworld, instead of Hades himself. Persephone is yet another female figure (death itself) engaged in the hero's homecoming. Even Tiresias' wisdom (after his death) comes from Persephone. The cow/calf simile (10.410–415) here applies to Odysseus, as well as his companions: they are the calves, who out of necessity eagerly await their mother for security and safety. Odysseus must now renounce his Iliadic world before he can ascend to his new role as unifier. In Hades, at the junction of the twin rivers Pyriphlegethon and Cocytos (tributaries of the Styx),[11] which flow into Acheron,[12] Odysseus is to dig a pit in preparation for Tiresias' meeting and dedicate a black ram to him. He must then keep the dead at sword's length to prevent them from approaching the pit until Tiresias arrives. Once Tiresias drinks from the pit, he will inform Odysseus how to complete his *nostos*.

At dawn Odysseus sails but fails to mention the trip to his men. He often holds back information from them, mostly to prevent mutiny and perhaps even to spare them extra anguish. He will do so again later by overlooking the risks involved when encountering Scylla and Charybdis, an adventure he is forewarned will cost him more lives. Keeping the truth from his followers, however, will cause him undue pain, as when he refused to inform his crew that Aeolus' bag contained adverse winds rather than treasure. As Odysseus readies to depart, Elpenor, his youngest companion, who is asleep on Circe's roof, falls and breaks his neck. The fall goes unnoticed, and Elpenor's soul descends to Hades before Odysseus sails. Elpenor, the third of three characters introduced in this book,[13] will play a larger role in *Od.* 11, where his shade appeals to Odysseus to return to Circe for his burial (11.51–80). Odysseus finally informs his men that, before reaching home, they must visit Hades to consult Tiresias. The men, caught by surprise at the news that they must visit the dead (and thus metaphorically die themselves), sink to the ground in grief and then board the ship weeping.

Selected Bibliography: *Od.* 10

Ahl and Roisman, "*Odyssey*," 122–136.

Alexander, "Note."

Apthorp, "Nochmals."

Arans and Shea, "Fall."

Beck, Deborah, "Odysseus."
Birge, "Ambiguity."
Brilliant, "Kirke's."
Buchan, *Limits*, 133–180.
Clarke, *Art*, 45–66.
Clay, "Aeolia."
Davidson, "Tragic."
Garrison, "Great."
Louden, *Homer's*, 135–163.
MacDonald, "Luke's."
Marinatos, "Circe."
McClymont, "Character."
Most, "Structure."
Nishimura, "Circe-Episodes."
Page, *Folktales*, 23–48, 49–91.
Parry, Hugh, "*Apologos*."
Pocock, "Note."
Reece, *Stranger's*, 101–122.
Reinhardt, "Adventures," 63–112.
Reinhardt, "Homer."
Roessel, "Stag."
Said, *Homer*, 150–188.
Schmoll, "Odysseus."
Scodel, "Odysseus and Stag."
Scully, "Doubling."
Warner, "Enchantments."
Further commentary on *Od.* 10 in General Bibliography I.

Book 11

Od. 11 is on a single adventure, the *Nekyia* (a second *Nekyia* occurs in 24.1–204), a spiritual journey to the land of the dead, who live in darkness, lack mental powers (*noos*) and strength (*menos*), and are merely insubstantial shadows or dreams without material existence. *Od.* 11 serves also as a mythological encyclopedia, introducing material from sources other than the Trojan cycle. The book divides into two parallel halves of three parts each, separated by an intermezzo.

I. Hades: arrival (8%)
II. Elpenor, Tiresias, and Anticleia (27%)
III. Catalog of women (17%)
IV. Intermezzo (9%)
V. Agamemnon, Achilles, and Ajax (28%)
VI. Catalog of men (10%)
VII. Hades: departure (1%)

I. Hades: Arrival, 1–50

"First of all, we dragged the ship down into the bright water" (11.2),[14] and favorable winds drive Odysseus to the underworld entrance—the land of the Cimmerians (11.14).[15] Traditionally, Hades (the underworld) is located under the earth, but here Odysseus does not seem to descend (a *katabasis*, going under). Instead he travels horizontally to the land of the Cimmerians at the edge of Ocean, which surrounds the earth. Having crossed Ocean, he enters Persephone's groves, Hades' home (10.508–515). There, at the conjunction of two rivers (see notes 11 and 12 in the present chapter), lies Erebos (a general name for the land of the dead), the place Circe sends Odysseus. There he digs a pit and performs the ritual as directed by the goddess (11.13–22). As swarms of spirits approach out of Erebos (11.37; signaling that Odysseus has not yet descended deep into Hades), Odysseus, sword in hand, keeps the hordes of dead from approaching until Tiresias comes to drink first.

II. Elpenor, Tiresias, and Anticleia, 51–225

While Odysseus waits for Tiresias, Elpenor's soul, yet to be missed, stands lamenting before Odysseus, explaining how, startled and drunk with wine, he stepped off Circe's roof and broke his neck. Elpenor, whose only feat in the entire epic is to have his neck broken, wants to be remembered merely as one who rowed with his companions.[16] He implores Odysseus to return to Aeaea, burn his body with his armor, and place an oar on his burial mound. Odysseus promises to carry out his wishes (which he does at 12.15) and continues to brandish his sword over the sacrificial blood to keep other phantoms from approaching. The oar on Elpenor's grave signifies a kind of self-burial, an acceptance of death as a determinant in his life, and reminds the reader of Tiresias' prophecy to Odysseus (11.129–134), who upon his return to Ithaca must also plant an oar in the ground and render sacrifice to Poseidon and the other gods.

1. The Elpenor scene serves as a gradual transition from the world of the living to the world of the dead.
2. Since his unburied body's soul exists in limbo, Elpenor does not need to drink blood to speak.
3. The scene highlights Homeric man's longing for immortality and fame, whether that man is Odysseus or a blunderer like Elpenor. An oar planted on his grave gives him the little recognition needed to be remembered as one of Odysseus' crew. Elpenor exemplifies the instinctual man (Odysseus' crew). His qualities (lack of self-control, lack of heroism, failure to heed the gods' commands), opposite to Odysseus', emphasize why he and his companions fail to achieve their homecoming. In this respect, Elpenor's shortcomings comment not only on his and his companions' fate but also on that of the suitors'.
4. The scene illustrates the dead's foreknowledge of the future, as exhibited by Elpenor, who predicts Odysseus' return to Aeaea (69–70).

Odysseus, approached by his mother, Anticleia, whom he last saw thirteen years earlier, refuses to allow her near the pit until Tiresias approaches. It is the first time Odysseus hears of his mother's death, and he is anxious to question her about it but holds back until Tiresias arrives, which draws attention to one of his major traits—his ability to control his most urgent longings until the right time to act arrives. This ability to bide his time is especially evident in the latter part of the epic, where he patiently waits for many books before he discloses his identity. The prophet, who instantly appears, asks Odysseus to step away from the pit so he can drink the blood and speak the truth (11.96). However, he has already spoken without tasting the blood. It seems he only needs to drink it to forecast Odysseus' future, but his prophecy does not provide the information Circe promised (how to return to Ithaca [10.539–540]). Instead, Tiresias predicts the stages that will guide him from the present to his death at a ripe old age.

1. His path home will be long, since Poseidon intends to continue punishing him.
2. His return will come after much suffering, if he can control his companions and his own instincts.
3. The sun's cattle will be the final test for both his and his men's survival, where uncontrollable instincts will account for his misfortunes, a warning that goes unheeded by his companions.
4. Once home, he will kill the suitors in a proper and ordained massacre.
5. Having regained his kingdom, Odysseus will leave Ithaca for a second time.[17] He will travel with an oar to a place lacking knowledge of the sea. When someone mistakes his oar for a prong to separate grain from chaff (11.28; "winnow-fan"), he will plant it and render sacrifices to Poseidon and, once home, to all the other gods.
6. His death, gentle and painless, will come in Ithaca at an advanced age.

Tiresias' prophecies fail to inform Odysseus of the difficulties he must still face other than to warn him of Helius' (the sun god's) cattle. It is left to Circe to provide detailed directions for his return home (12.25–26). Why then is the trip to Hades necessary? In addition to allowing Odysseus to learn of his future, it more importantly allows him to confront his past. In reexamining the actions and regrets of his warrior past and listening to the stories of the fallen Greek warriors (Agamemnon, Achilles, and Ajax), he is better able to confront that past before shifting to the more domestic problems of his post-Troy world.

Odysseus breaks off Tiresias' predictions, anxious to know how to communicate with his mother, who sits in silence. The prophet cautions that to speak, the dead must drink from the blood pit, and Odysseus patiently waits for his mother's ghost to approach. Once she tastes the blood, she instantly recognizes her son, and in the next seventy lines (11.155–224), Odysseus and his mother converse within the narrative Odysseus is reciting to the Phaeacians. Anticleia is surprised to see her son in Hades while he is still alive. He explains he came to consult Tiresias but prefers to learn about his family—mother, father, son, and wife.

1. His mother: Did she die of a long illness or by Artemis' "painless shafts" (11.173)[18] out of sorrow for his absence?
2. His father and son: Is the inheritance he left behind intact in their possession or with some other man?
3. His wife: Did Penelope stay faithful to Telemachus and guard their property, or is she married to someone else?

Anticleia responds to the questions in reverse order, as is Homer's custom.

1. Her first concern is the faithfulness of Penelope, whom she presents as being in a constant state of weeping, waiting for her husband.
2. His inheritance is safe with Telemachus, who administers his estate as a man with authority (11.186–187), a more mature picture of Telemachus than seen previously in the *Telemachia* or anywhere else in the *Odyssey.* It seems that before Anticleia's death, the suitors had not yet descended on the palace.

3. Laertes remains on his estate, never ventures into the city, and lives like a vagabond, grieving and longing for his son.
4. The cause of her own death was longing for her son's absence.

Anticleia makes no mention of the suitors. Aside from her description of Penelope's distress at her husband's absence, Anticleia paints a positive portrait of conditions at the palace—the inheritance remains intact, and Telemachus not only is in charge but is a man of authority who is relied on by others (a little hard to believe for one so young). Over half of Anticleia's response, however, concerns her husband's and her own sorrow at Odysseus' absence. Laertes lives like a vagabond, sleeping at his estate in the dirt with his servants, and she died grieving for her son. For the first time since leaving Ithaca, Odysseus confronts the serious damage his absence has caused his parents. The *Nekyia* serves to redirect his morality away from his Iliadic past (military identity, glory) to what really matters in the post-Troy world—family. Upset at what he hears about his parents, Odysseus tries to embrace his mother's soul, but three times she flutters out of his hands (11.207–208). Frustrated, he asks why he cannot embrace her, and she demystifies for him the nature of the soul: when one is cremated, the flesh disappears, leaving only bones and ash, but the spirit flies away like a dream to the underworld. Anticleia, however, is anxious that her son leave the darkness for the light and reminds him to remember her to his wife.

III. Catalog of Women, 225–330

The catalog of women (106 lines) is the first of two catalogs in *Od.* 11; the second catalog, that of men, appears after the intermezzo. While Odysseus is conversing with his mother, Persephone sends a group of women toward him, who approach Odysseus in two groups, each group comprising two subgroups.

Group 1: Eight mortal women who gave birth to mortal or semidivine sons

Subgroup a: Tyro, Antiope, Alcmene, and Megara, who gave birth to sons (except Megara) by Poseidon or Zeus

Subgroup b: Epikaste, Chloris, Leda, and Iphimedeia, who gave birth to sons by mortal men

Group 2: Six women, with emphasis only on the third in each subgroup

Subgroup a: Phaedra, Procris, and Ariadne

Subgroup b: Maira, Clymene, and Eriphyle

Odysseus holds at bay the first subgroup of these women (1a), allowing each to approach and be questioned by him. The first woman, Tyro, identifies herself as the daughter of Salmoneus and wife of Cretheus, the son of Aeolus.[19] She loves the river Enipeus, but Poseidon, disguised as the river, raped her and she conceived two sons, Pelias and Neleus (the father of Nestor). She also gave birth to Aison, Pheres, and Amythaon by her husband.[20] Antiope bore Zeus Amphion and Zethos, two sons who laid the foundations for Thebes. Alcmene, the third woman to speak to Odysseus, is identified as Amphitryon's wife, who, lying in the embrace of Zeus, gave birth to Heracles. The fourth woman, Megara, daughter of Kreion, married Amphitryon's son (269–270).[21] All four women are classical heroines who produced sons by Zeus or Poseidon, with the exception of Megara (whose husband, Heracles, does become a god in later tradition). Since the *Odyssey* is preoccupied with relationships between husbands and wives (Odysseus and Penelope, Agamemnon and Clytemnestra), sons and their mothers (Telemachus and Penelope, Orestes and Clytemnestra), and fathers and sons (Odysseus and Telemachus, Agamemnon and Orestes), these myths are paradigmatic of what Odysseus, Penelope, and Telemachus could face and thus represent pitfalls to avoid. For Penelope, the women serve a double warning: first, to exercise extra care in accepting the beggar as her husband so as not to be duped by a god as Tyro, Antiope, and Alcmene are; and second, to avoid Clytemnestra's fate at the hands of her son and Megara's at the hands of her husband.

Tyro's is the longest exposition of the women considered in the catalog, and it likely serves as an example for Odysseus of the fate that can befall a wife left without a husband for a long period of time. Unbeknownst to her husband, Cretheus, a god, mistaken by Tyro for her lover (Enipeus), takes advantage of her. Penelope's reluctance to accept the beggar as her husband when all signs point to his identity is due to her fear that he might be someone (often a god) in disguise. The fact that Tyro has a lover (Enipeus) while married to Cretheus is reminiscent of Clytemnestra's taking Aegisthus as her lover while she is married to the absent Agamemnon. The appearance of Poseidon, the archenemy in Odysseus' homecoming, further adds intrigue to this story of a disguised god approaching Penelope. Thus, Tyro and the women who follow her (Antiope, Alcmene, and Megara) are all duped by disguised deities.

Epikaste,[22] the first of the second set of four women (1b), is the wife/mother of Oedipus. In Homer, Epikaste, in ignorance, marries her own son after he kills his father, and she hangs herself in shame for her monstrous deed (Oedipus, by contrast, remains king of the Cadmeans, unlike in Sophocles' tragedy,[23] in which he blinds and exiles himself from Thebes). Here the emphasis is placed on women who, acting out of ignorance, cause tragedy. An alert mind like Penelope's can avoid calamity, whereas a weaker mind like Clytemnestra's cannot. Chloris,[24] the second of the foursome, is given the second-largest space in the catalog of women (11.281–297). The wife of Neleus and mother of Nestor, she bore Neleus three sons in Homer's version (Nestor, Chromios, and Periclymenus) and one daughter (Pero).[25] The remainder of Chloris' tale (11.288–297) focuses on her daughter's courtship, which is briefly summarized by naming only two of the key characters, Iphikles and Melampous, leaving the myth incomplete. Since Homer returns to this myth later (*Od.* 15), it is probable he feels it is well known and no further narration is required. Here Pero's courtship and the many suitors who pursed her are highlighted. Her father's refusal to accept a bridegroom unless he could perform an assigned task led to fateful events linking this tale to the predicaments in Ithaca with Penelope's suitors. Leda, the third woman of the second group, is the mother of heroic sons by a mortal man, Tyndareos.[26] The fourth woman (11.305–320) and the last of the eight considered in some detail is given the third-largest consideration, after Tyro and Chloris. Iphimedeia, wife of Aloeus (little else is known of him), bore two sons to Poseidon, Otos and Ephialtes, the tallest men on Earth, known as the Aloads (after Aloeus, their mortal father). These two adolescent giants, considered to be nine cubits wide (about fourteen feet) and nine fathoms high (fifty-four feet), threatened to fight the gods on Olympus by piling the mountains Ossa and Pelion on top of Olympus to reach the sky, but before coming to maturity, they were killed by Apollo, Zeus's son. Both Leda's and Iphimedeia's tales deal with the loss of sons while carrying out their missions. Of special interest is the fate of Iphimedeia's two giant sons by Poseidon. In this tale we are reminded of the Cyclops, another of Poseidon's sons, who is blinded by mortals for his cannibalism. Thus, the catalog of eight women, which began with a consort of Poseidon (Tyro), ends with another of his consorts, bringing the group full circle back to Poseidon.

The catalog of women continues with two subgroups of three women each, though only the third woman in each subgroup is given any consideration. The first two women in each subgroup are merely named. In the tale told of the first of these two subgroups (2a; Phaedra, Procris, and Ariadne), Theseus brings Minos' daughter Ariadne to Athens from Crete, but she is killed on the way by Artemis. This is all Homer says about Ariadne.[27] The second subgroup (2b) is dismissed in two lines (326–327).[28] These three women have little in common except as mothers or daughters of heroes. Clymene, the daughter of Minyas, wife of Phylacus, and mother of Iphicles, has ties to the Chloris myth mentioned earlier (2a). The lesser-known Maira is the daughter of Proetus and a great-granddaughter of Sisyphus, whose punishment in Hades is described later in this book (11.593–600). The stories of the two women given any attention (Ariadne and Eriphyle) serve as a contrast to Penelope and Odysseus' situation. Ariadne, after saving her lover Theseus from the Minotaur, was abandoned and later killed by Artemis. Eriphyle was bribed, caused her husband's (Amphiaraus') death, and was later avenged by his son Alkman. Both tales call for caution and serve as a warning for both parties, as well as complementing the Atreus myth central to the *Odyssey*.

IV. Intermezzo, 330–384

Odysseus breaks his narration, arguing that he cannot possibly name all the wives and daughters of heroes he saw, and asks to retire for the evening. The Phaeacians, spellbound by his stories, remain silent until Arete, who has not spoken since *Od.* 8 (443–445), breaks the silence by complimenting Odysseus on his beauty and mind and urging those gathered to honor him with more gifts. Impressed by his performance, Arete asks him to delay his departure to allow the Phaeacian nobles to collect more gifts. Perhaps it is the tales of the chosen women, the meeting with his mother's ghost, and the sensitivity shown to Elpenor's ghost that so impress the queen. Echeneus, the Phaeacian elder, agrees that the queen's request should be respected, for her actions are exactly what her subjects expect of her, but he warns that the rulership belongs to Alcinous (11.346). The queen's generosity is appreciated, but lest anyone misunderstand, Alcinous is king and ultimately in control, a response perhaps to Nausicaa's comment that Odysseus' safety rests in Arete's hands. Alcinous echoes Echeneus' words when he states that whether Odysseus will receive more gifts is his decision as long as he rules the Phaeacians (11.348–349). Declaring his sole authority (11.353), he asks Odysseus to remain another day to collect more gifts. Odysseus acknowledges the king's authority and agrees to postpone his journey even for a whole year if it means greater respect and popularity when he returns to Ithaca.

The king implores the hero to continue his recitation, for he performs like an expert singer and is not deceptive like one who makes up lying stories (11.366). In complimenting Odysseus' skills as a singer of tales, Homer, through Alcinous, compliments himself again but is careful to distinguish between professional singers and amateurs who make up tall tales. The exchange is full of irony since Odysseus, in the Ithacan books (*Od.* 13–24), will use elaborate lies, sung as a professional would, to win his way home. It is even possible that the tales he is reciting so expertly to the Phaeacians are embellished to win them over. Alcinous offers to hold out until early dawn if it means listening to more of Odysseus' dismal sorrows. He asks whether Odysseus met any of his comrades in Hades, providing the transition between the first and second parts of the hero's underworld episode. Odysseus, yearning for sleep, nevertheless relents and turns to the catalog of men.

V. Agamemnon, Achilles, and Ajax, 385–566

As Persephone scatters the hordes of women waiting to approach Odysseus, the grieving soul of Agamemnon appears, accompanied by those who perished with him at the hands of Aegisthus. Weeping at the sight of him, Odysseus asks after his undoing; Agamemnon's three-part response is the longest episode devoted to a single figure in this book (11.385–466).

1. He explains how he was killed by Aegisthus with the help of Clytemnestra.
2. He launches into a condemnation of his unfaithful wife and all women.
3. He inquires about his son Orestes.

Thus far in the *Odyssey*, the references to the Atreus myth deal with Aegisthus' treachery (11.409–410). Of the seventeen references to the myth in the epic (see chapter 1, note 8), only four implicate Clytemnestra in his murder (3.234–235, 4.90–92, 24.96–97, and 24.199–202), but in Hades Agamemnon holds her equally responsible for both his and Cassandra's[29] deaths. Of the eighty-two lines devoted to Agamemnon in Hades, almost two-thirds (11.405–456) deal with Clytemnestra's involvement and the treachery of women in general. Misogynistic comments, absent in the catalog of women, are now abundant, perhaps intentionally on Odysseus' part, as he is careful not to annoy Arete until he is assured of her approval.

Agamemnon's depiction of his death's carnage parallels Amphimedon's description of the suitors' slaughter (24.184–185) and warns Odysseus of his own homecoming. Agamemnon's vehemence against women continues, for he longed to greet his son and household servants but had his expectations betrayed by his wife's grisly acts. For Odysseus, Agamemnon's comments hark back to the destructive nature of the House of Atreus,[30] which caused the Trojan War. Agamemnon persists in defaming even virtuous wives, who must be considered suspect and kept from one's plans. He admits that Odysseus has little to fear from Penelope, a virtuous woman with good thoughts, but even with her caution is needed. He warns Odysseus to return in secret for there is no trusting women, but anxious to hear news of his son, he asks after Orestes. However, Odysseus, ignorant of Orestes' state of affairs, has nothing to say (11.464).

Achilles' soul, accompanied by three fellow warriors who remain silent throughout (Patroclus, Antilochus, and Ajax),[31] interrupts to ask why Odysseus came to Hades. Odysseus responds that he came to consult Tiresias for directions to Ithaca. He praises Achilles as more blessed than any other man, since all his companions honored him as they did the gods, who even in Hades hold authority over the dead. Achilles' response contains three of the most famous lines in the *Odyssey*:

> I would rather follow the plow as thrall to another
> man, . . .
> than be a king over all the perished dead.
> (11.489–491)

The *Iliad*'s greatest warrior concludes that it is preferable to live as a nobody than be a dead somebody, a sentiment that captures the gulf between the *Iliad*'s and the *Odyssey*'s values. In the *Iliad* Achilles is willing to give his life for fame and glory, aware of his fate: a long, prosperous life if he evades Troy or a short, glorious life if he does not. He opts for the latter, but his admiration for courage and prowess has still not abated, as the two questions to Odysseus demonstrate: Did my son fight like a champion, and does my father, Peleus, still rule? Achilles here is reminiscent of Hector in the *Iliad*, who, bound by the Iliadic ethos while still alive, prays that his infant son will become a greater warrior than his father, although he is aware of the futility of war:

> There will come a day when sacred Ilion shall perish,
> and Priam, and the people of Priam. (*Il.* 6.448–449)

In like manner, Achilles in death comes to understand the meaningless of *kleos* but still cannot rid himself of the overpowering desire for his living son to gain fame. Odysseus responds in reverse order. He has nothing to report on Peleus but plenty on Neoptolemus:

1. At counsel, he ranked only behind Nestor and Odysseus.
2. In battle, he was among the best, killing many. Of those he killed, one stood out: Eurypylus, son of Telephus,[32] a warrior greater than Memnon.[33] By comparing him to the great Trojan warrior Memnon, Odysseus enhances the heroism of Neoptolemus' deed in killing Eurypylus.
3. Neoptolemus was one of the chosen warriors in the wooden horse, and he begged Odysseus to let him spring out and fight the Trojans.
4. Having sacked Priam's city, Neoptolemus, still unscathed, boarded his ship with his fair share of the booty and sailed home.

Hearing such praise lavished on his son, Achilles proudly stalks away, assured that the Aeacides' (*Od.* 11.538)[34] line of distinguished warriors is preserved by Neoptolemus' performance. Odysseus' own warrior pride, however, is not obscured by Neoptolemus' feats. While praising him, he is conscious of his own part in the war (11.523). Those in the wooden horse were under his command. If Achilles' warrior pride is still intact, so is Odysseus'. Most of all however, this episode stresses the pride that each of the two fathers (Agamemnon and Achilles) feels for his son, whose achievements bring fame to the father. In like manner, Telemachus will bring renown to the Arcesiads.

Once Achilles leaves, other souls crowd around Odysseus. It is not clear whether these souls, including Achilles, drink from the blood pit or whether Odysseus has moved closer to the interior and the sacrificial blood is no longer required for speech. Nevertheless, only Ajax's soul stands at a distance, silent and angry at his loss of Achilles' arms. Although Ajax was favored, Athena and the captive Trojans, acting as judges, awarded the armor to Odysseus in order to humiliate Ajax, who later commits suicide.[35] The Trojans, as officiating judges, were likely to select an undeserving individual to inherit Achilles' armor, knowing the contention it would create among the Greek warriors and the humiliation it would cause Ajax. Odysseus accepts Zeus's role in Ajax's death as payment for the Greeks' overzealousness in Troy's destruction, but he continues to compliment Ajax's achievements and begs his forgiveness. Ajax, unrelenting in his wrath, remains mute and strides off into the darkness. The humiliation of the second-greatest warrior after Achilles losing a contest to an inferior fighter like Odysseus is too great for Ajax to endure. In listening to these heroes articulate their disillusionment with the *Iliad*'s warrior ethic, Odysseus reappraises it himself and, like them, finds it lacking. The Greeks' "best of the Achaeans" (Achilles), who chose death over life, realizes he was wrong. The commander-in-chief of the expedition forfeits his own life and wife to retrieve a woman whose adopted people he now finds deadly and vile. Ajax, second in prowess only to Achilles, stands mute, apart from the others, having abandoned his great acts of valor for a reward denied. In death these heroes denounce Achilles' deeds for family. Achilles feels pride in a son he never knew, and Agamemnon asks for news of a son he will never see. He laments the ritual a wife owes a husband on his deathbed, while Ajax dies alone for an ill-placed pride. Odysseus is still alive and will eventually return to Ithaca to claim everything these warriors have lost. Peace and family are preferable to war, values worth fighting for. For now he will return to Circe and endure as he must whatever the gods still demand, for nothing is sweeter than home (9.34; *ouden glykion patridos*).

VI. Catalog of Men, 567–635

Odysseus, anxious to visit with the souls of the other dead, cuts off his one-sided conversation with Ajax to encounter six more figures, who are presented in three groups:

1. Two legendary mythic figures (Minos and Orion)
2. Three famous sinners punished in Hades (Tityus, Tantalus, and Sisyphus)
3. Heracles, the greatest hero of the generation before Odysseus

Odysseus must now have moved deep into inner Hades, otherwise he could not have seen Minos[36] and the gathered souls awaiting judgment. The geography of Odysseus' visit to Hades is not clear, perhaps left intentionally vague and dreamlike, like a trip into the unconscious more than a physical journey. Leaving Minos (he now seems to be moving vertically, if he is moving at all), Odysseus sees the giant Orion[37] in the meadow of asphodel[38] holding a brazen club and rounding up animals he killed in life. After these two legendary figures, he encounters three of Hades' famous sufferers. The first is another giant, Earth's son Tityus,[39] who is sprawled over nine acres, his liver torn by two vultures as punishment for raping Zeus' consort Leto. The second sinner, Tantalus,[40] suffers eternal punishment in a lake whose water extends up to his chin. Thirsty, he bends to drink, but the water drains away and disappears. Hungry, he reaches over his head to lofty trees laden with fruit, but the wind tosses the branches into the clouds. Sisyphus,[41] the most cunning and scrupulous of mortals, struggles to push a monstrous stone to the crest of a hill; the moment it reaches the hill's peak, it rolls back down. What these sinners have in common are crimes against the gods (not mentioned by Homer), which Odysseus must avoid if he is to complete his *nostos.*

Odysseus next sights Heracles' (Hercules') image. After his death, Heracles joined the gods on Olympus, where, reconciled with his archenemy, Hera, he married Hebe, Hera and Zeus's daughter. Why then is he in Hades? If this famous hero is to be included among the dead in order to parallel his sufferings with those of Odysseus, he must occupy both Olympus and the underworld. He, like Odysseus, suffered many hardships, descended to Hades, and ascended to Earth to be reunited with his wife and live in peace and prosperity. Only his image (*eidolon*) appears in Hades, not his soul (*psychē*), since he is alive. Heracles asks whether Odysseus is pursuing some wretched destiny (his homecoming), as he himself did when alive, but before Odysseus can respond, Heracles pours out his angst. Though Zeus's son, he served as a bondsman to an inferior man.[42] He then relates his twelfth labor, perhaps the most demanding, which required him to enter Hades and bring to Earth Cerberus[43] (11.623). Like Heracles, who was forced to descend to Hades before he could finally reach home, Odysseus must survive a descent to the underworld and serve as a bondsman (a beggar) to the inferior suitors before his return to his home.

VII. Hades: Departure, 636–640

Having voiced his complaint, Heracles returns to the realm of Hades; Odysseus waits, hoping to speak to heroes of the generation before him, Perithous and Theseus,[44] but as he waits, hordes of dead begin to crowd about him. Seized by fear that Persephone might confront him with some Cerberus from Hades, he returns to his ship with his companions, who are miraculously present (is he awakening from a nightmare?), and a fair wind carries them down the Ocean river.

Selected Bibliography: *Od.* 11

Ahl and Roisman, *"Odyssey,"* 122–136, 137–151.

Beck, Deborah, "Odysseus."

Clarke, *Art*, 45–66.

Doherty, "Athena."

Doherty, "Tyro."

Edwards, Anthony, "Homer's."

Garrison, "Great."

Griffith, *Mummy Wheat*.

Griffith, "Voice."

Gutting, "Emendation."

Hansen, "Odysseus."

Karanika, "End."

Katz, *Penelope's*, 48–53.

Larson, "Boiotia."

Louden, "Extended."

Louden, *The "Odyssey,"* 31–49.

MacDonald, "Luke's."

Martin, Bridget, "Blood."

Most, "Structure."

Pache, "Odysseus."

Parry, Hugh, "*Apologos*."

Reece, "Homer's."

Reece, *Stranger's*, 101–122.

Reinhardt, "Adventures."

Rutherford, *Homer* (1996), 82–104.

Said, *Homer*, 150–188.

Scully, "Doubling."

Segal, *Singers*, 187–194.

Stephens, "Thoughts."

Tsagarakis, "*Odyssey* 11."

Tsagarakis, *Studies in "Odyssey" 11*, 19–144.

Vernant, "Death."

Further commentary on *Od.* 11 in General Bibliography I.

Book 12

In *Od.* 12, as in both *Od.* 9 and Od. 10, two short tales follow a long one. Odysseus is in the thirty-third day of the *Odyssey* narrative, but the three adventures he narrates occur over a period of fifty-one days[45] during the twelfth year of his absence. After Thrinacia, the third adventure of *Od.* 12, he sails to Calypso's island (*Od.* 5), where he remains seven years. He arrives in Ithaca on the thirty-fourth day, the day after he concludes his *apologoi* to the Phaeacians.

I. Return to Aeaea (31%)
II. Odysseus' adventures (61%)
  A. Sirens
  B. Scylla and Charybdis
  C. Thrinacia
III. Arrival at Ogygia (8%)

I. Return to Aeaea, 1–150

Odysseus returns to Circe's island, which he now locates somewhere in the East. The island's locale is significant, for Odysseus and his companions are returning from the West, where the sun sets, back to the East, where the sun rises, thus moving from darkness to light, from death to life. On his first full day on Aeaea, Odysseus sends his men to Circe to retrieve Elpenor's body, which they cremate, then bury the ashes and plant his oar on top of the grave. Circe then welcomes them as men who die twice, whereas the rest of humankind dies once, and promises directions for their journey home the next day. With his Iliadic past dead, Odysseus has resurfaced as the Odyssean postwar hero of the present. Taking him aside, Circe reveals the journey yet to come. First, he must face the Sirens—enchantresses who captivate men and persuade them to neglect their journey and idle their lives away, enchanted by their songs (earlier they were enticed by the lotus flower [*Od.* 9]). Mortals must opt for life and not be tempted to exchange it for oblivion. To evade these enchantresses, Odysseus and his companions must plug their ears. However, Odysseus craves their knowledge but wants to escape the deadly effects of their songs. As in his other adventures, he refuses to succumb to inertia and leave his thirst for knowledge unfulfilled. He has himself tied to the ship's mast in order to exchange anguish for knowledge. The Phaeacians listening to Odysseus' stories are like those passive sailors who, having exchanged action for inaction, now litter the Sirens' beach with their bones. Unlike Odysseus, who rejects immortality, the Phaeacians accept it; isolated from reality, they experience life through others' songs (deeds).

Once past the Sirens, Odysseus faces two choices. The first is the Planctae (12.61),[46] an impossible route, for not even doves could traverse it (12.63). No ship ever slipped through these rocks except the *Argo*,[47] Jason's ship, which was saved by Hera's love for him. The second route passes next to two huge crags on opposite sides. The first, which is unscalable, is where Scylla, a female monster (with twelve legs, six long necks, and six heads, each with a triple row of sharp fangs), lurks. Stuck in her cave from the waist down, she extends her long necks, searching Amphitrite (the sea) for food. Attack is futile, escape with casualties possible only if one races past her. On the second, lower crag grows a fig tree, below which is Charybdis,[48] an enormous whirlpool that gulps and vomits water three times a day. The best route is to hug Scylla's crag and sail past her at top speed, for from the whirlpool no one can be saved, not even with Poseidon's help. Odysseus will encounter losses, one man to each of Scylla's awesome mouths.

If the best route is past Scylla, why mention the Planctae and the *Argo*? Is it to be inferred from this reference and several in the *Iliad* (7.468–469, 21.41, and 23.747) that the *Argonautica* is a source for some of Odysseus' adventures? Odysseus identifies Circe as Aeetes' sister (*Od.* 10.137; see note 8 of the present chapter), a major player in the *Argonautica* and Jason's journey. Circe's own location near where the sun rises (12.4) is closer to the area of the *Argo*'s voyage than that of Odysseus' wanderings, which take place mostly in the western Mediterranean. In addition, Artakiē, mentioned in reference to the Laestrygonian Antiphates' daughter, who had gone to the spring by that name (10.107–108), is a place-name from the *Argonautica* (see Ap. Rhod. 1.957). Yet these references do not explain why Circe believes the *Argo*'s voyage through the Planctae is an impossibility for Odysseus. The implication that Jason, who accomplishes the impossible, is a greater hero than Odysseus does not seem likely. It appears, then, that Odysseus' choice is somehow superior to that of Jason. Jason survives the passage through the Planctae only because of Hera's assistance. Odysseus survives his ordeal through *mētis* (intelligence) and *tlēmosynē* (mental and physical endurance), terms that further define Homer's post-Troy hero. *Mētis* and *tlēmosynē* also aid him in his escape from Charybdis, an undertaking in which not even Poseidon can assist. Odysseus even considers fighting Scylla rather than risk losing six men, but Circe reprimands him (12.116–117). He has no means of defense against such bloodthirsty forces. To fight Scylla is to imperil another set of six men. Nevertheless, Odysseus will reject Circe's advice and arm himself (12.225–229) but is unsuccessful against Scylla. Beyond Scylla, Odysseus will reach Thrinacia and come upon seven herds of oxen and sheep, immortal animals that neither give birth nor die and are tended by Helius'[49] two nymph daughters, Lampetia and Phaethousa.

Thrinacia, the only adventure mentioned in the epic's proem (1.6–9), is significant for absolving Odysseus from any responsibility for the actions of his companions, who are destroyed by their own recklessness (1.7; *atasthaliē*, reckless folly). This term, used by Zeus in line 1.34, underscores the element of choice. The choices one makes decide one's fate, and neither the gods nor Odysseus (struggling for his life and his companions') can be blamed for his men's shortcomings. Tiresias warns Odysseus to curb both his and his men's cravings on Thrinacia (11.104–109); Circe likewise warns him that if any harm comes to the cattle, destruction for both his ship and his companions will follow. Circe predicts the outcome of Odysseus' journey, just as the gods predicted the outcome of Aegisthus' marriage to Clytemnestra (1.32–43). By neglecting the gods' warnings, Aegisthus lost his life at the hands of Orestes, as Odysseus' men will lose theirs at the hands of Zeus. Thus, the Thrinacia episode is central to the epic's themes, underlining two qualities necessary for survival—*mētis* and *tlēmosyne*—as a form of control over humankind's *atasthaliē*, a word that describes the actions of both Odysseus' companions and the suitors. Odysseus warns his men that no one should kill any of Helius' flocks in reckless action (*atasthaliēsi*) (12.300–301). In *Od.* 22, after the suitors' slaughter, Odysseus tells Eurycleia that, by their own recklessness (*atasthaliēsin*), they found death (22.416–417).

II. Odysseus' Adventures

II.A. Sirens, 144–200. Odysseus encounters the Sirens and Scylla and Charybdis on the third day after his return to Aeaea. On board his ship, he warns his men of the imminent dangers, plugs their ears with wax, and is himself bound to the mast. When he encounters the enchantresses, he is driven to a frenzy and begs to be untied, but his pleas are disregarded. The songs Odysseus hears assault his instincts and play on his emotions in the same way Demodocus' songs moved him to tears. Like Demodocus' songs, the Sirens' deal with memory, feats performed, companions loved and lost, and the pride of past accomplishments already become legends and sung for the enjoyment of others. The Sirens, themselves immortal singers of tales, captivate audiences as Odysseus' tales hold the Phaeacians captive. Once the Sirens' divine music fades, the companions remove the wax from their ears and unleash Odysseus from the mast, saved from feelings of longing that keep the Sirens' audience captives of their past.

II.B. Scylla and Charybdis, 201–259. Terrified at the thunder of heavy surf, the men stop rowing. Odysseus encourages his men not to surrender to fear, reminding them of the horrors of the Cyclops' cave and how his courage, counsel, and intelligence saved them. He orders them to keep clear from the surging breakers (Charybdis) and to hug Scylla's crags on the opposite side. Deeming ignorance to be best for the crew, he keeps from them the fate of the six men Scylla will devour. Disregarding Circe's advice not to arm himself, he takes up two spears and bestrides his vessel. Always independent and carefully considering his options, as in the Ino episode (5.343–347), he opts for action rather than remaining passive but is unable to stop Scylla, who snatches six men from the vessel. A simile compares the men to small fish caught in a fisherman's rod and cast on the beach writhing and gasping for breath.

II.C. Thrinacia, 260–419. As they near Thrinacia, Eurylochus vehemently objects to navigating in the dark. He proposes they spend the night on the island, a plan his companions embrace. Odysseus realizes that all that happens is predetermined by the gods, but he refuses to acquiesce without a struggle. Supposing there is a chance to save his companions, he has them swear that none of the animals on the island will be touched; they will feast on the plentiful provisions provided by Circe. A supernatural storm (12.314) that night prevents them from sailing the following morning, and Odysseus again warns against harming the animals. His men, agreeing to obey, confirm their earlier oath. However, the monthlong storm depletes their food supplies, and the men turn to hunting and fishing. Hoping to find a solution to their food shortage, Odysseus goes off by himself to pray but falls asleep, an act he attributes to the gods. During his absence, Eurylochus counsels butchering some cattle, sacrificing to the gods, and later in Ithaca building a temple to the sun god in appreciation. If not acceptable, the god can wreck their ship, for drowning is preferable to hunger. The Thrinacia episode reinforces a number of the *Odyssey*'s themes:

1. Absence
    a. Poseidon's absence from the gods' council enables Odysseus' *nostos*.
    b. Agamemnon's absence from Mycenae costs him his kingship and his family.

   c. Odysseus' absence from Ithaca creates chaos and threatens the Arcesiad line.
   d. Menelaus' absence prevents him from avenging his brother.
   e. Telemachus' absence from Ithaca threatens his inheritance.
   f. Odysseus' absence in Thrinacia turns mutinous.
2. Blind decisions. Odysseus always weighs his options before deciding on what action seems best (e.g., how to approach Nausicaa). In Thrinacia his companions act without seriously considering the consequences.
3. Acting on instinct rather than *mētis*. Odysseus controls his physical needs, as opposed to the suitors and his companions, who satisfy their physical needs first and consider their actions later.
4. False prayers and sacrifices. Like the suitors, Eurylochus and crew recklessly commit unlawful acts and try to conceal them through false prayers and sacrifices. In Thrinacia they make a mockery of the sacrifices due the gods; instead of barley, they use oak leaves, and instead of wine, they use water to purify their offerings. These acts seal their fates even before they taste the sacred meat, an act so transgressive that Odysseus instantly recognizes it as reckless and monstrous when he wakes and smells the cooking meat.
5. Hospitality. In Thrinacia the companions abuse Helius' hospitality. Offered sanctuary by the god, they mistreat their rights as guests by taking advantage of his property (as the suitors take advantage of Odysseus').
6. Transgression against the gods
   a. Odysseus' wanderings are due in part to his sacking Troy's sacred citadel and injuring Poseidon's son.
   b. His fellow warriors suffer delayed homecomings due to Athena's anger for the rape of Cassandra in her temple, which causes the Lesser Ajax's death.
7. Hubris
   a. Eurylochus' whimsical comment about Helius wrecking Odysseus' ship if he wants belittles the god.

b. Lesser Ajax's boast that, despite the gods, he escaped the sea's wrath (4.504) angered Poseidon, who split the rock on which he perched, killing him.

Threatening to shine in Hades but no longer on earth, Helius pleads with Zeus and the other gods to punish Odysseus' men.[50] Heeding the sun's warning, Zeus promises to dash Odysseus' ship to pieces, forecasting the demise of the remaining companions. At this point Odysseus interrupts his *apologoi* to explain to his audience that the details of what transpired between Zeus and Helius were acquired from Calypso, who heard them from Hermes.

Returning to camp, Odysseus finds the cattle butchered and his men blaming each other. In the surrealistic scene that follows, the signs of their sacrilegious acts are apparent:

1. The skins of the butchered crawl.
2. The meat stuck on the spits bellows.
3. The noise permeating the camp is like the lowing of cattle.

The men continue to feast on the cattle for six more days, and on the seventh, when the winds abate, they set sail. Once out at sea, the island no longer visible, the sky darkens; the wind splits the mast pole, killing the steersman; and a thunderbolt shatters the ship, drowning all the men.

III. Arrival at Ogygia, 420–453

Odysseus, the sole survivor, holds on to a broken mast and is transported through the night back to Charybdis. His mast swallowed, he uses his own initiative in a situation from which even Poseidon could not rescue him (12.107) by grabbing onto a fig tree branch growing from the cliff above. When the whirlpool regurgitates the mast, Odysseus releases his hold, lands on it, and paddles with his hands away from Charybdis and Scylla. A simile (12.438–441) compares both Odysseus and Charybdis to a judge who, after a long day at court judging disputes, returns home for dinner exhausted. Like the judge, Charybdis is working on a final judgment on Odysseus' case, which arrives after a long delay—a verdict of life or death. Like the judge, Odysseus, exhausted, holds on to the fig tree awaiting the trial's end so he can go home. Once Charybdis disgorges the mast and Odysseus mounts it, the verdict is set and his trying experience over. He drifts for nine days toward Calypso's island, where the gods decreed his homecoming (*Od.* 5), reaching Ogygia on the night of the tenth. Here Odysseus concludes his *Alkinou apologoi*.[51]

Selected Bibliography: *Od.* 12

Aasved, "Sirens."
Ahl and Roisman, *"Odyssey,"* 137–151.
Beck, Deborah, "Odysseus."
Blanchot, "Song."
Buchan, *Limits*, 133–180.
Buchan, "Looking."
Clarke, *Art*, 45–66.
Cook, *"Odyssey,"* 111–127.
Davies, "Sirens."
Friedrich, "Thrinakia."
Garrison, "Great."
Germain, "Sirens."
Gresseth, "Homeric."
Hopman, "Narrative."
Kafka, "Silence."
Louden, *The "Odyssey,"* 31–49.
Louden, *Homer's*, 222–243.
MacDonald, "Luke's."
Most, "Structure."
Neils, "Les Femmes Fatales."
Nugent, "Sounds."

Page, *Folktales*, 71–91.

Parry, Hugh, "*Apologos*."

Pucci, "Song."

Reece, *Stranger's*, 101–122.

Reinhardt, "Adventures."

Roessel, "Stag."

Said, *Homer*, 150–188.

Schmoll, "Odysseus."

Schur, "Silence."

Scully, "Doubling."

Segal, *Singers*, 195–228.

Stephens, "Thoughts."

Further commentary on *Od.* 12 in General Bibliography I.

PART II

FROM WONDERLAND TO ITHACA

CHAPTER 4

ODYSSEUS AND TELEMACHUS AT EUMAEUS' HUT (*OD.* 13–16)

Book 13

The final twelve books of the *Odyssey* relocate the reader from the mythic to the real world of Ithaca. In *Od.* 13 Odysseus both departs for and arrives in Ithaca:

I. Departure for Ithaca (20%)
II. Arrival in Ithaca (80%)

Upon his arrival at *Od.* 13.93, Odysseus completes his outer journey (striving for home) and begins his inner journey (regaining his kingdom).

1. Except for *Od.* 1–4 (*Telemachia*), the first twelve books occur in a mythic world; the second twelve (the Ithacan books), in the factual world.
2. The first twelve books occupy Odysseus' (and Telemachus') wanderings away from Ithaca; the second twelve books consist of their return to Ithaca, as well as the lies Odysseus employs to test the allegiance of those around him.[1]

3. In the first twelve books, Odysseus appears as himself; in the second twelve, he appears in disguise until he reveals himself to the suitors at 22.1–2.
4. In the first twelve books Odysseus' *mētis* helps him return to Ithaca; in the second, his *mētis* helps him to remain in Ithaca.

I. Departure for Ithaca, 1–92

It is evening of the thirty-third day of Homer's narrative, a day that began in *Od.* 8 and ends when Alcinous' court retires (13.17). Odysseus' narration now ends, and Homer's narration begins again. Alcinous confirms Odysseus' homecoming and entreats his dignitaries to offer him more gifts, promising to recompense their worth by taxing his people. The following morning, the thirty-fourth day, Odysseus leaves for Ithaca with his gifts stowed. A simile compares Odysseus' state of mind to that of a laborer, who, plowing his fields all day, exhausted by his labor so that his knees fail him, is anxious to return home and have dinner. Like the laborer, Odysseus, weary, his wanderings brought to completion, is ready to return home. The entire passage of the hero's farewells is filled with prayers and libations to the gods (twice by Alcinous and once at Odysseus' request). Odysseus also offers separate toasts to the king and queen, wishing the king comfort and cheer for his wives and children (the plural "wives" sets the Phaeacians apart from the monogamous Greeks). Odysseus, released from further roaming, has come to understand life's significance—happiness and contentment among one's family and household and the ability to bring peace and prosperity to one's people. The Phaeacian enchanted ship flies to Ithaca through the night like a hawk. Odysseus' former self has metaphorically died (13.79–92) and wakes as the avenging king who brings peace and justice.

II. Arrival in Ithaca, 93–440

Early on day thirty-five, the ship makes shore in the harbor of Phorkys,[2] which is closed in by two high promontories that protect unsecured vessels from strong winds. At the head of the harbor, there is an olive tree (13.102–103), and nearby there is a cave sacred to the nymphs (13.104; the Naiads),[3] the three sites (harbor, olive tree, and nymphs' cave) that allow Odysseus to recognize his homeland. The harbor of Phorkys is a transitional point from Odysseus' mythic world to the real world of Ithaca, a place where the primitive and the human meet. The cave, emblem of the Cyclops' home, now houses nymphs, minor female deities friendly to humans. The two cave entrances also suggest their intermediate status between the human and divine, as do the cave's contents: bowls and jars where bees deposit their honey. The nymphs (*numphe*, a word that also means "bride"), who also weave, symbolize a return to Ithaca and Penelope. The enclosed harbor further reminds one of the Laestrygonians, whose harbor traps Odysseus' eleven ships. Here, however, the harbor offers a safe haven from Odysseus' adventures. Odysseus, still asleep, is laid on the sand, and his possessions, protected from wayfarers, are placed at the trunk of Athena's sacred olive tree. The olive tree, symbol of the goddess herself, now guards Odysseus' wealth just as the olive wood saved Odysseus from the Cyclops' cave, the two olive trees protected him from the elements in Scheria, and the olive trunk on which his bed was built saved his marriage.

On Olympus, Poseidon vents his anger at Zeus, taking offense at those who conveyed Odysseus to Ithaca with gifts and without further suffering. Aware that he cannot prevent Odysseus' homecoming, Poseidon wants the hero to undergo more adversity, which the Phaeacians impeded. Zeus assures him he is free to punish anyone who slights him. Encouraged, Poseidon promises to stun the Phaeacian vessel as it nears Scheria, preventing it from ever conveying other strangers in the future. Furthermore, he will hide their entire city under a mountain. Zeus agrees but suggests a less extreme ploy: petrify the ship as it sails into port and fling a mountain around their city (158; "*mega de sphin oros polei amphikalupsai*," a controversial phrase).[4]

Gratified, Poseidon strides off to Scheria and petrifies the ship as soon as it arrives. Witnessing this act in amazement, Alcinous reminds the

Phaeacians of his father's prophecy and declares an end to conveying strangers. He pledges a sacrifice (to which no response is given) in the hope that Poseidon will take pity and prevent the second part of the prophecy. However, since Zeus gives Poseidon a carte blanche, there is little reason to doubt that this prophecy will come true. Homer leaves the Phaeacians sacrificing to Poseidon that he might take pity on them and returns to Odysseus, who is not aware he awakes in his own homeland.

As Poseidon's involvement in the *Odyssey* recedes into the background, Athena, disguised as a young shepherd, takes central stage. But before her appearance, she pours a mist over the landscape, rendering it unrecognizable. Odysseus, fearing another harrowing adventure, utters the same three lines used previously when encountering a new adventure (13.200–202). His first concern, even before his own safety, is his gifts, which translate into his *kleos* (honor)—thus his anxiety in leaving the treasure exposed and unprotected. Convinced the Phaeacians did not deliver him in Ithaca, Odysseus prays to Zeus to punish them and turns for a third time to the gifts to confirm that the Phaeacians did not carry some off. Here Odysseus' suspicious mind is again apparent, as he greets positive events with skepticism or disbelief. One recalls Calypso's words, "Now I will send you on, with a good will" (5.161), which Odysseus suspects as inauthentic and demands the goddess authenticate (5.173–179). It is this mentality that has been a key to his survival.

Odysseus' first words to the shepherd disclose his distress. He fears the shepherd might steal his booty and entreats his help in rescuing both him and his spoils. Approaching the shepherd as he would a god, he asks three questions: (1) What land is this? (2) What neighborhood (*demos*)[5] is it? and (3) What people live here? At the shepherd's mention of Ithaca, Odysseus, overjoyed, begins his first lie to discourage the shepherd from stealing his gifts. He identifies himself as an unnamed exile from Crete who, unwilling to serve as Idomeneus'[6] henchman, fled after killing Idomeneus' son Orsilochus.[7] A rich man, he alleges he left behind for his sons as much wealth as he is carrying. He killed Orsilochus for trying to deprive him of his plunder from Troy and slipped out in the dark of night unnoticed. He paid Phoenician sailors to take him to Pylos or Elis, but they were forced toward Ithaca by bad weather, not because the sailors intended to deceive him. While he slept, the Phoenicians unloaded his possessions, set them close to where he lay, and sailed on to Sidon. His tale offers a number of points that he believes will clarify his position and help protect his wealth:

1. He is an exile from Crete, a land so distant from Ithaca that his anonymity can be kept safe.
2. He is a rich and important man who fought in Troy and commanded others.
3. He has sons to avenge him should something happen to him.
4. He killed Orsilochus for trying to steal his wealth, even though the latter was swift footed (13.260). In other words, not even the fastest of mortals could escape the Cretan's wrath.
5. He is affiliated with a royal family, since Idomeneus wanted him to serve as his loyal subordinate.
6. The Phoenicians, who elsewhere in the *Odyssey* are portrayed as thieves and pirates, are here honorable men who were ready to deliver the exile to Pylos or Elis had the storm allowed; when they disembark in Ithaca, they do not defraud him.

Odysseus' lie is a warning against stealing his gifts; he is capable of killing, even guilefully, anyone who tries. Moreover, he has sons to avenge him if necessary, a fact meant to discourage the shepherd from foul play, since even those known for piracy, the Phoenicians, thought better than to treat him dishonorably. Taking a woman's shape, Athena smiles, strokes him, and compliments him on his cleverness. She is surprised he does not recognize her, since both are known for wit and sharpness, he among mortals, she among immortals. Now she will help hide his possessions and advise him of the future, just as she previously caused the Phaeacians to love him. However, he must endure more grief in silence, for no one must know of his return if he is to face the suitors.

Odysseus complains of the difficulty in recognizing a goddess who continually conceals herself. Disappointed that Athena abandoned him during the years of his wanderings, he reminds her how she stood by him in Troy but, once the Achaeans sacked the city, she vanished until Scheria. Always cautious, he still doubts he is in Ithaca and asks for reassurance. Athena again compliments him on his mind, his fluency, and his reasoning, qualities that kept her by his side. Anyone else would have rushed to his family, but it is his nature to first test those he meets and ask questions. Her absence until he reached Scheria was due to her unwillingness to disavow Poseidon's hatred. Once Odysseus is in Ithaca, Poseidon is no longer a threat; now Odysseus needs a cunning and agile mind (Athena's assistance as the goddess of wisdom) to defeat the suitors.

Athena dissipates the mist hiding Ithaca, and Odysseus rejoices at the sight of his country. Kissing the ground, he lifts his hands to the nymphs in prayer (the Naiads who occupy the cave), promising them gifts, if only Athena grants life to both him and his son. Accepting his dependence on the gods since his near-death experience in the river (*Od.* 5), he freely admits his reliance on her not only for himself but also for the survival of his son, whose well-being is required for his honor (as Orestes' was for Agamemnon's) and for the perpetuity of the family name. The goddess vows her support, and the two plot the suitors' deaths under the trunk of the olive tree, Athena's guarantee that he will not perish like Agamemnon.

Tapping the hero with her wand, she transforms him into an old beggar so that neither the suitors nor his wife and child will recognize him. Disguised as a beggar, he will go to the swineherd Eumaeus, who remained faithful throughout his master's absence, to question him about the suitors; Athena will go to Sparta to arrange for Telemachus' return. Hearing of Telemachus' journey for the first time, Odysseus, somewhat irritated, questions the goddess. Why did she not tell Telemachus herself about his father, since she knew where he was? Did she want him to suffer hardships like his father while his inheritance was being depleted at home? Athena's response presents her in complete control of the situation:

1. She sent Telemachus to Menelaus to gain maturity, education, a reputation, and a sense of identity.
2. Telemachus did not experience hardships, for she was constantly at his side. He is presently enjoying Menelaus' hospitality.
3. Although the suitors are waiting to kill him on his return, they will not succeed.

The beggar/Odysseus leaves for Eumaeus' hut and the goddess for Lacedaemon to fetch the prince. Telemachus' journey, which early in the epic seemed unrelated to the larger narrative of Odysseus' *nostos*, now becomes part of Athena's grand design to reclaim Odysseus' throne.

Selected Bibliography: *Od.* 13

Ahl and Roisman, *"Odyssey,"* 152–166.
Byre, "On the Description."
Clarke, *Art*, 67–85.
Clayton, *Penelopean*, 53–82.
Emlyn-Jones, "True."
Finley, John H., Jr., *Homer's*, 159–184.
Friedrich, "Zeus."
Haft, "Odysseus."
Katz, *Penelope's*, 55–63.
Louden, *Homer's*, 135–163.
Marks, *Zeus*, 36–61.
Maronites, *Homeric*, 147–163.
Reece, "Cretan."
Reece, *Stranger's*, 101–122, 145–164.
Roth, *Speech*.

Said, *Homer*, 189–222.
Schmoll, “First.”
Scott, John A., “Odysseus.”
Segal, “Phaeacians.”
Stanford, “Lies.”
Thalmann, *“Odyssey,”* 95–132.
Trahman, “Odysseus’.”
Walcot, “Odysseus.”
Walcot, “Odysseus’ Lies.”
Further commentary on *Od.* 13 in General Bibliography I.

Book 14

Odysseus’ lies to Eumaeus and their aftermath occupy over half of *Od.* 14; it is still the thirty-fifth day of the narrative.

I. At Eumaeus’ hut (35%)
II. First lie (50%)
  A. Crete
  B. Troy
  C. Egypt
  D. Phoenicia
  E. Thesprotia
  F. Doulichion
  G. Ithaca
III. Second lie (15%)

I. At Eumaeus’ Hut, 1–190

Odysseus finds Eumaeus admiring the enclosure he constructed to house his master’s pigs, whose numbers the suitors’ gluttony has diminished. Throughout this book, the swineherd’s diligence, honesty, and care in managing his master’s pig farm are contrasted with the suitors’ gluttony, which forces him to supply them with pork daily. The fact that he diligently cares for the pigs at such a distance from Penelope and Laertes proves his good intentions, and he is not to be blamed for the waste. His frugality in manufacturing his own shoes from a piece of ox hide to cut costs is testament to his honesty. Later in the book he even tells the beggar/Odysseus that he and the other four swineherds under his control are forced to eat only young pigs, since the fat ones are devoured by the suitors. Eumaeus' care in managing Odysseus' farm not only is a credit to his good stewardship but also serves also to highlight his master's great wealth, since not even twenty men combined could claim as much. Catching sight of the stranger, the four dogs Eumaeus raised charge Odysseus. Eumaeus drops his work to chase the dogs away, apologizing, for any harm to the stranger would cause him shame, revealing his good manners as well as the importance he places on being perceived as an ethical and virtuous man. He expresses his grief and pain at the absence of his master and resents caring for Odysseus' pigs for the suitors' consumption while Odysseus, among alien people, might be in need of sustenance.

Eumaeus' hospitality is as generous as Alcinous', each man offering what his station allows. Odysseus thanks the swineherd for his generosity, and Eumaeus claims he would do the same for anyone in dire straits, for under Zeus Xenios all strangers deserve hospitality, even from servants like himself, implying that it is more difficult for a servant to be hospitable than it is for a master. Eumaeus hints at a slave's lot under the control of those more fortunate than he and the humiliation a slave must bear to kowtow to younger masters who lord it over him. The loss of a kind master like Odysseus makes Eumaeus' situation more intolerable. The swineherd feels short-changed, for a faithful slave like himself expects to receive a home, a plot of land, and a wife, stressing the degree to which a slave owes every aspect of his life to his owner. But why does Eumaeus air such personal concerns with a total stranger? Is it because Eumaeus harbors disappointment at being deprived of such possessions? Would he confess his regrets to anyone? Does he find the beggar approachable, one easy to confide in? Or can it be that he intuits something? Perhaps he senses Odysseus' presence and hopes to learn more about the stranger's identity by continuing to voice the belief that his master is dead. If Eumaeus indeed harbors suspicions, he could be voicing what he hopes to gain from his many years of honest service. He is among those most likely to recognize Odysseus, along with Laertes, Penelope, and Eurycleia. Both he and Eurycleia have known Odysseus from an early age, as indicated later. Eurycleia nursed Odysseus from infancy, and Eumaeus was raised almost as his brother. However, no concrete evidence of recognition is given other than the swineherd's treatment of the stranger. It is possible that Eumaeus, Eurycleia, and Penelope at some point recognize Odysseus and, to safeguard his identity from the suitors, resort to a disguise of their own, "the only disguise they have available: disguise of their recognition of him" (Ahl and Roisman, "*Odyssey*," 173).

Eumaeus, in strong language, blames his master's loss and the loss of all those who perished in Troy on Helen and her family. Registering such sentiments through an ethical and virtuous slave heightens the sense of distance between the Trojan War and the postwar resentment of the common man. He disdains the suitors, who lack pity for everyone but themselves. His affirmation that the gods detest pitiless action and reward only justice and what humans do that is lawful amplifies his deep-seated philosophy of what constitutes right and wrong (*themis*; see chapter 1, note 14). Even pirates who loot and rob are aware of the unlawfulness of their actions and fear retribution. Listening, the beggar/Odysseus takes note of the swineherd's strong belief in a universal order in which good is rewarded and bad punished. His own lie to Eumaeus will be based largely on what he already knows about this servant's past, and what he understands his beliefs to be at the present.

Tightening his belt (indicating a loss of weight due to the suitors' gluttony, perhaps?), Eumaeus selects two pigs, prepares Odysseus' dinner, and urges the stranger to eat what is left for servants after the suitors have had their fill. As the swineherd continues to set forth his views, the beggar eats quietly without speaking, devising evils for the suitors. He asks to learn more about the man who bought Eumaeus, hoping to gain the swineherd's confidence without being recognized and to persuade him that he has information concerning his master's return. To gain his confidence, the beggar/Odysseus begins to address Eumaeus as *phile* (14.115; friend), whereas previously he addressed him as *xeine* (14.53; stranger). Emboldened by his servant's forthrightness and honesty, he continues prodding, claiming he might know his master, might have seen him, and might have news of him, since he traveled to many places (14.118–120).

Eumaeus, however, remains suspicious, since other vagabonds in need of sustenance have lied about Odysseus' homecoming. He is not willing to listen to any more lies. Such fabrications, offered for personal gain, bring false hope to his mistress and increase her suffering. Perhaps the beggar wishes to spin a well-made story for a cloak or a tunic. Reluctant to mention his master's name until now (a frequent pattern in the *Odyssey*—e.g., the narrator's postponing naming Odysseus in the proem; Odysseus' refusal to identify himself to the Phaeacians until long after his arrival in Scheria; Odysseus' withholding his name from the Cyclops), he expresses his longing for Odysseus, a yearning stronger than for his own mother and father, and states that he is grief-stricken that he will never again have a lord as kind as Odysseus. Again addressing the swineherd as *phile* (14.149), the beggar/Odysseus asserts that he is not among those who lie for gain. He vows Odysseus is on his way home. Although he is in need of a tunic or a cloak against the cold, he will not accept one until Odysseus returns, for he knows he is on his way. Thus, the beggar tries to convince the swineherd of his master's imminent return without revealing himself and at the same time takes the opportunity to repeat an earlier request for a cloak. He again affirms his honesty by declaring his loathing for those who, under the constraint of poverty, engage in falsehoods (14.156–157), a comment that parallels Achilles' in *Il.* 9.312–313:

> For as I detest the doorways of Death, I detest that man, who
> hides one thing in the depth of his heart and speaks forth another.

In that context, Achilles, aware that Odysseus was sent to persuade him to return to battle, realizes he is not accurately conveying Agamemnon's message. In fact, Odysseus edits Agamemnon's words, hoping for a positive response. Is Odysseus promising Eumaeus his master's return within the year in order to win his confidence or to have him suspect the beggar's identity? How can the beggar be so adamant about Odysseus' return that he is willing to wait for him before accepting clothing against the cold? Odysseus is manipulative here in the same way he is in the *Iliad*. However, in both instances, he lies for a purpose, and in the present instance, as he is Odysseus in disguise, he is in fact telling the truth. Appearance versus reality is another *Odyssey* theme that permeates the epic. The beggar is not who he pretends to be, nor are the characters Odysseus impersonates in his adventures and in his lying tales.

If the beggar/Odysseus' insistence that Odysseus will presently return is a signal, Eumaeus does not recognize it, but he does begin to confide in the beggar. The swineherd rejects the stranger's oath not to accept clothing until Odysseus returns, for hospitality does not allow mistreatment even at a cost, but he requests not to be reminded of his master's return, since it distresses him, even though he hopes for it. Eumaeus' attitude toward the beggar grows more accepting throughout *Od.* 14, as the vocatives used to address him illustrate. Early in the book, the swineherd refers to him as "old man" (*geron* [14.37]), then as "stranger" (*xeine* [14.56, 80]), before returning to "old man" (*geron* [14.122, 166]; *geraie* [14.131, 185]). After Odysseus tells his lying tale, however, the vocatives become more intimate: "poor stranger" (*deile xeinōn* [14.361]); "old man of many sorrows" (*geron polupenthes* [14.386]); and, finally, "divine stranger" (*daimonie xeinōn* [14.443]). Thus, the beggar slowly persuades Eumaeus of the possibility of his master's return, but in spite of this growing intimacy, the beggar is still unsuccessful in procuring a cloak.

Eumaeus, still skeptical, also grieves for Telemachus, who went seeking news of his father and whom the suitors are plotting to kill upon his return. Both of these details were known only to Eurycleia, Telemachus' nursemaid, and the suitors. It is difficult to conceive how Eumaeus obtained this news, being far removed from Ithaca and one who, by his own admission, stays away from the city. It is either one of the epic's inconsistencies or a detail Homer considers irrelevant. Nevertheless, his concern regarding whoever, man or god, convinced the prince to make such a trip and his anguish for the prince's welfare underscore the important position Eumaeus holds in Odysseus' household. Telemachus is a surrogate son for Eumaeus, as the simile in *Od.* 16.17–21 demonstrates. Leaving Telemachus' fate in Zeus's hands, Eumaeus returns to the beggar to ask how he came to Ithaca and to reveal his identity.

II. First Lie, 191–456

Odysseus presents his first lie to Eumaeus in seven parts, each describing a single aspect of his invented journey. He begins by promising to respond accurately to all that he is asked (14.192), another clue to his true identity if Eumaeus only listens closely to each of the tale's details, which correspond to his own life, but at the same time, the beggar/Odysseus' use of "accurately" is a clue to the audience that he is about to lie.

II.A. Crete, 199–239. His origin again is Crete, and he is one of a rich man's many sons. Nameless, as in his lie to Athena, he is illegitimate, but his father, Castor, treated him as he did his other sons. Once Castor dies, his legitimate sons divide the inheritance among themselves and grant him little. The beggar, self-reliant and courageous, acquires a wife, becomes a great soldier who prefers ships and wars, and becomes so wealthy that among the Cretans he is feared and respected. When the Achaeans sail for Troy, he leads the Cretans, along with Idomeneus.

II.B. Troy, 240–246. After nine years, Troy is sacked on the tenth. He suffers many ordeals but arrives home safely. After a month at home enjoying his wife and children, he is again anxious to go to sea and sails for Egypt.

II.C. Egypt, 246–286. With few variations, the beggar/Odysseus recites his own experiences since Troy. As Tiresias prophesies in *Od.* 11, once Odysseus reaches Ithaca, he leaves again to travel inland. In his false tale, he sets out for Egypt and reaches the Nile with nine ships. Once there, he urges his companions to remain close to the ships, but they plunder the Egyptians, carrying off women and children and killing the men (as in the Cicones episode). Fellow Egyptians, hearing the outcry, come to the rescue, but instead of losing seventy-two men (as in the Cicones episode), the entire crew is either killed or taken into forced labor. The beggar grovels before the Egyptian king and asks forgiveness, cowardly behavior for a Homeric warrior whose honor comes from prowess in battle (see *Il.* 12.328). Why then such an about-face by the beggar, who earlier boasts of being endowed with courage by Ares and Athena (*Od.* 14.216)? It seems he is reacting to Eumaeus' earlier comments about the gods' hatred for crime and their love for justice—even those to whom Zeus grants spoils and plunder deserve punishment. The same holds true for the Achaeans who plunder Troy at war's end. They are punished for their lawlessness like the beggar, who, realizing his heinous acts, throws down his weapons and asks forgiveness.

The Egyptian king saves the Cretan, honoring Zeus Xenios, who is outraged at evil dealings. The beggar/Odysseus is careful in his lie to follow not only the theodicy Eumaeus expressed earlier but also Eumaeus' own life story, with which he is familiar (*Od.* 15). In his false tale, he incorporates Eumaeus' beliefs and expresses an attitude antithetical to the warrior code of the *Iliad*, preferring a slave's life to a hero's, the sentiment voiced by Achilles in Hades (11.489–491). Set free by the Egyptian king, the Cretan remains in Egypt seven years, accruing great wealth (comparable to Odysseus' seven years in Ogygia).

II.D. Phoenicia, 287–313. In the eighth year of his Egyptian exile, a Phoenician persuades the Cretan to accompany him to Phoenicia and then to Libya, promising him a lucrative deal but instead intending to sell him for a profit. Although suspicious, the Cretan is forced to accompany the Phoenician to Libya. A storm develops once land is out of sight, and everyone drowns except the Cretan, who clings to the ship's mast and escapes (reminiscent of the Helius episode [*Od.* 12]). The Phoenicians here are evil like those responsible for Eumaeus' own slavery in *Od.* 15. In Odysseus' previous lie to Athena, the Phoenicians were honorable men who set him ashore with all his gifts intact. In that lie, worried about the fate of his wealth and whether the young shepherd had designs on it, Odysseus used the Phoenician sailors' treatment as an example of how he wanted to be treated by the shepherd/Athena. In the present lie, familiar with Eumaeus' past, he paints them in a negative light, hoping to win Eumaeus' approval.

II.E. Thesprotia, 314–333. As the sole survivor from the Phoenician ship, the Cretan is swept along for nine days until he is washed ashore in Thesprotia on the tenth. There he is rescued by King Pheidon's son, who carries him to his father (reminiscent of the Nausicaa-Alcinous episode [*Od.* 6]). Cold and exhausted, the Cretan is given a mantle and tunic by Pheidon, another subtle reminder to Eumaeus that he is still in need of a cloak.

The beggar tells Eumaeus that it was in the court of Pheidon that he first heard of Odysseus, whom the king had entertained. Pheidon kept Odysseus' possessions while the hero was at Dodona to consult Zeus's oracle on his voyage home. While at Pheidon's court, Odysseus showcased for the king his many possessions. The Cretan seems compelled to mention Odysseus' enormous wealth, a compliment he is paying himself—his *timē* and *kleos* remain intact. His twenty-year absence was not in vain, since he accumulated wealth to feed ten generations. When he returned from the oracle, a ship and crew stood ready to carry him to his own country.

The Thesprotian episode holds a number of clues for Eumaeus to consider. Why does King Pheidon take the Cretan into his confidence to tell him (a stranger) of his friendship to Odysseus? All Pheidon knows of the Cretan's former self is that he was a rich man's illegitimate son, he was a great soldier who fought in Troy, and he was once wealthy. More to the point, why should Pheidon want to disclose the fact of the absent hero's stored treasure to him? Why inform the Cretan not only of Odysseus' trip to Zeus's shrine at Dodona but also its purpose (how to return to Ithaca—secretly or openly)? Why need Pheidon "swear" to the Cretan that the ship and crew were ready to transport Odysseus to Ithaca? King Pheidon clearly welcomed the Cretan into his complete confidence as King Alcinous welcomed Odysseus by the end of his stay in Scheria, once the hero divulged his identity. If the Cretan is not Odysseus himself, he must be of equal stature to have a king confide such intimate details to him. As a stranger at Pheidon's court, there is no need for him to know Odysseus' personal affairs.

II.F. Doulichion, 334–347. Pheidon sends the Cretan to King Akastos on a Thesprotian ship bound for Doulichion, but the sailors decide to enslave him. They remove his clothing and give him the vile rag and tattered tunic he is now wearing, yet another subtle prodding for Eumaeus to provide a cloak.

II.G. Ithaca, 348–359. That same evening, the Thesprotian ship docks in Ithaca, but the sailors leave the Cretan bound on the ship. The gods themselves untie the Cretan's knots (their help is proof of his goodness), allowing him to swim ashore. When the sailors discover his absence, they search the shore unsuccessfully and resume their journey. The Cretan hides in a thicket before starting out for Eumaeus' hut. By acknowledging his transgressions, the gods not only forgive the Cretan for his unlawful ways but in fact reward him by loosening his bonds and hiding him from his captives. However, if such outlandish events (the Cretan's sojourn in Troy, the Thesprotian king's loyal reception, the Cretan's sufferings on the way home, and his miraculous escape) affect Eumaeus, he does not make it known. He is, however, moved by the beggar's tale, but, like Telemachus in reaction to Athena's tales (*Od.* 1), he still believes (or pretends) the stranger is lying about his master, whom the gods did not allow to die in Troy and win honor for himself and his family.

Since an Aetolian arrived at Eumaeus' hut claiming he saw Odysseus with Idomeneus among the Cretans, the swineherd no longer trusts anyone alleging to know his master's whereabouts, and Eumaeus shuns the palace lest Penelope question him. The Aetolian had disclosed that Odysseus was repairing his ships and would arrive in Ithaca with his companions by summer or autumn, bringing many gifts. Given that the beggar/Odysseus' Cretan story is a lie for the purpose of gaining Eumaeus' trust, is it possible that the swineherd's Aetolian tale is a lie to obtain more information from Odysseus? Was there in fact an Aetolian whose story so closely resembled the beggar/Odysseus' lie? Whatever the truth, it remains unresolved. Eumaeus tells his tale to show he has no need for lies in order to offer hospitality; he does so out of fear of Zeus and out of his own pity toward the beggar. The beggar/Odysseus now suggests taking a stronger oath with the gods bearing witness: Eumaeus can offer clothing and send him to Doulichion only *after* his master arrives. If his master does not arrive, the beggar will not accept clothing and, more importantly, Eumaeus' men can throw him to his death over a cliff. The beggar's willingness to suggest such an oath, together with his insistence that he has knowledge of Odysseus, perhaps alerts the swineherd that the stranger might be someone other than a mere vagabond. The beggar/Odysseus, on the other hand, cannot say more without risk of exposure. Perhaps he is signaling who he is, as one might assume he does to Penelope in *Od.* 19, but the swineherd does not give any indication he understands. The beggar's offer to be murdered is against the laws of hospitality. Eumaeus cannot invite a stranger into his home, entertain him, murder him, and then pray to Zeus.

When Eumaeus' fellow swineherds return from the fields, he asks them to butcher the best pig for their guest. Earlier, only the suitors received the best. On first meeting the beggar, Eumaeus offered him pork of the quality he himself eats, but now, after his guest ends his false tale, Eumaeus offers him the best pig. Is this a sign that Eumaeus suspects the beggar to be someone other than he lets on? Has the beggar calmed Eumaeus' fears about Odysseus' homecoming? After killing the fat five-year-old pig and sacrificing to the gods, the swineherd prays that Odysseus should have his homecoming. Eumaeus no longer insists that his master will not return but hopes he will and treats the stranger as one deserving pork reserved for the suitors. Laying a portion of the slaughtered pig aside for the nymphs and Hermes, Eumaeus distributes equal shares to his men, but the best cut is placed before the beggar. The swineherd's constant praying and pouring of libations to the gods while performing his chores throughout this episode reminds the reader of Nestor's piety in *Od.* 3. Both king and slave are rewarded by the gods for their devotion. Nestor receives a painless return from Troy, many sons, and health for all his family. Eumaeus will receive a wife, a house, and property (*Od.* 21.214–215). The beggar/Odysseus, delighted by Eumaeus' treatment, calls him for the first time by name and hopes that Zeus's love for him is as great as his own—excessive praise for a stranger to bestow on someone he just met. At this point, the swineherd speculates that the stranger is at least someone who might know the whereabouts of his master. After more offerings to the gods, Mesaulius, Eumaeus' personal slave,[8] clears the table and they all retire.

III. Second Lie, 457–533

The night is cold and windy, and the beggar/Odysseus takes the opportunity to ask Eumaeus again for a cloak. Using the pretext that the wine made him tipsy, he feels a need to boast and begins a second false tale, in which he pretends to be one of three Achaean leaders who led an ambush detail in Troy. These three leaders (Odysseus, Menelaus, and the beggar) find themselves huddling under Trojan walls on a freezing night. All but the third leader (the beggar), who forgot his cloak, sleep with their mantles and tunics wrapped about them. By early morning, the third leader, freezing, nudges Odysseus, who comes to his rescue. He asks for a volunteer to return to Agamemnon for more troops, saying he saw this need in a dream. Thoas volunteers and removes his mantle to run back to camp. The third leader picks up Thoas' mantle and rests comfortably the remainder of the night. Having finished his tale, the beggar/Odysseus reminds the swineherds of his advanced age; he would welcome a mantle given out of respect for a warrior.

While stressing his need for a mantle, the beggar emphasizes his intimacy with Odysseus, making the prospect of his return more plausible for the swineherd. Eumaeus, no longer able to ignore the beggar's request, temporarily loans him a mantle, for each man possesses only one. Although Eumaeus believes he sees through the beggar's tale, he is at the same time duped to do his will. In any event, the beggar now has a mantle, and he is promised a permanent one once Telemachus returns, along with the freedom to go wherever he wants. Eumaeus then prepares him a bed, covering him with his own extra mantle kept for extreme weather, and retires outside to guard his pigs. Noting the herdsman's devotion to his duties, Odysseus is happy to see his property so well cared for in his absence.

Eumaeus is conscious that the beggar's tale was made up for personal gain, for earlier he explained that many vagabonds lie about Odysseus' homecoming for food. Why then does Eumaeus accept the false tale? It seems the beggar is being rewarded for his storytelling ability as much as for convincing the swineherd. The beggar makes it clear that the wine gave him the desire to sing like a bard, one who captivates his audience with the beauty of his words (*epos*; 14.463, 466), rather than with the story's contents. As one scholar remarks, "The story is told in a persuasive manner as poetry" (Brennan, "Ethnic," 3).

Od. 14 ends with renewed hope for Odysseus' return and the possibility that the beggar not only knows Odysseus is alive but even has knowledge of his whereabouts. In the beginning, the swineherd's doubts are mingled with pity, but after the first false tale, his pity is tinged with admiration. By the end of the second false tale, a closeness develops between the two characters and Eumaeus' trust in the beggar's predictions grows.

Selected Bibliography: *Od.* 14

Ahl and Roisman, *"Odyssey,"* 137–151, 167–181.
Brennan, "Ethnic."
Clarke, *Art*, 67–85.
Kadletz, "Sacrifice."
King, "Rhetoric."
Louden, "Eumaios."
Marks, "Alternative."
Newton, "Cloak."
Olson, *Blood and Iron*, 120–139.
Petropoulos, A., "Sacrifice."
Reece, *Stranger's*, 145–164.
Roisman, "Eumaeus."
Rose, Gilbert P., "Swineherd."
Said, *Homer*, 189–222.
Segal, "Phaeacians."
Segal, *Singers*, 164–183.
Segal, "Wanderer's."
Further commentary on *Od.* 14 in General Bibliography I.

Book 15

Telemachus is sleeping uneasily in Sparta on day thirty-five, soon to dawn as day thirty-six. *Od.* 15 ends at dawn on day thirty-eight as Telemachus arrives at the swineherd's hut. Two-thirds of the book deals with Telemachus' journey home and one-third with the prince's visit at Eumaeus' hut.

I. Telemachus' return, part I (54%)
II. At Eumaeus' hut (35%)
III. Telemachus' return, part II (11%)

I. Telemachus' Return, Part I, 1–300

Athena comes in a dream to Telemachus in Lacedaemon[9] and advises him to return home, for his mother's father and her brothers[10] are pressing her to marry Eurymachus, who is showering her with gifts. Athena warns that if he lingers in Sparta, he will lose his property, for once married, women, even Penelope, are not to be trusted. Their main concern is to augment their husbands' household, forsaking children and former husbands.[11] He must stop pursuing news of his father and turn to the more pressing affairs in Ithaca. Not completely awake and aware of the pressures compelling his mother to marry, Telemachus worries about her allegiance in a new relationship. If she weds, will she want his inheritance for her new husband? In his dreamlike state, he contemplates how to preserve his inheritance.

1. He must delegate it to a trustworthy servingwoman until he marries.
2. He must be watchful of the suitors waiting to kill him, although Athena alleges they will not fulfill their goal.
3. He must send his ship to the city, make his way to Eumaeus' hut to spend the night, and send a messenger to inform his mother of his safe arrival.

If Athena's presence represents the prince's racing thoughts, his maturity since he was last seen in 4.624 is remarkable. He is now a young version of his father, cautious and mistrustful even of his mother until he settles on a scheme. Of the two leading suitors, Eurymachus, who is more restrained in dealing with the prince, engages his mind. The reader is already privy to Eurymachus' true feelings, no less lethal than those Antinous harbors. As the prince plans his homecoming, he becomes aware of the danger Eurymachus poses; he is the one most likely to marry Penelope and rule Ithaca. Telemachus' instincts will prove true (16.435–449); even though Eurymachus promises to defend Telemachus, he is planning his murder.

Once Athena leaves, Telemachus alerts Pisistratus that he must return to Ithaca. Pisistratus reminds the prince that driving at night is difficult, and that it is rude to leave before thanking Menelaus and Helen for their hospitality. Mindful of his manners, Telemachus agrees, and as soon as Menelaus and Helen wake, he asks approval to be on his way. In a scene full of irony and comic relief, Menelaus promises not to detain him, saying he disapproves of excessiveness in friendship and prefers balance in all things. However, no sooner does he ask for balance in all things than he detains Telemachus not only to load the promised gifts in the chariot but to further honor him at a banquet. He then suggests detaining him even longer to escort him on a tour throughout the country to collect more gifts. Telemachus, whose thoughts are now focused on his personal affairs, begs Menelaus to speed him on his way. He can no longer continue to search for a father who might be dead; he must look after his own affairs rather than ruin himself chasing a ghost. Telemachus' decision to terminate his search for his father and his refusal of Menelaus' invitation to acquire more gifts, an opportunity few heroes would resist, give further weight to the prince's growing maturity. He heeds Nestor's warning not to wander far or stay away long from home (3.313–314) lest the suitors take possession. Menelaus had earlier expressed the same sentiment, reminding him that while Menelaus was wandering in Egypt amassing wealth, another man killed his brother (4.90–91). The prince now takes Nestor's and Menelaus' advice to heart. Wanting more could leave him with less. Delaying his journey home could jeopardize his property, negating his journey's purpose. Menelaus agrees to speed Telemachus on his way, but not before he holds a banquet and offers more gifts. Pisistratus, a prince and a guest whose father Menelaus admires as much as Odysseus, is offered none. This, however, is not an oversight; Pisistratus is merely a facilitator who accompanies Telemachus to Menelaus' palace. The journey, after all, is intended for Telemachus' growth; Pisistratus is another Orestes used to measure and advance his education.

The two men are again detained by Menelaus, who now offers a libation for the princes' safe journey. Once on the road, Telemachus must return with Pisistratus to Pylos, for not to do so would be an insult to Nestor, who expects to entertain his son's friend before he embarks for Ithaca. Telemachus, hoping to avoid further delays, searches for a proper way to bypass Pylos. The first half of *Od.* 15, like the second half of the *Telemachia* (*Od.* 3 and 4), is permeated with hospitality, prayers, and libations to impress on the reader not only the importance of these rituals in a world of peace and harmony but also the proper behavior among humans and gods. The difference between a tranquil world (Nestor and Menelaus') and one of chaos (Ithaca) is due to humans of good counsel who observe the gods' ordinances. Accentuating these values not only furthers Telemachus' education but also contrasts them with the suitors' values, which are found wanting. The greater the emphasis on proper behavior, the greater the guilt of those who ignore them and thus the more deserving they are of punishment. Of equal importance for the prince is how to separate himself properly and graciously from such a world of hospitality and rituals without causing offense. Weighing his options (as his father would do), Telemachus breaks protocol for the more important issues facing him in Ithaca.

The princes' journey is interrupted again by an omen. An eagle flies past Telemachus on the right, carrying a white goose in its talons. Foreshadowing Penelope's dream (19.535–550), Helen intervenes to prophesy. Odysseus, the eagle, already in Ithaca, will kill the suitors, the goose. Since the eagle flew on the right (a positive sign) and Helen's prophecy was inspired by the gods (15.172–173), her prediction will be fulfilled. Rejoicing, Telemachus and Pisistratus take their leave, reaching Pherai by the end of day thirty-six, and spend the night at Diocles'[12] house as they did on the incoming journey (the same phrase describes Diocles in both cases [15.187, 3.489]). His only function in the epic is to provide a pit stop for Telemachus' jaunt between Pylos and Sparta. The two princes near Pylos on day thirty-seven, and Telemachus reluctantly requests to be excused from continuing to Nestor's. Not to further delay his return, he prefers to go directly to his ship but is embarrassed to deny the most devout man in the *Odyssey* the chance to perform the rituals of hospitality. That the prince is willing to chance the insult shows great maturity, as it demonstrates his decisiveness in choosing between two important options. Pisistratus, showing great strength of character since he knows his father will be angry with him, acquiesces to Telemachus' wishes and urges speed, so by the time Pisistratus reaches Pylos, Telemachus will be some distance from the city. Out of friendship, Pisistratus is willing to lay the blame on himself for Telemachus' absence, knowing he must confront his father's anger (15.212).

When Telemachus is ready to set sail, he is greeted by a fugitive, a prophet from Argos who killed someone and is fleeing the man's relatives. Common to both the *Odyssey* and *Iliad*, fugitives are generally people from good families who intentionally or mistakenly kill a relative or acquaintance from their district and are given two choices: either reach a monetary agreement with the victim's family or, if an agreement is not acceptable, exile themselves from the district. Such exiles find residence as guests or servants in noble families far away from their parental homes.[13] The fugitive here is Theoclymenus, whose genealogy Homer condenses in the ensuing lines (15.222–286).

1. He is a prophet from Melampus' line, a rich man from Pylos.
2. Melampus was fleeing Neleus for loving his daughter, and Neleus forcibly confiscated his property for one year.
3. Melampus was held prisoner and tortured in Phylacus' house.
4. Melampus escaped and drove the cattle from Phylace back to Pylos, completing the labor imposed on him by Neleus.

5. Melampus returned Neleus' daughter to his brother's house.
6. Melampus settled in Argos and became lord over the Argives.
7. In Argos, Melampus had two sons, Mantius and Antiphates.

Having traced Melampus' line, Homer now traces Antiphates' genealogy, which leads to Amphiaraus, who inherits Melampus' prophetic mantle (the second of the four prophets dealt with in this digression).

8. Antiphates had a son, Oicles.
9. Oicles had a son, Amphiaraus, who was killed in Thebes because his wife was bribed (15.246–247).[14]

Before continuing with Theoclymenus' genealogy, Homer pauses to acknowledge the prophetic skills of Melampus' great-grandson Amphiaraus, a central figure in the Theban Cycle.

10. Amphiaraus had two sons, Amphilochus and Alcmaeon.

Having traced Antiphates' genealogy leading to Amphiaraus, Homer returns to Melampus' first son, Mantius (see no. 7), to trace his lineage, which will produce the third great prophet, Polyphides.

11. Mantius has two sons, Polyphides and Clitus (abducted by Dawn because of his beauty).
12. Apollo makes Polyphides a prophet, the best among mortals after Amphiaraus dies.
13. Polyphides, angry at his father, lived in Hyperesia as a fugitive.
14. Theoclymenus (the fourth prophet) is Polyphides' son.

In this line of succession, the powerful prophetic dynasty begins with Melampus and passes from the second son's line to the first's. Theoclymenus, Polyphides' son, inherits the prophetic powers of Melampus from his father and becomes the final link in this line of powerful seers. Homer's route in tracing this prophetic family underscores Theoclymenus' abilities and the important predictions he makes concerning Odysseus' homecoming.

This digression,[15] used to introduce the fugitive and highlight his importance to the larger narrative of Odysseus' *nostos*, is a good example of the way Homer handles such para-narratives in the *Odyssey*. In the present case, the digression provides a long, reliable line of prophets in the fugitive's ancestry, thus vouching for his legitimacy. At the same time, Melampus, the forerunner of this line of prophets, provides parallels to Odysseus' own situation. Melampus leaves his home out of necessity, and his property, like Odysseus', is seized. Like Odysseus, Melampus returns home to reclaim his wealth once he suffers an imposed labor. The fugitive's genealogy, however, is minimally sketched to establish Theoclymenus' credentials as a prophet. This kind of condensation leaves those unfamiliar with the myth confused. For example, how does Melampus' brother figure in the story? What is the role of Neleus' daughter in the myth? Why is Melampus forced to flee Pylos? How does the cattle at Phylace figure in Melampus' suffering? None of these questions are clarified. Homer either considers the suppressed details unnecessary or supposes his listeners are acquainted with the original myth, making further explication unnecessary.[16] The Melampus myth, first discussed in abridged form in the underworld's catalog of women (11.281–297) in order to introduce Chloris, is now selectively cited here to illustrate Theoclymenus' legitimacy as a prophet.

Theoclymenus, the fugitive, who approaches Telemachus before Homer digresses to narrate his genealogy, asks Telemachus his name, his place of birth, and the names of his parents. The prince responds politely that he is from Ithaca and seeks news of his long-absent father. The prophet confesses that he, too, is away from his country, for killing a man who had many powerful relatives. To avoid their wrath, he has become a fugitive and now begs asylum, lest they come after him and kill him.

Telemachus welcomes him aboard his ship and relieves him of his spear (15.283–284), an action reminiscent of the kindness he extended to Athena (1.121–122).

II. At Eumaeus' Hut, 301–495

In the meantime, at the pig farm, the beggar/Odysseus tests Eumaeus, hoping for an invitation to remain at the hut. He claims he is eager to go to the city to beg so as not to impose on the swineherd and his men, but he will need a guide to lead the way in the morning. He intends to beg in the streets and then make his way to Penelope to deliver news of her husband and mingle with the suitors, hoping for a hand out. He claims he is skilled in all domestic tasks, which will allow him to stay with the suitors.

Eumaeus, addressed in the vocative (15.325; *Eumaie subota* [O swineherd Eumaeus]),[17] is outraged that Odysseus is considering leaving the hut to compete with the young servingmen who work for the suitors and advises him to stay. Relieved that his ruse worked, the beggar/Odysseus takes the opportunity to comment on one of Homer's themes: homelessness and hunger. Mortals continue to endure even as homeless drifters because of desperate hunger. When the beggar inquires about Odysseus' mother and father, Eumaeus reminisces about Anticleia, who raised him alongside her daughter Ktimene as one of her own, and describes his treatment growing up as loving. He regrets his present situation far from Ithaca and longs for his past conversations with Penelope. Painting a picture of loneliness and one full of memories, he laments not being accepted as part of the family of his youth, when he was treated almost as an equal to Ktimene. However, once he came of age, Ktimene married, and he was sent to manage the swine farm. Eumaeus' reminiscences attest to what slaves endured during Homer's time. Even in Odysseus' household, slaves experience disruption, an internal form of exile, and treatment that necessitates stoic endurance. These themes of exile and a loss of innocence are revisited again in the story Eumaeus later relates to the beggar/Odysseus.

Although intimate with Eumaeus' background, Odysseus asks the swineherd to tell his story, which explains for the external audience his lie's merit. As Eumaeus narrates his life, it becomes apparent that the beggar/Odysseus' lie to Eumaeus is based on the servant's own life in order to win his approval and goodwill.

1. Eumaeus, son of King Ctesios, comes from Syria, located above Ortygia,[18] a mythical land lacking hunger and illness, an island paradise without human suffering in many respects not unlike Ogygia. Eumaeus is not only descended from a noble family but in fact comes from a country favored by the gods, one free of hunger and illness. The special circumstances of his origins are proof of his goodness and faith. In the *Odyssey*, humaneness derives from one's pedigree.
2. Eumaeus' Phoenician nanny, the daughter of Arybas, a rich man from Sidon, was abducted by Taphian pirates and sold to Ctesios.
3. The nanny's Phoenician lover promises to deliver her to her parents; she accepts and promises to abduct Eumaeus.
4. After one year the Phoenician lover escapes with the maid and Eumaeus.
5. On the seventh day of their escape, Artemis strikes down the maid for her evil ways and the sailors throw her overboard.
6. Once the ship reaches Ithaca, Eumaeus is sold to Laertes.

Unlike in Odysseus' first lie to Athena, in his lie to Eumaeus the Phoenicians are culprits, since they were responsible for Eumaeus' enslavement. Eumaeus was sold into slavery to a good man, as the beggar/Odysseus was saved by the Thesprotian king. The beggar's enslavers are drowned in a storm, just as Eumaeus' kidnapper is killed by Artemis. Since for Eumaeus bad acts are always punished, Odysseus is careful to base his lie on the swineherd's beliefs. Thus, by the time the beggar and swineherd finish each other's life stories, they bond, two men with similar life experiences—both from nobility, both suffering the same losses, both pious and brought low by fate and the will of Zeus.

III. Telemachus' Return, Part II, 495–557

When Telemachus' ship reaches Ithaca on the evening of day thirty-seven, it stops to disembark Telemachus, who will visit Eumaeus to inspect his holdings before his companions continue on to the city. Theoclymenus asks whether he will stay with Penelope; the prince advises against it. Penelope rarely leaves her chambers, and the suitors are not hospitable. He recommends Eurymachus as host for two reasons: he is thought of highly by the Ithacans, and Telemachus considers him the dominant suitor, the one most likely to marry his mother and acquire his inheritance. However, it is obvious that Telemachus' recommendation is the result of the threat he intuits in Eurymachus, for he is quick to add that only Zeus knows what the future holds. He follows that comment with wishful thinking: Eurymachus might die before marriage. Just then a falcon flies on his right, carrying in his claws a dove whose feathers drift down between the prince and the ship, which Theoclymenus interprets as a positive sign for the Arcesiads (15.533–534). Heartened, Telemachus promises gifts and friendship should the prediction come true. He immediately retracts his previous offer and asks his friend Piraeus to take the seer to his own home and offer him hospitality until he can perform his duties as host himself. As Piraeus and crew cast off for the city, Telemachus sets off on foot for Eumaeus' hut, reaching the farm on the morning of day thirty-eight.

Selected Bibliography: *Od.* 15

Ahl and Roisman, "*Odyssey*," 182–188.

Brown, Edwin L., "Eumaeus'."

Clarke, *Art*, 67–85.

Katz, *Penelope's*, 55–63.

Levine, "Theoklymenos."

Minchin, "Homer Springs."

Muse, "Don't Dally."

Olson, *Blood and Iron*, 120–139.

Reece, *Stranger's*, 59–70, 71–100, 145–164.

Rose, Gilbert P., "*Odyssey*."

Said, *Homer*, 189–222.

Segal, "Phaeacians."

Segal, *Singers*, 164–183.

Further commentary on *Od.* 15 in General Bibliography I.

Book 16

A book of recognition and strategy, *Od.* 16 concludes Odysseus' and Telemachus' journeys at Eumaeus' hut. Three-fourths of the book is set there, with an interlude on the suitors' disappointment at the arrival of Telemachus' ship. In the first of three sections, Telemachus is reunited with his father. The interlude covers the suitors' failed interception of the prince's ship and Penelope's questioning the suitors about her son's fate. In the third section, Eumaeus returns from Ithaca to his hut with news on the suitors.

I. Eumaeus' hut, part I (67%)
II. Odysseus' palace (27%)
III. Eumaeus' hut, part II (6%)

I. Eumaeus' Hut, Part I, 1–320

When Telemachus arrives at Eumaeus' hut, the startled swineherd embraces and kisses him. A simile (16.17–21) of a father welcoming his son after a ten-year hiatus follows. Ironically, in the simile Eumaeus becomes a surrogate father who welcomes his only son when it is Odysseus who, after a long absence, should be embracing him. Perhaps it should be Laertes hugging his own sole son, Odysseus, upon his return from his wanderings or even Eumaeus embracing Odysseus upon his return from Hades.

The swineherd clings to Telemachus as if he has escaped death, which in fact he has by bypassing the city. Eumaeus, like a loving father, complains of how infrequently the prince visits the farm. However, it seems Telemachus is a regular visitor, since the dogs, instead of barking, fawn on him when he approaches the hut. Telemachus reassures the swineherd he came for his sake, but it was Athena (16.36–42) who urged him to avoid the suitors and the city. Athena's dream still fresh in his mind, the prince inquires about his property and whether his mother married, but the swineherd reassures him that she still holds off the suitors, hoping for her husband's return. As the beggar/Odysseus rises to yield his seat, the prince's good breeding stops him, and he looks for another seat. After dining on the leftovers Eumaeus served earlier, Telemachus again shows his nobility by addressing the stranger neither by age nor by condition but as "stranger" and "friend." The prince asks for the stranger's identity, which Eumaeus summarizes for him.

In Eumaeus' stripped-down version, the beggar is a Cretan whose wanderings took him to many cities before he arrived fleeing a Thesprotian ship, but Eumaeus fails to mention the beggar's news concerning Odysseus, his aristocratic background, or his kind reception by King Pheidon. Does Eumaeus neglect to mention news of Odysseus intentionally? Perhaps after spending an evening with the beggar, he is conscious of more than he is willing to share. Moreover, Eumaeus would rather turn over the responsibility to the prince. Should the beggar have valid information on Odysseus, then the prince and the palace should hear it from him. The swineherd's suggestion upsets Telemachus, who lacks the means to entertain guests. He gives two reasons for his reluctance to accept responsibility. First, he is too young and inexperienced to take on such a task, and he does not have the power to defend the beggar. Second, he still does not completely trust his mother with a stranger, as previously noted in Theoclymenus' case. Telemachus finds his mother conflicted as to whether to remain faithful to her son, husband, and home and respect the people's voice or take on a new husband and hope her choice is the right one. All the prince can offer the beggar is a mantle, a tunic, sandals, a sword, and his freedom. A better solution is for the stranger to remain at the hut; Telemachus will send clothing and provisions to unburden the herdsman's obligation. However, he cannot allow the stranger among the suitors, for they are too violent and will insult him, causing the prince great sorrow. Telemachus, at this point of his development, is still groping to discover how to proceed with two matters that plague his mind:

1. He feels inapt to take on the suitors on his own.
2. He is conflicted about his mother's intentions.

Odysseus, visibly upset at his son's lack of courage and unable to hold in his anger and disappointment in him, asks why he allows the suitors to bully him. He wonders whether the Ithacans have turned against him to allow such dreadful occurrences to continue. He questions whether Telemachus lacks supporters in a time of need. What prevents the prince from taking charge, since he seems physically capable? If the beggar were as young as he feels in spirit, he would rather fight alone and die than endure such shameful activities. Eumaeus does not question how the beggar knows about the suitors' abuses. Perhaps he feels the beggar assumes such transgressions from earlier conversations. We are not told, but with each passing moment Eumaeus' relationship with the beggar grows stronger.

Addressing the beggar as "friend," Telemachus explains his inaction is based mostly on the Arcesiads' small numbers. His great-grandfather had one son, Laertes, who in turn bore a single son, Odysseus, who himself left behind a single son, but their enemies are many, the most powerful men from the neighboring islands. A single son cannot face the suitors alone. His mother, whom the suitors want to marry, neither refuses them nor is able to accept them. This uncertainty causes the prince's angst over his inheritance. In the meantime, the suitors continue consuming his wealth and plan his destruction. He has no alternative but to remain at the hut while Eumaeus secretly alerts Penelope of his safe arrival.

The swineherd asks whether he should also inform Laertes, whose condition has worsened since Telemachus' trip. Telemachus' priority, although he is upset at his grandfather's condition, is his father's return. He thinks it best to let Penelope send the housekeeper (a reference to Eurycleia) with the news. It is not clear why the housekeeper should be the one to inform Laertes of his grandson's return. Perhaps her presence will comfort the old man, since he favored her as much as his own wife (1.432–433). Telemachus' mention of and interest in his grandfather, his longing for his father, his feeling of incompetence before the suitors, and his uncertainty regarding his mother's intentions are signs not only of his growing attention to Ithaca's affairs but also of the pressing need with which these matters now engage his mind.

Once Eumaeus leaves, Athena appears before Odysseus as a tall, beautiful woman, unseen by Telemachus; only Odysseus and the dogs, which silently cower away, are aware of her presence. Odysseus exits the hut and stands before her, attentive to her commands:

1. Reveal yourself to your son.
2. Prepare a plan with Telemachus to bring about the suitors' death, in which Athena will assist.

Tapping him with her golden wand, she transforms his appearance as she did earlier, but this time she makes him younger.[19]

Telemachus, startled at the beggar's transformation, ponders whether he is in the presence of a god and promises offerings and gifts if only the divinity will be merciful. Odysseus, in a pun[20] identifying himself as a father and not a god, assures him, *"Ou tis toi theos eimi"* (No, I am not a god), *"alla pater teos eimi"* (but I am your father [16.187–188]). Weeping, he kisses Telemachus, but the prince is hesitant; what if a divinity is deceiving him? Can an elderly person become young unless an immortal hand is behind it? Odysseus reassures him that no other Odysseus than the one before him will ever return (16.203–204). At that, Telemachus embraces his father, a reunion captured in a simile in which father and son are compared to vultures whose young are stolen, comparing a happy moment of recognition to a painful event of loss and sadness. Their crying is likened to the shrill lamentation of birds of prey, equating emotions experienced in loss and death to those of renewal and rebirth. Father and son rejoice as if the dead have come to life. Odysseus and son, like vultures (*aigupioi*), will eventually take vengeance on the suitors.

The prince remains doubtful and is curious to know how Odysseus landed in Ithaca. Odysseus explains that the Phaeacians brought him to the island with gifts that are now stored in the nymphs' cavern. He came to Eumaeus on Athena's orders so that together they could plan their enemies' deaths. He asks for their numbers to assess whether they alone will be able to face them or whether they will need assistance. Aware of his father's deeds of prowess, Telemachus nevertheless is taken aback at his father's suggestion that the two of them can defeat so many.[21] The prince, his maturity in full view, wants to know whether Odysseus has allies in mind. First, although he acknowledges his father's presence, he is cautious to question his identity further. Second, he reconsiders his father's plan and finds it unfeasible. Third, he asks for possible reinforcements. Odysseus, irritated that his son mistrusts his judgment, asks whether Athena and Zeus's participation would be sufficient. Telemachus admits the gods' assistance would be enough if they can depend on gods so far away who are responsible for all humankind. Odysseus maintains that, although far away now, the gods will be near when needed. Telemachus relents, and Odysseus asks the prince to return to the suitors until Eumaeus and he, as a vagabond, arrive. Telemachus must then ignore the beggar and abide his mistreatment; he can, however, try to restrain the suitors' behavior toward him. When Athena signals, Odysseus will nod to his son to clear the great hall of weapons and store them in some corner, offering two reasons for their removal: first, to keep them safe from the smoke, and second, for safety in case of a drunken rage, which could spoil the suitors' feasting. However, the prince must leave behind a pair of swords, spears, and shields for himself and his father. Odysseus is confident that the presence of Athena and Zeus to daze the suitors' wits, along with his son's assistance, is sufficient to handle 108 men.[22] However, at the time of the attack, the swineherd and oxherd will join the fight. The pair of swords and shields Odysseus asks for here will not be present (a contingency and maneuver that does not come to pass). Instead, Telemachus will go to an inner room where the weapons are stored to take four shields, eight spears, and four helmets (22.110–111).

Odysseus warns he must remain incognito even from Laertes, Eumaeus, and Penelope. The two of them alone will judge the faith of the palace staff. Telemachus again questions his father's recommendation. He concedes the necessity of testing the innocence of the women, but he finds traversing the estate to test the men excessive; that task can be carried out after the suitors are dealt with. Their priority should be the suitors when Zeus gives the sign to act. Again, Telemachus displays his growth in refusing to accept his father's counsel blindly; he is confident enough to trust his own opinion. We can only assume Odysseus takes Telemachus' advice, for while they are still conversing, the narrative crosscuts to Ithaca as Telemachus' ship arrives.

II. Odysseus' Palace, 321–451

The narrative now continues from the point abandoned in *Od.* 4.847, where the suitors wait to ambush Telemachus, and moves at a feverish pace, creating an anxious, hurried atmosphere.

1. Telemachus' companions hull their ship on land and carry the gifts to Piraeus' house.
2. The companions send a herald to Penelope to inform her of her son's arrival.

3. The dispatched herald arrives at the palace at the same time as the swineherd, and before Eumaeus delivers his secret message, the herald openly announces Telemachus' return.
4. Eumaeus whispers Telemachus' message to the queen and quickly departs.
5. The suitors who doubted that Telemachus would complete his voyage are discouraged.
6. Stunned, Eurymachus recalls the suitors' ship, which is sheltered in Asteris.
7. Amphinomus catches sight of Telemachus' ship in the harbor before Eurymachus' recall can be carried out. Smiling (a sarcastic smile that signals that some divine power is acting behind the scenes), Amphinomus suggests the suitors' efforts to kill the prince are foiled.
8. The suitors waiting to ambush Telemachus return to the assembly.
9. Antinous encourages killing Telemachus before he retaliates. He too is aware of the prince's growth (16.374). He fears Telemachus is now capable of convincing the populace of the suitors' crimes and the need for their exile. He recommends they secretly eliminate the prince outside the city, divide his estate among themselves, and allow Penelope to keep the palace for the man she weds. Alternatively, if Antinous' counsel is found offensive, allow Telemachus to live, abandon the palace, and strive to win Penelope through gifts of courtship.
10. Amphinomus (who pleased Penelope most) argues against killing the prince, since to kill someone of royal blood is unlawful. If Zeus approves the murder, he will sanction it, but if the gods disapprove, the suitors must give up their plans to murder him. His counsel meets the suitors' approval, and they return to their accustomed places in the great hall.

By now the situation in Ithaca has reached a critical point. Penelope, informed by Medon of her son's impending death, appears before the suitors to address Antinous as a brute and a criminal disregardful of Zeus's wrath. She tries to mollify his rage, digressing to tell how Odysseus saved Antinous' father's life when he came to Ithaca as a fugitive pursued for piracy and about to lose his livelihood to the people's fury. Odysseus stayed their hand and saved him. Antinous, like the people after his father's wealth, is now attempting to squander Odysseus' instead of protecting it. He should ask the suitors to do the same instead of repaying Odysseus' kindness by wasting his property, courting his wife, and attempting to murder his son. Eurymachus tries to appease Penelope, maintaining he will not allow any harm to come to Telemachus even if he must kill the perpetrators himself. He continues in his duplicitousness, reminding her that, as a young boy, Odysseus rocked him on his knees and fed him roasted meat and wine, reassuring her that Telemachus need not fear the suitors, while at the same time plotting his murder. Antinous' and Eurymachus' remarks also make us aware of the age discrepancies between Penelope and many of her suitors. Odysseus is closer to Antinous' father's age (he saved him from the Ithacans), and Eurymachus' reminiscences of Odysseus establish at least these two suitors as Telemachus' contemporaries, which lends support for the supposition that the suitors' intended prize is the property and the power they hope to gain and not Penelope.

III. Eumaeus' Hut, Part II, 452–481

By evening, Eumaeus is reunited with the beggar/Odysseus and Telemachus at the farm. The prince is anxious to hear whether the suitors are still lying in wait for him. Although Eumaeus' responsibility was to deliver a message and return, he did see a ship with many men on board pulling into the harbor, loaded down with weapons. Catching his father's eye but avoiding the swineherd's, Telemachus smiles (16.477), a knowing smile of recognition between father and son (an early instance of secret communication, which is a hallmark of *Od.* 13–24). Happy to have avoided the suitors' ruse and aware of their intentions, father and son are prepared to face them.

Selected Bibliography: *Od.* 16

Ahl and Roisman, "*Odyssey*," 189–204.

Clarke, *Art*, 67–85.

Katz, *Penelope's*, 72–76.

Reece, *Stranger's*, 145–164.

Rood, "Implied."

Said, *Homer*, 189–222.

Segal, "Phaeacians."

Further commentary on *Od.* 16 in General Bibliography I.

CHAPTER 5

ODYSSEUS AND TELEMACHUS STRATEGIZE AT THE PALACE (*OD.* 17–20)

Book 17

The first book of the fifth tetrad returns to Odysseus at his palace, where he observes and tests the suitors, his household staff, and his wife, leading to Penelope's recognition of him in *Od.* 19. The pace is slow and deliberate, allowing Odysseus to reclaim his identity slowly and affording ample time not only for Odysseus and Telemachus to relish the revenge they exact from the suitors but also to underscore the crimes the suitors perpetrated. *Od.* 17 is filled with forebodings, predictions, prophecies, Odysseus' impact on the suitors, and the effect his presence has on Penelope. Telemachus has already recognized his father; Eumaeus suspects the stranger is not a mere beggar; and Penelope begins to suspect that her long-absent husband could be near. This optimism is bolstered by Theoclymenus' predictions and the beggar's news of Penelope's husband, which she acknowledges: *"Ouk aphrōn ho xenos oietai"* (17.586; The stranger is nobody's fool).

In the book's three-part division,[1] the first and third sections, on Telemachus and Penelope, frame a second, longer one, which follows the beggar from Eumaeus' hut to the palace to expose his treatment by the suitors (especially Antinous). The first section plots Telemachus' journey from Eumaeus' hut to the palace and his interaction with the suitors, while the third presents Penelope's reaction to her son's return and the suitors' mistreatment of the beggar.

I. At the palace: Telemachus and Penelope, part I (30%)
II. At the palace: Odysseus (51%)
III. At the palace: Telemachus and Penelope, part II (19%)

I. At the Palace: Telemachus and Penelope, Part I, 1–182

The thirty-ninth day of the *Odyssey* narrative occupies almost the entire fifth tetrad, up to 20.90. Telemachus sets out to visit his mother, but in truth, he must arrive at the palace first to prepare for his father. For now, he must play the part of an inhospitable host and ask Eumaeus to lead the stranger to the city to beg, arguing that his situation makes it impossible to host every stranger, although he is aware that he is ignoring Zeus's law by turning away a vagabond. Eumaeus is disappointed in him, but the beggar/Odysseus, standing next to the prince, is clear on the false role his son must play and comes to his rescue as he does for Nausicaa before her parents in *Od.* 7. He casts blame on himself for wanting to beg in the city, attributing the difficulty of earning a living as a farmhand to his advanced age. He states that he trusts Eumaeus will lead him to the city after he warms himself, for his clothes are poor and the morning frost undoes him, calling attention again to his scant clothing as he has done throughout his stay at the farm.

Eurycleia, first to greet Telemachus, bursts out in tears as she and the maids rush to embrace him, while his mother descends, looking like both Artemis and Aphrodite (17.37). Homer highlights Penelope's beauty by comparing her not only to Aphrodite, the goddess of love (making her desirable), but also to Artemis, the goddess who most guards her virginity and independence (stressing her purity and faithfulness). Embracing him, she bursts into tears, eager for news. Telemachus, exercising his newly found masculinity and aware of his father's presence, is not ready to divulge any news to his mother. In a serious tone of one who has embraced his manhood and must deal with pressing matters, he asks his mother to return to her chambers, bathe, dress, and pray to the gods for revenge. Telemachus is anxious to summon his guest from Piraeus' home. Sensing his earnestness, Penelope returns to her rooms to pray for the hour of their deliverance. Perhaps Penelope is also more hopeful of Odysseus' return as she ponders who the guest from abroad might be. As the prince departs to summon his guest, he is described with the identical phrase used in the Ithacan assembly at *Od.* 2.12 (spear in hand and accompanied by a pair of dogs). In both cases, the dogs accompanying Telemachus grant him stature and create an aura of power, which is further enhanced by Athena's involvement. However, in this instance, not only is he more comfortable with himself, but those present take him more seriously as they wait for answers to their questions. The suitors, harboring murder in their hearts, cluster around him, uttering pleasantries. The prince gives them a wide berth and takes a seat beside some of his father's old friends. Piraeus approaches with Theoclymenus, anxious to have Menelaus' gifts transferred to the palace. The prince, preoccupied with the suitors' threat to kill him, asks Piraeus to hold the gifts. If he survives, his friend can return them for their mutual pleasure; otherwise, Piraeus can enjoy them with their companions. Without harboring any delusions, Telemachus, like an adult, is ready to face the serious matters that confront him.

Penelope, respecting the control Telemachus has exhibited since his return, waits patiently for her son and his guest to finish dinner so that she can learn why he is avoiding her, anxious to hear the outcome of his journey and the identity of his guest. Perhaps she suspects that the guest is someone special and that Telemachus has news of his father. After all, she rarely leaves her chambers or shows herself before the suitors, yet she now sits alone in the great hall, risking exposure. Telemachus finally relents and summarizes his journey.

1. Nestor treated him as a father would but knew nothing about Odysseus. He sent him to Menelaus, newly arrived from Troy.
2. Telemachus recalls Helen's graciousness; whatever suffering she caused was the gods' will. It is interesting that Telemachus' first memory of Sparta, and the first thing he mentions, is Helen, a testament to her beauty that recalls the old Trojans' reaction in *Il.* 3.154–158. Helen's charisma must have captivated the prince, as he offers voluntarily that the suffering she caused could not have been her own doing.
3. Menelaus reacted to the suitors' shameful behavior and was hopeful that the Odysseus who wrestled and defeated the undefeated Philomelides (see chapter 1, note 27) would return among the suitors, who would find a quick death. Telemachus also recalls Menelaus' lion/doe simile (4.333–348 and 17.124–139), which he repeats verbatim, perhaps covertly joyful at the presence of his father, who, like a lion, will soon destroy the suitors who presently occupy his den.
4. He mentions what Menelaus heard from Proteus: Odysseus, detained by Calypso on her island by force, lacks the means to sail home.

Theoclymenus, seeing Penelope visibly moved by her son's report, makes his own prophecy. Taking an oath before Zeus as a suppliant at Odysseus' hearth, he predicts that Odysseus is already in Ithaca. The bird omen he interpreted earlier (15.525–534) informed him of what he now forecasts. Penelope must wonder how this young prophet already knows of Odysseus' presence. Is it by chance or design that he came aboard Telemachus' ship? She now has news of Odysseus from two reliable sources: Menelaus' report and Theoclymenus' prediction. The warmth and generosity with which she receives the young prophet's predictions should they come true seems to indicate that she is entertaining the possibility of her husband's return. Though she is still unable to accept these assurances at face value, she is more hopeful than ever before. Penelope now takes control of her own fate; she will question the beggar/Odysseus privately and actively work to bring about the suitors' demise. To enhance the righteousness of Theoclymenus' predictions, Homer crosscuts to the unruly suitors, who are amusing themselves without any concern for others. When Medon calls them to their feast, they accept his invitation but neglect to give the gods their due, a disregard for which they will be held accountable.

II. At the Palace: Odysseus, 182–488

Although Eumaeus feels the journey to the palace is ill advised, he will not chance a scolding from Telemachus. In consideration for his guest, he suggests starting out immediately in order to avoid the chill at sunset. A digression provides a brief history of the city fountain (17.204–212), the setting for Odysseus' encounter with the goatherd Melanthius, which slows the episode's pace, anticipating the main action to follow. Melanthius enters, herding the pick of his goat flocks for the suitors' meal. Spotting Eumaeus and the beggar, he breaks out in foul language, challenging the beggar to work for a living rather than scrounge for food, and as he passes, kicks him in the hip. The beggar/Odysseus, unshaken, ponders whether to bash his head on the rocks or wait for a more favorable opportunity. Angered at Melanthius' abuse, Eumaeus prays to the fountain nymphs for Odysseus' return. Melanthius' punishment is inevitable, for like the doe in Menelaus' simile (4.333–348), he enters the lion's den mindlessly, without any thought of danger. His thoughtlessness is echoed a second time when he vents his animosity at the beggar and prays to Apollo to strike down Telemachus and be rid of both father and son, but Apollo refuses him because his prayer is self-serving.

Odysseus, at the palace for the first time since his return to Ithaca, listens to Phemius and is overcome with emotion. Admiring his palace as a beggar, he is at the same time scrutinizing every detail of his surroundings, mentally preparing himself for his assault on the suitors. He mentions the music and the ongoing festivities to Eumaeus not only to give cover to his true identity but also to comment on the suitors, since this type of merriment indicates a feast for an important event. Athena expressed the same confusion in *Od.* 1.225–226 to indicate the inappropriateness of holding a feast for no singular event. When Eumaeus asks how they should enter the great hall, the beggar/Odysseus already has the solution at hand. Eumaeus will enter first, and he will follow. He will weather any blows he might receive, for there is no way to hide a hungry belly. Homer, who never misses an opportunity to mention the evils hunger bestows on humankind, has the beggar/Odysseus add that it is the curse of hunger that necessitates building ships to travel great distances in order to acquire food by raiding. Humans are capable of withstanding, as well as dealing out, a great deal of punishment to satiate hunger, which cannot be suppressed.

Argus, Odysseus' dog, who was abandoned when his master sailed to Troy, is lying nearby and raises his head at Odysseus' voice. This small cameo is the first recognition scene in the epic, which anticipates the more elaborate ones to follow. Each of these recognition scenes adapts to whoever is recognizing Odysseus. Argus, a cherished pet which has been neglected and is lying in a pile of dung, too weak to stand or move, instinctively wags his tail and dies, a symbol of Ithaca's deterioration in the absence of its king. Fearful of revealing himself, Odysseus admires the dog's handsome physique, sheds a secret tear, and asks the swineherd about its owner. In reply, Eumaeus is given an opportunity to comment on slavery. The household staff fails to care for the enfeebled and powerless, for once the master is out of sight, slaves refuse to perform their duties. Zeus robs a man of half his virtue on the day of enslavement. Once freedom is gone, human status is degraded, and without a strong leader to keep order, apathy sets in.

Telemachus, first to notice Eumaeus, nods and motions to the swineherd, who picks up a stool and sits next to him. The beggar enters soon after and sits on the threshold, propping himself on his cane and looking old and haggard. Telemachus, noticing his father, asks Eumaeus to take a portion of meat and bread to him and urge him to circulate among the suitors, for there is no shame for one in need. This comment is voiced by Telemachus to protect his father's disguise but is also another Homeric pronouncement on hunger. The beggar accepts the food with a prayer calling for his son's prosperity and anything his heart desires, another prediction of what is to come. Athena, standing at his side (perhaps in his thoughts, since she is not present in disguise), urges the beggar/Odysseus to move among the suitors to mark the innocent from the guilty. It is a strange request from the goddess, since she has no thought of delivering any of the suitors from disaster (17.364). However, since in *Od.* 1.32–34 Zeus states that the gods assist and advise mortals who are left to their own designs, Athena here advises Odysseus, who, unlike Aegisthus in *Od.* 1.37–43, heeds her. Being of one mind with the hero (intelligent, wise), she knows Odysseus will do as she asks, identifying the suitors and, by his choice alone, sparing two of them. Unlike in a modern whodunit, where the outcome is not revealed until the very end, in the Homeric epics, the outcome is known from the beginning.

Melanthius continues to blame Eumaeus for the stranger's presence, while the suitors question his identity. In an ironic twist, Antinous lashes out at Eumaeus for dragging vagabonds into the hall to consume Odysseus' food, though he himself is the prime culprit for the wastefulness. In retaliation, Eumaeus points out that guests are invited to perform a function—to prophesy, to heal, to entertain, and to serve the household, indicating that the stranger is there for a purpose, the purpose ironically being Antinous' own demise. Eumaeus calls Antinous' behavior toward the master's servants contemptible, although Eumaeus remains undaunted by his insults as long as the queen and prince are alive, subtly reminding Antinous that the palace still remains in his master's control. These exchanges between Odysseus' supporters and his enemies further identify the disintegrating conditions in the palace and sanction Athena and Odysseus' resolve to do away with the suitors.

Telemachus, manifesting great authority as master of his domain, interrupts Eumaeus, telling him not to waste his breath on a man intent on creating discord. Turning to Antinous, the prince ironically compliments the suitor for treating him as a father treats a son (17.397–398), implying that the suitor's disdain for the beggar is out of concern for the prince's property. Yet Telemachus will not drive a stranger from his home. He prods Antinous to offer the beggar something, adding ironically that he can spare the gesture, since he is giving away Telemachus' food. In a commanding voice missing in the *Telemachia*, the prince accuses Antinous of gorging himself and charges him of selfishness toward his mother, household slaves, and people in general. The suitor counters, calling the prince high and mighty and stating that he has a nasty temper. He then promises a gift to keep the beggar from the palace for three months and, grabbing a stool, lifts it up for all to see but fails to act on the threat, which he carries out later. It is clear by now that Telemachus has reached the maturity necessary to rule and is further emboldened by his father's presence to hold his own against the suitors, who now take him as a serious threat.

The beggar/Odysseus baits Antinous that since he looks more prosperous than the others, his gift should be greater. He narrates a short version of the lie told to Eumaeus to underscore life's unpredictability: he too went from prosperity to poverty. Once a rich man, he had many servants and the advantages that go with wealth, but Zeus, for reasons unknown, had him lead a roving band of pirates to Egypt, where, in their recklessness, they plundered the countryside, killing the men and enslaving the women and children. The cries of the slaughter reached the city, and by daybreak his troops were either killed or enslaved; only he was captured and taken to Dmetor, the king of Cyprus. From there he came to Ithaca, suffering hardships. The lie becomes a cautionary tale for Antinous: A leader who loses control of his men risks their death and enslavement. Instead of making him wealthier, his greed, reinforced in the actions of his men, made him a slave. Antinous would do well to take heed; as a leader among the suitors, his greed and self-interest are leading him and the others to destruction.

Eumaeus withholds comment until summoned by Penelope to inquire about the stranger. He must wonder why the beggar changed his story, or he realizes there is an ulterior motive. In the present lie, the beggar/Odysseus claims to be not a rich man's son but rather someone prosperous; nor does he mention Crete, Troy, or a nine-ship expedition. He willingly sails with pirates to Egypt, where they kill many and are themselves killed or enslaved; he is sold to the Cyprian king. Without further detail, the narrative thereafter places the beggar in Ithaca, neither taken captive by the Egyptian king nor following a Phoenician to Libya; neither shipwrecked nor saved by the Thesprotian king; neither hearing of Odysseus nor escaping Thesprotian sailors once he reaches Ithaca. In Penelope's presence, Eumaeus later emphasizes two points concerning the beggar/Odysseus' lie. First, he is a great storyteller whose tales can charm one's heart. Second, he heard Odysseus is alive, near, and returning with many gifts. Eumaeus now finds the beggar's story credible and is more admiring of him. Have the beggar's two versions raised doubts regarding his identity? After his meeting with Penelope, Eumaeus' opinion of the beggar changes; he takes him to be an exceptional man and storyteller who selectively uses his background for a purpose. Does he suspect that the beggar is more than he lets on?

Antinous, calling the beggar brazen, shameless, and always hoarding, orders him to stay clear of his table or end up again in Cyprus or Egypt. The beggar retorts, calling Antinous an idiot who would not give even a grain of salt to his own servant even though he freely lounges at another man's table. The beggar/Odysseus' sharp-witted response risks exposing his disguise, but before he can say more, the suitor picks up the footstool he raised earlier and hurls it, striking him under the right shoulder. The beggar/Odysseus bears the blow, returns to the doorsill, and points out that there is no shame in being wounded in defense of one's country or possessions, yet Antinous causes him physical pain not for either of these but for hunger, which brings men suffering, yet another opportunity for Homer to preach about his pet peeve, hunger. To abuse someone defenseless for status is to disrespect his humanity. If the gods exist for all people, and if there are Furies to right wrongs, Antinous' death will come before his marriage.

Antinous is unrelenting. He orders the beggar to eat quietly or leave lest his behavior tempt the younger suitors to drag him through the halls and flail him. The suitors, outraged at Antinous' threats and fearing the beggar a god in disguise, since gods often appear to test humans, object to his disregard for gods and laws. Telemachus, anguished at the blow his father received, keeps silent, contriving ways to repay the suitor. By this point, matters in the great hall have reached a crisis. Antinous' true nature is exposed to the point that other suitors begin to question his actions. Odysseus' and Telemachus' anger is at a breaking point, threatening to expose the beggar's disguise. It is usually at such crucial moments that Homer comes to a sudden stop to crosscut to another scene before returning to the previous one (e.g., the footbath scene in 19.392–393).

III. At the Palace: Telemachus and Penelope, Part II, 489–606

Penelope, probably made aware by her servants of the beggar's mistreatment, prays that Apollo's arrows reach Antinous as his missile reached the beggar (foreshadowing the first arrow from Odysseus' bow that will strike him [22.8]). Eurynome, echoing Penelope's sentiments, increases the foreboding. The queen summons Eumaeus to order (17.508; *ercheo*) the beggar to come to her for questioning. The swineherd, anxious to impress on his mistress the stranger's positive qualities, offers a simile comparing the beggar to a divine singer, a man whose skill in holding audiences spellbound comes from the gods. Not only does the beggar delight like a Phemius or Demodocus, but he is inspired by the gods to celebrate in song the truth. Eumaeus' engrossment shows he has taken the beggar's tales to heart. He is anxious for Penelope to notice the difference from those she questioned in the past and adds that Odysseus is close by (17.525–526), is alive (17.527), and returns with many gifts (17.527). The swineherd's opinion of the beggar has intensified. Earlier he was cautious and expressed disbelief. Now he seems convinced that given his speech, his cleverness, and his demeanor, this special stranger is telling the truth. Penelope again commands Eumaeus to have the beggar come (*ercheo*) to her, but with greater urgency than before. Eumaeus points out that the suitors' clamor will make it difficult to speak to him, but she insists on his immediate presence, regardless of the noise.

Penelope is finally able to vent her frustration at the suitors' squandering. She feels empowered to make bold accusations and to bolster her suspicions as a result of the positive signs and predictions she is given. When Telemachus sneezes (17.541–542), the queen laughs at her good fortune and again orders Eumaeus to summon the stranger (17.544). She hopes the sneeze, a divine sign, means death for all the suitors. She is now ready to declare her hatred for the suitors openly and considers Odysseus to be near, predicting that if what the beggar says is true, she will bestow on him a tunic and mantle. Both Eumaeus and Penelope are by now swayed that the beggar knows more than he admits; it is now up to the beggar to allow Penelope to discover his identity without exposing himself, a process that will take the reader through *Od.* 19. It should be noted, however, that the narrator nowhere states that Penelope has recognized Odysseus before the end of *Od.* 23. Homer is clearly at pains to keep this question in the realm of ambiguity. At most, he has deliberately and self-consciously made the matter ambiguous and suggestive, which makes possible the reading of an early recognition.

Eumaeus delivers Penelope's order, addressing the beggar as *xeine pater* (17.553; friend and father), thus indicating the respect he holds for him. The beggar/Odysseus' response to Penelope's invitation, however, sounds rude and out of character. He tells Eumaeus he will speak the truth to Icarius' daughter (17.562), ignoring the more intimate phrase *meter Telemachio* (mother of Telemachus) used by Eumaeus (17.553–554). Second, the beggar admits he knows a lot about Odysseus, since they suffered the same sad story (17.563), equating himself with the hero. Third, he states that Penelope should not expect him until after the sun sets because he fears the suitors' abuse. His use of the imperative of *anōga* (*anochthi*) seems out of character here; it has a stronger meaning than "advise" or "urge" and is closer to "command" or "order." The beggar is ordering Penelope to postpone the meeting until evening; a stranger is commanding the queen to do his bidding by way of his host, now become his servant. He also appeals to the queen to offer him a seat near the fire, giving as an excuse his scanty clothing, thereby putting himself forward as someone of authority who is certain of himself and in control of his beliefs and thus risking exposure.

Penelope is surprised that Eumaeus returns without the beggar. She is disappointed at having her request ignored and asks herself whether the beggar's behavior is due to fear, bashfulness, or embarrassment. Eumaeus agrees that it is better for both Penelope and the beggar to avoid drawing attention to themselves and wait until the suitors leave the hall. He argues that an evening meeting puts a halt to further violence and prevents gossip. Penelope, satisfied with Eumaeus' reasoning, agrees that the stranger makes good sense (17.586; *ouk aphron ho xeinos oietai*). Both admit that the beggar, like Odysseus, has a quick and agile mind and considers all possibilities before he acts.

Eumaeus returns to the *megaron* to inform Telemachus he is leaving for the farm and caution him to be conscious of the suitors, who mean him harm. He ends with a parting wish that has been the mantra of the beggar, Penelope, Telemachus, and the household servants: "May Zeus destroy them before they can make any harm befall us" (17.597), a prediction and a prayer the gods will honor. Addressing him as "father," Telemachus endorses Eumaeus' wish and assures him that matters should now be left in his and the gods' hands.

Selected Bibliography: *Od.* 17

Ahl and Roisman, *"Odyssey,"* 189–204, 205–214.

Clarke, *Art*, 67–85.

Coughanowr, "Meaning."

Emlyn-Jones, "Reunion."
Frank, "Homer's *Odyssey*, Book 17."
Jacobson, "Homer, *Odyssey* 17.221."
Katz, *Penelope's*, 114–154.
Lateiner, "Telemakhos."
Newton, "Odysseus and Melanthius."
Newton, "Poor Polyphemus."
Pedrick, "Eurycleia."
Reece, *Stranger's*, 145–164, 165–188.
Said, *Homer*, 189–222.
Scodel, "Odysseus' Dog."
Scott, John A., "Eurynome."
Segal, "Phaeacians."
Further commentary on *Od.* 17 in General Bibliography I.

Book 18

Od. 18 continues day thirty-nine in the three-part structure explained earlier (note 1 of the present chapter): the two halves of the beggar/Odysseus' stay in the *megaron* frame a middle section on Penelope among the suitors. This symmetry persists within each of the two end sections (I and III)—episodes on a low-class character (Irus [I] and Melantho [III]) followed by episodes on a high-class one (Amphinomus [I] and Eurymachus [III]). Further parallelism is found in the relationship of each set of characters to the hero; Irus and Melantho, a beggar and a servant, are both followers of the suitors who abuse Odysseus in the *megaron*. The two suitors, Eurymachus and Amphinomus, are considered the best choices for marriage to Penelope: Eurymachus by Penelope's father and brothers (15.16–17), and Amphinomus by Penelope herself (16.397–398). The middle section (II) on Penelope consists of four exchanges she has, one each with Eurynome, Telemachus, Eurymachus, and Antinous. All three sections (I–III) serve as a retardation device to postpone the meeting between

Odysseus and Penelope (initially delayed by the beggar/Odysseus in 17.586), a meeting that will not take place until *Od.* 19.

I. Odysseus in the *megaron*, part I (37%)
II. Penelope among the suitors (34%)
III. Odysseus in the *megaron*, part II (29%)

I. Odysseus in the Megaron, Part I, 1–157

A short introduction of Irus, a public vagabond known for his ravenous appetite and for scrounging a living on the streets of Ithaca, opens the book. This is a light-hearted episode that offers some comic relief following the highly charged previous book. It allows the internal audience to further question the stranger's identity, which becomes more pronounced in his fight with Irus. It is rife with irony when the suitors congratulate the beggar/Odysseus on his victory, wish him well, and invite him to their feasts. The bout between the false and true occupiers of Odysseus' *megaron* becomes a mock replay of the bow contest still to come between the suitors and Odysseus. The chuckles and laughter of the suitors intensify and contrast with the sullenness to follow.

Irus, whose given name is Arnaeus, is called Irus because he willingly performs errands for the suitors and thereby puts them in mind of the messenger goddess Iris.[2] His given name alludes to the Greek word *arneios* (sheep or lamb), which speaks to his character—a braggart but in fact docile. Big in size but small in strength, he comes to the palace to chase the beggar from the *megaron*, which he considers his private preserve. In boasting that he is ashamed to use force on one so old, he reminds the reader of the suitors' boasting of their superiority over Odysseus. The beggar/Odysseus warns him that, should they come to blows, Irus will never again return to the palace. Angered at the beggar's threat, Irus, spewing invectives, prepares to smash out all the stranger's teeth. As the tongue-lashing continues, Antinous, laughing, goads them on for the suitors' amusement. The other suitors, laughing[3] in agreement, gather around as

Antinous sets the rules for a fight. The winner of the bout will receive a goat sausage and will be allowed to dine with the suitors. The beggar/Odysseus, preserving his identity, feigns doubts about fighting a younger man, finds an opportune moment to blame his ravenous belly for even considering it, and beseeches the suitors not to interfere. Antinous and the others shout their approval, and Telemachus promises that if the beggar is determined to fight Irus, the prince will vouch for his safety, as will Antinous and Eurymachus.

The beggar pulls his rags about his thighs, Athena fleshes out and magnifies his limbs, and the suitors gasp at his physique, saying, *"E tacha Iros Aïros"* (18.73; Iros will soon be unIros).[4] Hearing them, Irus trembles with fear and is forcibly dragged into the fight. Antinous, disgusted at Irus' behavior, scolds him for fearing an old man and threatens to send him to Echetus[5] should he lose. Antinous will use the same threat in *Od.* 21.307–309 against Odysseus, which ironically forecasts the grim end of one of his staunchest supporters, Melanthius (22.474–476).

Irus, terrified, is hauled into the ring as the beggar/Odysseus ponders whether to finish him off with a single blow or merely knock him to the ground with a light jab. Since the second option seems best for preserving his anonymity, he hits him below the ear, shattering the inner bones. As Irus falls to the ground, writhing in pain, the suitors die laughing (18.100; *gelōi ekthanon*). The suitors' laughter, an ironic comment on their own fate, points to their hubris in taking pleasure at others' pain. When Eurycleia later also rejoices on first seeing the suitors' slain corpses, Odysseus checks her glee, warning that it is profane to glory over slain men (22.411–412).

The suitors' blindness in refusing to recognize their illegitimacy is as tenuous as Irus' right to be the undisputed beggar of the *megaron*. Their lack of insight is effectively illustrated by their constant laughter mocking Irus' self-appointed stature. The fight between the two beggars, moreover, increases the tension that exists in the great hall, which leads the suitors and the household staff to behave in unexpected ways, puzzled by the uncommon behavior of a stranger who speaks and acts unlike any beggar to come before them. The beggars' fight also reaches Penelope, who, puzzled by the stranger's actions, is more curious than ever to question him regarding his identity.

The suitors, laughing (18.111), toast the beggar's win and wish him whatever his heart desires (18.112–113). He welcomes their words as an omen sealing their fate, since what he wants most is their quick demise. Antinous offers him the promised goat sausage, and Amphinomus presents two loaves of bread and toasts the beggar's health, wishing him prosperity. Amphinomus' sincerity moves the beggar/Odysseus, and he tries to repay the kindness with a warning that could save him from his doom. He starts by citing one of Homer's most beautiful passages (18.130–135)[6]—nothing is more helpless than humans, for as long as they prosper, they feel immune to misfortune, but when hard times befall them, they must steel their hearts and endure adversity. He accuses the suitors of disrespecting the queen and carving away at Odysseus' wealth, reiterating the same list of abuses of hospitality that Athena accused them of (courting Penelope [13.378] and wasting Odysseus' property [13.396, 428]), which Odysseus will refer to again in *Od.* 22.36–38 (ravaging his home and pursuing his wife). He warns Amphinomus to go home before he meets Odysseus face to face. Amphinomus, saddened by the beggar's words, returns to his seat visibly shaken by what he has heard. Puzzled by the beggar's identity, he realizes that his words are right and the suitors' actions wrong. However, he does not have the means to escape his fate, for Athena has marked him to die by Telemachus' spear (18.155–156). Amphinomus, dissatisfied with his lot, has given in to unrighteous ways and will pay; there is no escape from abusing Zeus's law.

The difference here between Odysseus' willingness to save Amphinomus for his kindness by sending him home before the suitors' slaughter and Athena's inflexibility is a comment on the severity of the gods. Humans are more flexible in response to emotions than are the unpliable gods.

Athena, in her mounting anger, scolds Odysseus for holding back (22.224–230), which leads to his and his supporters' barbarity against the twelve immoral maids and Melanthius (22.465–476).

II. Penelope among the Suitors, 158–303

Penelope, having heard of the beggar's fight with Irus, is aware that he is unlike other beggars. His words, his actions, and even his physique point to someone special—a prophet, a god in disguise, perhaps Odysseus. Athena, on the other hand, has her own plans for Penelope, of which Penelope is not yet aware. The goddess intends to have her appear before the suitors so that her beauty, her cleverness, and the suitors' lust for her will provide Odysseus with greater resolve to carry out Athena's will. The goddess is ready to use her as bait to catch the suitors. Perhaps Penelope herself realizes that she must put herself forth to test the positive signs around her. Laughing uncannily (18.163; *achreion d' egelassen* [without a need she laughed]; perhaps a nervous laugh), Penelope feels an impulse to appear before the suitors. Aware of the suitors' intentions toward her son, she must embrace her situation and act. Encouraged by Theoclymenus' and the beggar's prophecies, Penelope seizes the moment for action. She tells Eurynome she wants to appear before the suitors even though she hates them. Perhaps, as her uncharacteristic laugh indicates, she has plans to trick the suitors, reducing the threat to her son's life or even preparing the way for her husband's entrance should the omens and prophecies prove true. Eurynome wants her to beautify herself before making an appearance, but the queen refuses. Manifesting her loyalty to Odysseus, she claims that whatever beauty she once had died when her husband left for Troy. She will allow two maids (Autonoē and Hippodamia) to accompany her, as is proper, to lessen her embarrassment. Penelope will remain true to her role as a faithful wife, although Athena puts her own plan in motion. She raises the tension between the beggar/Odysseus and the suitors in order to bring matters to a head, and she graces the queen with beauty to captivate the suitors.

When Penelope descends to the *megaron* with her attendant maidens, Athena's plan takes effect. The suitors are bemused with passion, each one waiting for the privilege to lie with her. The queen scolds her son for permitting their guest's abuse, since she is to meet him in the evening. Although Telemachus does not fault his mother for her anger, he cannot stand alone against the suitors, and he must obey his father's orders not to act or reveal the beggar's identity. Pleased at the outcome of the fight, something the suitors did not expect, he appeals to Zeus, Athena, and Apollo for the suitors' defeat, adding to the prayers and forecasts that fill this book.

Eurymachus praises the queen's excellence, but she brusquely waves any compliments aside, responding that whatever excellence (18.251; *aretēn*) and beauty she possesses disappeared the day her husband left for Troy. Noble bearing can be hers again only if her husband returns to cultivate it (18.254; *amphipoleuoi* [take care of]). Her value as a woman and as a wife comes from the man who can bring out this excellence, one equally minded (*homophrosunē*). She then recalls Odysseus' parting words to marry whoever pleases her once Telemachus comes of age (18.269). There is no way of knowing whether Penelope received these instructions from her husband, or whether she is lying in order to explain to the suitors why she has suddenly decided to marry. Like-minded as she and Odysseus are, both being prone to cunning and trickiness, she now discloses that it is time for her to do as her husband ordered, even though she dreads a new marriage. However, she is mortified at how the suitors are going about their courtship; in past times, when suitors rivaled to win the hand of a noblewoman, they showered her with gifts instead of devouring her fortune. The beggar/Odysseus, standing nearby and listening to his wife's clever speech, is delighted that she can procure gifts from the suitors when her intentions were otherwise (18.283). The beggar/Odysseus assumes that Penelope has other intentions in sweet-talking the suitors for presents. What these intentions are, we are not told. Perhaps for the queen this is just another delaying tactic (like the weaving trick) used to stall until she interviews the stranger. Perhaps she realizes, given all the omens, the prophecies, and the stranger whose actions and physique are not those of an old man, that events at the palace must come to a crisis. Setting herself up as a decoy might produce results. Perhaps Odysseus imagines that Penelope suspects his identity and that her current flirtations are a signal to that effect. Earlier she ordered him to meet with her, and he tactfully ignored her request. Perhaps his boldness in disobeying her gave her further notice of his identity.

Antinous agrees that Penelope can have all the gifts the suitors are willing to give her, but not one of them will return to his estate until she selects a husband. Penelope receives the gifts they offer and returns to her chambers, but the presents do not aid her in selecting a husband. Instead they send a signal that she is ready for action should anyone be present to heed her. The beggar/Odysseus, who is present, recognizes she is prepared to take on the suitors and must find a way of making it known to her.

III. Odysseus in the Megaron, Part II, 304–428

Homer now returns to the end of part I, where the beggar/Odysseus was last seen with Amphinomus. Three braziers set against the *megaron*'s walls provide the suitors with light as evening approaches. The beggar asks the maids to leave the premises and attend to the queen, promising to remain in the hall himself to fuel the fires for the entire night if necessary, a brazenness that makes the maids burst into laughter. Melantho, one of the maids, scolds him, and Homer digresses to introduce her. She is the daughter of Dolius (and sister of the goatherd Melanthius) but was raised by Penelope, who treats her like a daughter. Now Eurymachus' lover, Melantho has little sympathy for Penelope and mocks and taunts the beggar. She accuses him of drunkenness for talking so boldly. She warns him to be heedful lest a better man than Irus chase him out of the palace. Eyeing her menacingly, the beggar/Odysseus threatens to report her to Telemachus, which sends the maids scurrying, disclosing the prince's growing authority and acceptance as master of the house. With the maids out of the way, the beggar takes his post looking after the braziers, exposing qualities that continue to bring him to Penelope's attention and increasing her estimation of him.

Athena, anxious to provoke the suitors, incites them to greater insolence. Eurymachus calls attention to the beggar's bald head and claims it is a gift from the gods to light their way (18.354). Ironically, the beggar will soon enlighten the suitors with his identity. Eurymachus taunts the beggar by offering him work but then states that, given his propensity for loafing, he feels it would be useless. His comments irritate the beggar/Odysseus, who defies him by stating that, in a contest of labor or combat, he would be victorious and threatening that should Odysseus return, the palace's wide gates would be too narrow for Eurymachus' escape. The suitors are completely baffled by the stranger's brassiness. Stunned at his boldness, Eurymachus explodes in anger. Unafraid, the beggar/Odysseus becomes unmanageable, and as his anger rises, he is in danger of revealing more of himself than he intends. It is Athena's plan to bring the situation to a fever pitch, enabling the slaughter that follows. In frustration, Eurymachus picks up a footstool and throws it at the beggar, but the stool misses him and hits the wine steward's hand. The other suitors, irritated at the commotion, break into an uproar, wishing the vagabond had never come to spoil their feasting. Telemachus berates them for their insolence. Taking charge, he politely asks them to leave, careful not to drive away anyone against his will. Aware of his father's presence, he is doing his best to empty the great hall in preparation for his father's onslaught. His tone, however, surprises the suitors, but Amphinomus once again intercedes as he did earlier in the *megaron* (18.119–123), calling on all in the service of the king's household not to abuse the stranger. Telemachus, he concurs, can look after the stranger, since the beggar is in his home, thus acknowledging the prince's right to his inheritance. Assenting to Amphinomus' words, the suitors drink, first tipping their cups to the gods.

Selected Bibliography: *Od.* 18

Ahl and Roisman, "*Odyssey,*" 215–228.

Byre, "Penelope."

Clarke, *Art*, 67–85.

Clay, "Homeric."

Hölscher, "Penelope."

Katz, *Penelope's*, 78–93, 115–120.

Lateiner, "Telemakhos'."

Levine, "*Odyssey* 18."

Levine, "Penelope's."

Reece, *Stranger's*, 165–188.

Said, *Homer*, 189–222.

Segal, "Phaeacians."

Steiner, Deborah, "Diverting."

Further commentary on *Od.* 18 in General Bibliography I.

Book 19

Od. 19, the epic's fourth-longest book,[7] is devoted to the long-awaited meeting of Odysseus and Penelope. Occupying 552 lines, the book's second section (Odysseus-Penelope meeting) is as long as or longer than sixteen of the *Odyssey*'s twenty-four books. *Od.* 19 lends itself to a two-part division, a short section in which the *megaron* is cleared of weapons and the long Odysseus-Penelope episode. The meeting itself falls into three subsections: Odysseus' lie to Penelope (II.B), framed by Penelope's interview (II.A) and its aftermath (II.C). The largest of the three subsections, the interview's aftermath, occupies over half of the entire Odysseus-Penelope meeting (355 lines) and is presented in three parts—Odysseus' bath, Odysseus' scar, and Penelope's dream.

I. The *megaron* cleared of weapons (9%)

II. Odysseus-Penelope meeting (91%)

A. The interview
B. Odysseus' lie to Penelope
C. Interview aftermath
  1. The bath, part I
  2. The scar
  3. The bath, part II
  4. The dream

I. The Megaron Cleared of Weapons, 1–52

The beggar/Odysseus is finally ready to reveal himself and his plan to his wife, but he intends to further stir the minds of the maids and Penelope (19.45), a process that began in *Od.* 17.

1. He asks his son again to remove the weapons from the walls of the *megaron* as he requested in 16.284–285, omitting the two lines from his earlier request that specified that Telemachus should leave behind a pair each of swords, spears, and shields (16.295–296).[8] Should the suitors inquire about the removal, Telemachus is to stress his desire to prevent smoke damage and accidents.[9]
2. He orders Telemachus to have Eurycleia lock the maids in their quarters until he can stow the weapons in the storeroom. Eurycleia is concerned about lighting Telemachus' way in the storeroom. Exhibiting his father's caution, he tells her the beggar will do it to earn his keep.

As father and son haul the weapons into the storeroom, Athena, unnoticed, lights their way with a golden lamp. Dazzled by its radiance, Telemachus blurts out that an Olympian must be present, but Odysseus hushes him, explaining that the gods work in mysterious ways. Judging from Telemachus' reaction, the prince sees only the light and not the goddess. The beggar/Odysseus does not acknowledge Athena's presence but assumes this surrealistic light comes from the gods, which designates him as the messenger of the justice to come. Later, in reciting the Cretan tale (for the third time) to Penelope, he assigns a pseudonym to his character, Aethon, that signifies a fire or a burning (from *aithomai/aithō* = to burn), thereby identifying himself as the one who brings the blazing fire. This image of Odysseus as light is reinforced when he enters the palace to stoke and keep the braziers glowing.

II. Odysseus-Penelope Meeting, 53–604

II.A. The Interview, 53–163. After Telemachus retires, the beggar/Odysseus remains in the hall, and Penelope descends from her upper chamber and takes a chair near the fireplace. Throughout her husband's absence Penelope sleeps above the *megaron* and not in the master bedroom on the first floor. Since the queen enters the *megaron* after Telemachus retires, the arms are already removed. Has Penelope noticed the walls are now empty of weapons? No mention is made either way. If one assumes Penelope notices the naked walls, she is then aware that something strange is happening, which becomes apparent when she questions the beggar. For the time being, she keeps what she sees to herself.

Before the interview, Melantho lashes out at the beggar for a second time (19.66–67; the first is at 18.320–336). She orders him to leave the hall, threatening to remove him by throwing a torch at him. The beggar adopts the persona of a charitable, wealthy man now in need himself and again underscores life's unpredictability (see 18.130–135), which in time will obliterate the looks that make Melantho desirable. The beggar cautions that if Odysseus does not return to punish her, Telemachus will make certain her behavior does not go unpunished, thus acknowledging Telemachus' authority in his absence. The queen, overhearing the beggar's warning, reprimands Melantho, who was aware of her mistress's invitation to probe the stranger regarding Odysseus.

Turning to Eurynome, Penelope asks for a chair to be placed opposite hers so that the interview may begin. Abandoning protocol, the queen implores the stranger to identify himself, his city, and his parents (19.105).

She is anxious, puzzled that he responded to Eumaeus' invitation by postponing the meeting until sundown (*alla se meinai anōgen es ēelion katadunta* [17.582]). The word *anōgen* can more accurately be translated as "to order (or command)," rather than Lattimore's "he tells." Surprised at this command, Penelope pondered his identity for a whole day, which now leads her to dispense with protocol and ask who he is. The beggar, however, cannot openly reveal himself, since Melantho is in attendance and possibly the maids who earlier revealed Penelope's weaving trick (19.154). Even if the maids are not present, Penelope's ladies-in-waiting are, for they never leave her side.

The beggar, in a simile, compares her stature and faultless fame to those of a king's daughter (19.109–114), the kind of king her husband was among the Ithacans (4.689–693, 20.209)—a god-fearing and just one under whom his people prospered. The beggar seems to indicate that Penelope is like the king in the simile—like-minded (*homophrosunē*). In other words, he is indicating she is like her husband, but how does the beggar know her husband so intimately to make such a comparison? He then urges her not to ask him who he is, for the memory of his past would cause him pain. Is Odysseus suggesting he cannot reveal too much because of the maids' presence? Penelope's response, also veiled, references his compliment and reveals the urgency of her present situation. Her former self, along with her beauty and strength, was ruined the day her husband left for Troy. She can only regain that beauty and status if he returns. In her grief, she now spins schemes to put off all those noblemen seeking to marry her against her will. They not only wear her down but are also spoiling her house. Suppliants, strangers, and beggars no longer interest her, since she no longer hopes for Odysseus' return. She is being forced into a marriage she detests, while her heart melts for her missing husband. Penelope's remarks are more intimate than a queen should be with a stranger, and they reveal an urgency for advice and information. If by chance the beggar is Odysseus, she must be convinced of his identity. She explains the weaving trick she played for three years, until her maids reported her to the suitors and exhausted her delays. She can no longer escape them, for she is pressured into a union not only by them but also by her parents and her son. Odysseus must identify himself.

II.B. Odysseus' Lie to Penelope, 164–248. The beggar/Odysseus is ready to reveal himself, but not in the presence of others. He will surreptitiously signal his identity through his Cretan lie (using it for the fourth time). He begins by saying *ō gunai aidoiē Laertiadeō Oduséos* (revered wife of Odysseus), a phrase he uses four times (19.165, 262, 336, and 583) and the first two words of which Penelope claims he used to address her on his departure for Troy (18.259; *ō gunai* [wife]). Is his insistence on these words yet another signal? The beggar now decides to answer the question he avoided earlier. Since she will not stop asking for his identity, he will respond, but the answer will cause him great anguish and sorrow; it will bring back a flood of memories for a wanderer who endured hardships over many years (is he not talking about himself?). His homeland is Crete (was she expecting to hear Ithaca?). His lie will provide what she seeks, if she listens closely. After all, Odysseus and Penelope have their own private way of communicating, as Penelope later tells Telemachus in *Od.* 23.109–110.

He describes Crete and the city of Knossos and identifies the legendary king Minos as the father of his father, Deucalion, who raised two sons, Idomeneus, who led eighty ships to Troy (*Il.* 2.645–652), and the younger, Aethon, the name the beggar assigns himself. Aethon encounters Odysseus when the latter is swept off course at the cape of Malea on his way to Troy and lands on Crete, seeking the house of his hereditary friend Idomeneus, only to discover that the king left for Troy eleven days earlier. Aethon offers Odysseus hospitality, inviting him to his own home while he collects food from the public for his companions. In the lying tale, Odysseus and his crew remain with Aethon for twelve days until the north wind abates. Homer intercedes to praise the beggar/Odysseus for telling his lies like truths (*Od.* 19.203).

The beggar's tone moves Penelope, who begins to weep. In a simile (19.205–209), the narrator compares melting snow to Penelope's tears as she weeps for her husband, who is sitting by her side. The phrase "her husband sitting by her side," a fact known to the reader, acts as a premonition for the reserved queen, whose tensions are slackening as thoughts of her husband flood her memory. But it is not just the memory of Odysseus that causes her cheeks to stream with tears; she is allowing herself to relax, sensing that perhaps the waiting and the plotting are over. She indicated earlier that she was out of ideas. Seeing her in distress, the beggar/Odysseus pities her but tries not to show any emotion. Penelope composes herself, anxious to make sure that what she feels is not false. She decides to quiz him to make sure that the beggar did in fact host her husband and the men in his company. She poses a question that would be impossible to answer for someone who met her husband for the first time twenty years earlier and only spent twelve days with him. She wants a description, first, of the clothes he was wearing; second, of what he looked like; and third, of his companions. The beggar is expected not only to remember the clothing Odysseus wore two decades earlier, an unrealistic expectation, but also to recall his impressions of Odysseus' companions, with whom he had little intercourse, since he provided for them by collecting provisions from the public (19.196–197) but did not host them in his home. Nevertheless, the beggar/Aethon does not decline. First, he makes clear to Penelope the difficulty of recalling such details about someone he met so long ago. In other words, he is willing to respond to an untenable question, beginning by acknowledging that he did not know where the clothes came from or who gave them to him (perhaps for the benefit of those in attendance?) but will try to describe them. He, of course, is aware he is describing the clothes Penelope herself gave Odysseus before leaving for Troy, as she informs him at the end of his description (19.255).

The beggar/Aethon begins a description of Odysseus with a meticulousness that can only be a clue to his identity. He was wearing a purple fleecy cloak with double folds (19.225–226); the beggar notes not only the color of the mantle but also its double folds, and more precisely, he states that the brooch with double clasps that held it together was made of gold (19.226–227). In case such minuteness is not enough to convince her that he is the owner of the mantle, he provides more details: the brooch was a work of art on which was etched the image of a hound with a fawn struggling in its paws. The hound strangles the fawn as it tries to escape, a significant image that serves as yet another clue of what is to come and recalls the fawn earlier that ventures with her young into the lion's den (4.335-340). Odysseus' tunic (the garment worn inside the mantle) was sheer and soft like the skin of a dried onion (19.233–234). And the beggar/Aethon throws in for good measure that many women admired it (19.235), an irrelevant comment for a beggar to make to a queen. Is this a light-hearted effort to signal his true identity, and an attempt to flatter himself as a man admired for his looks? He tells Penelope that after offering Odysseus gifts (a sword, a double purple cloak, and a tunic [19.241–242]), he personally saw him off. If what he recounts is not sufficient to arouse Penelope's suspicions, he identifies Odysseus' valet, whose name he suddenly remembers and whom Penelope is likely to have known. The beggar recalls he was a man a little older than Odysseus, he was black, he had round shoulders and wooly hair, he was Odysseus' favorite from among his companions, and he was called Eurybates. Eurybates is the herald Odysseus used to communicate with his family and associates, a postman-messenger known to Penelope. But how does the beggar remember this man's name after twenty years? How does he know Odysseus prized him above all others? These details are too intimate for a stranger who knew Odysseus for only twelve days. Penelope, recognizing the signs the beggar is offering, has the urge to weep for a second time (19.250).

II.C. Interview Aftermath, 249–604. Penelope now asks the beggar, whom she earlier pitied, to remain in the palace as her respected friend. Admitting she herself gave Odysseus the clothes described and clasped the brooch on him herself, she openly asserts he will never again return to Ithaca.

Either she speaks for the maids' benefit, not to arouse their suspicions, or she is seeking further proof of the beggar's identity. Whatever conclusion Penelope reaches will mean life or death for her husband and an uncertain outcome for herself and her son. If the beggar is Odysseus, she must find out how he can dispatch the suitors alone. If, on the other hand, he is not Odysseus, she must marry one of the suitors to save her son's inheritance.

The beggar reassures her of her husband's homecoming and praises Odysseus as a husband any woman would desire. He cannot blame her for weeping for a man who was like the immortals. Is this another attempt at humor, or is Odysseus telling his wife that he is still the same man who left for Troy? He reaffirms that Odysseus' coming home is a certainty. How can the beggar be certain of Odysseus' homecoming, which he admits is hearsay in order to remain in character as a stranger? However, the forcefulness of his prediction (19.269) insinuates that it is not just hearsay. Odysseus is near at hand (19.271), he is still alive (19.272), and he is returning with many rich treasures (19.272).

The beggar/Odysseus then narrates Odysseus' wanderings from the point he left Thrinacia: the loss of his companions, being cast ashore in Scheria, and the Phaeacians' willingness to deliver him home. Diplomatically, he omits the Calypso episode, sparing his wife the details of his amorous seven-year sojourn with the goddess. The hero's homecoming could have been earlier, but he did not want to return empty-handed, a positive reason for his delay and praise for his uniqueness. To support his familiarity with Odysseus' personality and to prove his sincerity, the beggar introduces another character to his lie: Pheidon, king of the Thesprotians, who told him about Odysseus. By introducing Pheidon, the beggar retains his disguise and enhances his standing as an exceptional stranger, one hosted by a king who swore to him that the ship and crew were ready to carry Odysseus home. Why does Pheidon trust the beggar (Aethon) with information concerning another guest? Perhaps the event is made so outlandish that Penelope will see through it, but the maids will not. The beggar narrates how he was shipped off by the Thesprotian king on a boat heading for Dulichion, but before his departure, Pheidon displayed for him the treasure Odysseus amassed, large enough to feed a succession of heirs to the tenth generation. Odysseus was away in Dodona, the site of Zeus's oracle in Thesprotia (present-day Epirus), to consult the oracle regarding whether to return to Ithaca openly or in disguise. The beggar/Aethon is willing to swear that Odysseus is returning safely with a great deal of treasure; he is close at hand; he is not far from his country. He swears all he says will occur exactly as he reports. Odysseus will arrive within this very year.

The beggar/Odysseus swore the same assurances to Eumaeus (using the identical lines in 14.158–161 and 14.229–230); the prophet Theoclymenus swore before Penelope (17.155–157) that he told the truth, holding nothing back: Odysseus was already in Ithaca. Oaths in Homer are sacred and not to be taken lightly. By the time the beggar meets Penelope, Eumaeus has acknowledged the stranger's special qualities and might even suspect his identity. Penelope has now heard the same oath from a prophet and from the stranger, who provides her with multiple signs of his identity. The queen's immediate sensation is elation. If what the beggar says is true, he will have her undying gratitude (*philotēta*) and many gifts to go with it. Since the word *philotēs* can mean "love," "friendship," or "affection," one wonders how Penelope is using the term. Does she mean that the stranger's predictions endear him in her affections and cause her feeling for him to grow from sympathy to respect and finally to love? Harboring such thoughts, the queen catches herself and denies Odysseus will ever return. In the joy of the moment, she has forgotten the presence of the maids and now for their sake denies Odysseus will ever return.

II.C.1. The Bath, Part I, 317–391 Penelope wants the beggar to remain in the palace and instructs the maids to wash his feet (*aponipsate*) and prepare a bed for him. On the following day (bathed again, anointed, and freshly dressed), he is to dine with Telemachus. Why such special consideration for a beggar? To justify her special treatment of the vagabond, she attributes her actions to good manners, a course of action any intelligent person would take, which summarizes the significance of *kleos*. Life is short. It is better to perform acts of kindness, which travelers bring to the attention of many people to admire, than to perform acts of cruelty, which bring one mockery in life and curses in death.

The beggar/Odysseus refuses her offer of blankets and costly bedsheets, since he did without them over his many years of wandering. Nor is he interested in footbaths unless some aged and virtuous woman is present to carry out such a task. Odysseus and Penelope could be secretly communicating with each other while keeping the maids from realizing what is taking place. If the beggar is her husband, Penelope wants him in the palace to advise her how to handle the suitors. Odysseus, in turn, wants his wife to recognize him. His rejection of the footbath signals what needs to be done to throw off the maids. Once he states his reservations about being touched, he can safely accept an older woman to wash his feet. He knows three women who, if alive and in service, will recognize him: Eurycleia, who raised him; Eurynome, Penelope's nurse and housekeeper; and Actoris, Penelope's maid in charge of the couple's bedroom. Penelope catches the signal. She does have a sensible old woman who brought up her husband. She is now weak but strong enough to wash his feet. Of the two women still in her service, Eurynome and Eurycleia, Penelope chooses Odysseus' nurse, the one most likely to recognize his scar. She thus asks her to wash the feet of one who by now would bear resemblance to Odysseus (19.358–359). Is Penelope comparing the stranger to her husband intentionally for Eurycleia, or is she voicing what she is thinking without realizing it? In comparing the beggar to Odysseus, Penelope insinuates that the stranger could be Odysseus, and Eurycleia recalls her absent master as if addressing him:

> How helpless I am to help you, my child. Surely Zeus hated you
> beyond all other men.
> (19.363–364)

Sitting before the beggar ready to wash his feet, the nursemaid imagines Odysseus being mocked in his wanderings as the maids and suitors mock the beggar, and she believes that Penelope asked her to wash his feet instead of them in order to avoid this abuse. As Eurycleia nears the beggar, she marvels how alike the stranger's feet, voice, and appearance are to Odysseus'. The beggar, instead of refuting her, agrees that others have made the same observation and comments on her perceptiveness. Is this yet another signal for Penelope, who is sitting nearby? The beggar, sitting near the fire, turns away from her and the maids present, afraid that Eurycleia will immediately notice his scar and disclose his identity. His concern is not that she will recognize him, for in asking her to wash his feet, he expects both her and Penelope to have proof of his identity. Rather, he is fearful that once Eurycleia sees the scar, she will cry out and expose him in front of the maids; at this juncture the scene is frozen. Between the split second the maid spots the scar and the moment she drops the pan of water, seventy-five lines intervene (19.392–466) to describe the scar's origins.

II.C.2 The Scar, 392–466 As previously noted, Homer's digressions provide background information on objects that play a major role in the narrative. The scar is the undisputable sign that the beggar is Odysseus, as the bow, whose genesis is described in *Od.* 21,[10] is the instrument for the suitors' demise. Second, the digression provides suspense by freezing the action at a crucial moment. What will Eurycleia do now that she has noticed the scar? Will Odysseus' identity be discovered by the maids present, thus foiling his plans? What will Penelope do if Eurycleia cries out? How will the narrative be returned to its original course? Third, the digression provides further information concerning the hero's background and greater insight into his character—his first heroic act, the origins of his name, and his fearless determination. The boar hunt is not only a glimpse of Odysseus as a child but also a rite of passage, Odysseus' entrance into the heroic world. It is his *Telemachia*, a look at the hero on the verge of entering manhood.

The structure of the scar episode is a story within a story—Eurycleia's recollection of the incident. Eurycleia asks Autolycus,[11] Odysseus' maternal grandfather, to name his new grandson when he visits the child in Ithaca. It is not clear why the nursemaid is given this responsibility rather than the parents. However, since the nurse is narrating this incident, her involvement speaks to the intimacy between them. Of those present in the palace, Eurycleia would be the obvious choice to notice the by-now-fading scar. Autolycus, who in his travels caused pain (407; *odyssamenos*) for many people, proposed the name Odysseus, the son of pain, for his grandson and invited the newborn to visit him in Parnassus and receive gifts when full-grown. Coming of age, Odysseus is warmly received by his grandparents in Parnassus and is invited to a boar hunt by his grandfather and uncles. Running ahead during the hunt, he attacks a great boar whose tusk rips open his knee. Although wounded, young Odysseus nevertheless kills the boar and is showered with gifts by his grandfather and uncles for his initiation into manhood. He returns to his parents to proudly recount his hunting adventure and display his wound.

II.C.3. The Bath, Part II, 467–507 The narrative now returns to the instant Eurycleia notices the scar. Suddenly, she drops the beggar's foot into the washbasin (which left her hands some seventy-five lines earlier), tipping it over with a clang and spilling the water across the floor. Her eyes full of tears, Eurycleia reaches for the beggar's beard to whisper that she was not sure it was he until she touched his leg, indicating she suspected the beggar before she started to wash his feet. Her suspicion verified, she turns to get Penelope's attention. Athena, however, has Penelope turn her head aside (19.479), indicating ignorance on her part, a highly unlikely scenario, since she is sitting close by. More likely, Penelope, in her wisdom, feigns ignorance so as not to arouse suspicion. She thereby dismisses the overturning of the washbasin and avoids Eurycleia's eyes. Odysseus, fearful Eurycleia might scream and expose him, stifles her and, pulling her close, warns her not to betray him (19.482). He begs her to remain silent, threatening death if she does not. Eurycleia swears silence and even volunteers to name the unfaithful maids once Odysseus kills the suitors, an offer he refuses, since he intends to test the allegiance of his staff, as he indicated earlier to his son. He advises Eurycleia to put her trust in the gods and keep what she saw to herself. Later, Odysseus will, nonetheless, change his mind and ask Eurycleia to identify the innocent and the guilty (22.417–418).

Eurycleia leaves to fetch another basin, intending to finish washing Odysseus' feet. In the meantime, he draws his chair closer to the fire to keep warm, keeping his scar hidden under his rags. Penelope resumes her interview and seems to be unaware of what transpired. If she suspects that he is Odysseus, she wants to know how he intends to do away with the suitors. Failure to address a plan of action spells disaster for her, Telemachus, and him. Can he take on the suitors alone? Will she have to take a chance and commit to marriage? If she pledges to a marriage, can Odysseus prevent it? She seeks answers to these concerns and a way to communicate them to her husband without the maids' and suitors' knowledge. As late as it is, these thoughts so trouble Penelope that she wants to continue her conversation with the beggar a little longer.

II.C.4. The Dream, 508–604 Penelope is uneasy, and although it is time for bed, she needs to unburden herself, almost like a patient to her therapist. She is trying to authenticate the stranger's identity as Odysseus and at the same time entreat him for guidance on how to proceed if he is her husband. She presents her restlessness in a simile that compares her to Pandareus' daughter mourning her son, Itylos, whom she killed in a moment of madness (19.518–524).[12] The simile refers to an unnamed wife of Zethos who turns into a nightingale after killing her son. Homer does not provide further information on these characters, although tradition says that Zethos' wife killed her son by mistake, intending out of jealousy to kill a son of her sister-in-law, Niobe, who bore fourteen children to her one. The gods took pity on her grief and changed her into a nightingale, which now sings nightly for her loss. Penelope's comparison to Zethos' wife, then, refers not only to her grief in not knowing what action to take but also to the danger of having her son killed should she make the wrong decision. She can either remain at the palace, protect her son's property, remain faithful to Odysseus, and respect the peoples' wishes or marry one of the suitors. She is conflicted because Telemachus, fretting over his property, prefers she now leave the palace. If she marries against her will and that of the people, she fears for her son and jeopardizes her reputation as a faithful wife. The intimate details she shares with the beggar demonstrate that Penelope has taken him completely into her confidence, and she invites him to interpret a recent dream and listen to it[13] (19.535; *all' age moi ton oneiron hypokrinai kai akouson*). Penelope is asking for confirmation of what she believes to be her husband's intention—to kill the suitors. But did she actually have this dream, or is she making it up to allay her fears of what might happen?

In her dream, she sees twenty geese, which she loves to watch feeding from a water trough. A huge eagle swoops down and kills them, and Penelope weeps, sorrowing for her geese. The eagle in her dream returns, identifying the geese as the suitors and the eagle as her husband, already home and ready to destroy them. The eagle encourages her not to be afraid, for the dream is a vision that will come true, and Penelope wakes to discover the geese alive. The beggar assures her there is no other meaning for the dream: Odysseus will bring ruin to all the suitors, the identical foreboding voiced by Helen in *Od.* 15.174–178. The dream as related by Penelope seems self-explanatory since the eagle is identified as Odysseus and the geese as the suitors. Why then does she ask for an explanation? If Penelope is asking for assurance that her interpretation is correct, she is uneasy at having the suitors killed. Perhaps emotionally she is attached to her "geese" and likes having them around "feeding" after so many years. If, on the other hand, the beggar is Odysseus, she fears for his life, for it is not possible for one man to kill so many suitors. She is asking for verification, for dreams come through two gates. Dreams that come through the ivory gate are full of trickery and turn out to be false, while dreams that pass through the horn gate come true.[14] She does not believe her dream came through the horn gate, but both she and Telemachus wish it did. Although she prefers to avoid killing if possible, she is conflicted. If the suitors are ungoverned, they remain a threat to her son and the beggar, should he be Odysseus. Perhaps paradoxically she is not fully prepared for what she believes is about to happen. The beggar assures her that her interpretation is correct; Odysseus will kill the suitors.

Accepting the beggar's prediction of the suitors' end, Penelope must now uncover how Odysseus intends to accomplish the task. Recollecting how he often shot an arrow through twelve axes lined up in an unbroken row, she proposes such a contest to determine who her new husband will be. After all, only Odysseus was skilled in accomplishing such a feat. If the beggar is Odysseus, he will be the only one able to shoot an arrow through the twelve axes. On the following day, during the feast of Apollo, she will announce that whoever succeeds with Odysseus' bow will win her hand in marriage. That the contest will take place on Apollo's holiday is significant, since earlier, in *Od.* 17.497, when Antinous strikes the beggar with a footstool, Penelope prays that the famed archer Apollo strike the striker himself.

The beggar, delighted at her suggestion to confront the suitors, urges her not to delay the contest. He is in agreement that the suitors will fumble with the bow and will not be able to shoot it before Odysseus arrives. This is a plan Odysseus himself would have recommended, but he had to wait for his wife to propose it in order to protect his cover. Penelope will agonize over her suggestion in the books to come, uncertain how such a contest can succeed. She does not want to cause her family's ruin should Odysseus fail to destroy the suitors single-handedly. For now, she would like the beggar to entertain her all night long but needs sleep. She invites him to remain in the palace—either he can sleep on the floor or the maids will make a bed for him—and she leaves for her chambers, accompanied by her attendants, proof that the maids were present during her interview. Weeping at her state of confusion, she is yet unsure of the consequences of her proposal.

Selected Bibliography: *Od.* 19

Ahl and Roisman, "*Odyssey*," 215–228, 229–238.

Amory, "Gates."

Amory, "Reunion."

Anhalt, "Matter."

Atchity, *Critical*, 211–222.

Athanassakis, "Eagle."

Auerbach, "Odysseus'."

Bierl, "'Turn On.'"

Clarke, *Art*, 67–85.

Clayton, *Penelopean*, 53–82.

Combellack, "Wise."

De Jong, "Eurykleia."

DeSmidt, "Horn."

Emlyn-Jones, "Reunion."

Finley, John H., Jr., *Homer's*, 185–208.

Floyd, "Linguistic."

Goff, "Sign."

Haller, "Gates."

Harsh, "Penelope."

Havelock, "Intimate."

Heitman, *Taking*, 63–84.

Highbarger, *Gates*.

Katz, *Penelope's*, 93–113, 115–120, 128–145.

Köhnken, "Odysseus'."

Levaniouk, "Aithon."

Levaniouk, *Eve of Festival*.

Levaniouk, "Penelope and the Pandareids."

Louden, *Homer's*, 30–56.
Lowenstam, "Shroud."
McKay, "Studies."
Morrison, "Similes."
Myrsiades, "Early Recognition."
Pratt, "*Odyssey*."
Rankin, "Penelope's."
Reece, "Penelope's."
Reece, *Stranger's*, 165–188.
Richardson, Scott, "Case."
Rozokoki, "Penelope's."
Russo, "Interview."
Rutherford, *Homer* (1996).
Said, *Homer*, 189–222.
Segal, "Phaeacians."
Stewart, *Disguised*, 100–145.
Yamagata, "Penelope."
Vlahos, "Homer's *Odyssey*" (2009).
Vlahos, "Homer's *Odyssey*" (2011).
Further commentary on *Od.* 19 in General Bibliography I.

Book 20

Od. 20, full of omens and strange laughter, opens on the night of the thirty-ninth day. After the first ninety lines, the fortieth day dawns, a day that lasts until *Od.* 23.343 (De Jong, *Narratological*, 483). The book lends itself to the common tripartite division; each of the three sections is almost of equal size.

I. Odysseus and Penelope's restlessness (31%)
II. Apollo's feast day preparations (30%)
III. Apollo's holiday (39%)

I. Odysseus and Penelope's Restlessness, 1–121

Having refused Penelope's offer of a bed, the beggar lies awake on an ox hide in the entrance hall, plotting the suitors' death, while the maids skulk out of the palace to join their lovers. Angered at the sight, Odysseus is compared to a bitch defending her puppies from strangers. As the mother dog, he is anxious to safeguard his property (the maids) from intruders (the suitors), but at the same time it is the corrupt maids who are the interlopers from whom his moral values need refuge. He ponders whether to rush and kill them or allow them to lie with their lovers for the last time. He is furious not only at the maids' immoral behavior but also at the suitors who appropriate his wealth. Their unfaithfulness to a master on whose goodwill their livelihood depends is an affront to his person. To appease his anger, he recalls the Cyclops' cave and the loss of six companions before his *mētis* saved the others. In the same way, he will use his *mētis* while posing as a beggar, a Nobody, to trick the suitors at the bow contest.

Ensnared by the suitors in his own palace just as Polyphemus trapped him in the cave, he is at the same time both the Cyclops who bars his own doors to prevent the companions' (the suitors') escape and the Nobody who vanquishes the giant (the suitors) to escape his control. The outcome is dependent on the Ithacans, who will either support him or disregard him as the Cyclopes ignored Polyphemus. Tossing and turning in bed, he is compared to a cook and a sausage (20.25–27). Like the cook, he is impatient, constantly turning the sausage to roast it, thus delaying the eating of it; like a sausage, he squirms to and fro while his blood sizzles and strains hard to broil. How can one man face a mob? At that instant Athena, in the shape of a woman, appears, or perhaps it is his common sense or his intelligence that speaks to him, reminding him he is in his own house in the presence of the wife and the son he longed for. Odysseus should be thankful for what he has rather than regretting what he lacks. Although he agrees, he is still haunted by the suitors, for even if he defeats them, how will he escape their avengers? Athena, agitated by his faithlessness in doubting his ability under her watchful eye, reprimands him for his stubbornness. Most humans would trust even weaker mortal companions, but he has a goddess at his side who watches over him. Even if he were ambushed by fifty battalions of mortals hoping to kill him, he would escape. Having rationalized away the worries that plague him and having shifted his focus to the challenges that he must face on the following day, he falls asleep.

Meanwhile, Penelope wakes up crying and praying to Artemis for death. She too is preoccupied and confused by all that has transpired. She is now committed to marry one of the suitors, although she would rather die than have to please a lesser man. She dreams of her husband as she remembers him before Troy. However, her thoughts are less on the beggar as her husband and more on her solution (the bow contest): "I felt that it wasn't a dream but the truth at last" (90; my translation).[15] Odysseus, conscious of her crying, felt "she had already recognized him and was standing by his head" (93–94; my translation).[16]

What concerns Penelope is not whether Odysseus has come back but whether the Odysseus she knew is the same man who has returned. She prays to Artemis to put an end to her misery or to be carried away by storm winds like the daughters of Pandareus (19.518–523).[17] Penelope wants to be snatched away or shot by Artemis' arrows, which bring disease or sudden death to girls and women, to avoid a hateful marriage. The motivations for her death wish are twofold. First, it will prevent union with any of the suitors she detests and yet is reluctant to see killed. Second, it will spare her from the uncertainty of uniting with an Odysseus who might no longer be the same man she remembers. In an ironic twist, instead of Artemis' arrows ending Penelope's life, it is the arrows of Apollo, the archer god and brother of Artemis (both associated with the bow and arrow), that will end the suitors' lives.

Dreaming that his wife knows his identity, Odysseus is still uncertain of success. Doubtful of how he will carry out the suitors' slaughter, he prays to Zeus for further guidance. Although Athena promised him assistance and success, he needs to know whether the other gods feel the same way. He asks Zeus for two omens, an external one and an internal one, to secure his victory; Zeus grants both requests. First, he thunders from a cloudless sky, the external omen; then, from inside the house, an internal omen comes from a frail woman grinding grain. Trying to complete her quota for the day, she hears thunder from a clear sky, a sign of something to come. In her distress, she prays aloud to Zeus for relief, asking for the suitors' final feast in Odysseus' palace and incriminating them for her broken knees and heart-sore labor. Hearing her prayer, Odysseus rejoices at Zeus's positive signs.

II. Apollo's Feast Day Preparations, 122–239

In the morning, the scene shifts to preparations for the day's feast. Telemachus, knowing the beggar to be his father and displaying his newfound authority, questions his mother's treatment of their guest. Accusing his mother of acting on whims, he asks Eurycleia whether she neglected him. Eurycleia defends Penelope, calling her blameless; she states that Penelope even offered the beggar a cot, but he refused it. Telemachus' distrust of his mother's judgment at this point could be due to several reasons. He is concerned that his father be treated well after watching the abuse he received from the suitors and the maids. His comment that his mother favors the wrong man over the better one could stem from his grandfather's intention to marry her to Eurymachus, who wants to kill Telemachus (15.16–17), rather than Amphinomus, whose good sense pleased her more than the others (16.397–398). Perhaps as he is standing in for his father while he is incognito, the prince feels accountable for whatever transpires on his watch. Whatever his reasons, his control is demonstrated not only in his interest in the beggar's welfare but also in the way he marches off to the meeting grounds with spear in hand, followed by a pair of hounds. Early in the *Odyssey*, he is reluctant to face the Ithacans but, coaxed by Athena, he meets them in full regalia (2.10–11). Once back from his journey, he again goes before the assembly in his royal trappings (17.61–62), but this time in control of his authority. Now, for a third time, spear in hand and accompanied by a pair of dogs (20.144–146), he meets the assembly self-confident and as an equal.

With preparations for Apollo's festival under way, Eumaeus enters the palace with hogs for the suitors' feast. He initiates the first of three encounters the beggar/Odysseus has with each of his three herdsmen, which expose the state of deterioration in the palace and reveal the herdsmen's loyalty to their master. Eumaeus shows genuine concern for the beggar, whom he addresses as "friend," and inquires whether he is still abused or treated with respect. Although earlier the swineherd was adamant that his master would not return, he now prays with Philoetius for Odysseus' speedy homecoming (20.238–239). The beggar/Odysseus' second confrontation is with Melanthius the goatherd, who approaches with the pick of his flock for the suitors' pleasure. He addresses the beggar with cutting insults, threatening him with violence and demanding to know why he is still around and not begging elsewhere. He ends his tirade by threatening the beggar with a beating. The beggar/Odysseus acknowledges the herdsman's insolence but remains calm. His third and longest engagement is with Philoetius the loyal oxherd, who appears with his own offering—a heifer and some fat goats. Approaching Eumaeus to inquire after the beggar, Philoetius immediately shows compassion for the unlucky stranger who has a kingly look and the bearing of a lord. Unlike the negative Melanthius, who disregards the beggar's features, the more positive Philoetius sees in the beggar a man of nobility and greets him with respect. He then summarizes Homer's refrain on the unpredictability of life echoed elsewhere in the *Odyssey* (see 18.130–135): Zeus, the father of humanity, is destructive, for once he creates humans, he no longer takes pity on their pain but rather brings them to misfortune and suffering (20.201–203). The positive Eumaeus and Philoetius accept life's sudden reversals and look beyond appearances to the beggar's true attributes, while the negative and selfish Melanthius ignores the inner man.

Greeting the beggar, Philoetius senses[18] the presence of his master, who, if alive, must be wandering like the beggar, but if he is dead, Philoetius is grateful to have served him. Philoetius even considered moving the cattle elsewhere to prevent the suitors' wasting his master's fortune, but since Telemachus is still alive, such an action would be traitorous. Although he finds life unendurable, he prays his master return to scatter the suitors. Realizing the depth of the oxherd's loyalty to him, the beggar/Odysseus swears an oath (as he swore to Eumaeus in 14.158–161): Odysseus will return while the herdsmen are in the palace and they will watch him kill the suitors (20.233–234). The force with which the beggar stresses the validity of his claim[19] wins the two herdsmen's support and almost exposes his identity.

III. Apollo's Holiday, 240–349

The scene crosscuts to the suitors planning Telemachus' death. Antinous tried to convince the suitors to execute the prince's murder as early as 16.371–372, but Amphinomus delayed it in order to seek Zeus's approval (16.403). Now the suitors once again want Telemachus dead, but as they gather to consider how to go about it, Zeus sends a negative sign: an eagle carrying a pigeon flying on their left (20.242–243). Amphinomus warns the murder of Telemachus will fail and advises abandoning their plan, to which all agree. Amphinomus' interpretation of the omen reflects his own state of mind, since he expressed reluctance to kill one of royal blood from the beginning (16.401–402).

The suitors enter the *megaron* and begin butchering the animals brought earlier for their feast by the three herdsmen. However, at no time during these procedures do the suitors sacrifice to the gods as is customary. Such neglect on Apollo's holiday is further indication that their irreverence merits punishment. Telemachus, impatient to deal with the suitors, sits the beggar in front of a small table[20] and, in earshot of all those present, addresses him, promising him protection against abuse. Taking control of the *megaron*, he announces to all that they are not dining in a public place but rather in the house of Odysseus. Aggressively, he warns them to hold back their insults and reproaches them lest they quarrel and come to blows. Astonished by the prince's boldness, the suitors bite their lips. Nowhere else in the *Odyssey* has Telemachus shown such nerve (bolstered by his father's presence) or been presented so courageously. In a series of exchanges initiated by those gathered in the *megaron*,[21] Antinous is first to mockingly address the suitors. Since Zeus prevented them from dispatching Telemachus, they will bear his abuse and threats. It is apparent that the suitors still want Telemachus out of the way and are prepared to acknowledge their murderous intentions openly, but the prince ignores them, waiting for his father's signal.

The scene shifts briefly to the festivities outside the palace, where heralds drive a hundred animals through the town for Apollo's sacrifice. While the suitors feast inside during Apollo's holiday, the local residents outside sacrifice a hecatomb in his honor. Recalling Odysseus' companions in Thrinacia (*Od.* 12) who disregard Helius' decree and suffer Zeus's wrath, the suitors inside the palace neglect the god; no one among them burns thighbones or tips wine cups in his praise. The suitors turn a public festival in honor of Apollo into a private one honoring themselves.

Athena, intent on arousing Odysseus' bitterness, does not altogether let the suitors refrain from insults and abuse. The first insults come from Ctesippus of Samē, a man of great wealth who feels confident courting Penelope. Ironically, he points out that it is impolite to offer the beggar a portion smaller than their own and thus slight Telemachus' guest. He offers the beggar a guest gift that he can in turn offer "to the old bath-woman" (20.297; my translation)[22] who washed his feet or to anyone else. Why does Ctesippus mention Eurycleia (the bath-woman)? Has one of the maids reported the footbath to him? There are few secrets in the palace with the ever-present maids fraternizing with the suitors. Ctesippus' gift is an ox hoof, the third missile thrown by the suitors. The beggar/Odysseus dodges as the hoof hits the wall, and he clenches his fist and smiles a very scornful smile (20.302), the first of three smiles in these final books (also at 22.371

and 23.111), in each case to show cognition. His cynical smile (also translatable as malicious, cruel, or sardonic) signals that he is not about to forget the incident. In each successive case, the thrown projectile has become less effective, an indication of the suitors' diminishing power. Antinous' throw (a footstool) hits him in the right shoulder near the base of his back (17.462–463). Eurymachus' throw (a footstool) misses him and hits the cupbearer (18.394–396). By the time of Ctesippus' throw (20.299–303), the suitors' effectiveness has greatly decreased.

The prince again demonstrates his mettle when he scolds Ctesippus for his assault on the beggar. He considers it good luck that the suitor failed to hit the stranger. Had he not missed, Telemachus would have thrust his spear through his belly and, instead of looking forward to a wedding, his father would be attending his funeral. Turning to the suitors, he warns them to maintain a low profile in his home and not display any rudeness. He warns that being no longer an infant, he is aware of the offenses taking place, offenses he must bear, since one man cannot fight so many single-handedly. He then gives the suitors an ultimatum: either murder him or put an end to their shameful crimes. He would rather be dead than be privy to such outrages—guests treated to blows and men molesting the maids. Telemachus' unexpected ascendancy, acquired since his return and reunion with his father (16.188), again dumbfounds the suitors, for all fall silent.

The suitor Agelaus awakens to the fact that the prince must now be taken seriously and asks that no one get angry or argue with him, for what he said was fair. He asks the suitors to refrain from harming the stranger or anyone else in the palace and offers some friendly advice. No one can blame Telemachus and Penelope for holding off the suitors as long as there are signs of Odysseus' return. But since it is clear he will not return, Telemachus should coax his mother to wed whomever she desires so he can enjoy his father's estate in peace. Agelaus' advice is an attempt to enable the suitors' marriage to Penelope without the interference of the prince, who has shown himself to be a bigger stumbling block to their plans than anticipated. At the same time, his words expose the suitors' blindness, since all the signs point to Odysseus' imminent return. The greed and self-interest that have prevented them from rationally considering the facts before them will lead to the irrational behavior Athena soon elicits from them. Telemachus replies that far from delaying his mother's marriage, he welcomes it. His resistance is due to his reluctance to force her out of her own house, as he is ashamed to drive her out unwilling.

Without warning, an uncontrollable laughter (20.346; *asbeston gelō* [inextinguishable]) brought on by Athena takes possession of the suitors and drives them mad with hysteria: their plates run with blood, their eyes burst with tears, and they wail in grief. The supernatural character of the scene is reminiscent of similar happenings in *Od.* 12 after the suitors kill the cattle of the sun: the dead cow skins crawl, the meat on the spits bellows, and there is a noise like the lowing of cattle (12.395–396). The suitors' misdeeds are demystified by the gods; their punishment is inevitable, but they are unaware of their undoing.

Theoclymenus, whose arrival at the *megaron* remains unexplained, appears to interpret the meaning of this strange phenomenon. He is ever present the moment he is needed to prophesy the suitors' end, as when he appears before Penelope in *Od.* 17 at the very moment Telemachus reports the details of his journey. Appearing now before the hysterical suitors, the seer describes their state in visionary terms. Just as he predicted Odysseus' presence long before Penelope's interview with the stranger (17.157), he now predicts their deaths. His two appearances before Penelope vouch for her husband's return and the suitors' deaths at his hands. It is Theoclymenus' second prediction (20.368–369) that might have swayed Penelope to carry out the bow contest in *Od.* 21. The suitors continue laughing at the prophet's visions, and Eurymachus charges the younger men present to hustle him out of the palace into the daylight, since he claims everything inside the *megaron* is dark. The prophet counters Eurymachus' remarks by refusing an escort and marches out to return to Piraeus' home.

The suitors, oblivious to the prophet's words and indifferent to the forewarnings around them, continue to exchange snide glances and tease Telemachus by mocking him and pointing out his bad taste in guests. They accuse him of dragging into their midst a tramp and a charlatan who pretends to be a prophet. They suggest both the beggar and the prophet could fetch a good profit if sold to the Sicilians. Their disbelief and shunning of the dignity due to god and man bring them closer to extinction. Telemachus, paying little heed to them, rivets his eyes silently on his father, waiting patiently for him to give the signal to pounce on the suitors.

Penelope, eavesdropping for the first time in the epic, a sign of her concern over how the beggar will prevail, sets her chair just outside her door, listening closely to their every word. The suitors, rowdy and laughing aloud, are unaware of the groaning feast Athena and Odysseus are preparing for them. *Od.* 20 ends with the suitors targeted but not yet dead. Penelope is still trying to deal with her own confusion about the beggar's ability to carry out his task single-handedly, and she is still worried that she might be forced to wed one of the detested suitors even though she suspects her husband is the beggar, and deems she has verification of Odysseus' victory from Theoclymenus.

Selected Bibliography: *Od.* 20

Ahl and Roisman, *"Odyssey,"* 239–246.

Clarke, *Art*, 67–85.

Colakis, "Laughter."

Combellack, "Wise."

Finley, John H., Jr., *Homer's*, 185–208.

Guidorizzi, "Laughter."

Johnston, "Penelope."

Katz, *Penelope's*, 114–154.

Levine, "Odysseus'."

McDonald, "On Hearing."

Morrison, "Similes."

Rankin, "Penelope's."

Reece, *Stranger's*, 165–188.

Rose, Gilbert P., "Odysseus'."

Russo, "Homer."

Rutherford, *Homer and the "Odyssey."*

Said, *Homer*, 189–222.

Segal, "Phaeacians."

Further commentary on *Od*. 20 in General Bibliography I.

CHAPTER 6

REVENGE, REUNION, AND RECONCILIATION (*OD.* 21–24)

Book 21

Od. 21 continues the fortieth day from the previous book and focuses on the bow that will find its way into Odysseus' hands in preparation for the suitors' slaughter in *Od.* 22. The book tactfully delays the climax through retardations, digressions, and vignettes of the suitors and Odysseus' allies dealing with preparations for the contest. The book divides into two sections:

I. The bow contest: preparations (28%)
II. The bow contest (72%)

I. The Bow Contest: Preparations, 1–123

Athena inspires Penelope to hold the bow contest, which the beggar/Odysseus approves of as the best way of handling the suitors ("no longer put off this contest" [19.584; my translation]). In the meantime, Penelope agonizes and has second thoughts about it; she keeps crying and debating its merits. If the contest succeeds, she will be reunited with her husband and the suitors will be dead. If it fails, her husband and son will die, and she will be compelled to marry a suitor. Win or lose, people will die, not the outcome she desires, as she made clear in her dream. More importantly, Odysseus is to fight the suitors alone, an impossible feat in her mind. However, after eavesdropping on the suitors' murderous plans for her son and having witnessed the beggar's abuse at their hands, she has no alternative but to go ahead with her agenda.

Accompanied by her attendant women, Penelope takes the key in her thick (21.6; *pachus*) hand to unlock the storeroom containing the bow and the quiver filled with painful shafts. The thickness of her hand, gained from weaving Laertes' shroud, punctuates the length of time she wove before she was exposed by her maids. She is now ready to "weave" her final trick. Before Penelope unlocks the door to reveal the instruments of the suitors' deaths, the scene digresses to divulge the bow's background. In the next twenty-nine lines (21.13–41), Homer narrates in his unique way the myth behind the bow's procurement.

1. Bow and quiver were gifts from Iphitus, whom Odysseus met in Messene (Messenia) in Ortilochus' house.[1]
2. Odysseus traveled there in his youth on an errand to collect a debt. During a pirate raid, the men of Messene stole three hundred sheep from the Ithacans and abducted their herdsmen.
3. Iphitus went to Messene in search of a dozen lost nursing mares but was killed by Heracles (Hercules), who kept the mares[2] without regard for the rules of hospitality.
4. Iphitus was looking for these mares when he met Odysseus.
5. Iphitus gave Odysseus his father's (Eurytus') bow.[3]
6. Odysseus gave Iphitus a sword and a spear to mark the beginning of their friendship.
7. Odysseus and Iphitus never solidified their friendship, since Iphitus was killed by Heracles.[4]
8. Odysseus never took the bow on his journeys but kept it as a memento of friendship in his storeroom.

Homer assumes a basic familiarity with the myth. Thus, he presents only the pieces relevant to his digression. If parts of the myth were used in an earlier context, he does not repeat those parts in its current telling. The reader must then combine the different elements to get a sense of the whole. However, even then a certain amount of familiarity is required. Homer's digression here leaves out a number of basic facts about the bow's procurement that would fill out the myth. Heracles and Eurytus were expert bowmen who rivaled even Apollo[5] (Eurytus challenged Apollo, who killed him for his boasting). Heracles, having defeated Eurytus in an archery contest, was accused of stealing Eurytus' cattle (or mares) as revenge for not receiving the contest prize, Iole, Eurytus' daughter. Iphitus, Eurytus' son, was sent to retrieve the stolen cattle/mares and meets Odysseus in Messene on a mission to reclaim the three hundred sheep plundered by pirates. The two befriend each other and exchange gifts (Iphitus gifts Odysseus his father's bow). Iphitus ultimately recaptures the cattle/mares but is killed by Heracles while a guest in his home. The myth's purpose, as presented here, is twofold. First, it compares Odysseus as a hero and archer to both Eurytus and Heracles. Second, Heracles' treatment of a guest parallels Odysseus' treatment of the suitors, although the purpose in each case is vastly different. Is the point of this connection, then, to demonstrate the negative side of Odysseus' triumph? Penelope's abhorrence of the deaths to come supports such a reading. Odysseus is doing the gods' will, but at the same time he is breaking the laws of hospitality by killing guests (albeit uninvited ones). Is not Odysseus then also violating the rules of hospitality when he enters the Cyclops' cave uninvited and has his men help themselves to the giant's possessions? Is he not behaving like the suitors? Perhaps this is another reason for Odysseus' delayed *nostos*.

The scene returns to Penelope unlocking the oaken door to the storeroom to fetch the bow. A simile compares the opening door to the bellowing of a bull at pasture (21.48–49), anticipating Odysseus' deadly power once the bow is in his hands. She gently removes the bow from its case, handling it like a priceless musical instrument in preparation for a performance. Odysseus later examines the bow as one would a musical instrument (21.406–408). In this respect, Odysseus is compared to a bard who, inspired by the Muse, is invited to provide a valuable service. Eumaeus (17.382–386) places bards on the same level as healers and seers for their contributions to society. Their songs have the ability not only to confer undying fame (*kleos aphthiton*) on heroic and divine deeds (1.338) but also to teach proper conduct by exemplifying it in their songs. In the same way, Odysseus is inspired by the gods (Athena) to provide a valuable service—to bring order and peace to Ithaca by killing those who disrupt peace for chaos.

Penelope, overcome with emotion, approaches the suitors with the bow and quiver and in a condemning tone reveals her intention to hold a contest. She will marry whoever takes Odysseus' great bow in his hands, strings it easily, and shoots an arrow clean through all twelve axes. To avoid any misunderstanding should there be more than one winner, she stipulates the victor will be the one who accomplishes the task with the least effort (21.75). Both the swineherd and the oxherd burst into tears at the sight of the bow as Penelope hands it to Eumaeus to set before the suitors. Under the pretext that their tears upset the grieving Penelope, Antinous orders the herdsmen to take their sniffling outside, but it is the bow that most troubles him, as he realizes the difficulty in stringing it, since no one among them has Odysseus' skill. Nevertheless, Antinous is hopeful that he might be the one to string the bow and shoot through the axes. In an ironic tone, Homer adds that was not to be the case, for Antinous would be the first to taste Odysseus' arrow. Fate does not always respect one's hopes and dreams.

Penelope's announcement that she is finally willing to marry takes Telemachus by surprise, and he turns to the suitors with a nervous laugh, apologizing for his witlessness. He embraces his mother's plan, realizing that the purpose of her sudden change of heart is to provide his father with a weapon. He immediately begins to praise her as a prize worth their efforts. He offers her as a woman like no other in all of Ithaca or anywhere else in all of Greece, and he encourages them to start the contest right away. He even hopes to try his own hand at the bow as a test of his strength, anxious to prove his manhood. He begins setting up the axes expertly in a straight line, to the amazement of the suitors, who now greet his expertise as further proof of his having come of age. Antinous, on the other hand, has doubts about the suitors and his own ability to string the bow and believes the contest unfair (21.91), missing the irony of his comment. The contest will be "unfair" because the prize will be the suitors' lives.

II. The Bow Contest, 124–434

The contest begins with a number of delaying tactics before the onslaught of *Od.* 22.

1. Telemachus' continual growth, which now presents him as a younger copy of his father
2. The suitors' quibbling and shortcomings as they try to bend the bow
3. The beggar/Odysseus' maneuverings to gain possession of the bow

Telemachus tries his luck first, but three attempts later, he is still unable to string the bow. Hopeful that he can accomplish the task, he tries for a fourth and would have strung it (21.12), but a signal from his father stops him. Either Odysseus feels his son will upset his plans or he does not want the competition. Telemachus is the only one other than his father (who effortlessly strings the bow) to accomplish the task, albeit in four tries. His manhood is assured; he has become a young Odysseus. The fact that he is symmetrically positioned as the first contestant and Odysseus as the last suggests such a rite of passage. Also, given Telemachus' rivalry with his mother in the *Telemachia* in asserting himself as his father's surrogate (1.356–364), he is on the cusp of being the "suitor" for Penelope's hand before his father stops him, perhaps signaling Telemachus' desire to dominate his mother and become Odysseus himself. Demonstrating an ingenuity worthy of his father (the ability to size up the situation at hand), he sets the bow aside, calling himself a coward and a weakling because of his youth. Playing on the suitors' egos, he calls on them to try their luck (21.134). By belittling himself and stroking their vanity, the prince eliminates himself as a threat.

Antinous establishes the order in which each suitor will take his turn: from left to right until each is given a chance. Leodes, a weak but well-meaning seer who loathes his associates' reckless ways and disapproves their methods, is first but fails. He warns the bow will spell their end, since they cannot forever pursue a prize beyond their reach. As a seer, he is aware of the dangers inherent in the contest and advises that they abandon their hopes of marrying Penelope, pursue some other Achaean woman, and let the queen marry the one who brings the most gifts. His statement is full of foreboding and irony, for it is Odysseus who brings the most gifts (13.137). Too vain to consider himself a lesser man than Odysseus, Antinous scolds Leodes, observing that his inability to string the bow does not disqualify the others. He urges Melanthius to light a fire and heat lard to make the bow flexible, but even then, the suitors are unable to string it. Antinous and Eurymachus, the strongest among them, hold back, watching the others fail.

While the suitors preoccupy themselves with the bow, Eumaeus and Philoetius slip out of the hall. The beggar/Odysseus, seizing the opportunity to put his plan into action, follows them close behind to solicit their support and increase his odds against the suitors. He asks them whether they would support Odysseus if he suddenly appeared. Philoetius prays to Zeus for his master's return so all can witness his own power and strength. Eumaeus, following his lead, prays to the divinities for Odysseus' homecoming. Convinced of their loyalty, the beggar makes himself known—"In truth I am he, I am here before you" (21.207; my translation)[6]—and he pulls up his rags to reveal his scar. Recognizing the injury, they embrace him, but Odysseus cuts the greeting short lest someone exiting the palace catch sight of them and report it to the suitors. For their unwavering faithfulness, Odysseus vows to grant them the wives, possessions, and houses they longed for. For the present they must enter the hall, he first and they behind. Eumaeus will procure the bow while Philoetius secures the outer gate of the courtyard to prevent anyone from exiting or entering during the slaughter. At his signal, Eumaeus will bring him the bow, even at the suitors' objections; he will also inform the servingwomen to bar the doors to the *megaron* and keep them shut, regardless of what they hear inside.

The scene crosscuts to the suitors, who are still trying to make the bow more pliable. Eurymachus, frustrated at his lack of success, grieves not at failing to win Penelope, for there are many Achaean women from whom he can select a bride, but rather at the disgrace of being inferior to Odysseus and the shame it will cause him. If his feelings are a barometer for the rest of the suitors, his humiliation means a loss of *kleos* (fame)—the regard in which the world will hold him in the years to come. The queen, then, is desired more as a sign of the suitors' worth. To marry Penelope is to possess a part of Odysseus and his *kleos*, placing the suitors on par with him. If it were merely a question of marriage, as Eurymachus states, there are plenty of women available.

Antinous, refusing to admit weakness, chastises Eurymachus; he cannot expect defeat. He will string the bow and claim Penelope, and by replacing Odysseus as husband and master, he will win *kleos aphthiton* (undying fame). His fear of failure triggers a jolt of piety hitherto missing in Antinous' actions. He postpones the contest to gain more time, claiming it is not proper to hold a contest on Apollo's celebratory day. Acknowledging that without the god's help no one can string the bow, he entreats everyone to pay tribute to the god and claims that early the following day, they will burn the bones of Melanthius' goats in Apollo's honor. Necessity suddenly reminds Antinous the gods must have their due, but he has neglected the gods far too long for his newly found piety to take effect. Antinous' plan, nevertheless, pleases the suitors; they wash their hands, fill their bowls with wine, and offer the first drops from each cup to Apollo.

The beggar/Odysseus seizes the moment to begin maneuvering for the bow. First, he compliments Antinous' suggestion to honor Apollo. Second, he appeals to both Eurymachus and Antinous for a chance at the bow in order to amuse them. His request enrages them, for no matter how slim the possibility, they fear the beggar might string the bow and bring shame on them. Their main objection is the affront to their status; they would be mortified before Ithaca's citizens. Besides, the suitors are still uncertain of the beggar's identity and strength. He could be someone other than he claims, as they were made aware when he fought Irus (18.66–71), but they ignore the possibility just as they ignore the gods' signs. Antinous calls him a filthy drifter and chides him for considering such a request when he should be content with sharing their feast, listening to their conversations, and enjoying privileges no other beggar has ever been given. He must be in a drunken stupor to demand more favors.

The mention of intoxication leads to a digression—the myth of Eurytion the Centaur (21.295–304), which Antinous uses as an example for the beggar's behavior, for it was wine that also drove Eurytion to perform terrible acts.

1. Eurytion the Centaur came to the Lapiths at Perithous' house drunk and caused a great deal of harm.
2. Angered at his behavior, his hosts, the Lapiths, seized him and threw him out, cutting off his nose and ears. Since then, the Lapiths and the Centaurs have feuded.
3. It was the drunk Eurytion who started it all and thus met with disaster.

What happened to Eurytion is likely to happen to the beggar should he take part in the contest and string the bow, for then the suitors will dispatch him to King Echetus, who puts strangers to death, a threat Antinous and his companions made earlier against Irus (18.84–85, 115–116). Antinous compares Eurytion to the beggar, the guest abusing the hosts' hospitality.

The comparison, however, is ironic, for it is the suitors who, like the Centaurs, congregate in Odysseus' home to take his bride, and Odysseus, like Peirithous, punishes them for their indecent behavior. Had Homer disclosed the whole myth, the irony of the comparison between the Lapiths and Antinous would be more obvious. Eurytion and the other Centaurs came to Perithous' house as his wedding guests on his marriage to Hippodameia. Eurytion and his drunken troupe attempted to rape the bride, and his hosts, angered at their behavior, expelled them from the house; Theseus, an invited guest of the Lapiths, lopped off Eurytion's nose and ears, foreshadowing Melanthius' fate in *Od.* 23.474–476. The Lapiths and Centaurs battled (the *Centauromachy*), and the Centaurs were defeated.

Penelope intervenes to place the bow in the beggar's hands. She reprimands Antinous for his rudeness, reminding him the suitors should not interfere with any guest Telemachus chooses to invite, for even should the beggar string the bow, he does not expect to win Penelope as his wife (the irony being that the beggar does expect to win Penelope as his wife). Eurymachus agrees with Penelope but nevertheless fears the possibility of the beggar stringing the bow, which will bring shame and disgrace on them. For the second time now, Eurymachus expresses what the suitors fear most—shame. They fear the public's ridicule, particularly since superiority is measured by rank, wealth, and appearance. The queen cleverly reminds Eurymachus that he and the suitors have already accrued the shame they are avoiding by dishonoring Odysseus' home. Why deny a stranger who claims noble birth a turn at the contest? Should Apollo grant him success, she promises to give him clothing and a spear to ward off men and dogs (an ironic reference to the suitors perhaps?). She will then send him wherever he wants to go. Penelope here seems fully in accord with the strategy she and her husband have put into play. Her boldness and cunning become more and more apparent, revealing her resolve to go forward with the bow contest and take a chance on Odysseus' ability to deal with the suitors.

Unaware of whether his mother or Eumaeus knows the beggar's true identity (or whether they, in turn, know of Telemachus' or each other's recognition of Odysseus), the prince rudely interrupts his mother, either out of regard for his own authority or perhaps to protect her. Eager to get the bow into his father's hands and awaiting his signal, he takes charge of the situation and imposes his authority. He orders his mother and her attendants back to their quarters. The bow should be left in the care of men, more specifically in his care, for the power in the palace is his and his alone. Penelope, astonished at her son's maturity and singularity of mind, withdraws with her attendants, still apprehensive regarding whether the contest will turn out as planned.

Eumaeus, in the meantime, is trying to carry out his assigned task. He takes the bow and walks toward the beggar, but the suitors stop him. Fearing their threats, he balks and returns the bow to its source. From the opposite side, Telemachus, unaware that Eumaeus knows the beggar to be Odysseus, counters with his own threat. The prince, more for the benefit of the suitors than the swineherd, orders him to carry out his mission or be stoned to death by the prince himself. Telemachus' remarks are calculating, a cunning ploy to make his father proud, for, mean as he sounds toward the swineherd, he humbles himself before the suitors by undervaluing his strength to speed them out of his house. He not only clears the way for Eumaeus to carry out his task but also puts the suitors' minds at ease by subordinating himself to them. Telemachus' stratagem works, for all the suitors laugh happily and abandon their bitter rage against him. The prince demonstrates that he has truly developed into his father's son. The *homophrosunē* that binds Odysseus and Penelope now extends to Telemachus; agile minded as Odysseus, he carries off a three-way play:

1. He enables Eumaeus to deliver the bow to Odysseus.
2. He diffuses the suitors' anger by playing on their sense of superiority.
3. He reprimands the suitors under the cover of weakness.

With the bow in the beggar/Odysseus' hands, Eumaeus calls Eurycleia aside to deliver his master's message. Unsure whether she knows the beggar's identity, he tells her Telemachus orders all the doors locked. Perhaps in identifying the dispatcher as the prince rather than Odysseus, Eumaeus momentarily confuses the two. The housekeeper complies and bars the doors that lead from the *megaron*; at the same time, the oxherd quietly exits the hall to lock the courtyard gates. He fastens the gates with a cable found under the portico and returns, his eyes riveted on the beggar, who is holding the bow.

Concerned that worms bored through the bow of horn during his long absence,[7] the beggar/Odysseus probes it thoroughly while the suitors mock his actions. Some sneer at his close examination of the bow; others are uneasy that he might cause trouble. In the simile that follows (21.406–409), Odysseus is an expert bard ready to begin the evening's entertainment. His bow is the lyre that will "sing" the suitors' deaths. He strings the bow with the same ease with which a bard slips a lyre string over its peg and then plucks the string to test its pitch, which in this case sings like a swallow (21.411).[8] Phemius, whom the reader first met in *Od.* 1 unwillingly entertaining the suitors, now becomes Odysseus, who in *Od.* 21 is prepared to entertain them willingly for the last time. As the suitors watch the beggar handle the bow, regret seizes them and their faces pale. They realize the beggar is a threat, a feeling underscored by a resounding clap of thunder, an omen from Zeus. Rejoicing, Odysseus picks up an arrow from the table beside him, draws the bow string as far back as it will go, and shoots the arrow clean through the twelve ax heads. Turning to Telemachus, who is standing next to his father, now a warrior his equal, Odysseus nods, calling for "the feast" to begin, with music to follow later.

Selected Bibliography: *Od.* 21

Ahl and Roisman, *"Odyssey,"* 247–272.

Anhalt, "Bull."

Barrett, "Homer."

Borthwick, "Odysseus."

Brain and Skinner, "Odysseus."

Clarke, *Art*, 67–85.

Combdellack, "Wise."

Crissy, "Herakles."

Davies, "Homer."

Finley, John H., Jr., *Homer's*, 185–208.

Griffith, "Community."

Hoffer, "Telemachus'."

Katz, *Penelope's*, 114–154.

Losada, "*Odyssey.*"

Louden, *The "Odyssey,"* 31–49.

McLeod, "Bow."

Olson, "Telemachos'."

Page, *Folktales*, 93–113.

Perry and Perry, "Archery."

Ready, "ATU."

Reece, *Stranger's*, 165–188.

Roller and Roller, "Penelope's."

Said, *Homer*, 189–222.

Segal, "Phaeacians."

Van Nortwick, "Penelope as Double Agent."

Wyatt, "Penelope's."

Further commentary on *Od.* 21 in General Bibliography I.

Book 22

On the fortieth day of the narrative, Odysseus, bow in hand, begins the *mnēstērophonia* (the suitors' slaughter), which occupies *Od.* 22 and can be read in the tripartite format used in many of the previous books.

I. Odysseus' fight with the suitors (24%)
II. The suitors' retaliation (53%)
III. Aftermath of battle (22%)

I. Odysseus Fights the Suitors, 1–121

Stripping off his rags, the beggar/Odysseus shoots an arrow through Antinous' throat as the suitor lifts a cup of wine to his lips. In ironic contrast, Antinous dies drinking after having warned the beggar in the previous book of the dangers of inebriation. As he slumps on the floor, the cup drops from his grasp, blood spurts out of his nostrils, his foot kicks back his table, and food showers the floor. Having portrayed the suitors wallowing in gluttony throughout the epic, Homer now has them gagging and suffocating on their own food and wine. Their leader dead, the other suitors jump up and scan the empty walls for weapons. Thinking that Antinous was shot mistakenly, they turn their venom on the still-unrecognized beggar responsible for the death of the best among them. Unfazed by their threats, Odysseus makes himself known and denounces them for three of their five crimes: devouring his goods (22.36), ravishing his servingwomen (22.37), and wooing his wife behind his back (22.38). Later, he denounces them for a fourth crime: dishonoring his guests (22.414–415). Eurymachus names the suitors' fifth: their intention to murder Telemachus (22.52). They now pay for their crimes, fearing neither gods nor the resentment of future generations.

Odysseus' revelation seizes the suitors with terror; they look for avenues of escape, but Eurymachus dares to plead their case.

1. If the stranger is truly Odysseus, he has a right to his anger.
2. Since the responsible party, Antinous, is now gone, Odysseus should relent and listen to reason. Antinous' interest was to depose Telemachus, marry Penelope, and rule Ithaca. Now that he is dead, Odysseus can spare the suitors.
3. The suitors will replace Odysseus' losses by offering him twenty oxen each, paid in bronze and gold.

Like Achilles in the *Iliad* (9.168–655), who refuses Agamemnon's numerous gifts to battle the Trojans, Odysseus refuses any amount of wealth offered by Eurymachus in order to stop his slaughter of the suitors (*Od.* 22.61–63). Unlike Achilles' anger, Odysseus' is not an explosive wrath (*mēnis*) but a seething one. He is aware the suitors are trying to buy him as Agamemnon tried to buy Achilles. However, for Odysseus, the suitors' overriding crime is the assault on his very existence, the effort to eradicate all traces of his kingship (by appropriating his property, his wife, his son, and his household servants) and thereby to eclipse his memory and fame, a situation similar to the one he faced at Calypso's. She, too, in her offer of immortality, sought to place his human fame in jeopardy. He is not willing to accept Eurymachus' offer any more than Achilles could accept Agamemnon's. Eurymachus and Agamemnon did not understand what they were asking of these two heroes—selfhood from Odysseus and honor from Achilles. The suitors' abuse of the beggar, who depended for his existence on the kindness of others, denied him his very being, imposing on him a kind of anonymity. In like manner, the suitor Agelaus later claims (22.221–223) he will obliterate Mentor (Athena in disguise) from life and extinguish his entire family if he aids Odysseus. Conceding that Odysseus will not pardon their crimes, Eurymachus turns to the suitors and warns that as long as Odysseus holds bow and arrows, he will not be satisfied until he kills them all. Their only chance for survival is to attack en masse, hoping to reach the doors and seek help from the townspeople. Urging attack, Eurymachus draws his sword and hurls himself at the king with a savage cry; at the same time, Odysseus casts an arrow that pierces Eurymachus' nipple and lodges in his liver. Writhing in pain, he drops his sword before tumbling headfirst over his table, flinging food and wine all over the floor.

Amphinomus, heeding Eurymachus' call, rushes Odysseus with drawn sword to force him from the door. Telemachus casts his spear and strikes Amphinomus between his shoulders, causing him to topple to the ground, mortally wounded. His spear lodged in Amphinomus, Telemachus leaps away, fearing some other suitor might hack him down. It is interesting that the first suitor Telemachus kills is the one who most pleased his mother (Freudian perhaps?). The prince, taking notice of his father's diminishing arrows, offers to retrieve shields and armor from the storeroom for himself, his father, and the two herdsmen. Odysseus, pleased at his son's initiative, urges him to go quickly, while Odysseus can still defend himself. Telemachus returns with four shields, eight spears, and four helmets; dons his armor, as do Eumaeus and Philoetius; and flanks Odysseus, who is still firing his remaining arrows at the suitors. Odysseus, his arrows spent and having slaughtered many unnamed suitors, lays down his bow.

II. The Suitors' Retaliation, 122–389

The main struggle against the suitors begins once Odysseus lays down his bow and takes up two spears.[9] He orders Eumaeus to secure a side door leading to an alley. The suitor Agelaus calls for someone to slip through that door and call for help. Melanthius discourages him and proposes recovering arms from the inner chamber. When Odysseus sees the suitors arming themselves, his knees buckle, as he realizes that someone within his household is aiding them. Telemachus admits he mistakenly left the door ajar after he removed the armor. Eumaeus and Philoetius go to close the storeroom door and locate the traitor. In the meantime, Melanthius returns to the inner chamber to retrieve more weapons. Odysseus instructs Eumaeus and Philoetius to capture the goatherd and suspend him from the roof beams to suffer harsh torment. The two herdsmen seize him, wrestle him to the ground, bind his feet and arms, and hoist him to the rafters. Leaving Melanthius in his agonizing bindings, the two put on their armor (22.201; an oversight, since they had already put it on earlier [22.114–115]) and return to Odysseus and Telemachus to fend off the remaining suitors.

As Odysseus, Telemachus, and the two herdsmen battle against overwhelming odds, Mentor/Athena appears to remind Odysseus of his warrior past and encourage him to exhibit the same valor he showed in Troy. Odysseus, suspecting the goddess' presence, welcomes her assistance, but she turns into a swallow and perches on a roof beam to survey the parody of the Iliadic battle commencing below (22.241–329). Threatening

Mentor/Athena with extinction, Agelaus calls the suitors to action. Six of the suitors' best warriors join him in the attack, but all miss their marks, lodging their spears in the palace pillars, doors, and walls. Next, Odysseus' allies take their turn, each finding his mark in a scene with all the flavor of the *Iliad*—*parainesis*, vaunts, similes, divine interventions, and supplications (see note 9 of the present chapter). The remaining suitors shrink to the back of the palace, allowing Odysseus and his men to retrieve their spears from the corpses. The suitors then attack for a second time, but, distracted by Athena, they only cause minor injuries; the majority of their spear throws again end on pillars, doors, and walls. Odysseus' company retaliates, killing most of the holdovers. From the rafters, Athena wields her shield, bewildering the suitors and causing them to scatter. In a simile (22.299–301), they are presented as cattle maddened by horse flies—although unaware of the cause of their irritation, they stampede wildly in different directions. The pursuers, on the other hand, are compared to vultures (22.302–303) descending to pounce on smaller birds, which fly away yet have little chance against them. Likewise, Odysseus and his men give chase until the suitors' heads are broken and their blood covers the floor. Although the simile carries a note of censure, as the vultures are described as ravaging the smaller birds, their feeding on them for sustenance and survival is a natural act. The horror portrayed in these scenes, which are bathed in blood and full of horrible cries as heads are broken, would suggest something perverse about war; at the same time, there is also something comic, as the suitors' best warriors miss their marks each time while the herdsmen hit theirs.

The parody continues as Leodes rushes to clutch Odysseus' knees, pleading that he never wronged any of the women; he even tried preventing others from abusing them but could not. For his years of service as a diviner, he begs for mercy. Odysseus ponders how often Leodes prayed that the king might never return so he could marry Penelope and have her bear his children. Picking up Leodes' sword from where he dropped it, he severs his neck and his head drops in the dust, still speaking.

Phemius, clutching his lyre, considers two possible options to save his life: slip out of the *megaron* and crouch at Zeus's altar in the courtyard, or throw himself on Odysseus' mercy. The latter seems best, but before Phemius implements it, Homer again pays homage to his profession. The bard lays his lyre reverently on the ground for safety before rushing to grasp Odysseus' knees. Should he not be shown mercy, at least the lyre that immortalized the acts of heroes would be saved. He calls on Telemachus as witness, who hears Phemius' pleas and quickly intercedes on his behalf. He asks his father to spare both Phemius and Medon, the man who cared for him as a child. The herald, wrapped in a fresh ox skin and cowering under a table, emerges to hug Telemachus' knees and beg forgiveness. Odysseus, smiling, allays both men's fear, crediting Telemachus for saving them, and sends both outside to Zeus's altar. He surveys the *megaron* for any remaining suitors, but all lie heaped in piles of blood like fish caught in fishermen's nets, a simile implying again a natural activity; a daily catch that is needed for sustenance, piled on the beach and drying in the sun, is likened to the suitors, who, unaware of their crimes against the order of things, are caught and killed to preserve human life.

III. Aftermath of Battle, 390–501

Eurycleia finds Odysseus splattered in blood like a lion feeding on an ox (22.402–404). The lion simile here does not dwell on the hero's strength or draw a distinction between a lion's instinctive nature and Odysseus' more rational one, as in *Od.* 6.130–135, but rather points to the savagery that humans are capable of, whether they act in the name of justice or not. Eurycleia, surrounded by carnage, raises a cry of triumph, but her zeal is checked by Odysseus, who cautions her that it is not pious to glory over slain men. Unlike the lion to which he is compared, Odysseus, in a moment of anger, acts out of instinct, but once the anger has past, he recalls the respect due human life. The suitors' disrespect results in their deaths, for they paid attention to no one, whether base or noble. Odysseus now asks Eurycleia to assemble both the guilty and the innocent household servants. Earlier, in *Od.* 19.501–502, she promised to give Odysseus a list of unfaithful servants, but he declined in order to study each properly and learn of each himself. Without explanation, he changes his mind and asks her assistance; Eurycleia names twelve of the fifty maids as being guilty of immorality.[10] Dishonoring one's duty to the master breaks the chain of command and creates chaos and anarchy, a situation Odysseus must right if order and peace are to return to Ithaca.

Before Odysseus announces his presence to his household, he demands that the twelve maids be dealt with and his palace tidied up. Once the house is cleansed, Telemachus and the two herdsmen lead the unfaithful maids outside by the round-house[11] to kill them, but Telemachus, having considered the maids' immorality and the abuse shown his mother and himself, decides they deserve hanging, a harsher punishment than his father ordered (22.443). Telemachus here shows his complete independence, weighing the situation at hand like his father and opting for the choice he considers best, even if it counters his father's. After the maids are disposed of, Telemachus and the herdsmen torture and kill Melanthius. The excessive treatment of the unfaithful servants stresses the severity of their crimes, which, unchecked, cause the breakdown of social order, Homer's *themis*, the highly developed sense of what is fitting and proper in the world of the *Odyssey*. Odysseus, refusing clean clothing to replace his rags, sends for sulfur and fire to fumigate his home, intending to purify his palace before undertaking anything else.

Selected Bibliography: *Od.* 22

Ahl and Roisman, "*Odyssey*," 247–272.

Buchan, *Limits*, 133–180.

Clarke, *Art*, 67–85.

Davies, "*Odyssey*."

Finley, John H., Jr., *Homer's*, 185–208.

Fulkerson, "Epic."

Levine, "Odysseus'."

Morrison, "Similes."

Newton, "Odysseus and Melanthius."

Reece, *Stranger's*, 165–188.

Said, *Homer*, 189–222.

Scott, William C., *Artistry*, 112–118.

Segal, "Phaeacians."

Stewart, *Disguised*, 100–145.

Further commentary on *Od.* 22 in General Bibliography I.

Book 23

Od. 23 deals with Odysseus and Penelope's three-part reunion. The pre-reunion section (the fortieth day ends at line 347) takes up over half of the book, followed by the reunion (the night of the fortieth day) and culminating with the events following the reunion (early dawn of day forty-one).

I. Pre-reunion (55%)
II. Reunion (25%)
III. Post-reunion (20%)

I. Pre-reunion, 1–204

Eurycleia rushes to Penelope to announce Odysseus' presence and the suitors' deaths. The nurse's sudden news comes as a shock, since when the queen retired in *Od.* 21, the beggar/Odysseus had not yet had a chance at the bow. Eurycleia insists her news is true and volunteers that Telemachus knew of his father's presence for a long time. It is not clear how Eurycleia knows this fact or why she tells it to Penelope at this time other than to lend support to the validity of her news. Still skeptical, Penelope jumps out of bed and embraces Eurycleia, still bewildered how one man could stand up to so many. Eurycleia admits she did not actually witness the suitors' deaths but heard their cries and found Odysseus splattered in their blood. It is he who now summons her. Penelope longs to believe her but falters; it is too impossible a deed for a single man to accomplish. It must have been the work of an immortal in anger over their wicked deeds. Like Odysseus, she is cautious and mistrustful. Eurycleia confesses that while washing the beggar's feet, she noticed the scar, but Odysseus restrained her from exposing him. Now the maid is willing to stake her life on her news. Hesitant still, Penelope yields and follows the nurse to see for herself the man who killed the suitors. In a scene reminiscent of the interaction between Odysseus and Nausicaa in *Od.* 6, she debates how to approach the stranger: embrace him or keep her distance and question him. Using her husband's ruse, she will keep her distance until she is confident he is her husband. Her main concern is not merely whether the beggar is Odysseus and not some god in disguise, but more importantly, whether he is the same Odysseus who left Ithaca twenty years earlier. Is the external man who returned the inner man she married?[12] While Penelope sits in silence gazing at Odysseus, Telemachus (who recognized his father in *Od.* 16), impatient at her aloofness ("my mother cruel mother" [23.97; my translation]),[13] accuses her of being heartless and stubborn (100; *tetleōti thymōi*). Distraught, she is powerless to speak or look the beggar in the eyes and promises Telemachus that if he is truly Odysseus, she will recognize him through the secret clues they share (see 23.109–110)—the very clues they used to communicate in *Od.* 19, which led to the bow contest. Odysseus, thinking his foul rags and filth prevent Penelope from accepting him, smiles and advises Telemachus to give his mother time to examine him and she will presently know him.

In a digression, Odysseus' attention turns to the dead suitors (23.116–152), for killing even a single man demands exile, and Odysseus has killed Ithaca's finest men, so his next moves need great deliberation. Telemachus yields to his father's better judgment and vows that he and the herdsmen will cede to his decision. Hearing what he expects from his son, Odysseus posits his plan.

1. First, everyone will bathe and put on clean clothing.
2. Second, the bard is to lead all in a festive dance so that anyone hearing the music will think a wedding is taking place.
3. Third, no rumor of the suitors' deaths must escape the palace until they deal with the relatives.

The bard begins a celebratory tune to lead passersby to conclude the queen married (an irony, as the queen did not marry one of the suitors, but at the same time she is reunited with ["married to"] her husband). In the meantime, Eurynome bathes and anoints Odysseus with olive oil and dresses him, while Athena makes him taller with a headful of curls. A simile compares the alteration to that of a master craftsman who applies a coat of gold to silver (23.159), the identical simile used when Athena transforms Odysseus before Nausicaa and her maids (6.232–235), which the young princess accepts without question. However, Penelope's reaction is unlike Nausicaa's when Odysseus reenters the *megaron*; she is still unconvinced Odysseus is the man she married and not an immortal in his likeness. Her reluctance angers Odysseus, who assails her as his son had earlier: no other woman as stubborn (23.168; *tetlēoti thumōi*) would delay welcoming her husband. The phrase *tetlēoti thumōi*, used here by both Odysseus and Telemachus to express disapproval of Penelope's reaction, is more often used affirmatively. Menelaus and his men, lying among the seals (4.441–447), wait for Proteus with *tetlēoti thumōi* (translated as "enduring spirit" by Lattimore and "spirits steeled" by Fagles); later Menelaus holds on with *tetlēoti thumōi* to the shifting forms of Proteus (4.459). In *Od.* 9.435 Odysseus holds on with *tetlēoti thumōi* to a ram's underbelly when escaping from the Cyclops. In *Od.* 11.181 Anticleia, in Hades, informs her son that Penelope waits for him with *tetlēoti thumōi*, and Eumaeus in *Od.* 16.37 comforts the beggar/Odysseus that Penelope waits for him with *tetlēoti thumōi* (an enduring heart). Even Odysseus praises the man who, with *tetlēoti thumōi* (18.135; enduring spirit), accepts what fate offers.

Tetlēoti thumōi is high praise for a woman who cautiously weighs her options before rushing into a decision that might prove fatal.

Finding his wife's reaction annoying (23.166 *daimoniē*), he asks the nurse to set up a bed for him on the spot. Penelope replies using the same phrase (23.174; *daimoniē*); she knows well what he was like when he left Ithaca and intends to find out if he is still the same man. She approves his request that a bed be placed in the hall. Prepared to test his identity, she asks Eurycleia to bring out the bed that he himself built, though she is aware it is rooted in the earth. Her ploy is double-edged. First, she is blameless, since no other man has entered that bedroom but her true husband. Second, only the real Odysseus would know the bed's secret. If the man before her is her husband, he will realize the bed cannot be moved and at the same time know of her fidelity. Odysseus, knowing the bed Penelope wants moved was built around the thick trunk of an olive tree, is infuriated. Only a god could move it unless someone unearthed the olive stump and moved the bed elsewhere.

II. Reunion, 205–299

Odysseus' description of how he single-handedly built the bed (23.192–202) and his indignation that another man uprooted the symbol of his marriage convince Penelope. An immortal could fool her by taking Odysseus' physical qualities, but even a god could not imitate the deeply felt pain he expresses at the thought of another man invading his marriage. The secret of her bed was known only to her husband, the servingwoman, Actor's daughter (23.228), and herself. Constructed of olive wood and rooted in the earth, it symbolizes not only the strength and endurance of their marriage but also the fact that their marriage is endorsed and sanctioned by the goddess of wisdom. Penelope now asks forgiveness for not greeting him earlier. The spirit (215; *thumos*) deep within prevented her from accepting anyone for fear of being deceived. Penelope is contrasted with Helen, who ought not to have lain in love with a foreigner; had she exercised caution and considered the consequences, she might not have acted as she did. Lacking Penelope's *tetlēōs thumos*, Helen allowed a god to shame her. The reference to Helen reinforces Penelope's fear of being deceived by either god or mortal, but unlike Helen, Penelope thinks before she acts; like Odysseus, she takes great care to examine every possibility before giving in to her instincts.

The consummation of their reunion is expressed in a simile that reverses their roles and binds them into a single person (233–239). The simile begins with shipwrecked sailors striving to reach land after Poseidon has smashed their ship. As they battle the elements, only few succeed in attaining land. Up to this point, the reader is reminded of Odysseus struggling to reach the Scherian shore. However, in the last line, the comparison inverts to identify Penelope instead of Odysseus (23.239). Penelope then becomes the shipwrecked sailor being welcomed by Odysseus. Her twenty-year ordeal has come to an end like his. Her waiting and his wandering have united—opposite sides of a single coin. The couple is reunited but, being mortals, they can only expect more struggle as long as they are alive (23.249). Odysseus mentions Tiresias' prophecy (23.263–284), and Penelope will not sleep until she hears it. Athena prolongs the night so Odysseus can recount the prophecy (11.121–137) and summarize his wanderings (23.310–343).

For the Alexandrian scholars Aristophanes (ca. 257–180 B.C.E.) and Aristarchus (ca. 217–145 B.C.E.), line 23.296 marks "the end" (*telos/peras*) of the *Odyssey*, although these two words can also be translated as "climax." Aristarchus also discounts lines 23.310–343, the summary of Odysseus' adventures, and lines 24.1–204, the second *Nekyia*, as later additions to the epic. Ending the narrative at this point, however, leaves several points unresolved, chief among them the aftershock of the suitors' deaths and Odysseus' reunion with Laertes. The suitors' relatives are obviously a concern for Odysseus, for he questions how he and Telemachus will handle the relatives' intent to avenge their dead (23.117–140). This concern is present as early as *Od.* 20.41 when Athena appears in Odysseus' sleep to inquire about his restlessness: How is he to survive the aftermath? There is also Theoclymenus' vision of the suitors' ghosts huddled in the yard, ready to flock down to the underworld (20.355–356), a vision that foreshadows the second *Nekyia*. Also, in *Od.* 23.133–136, Odysseus tells Telemachus to use the bard Phemius as a subterfuge to keep passersby thinking a wedding is in progress until they make their way to their estate to plan how to handle the suitors' relatives. We can thus consider line 23.296 the climactic moment of the epic—the reunion of Odysseus and Penelope. But it still remains to resolve the threat the suitors' relatives pose to Odysseus' rule.

III. Post-reunion, 300–372

At last alone in bed, Odysseus and Penelope enjoy their lovemaking and take pleasure in telling stories. However, the stories they tell each other are briefly summarized by the narrator and not presented in direct discourse as are the *apologoi* (*Od.* 9–12) and Menelaus' and Helen's tales (*Od.* 4). Thus, what the reader hears is what the narrator tells us Odysseus said to his wife, that his wanderings happened. Slightly different portraits of the hero and his adventures, however, do emerge in the narrator's and Odysseus' versions. The Muse portrays the hero as one attentive toward Penelope's feelings and somewhat regretful of his earlier actions. He is prudent not to mention his affairs with Circe and Calypso and omits mention of Nausicaa altogether. He is sensible that mention of these women would be in bad taste at a reunion with his wife after a twenty-year absence. He is regretful that his *nostos* caused so much pain for others but takes little blame for his role in his companions' deaths. He cites his slaughter of the Cicones but fails to mention the seventy-two men lost in that campaign, whose loss was the result of his ineffective leadership. Passing over the Lotus-Eaters without comment, he is quick to praise his role in the Cyclops' undoing for devouring his men. However, he is silent concerning his two near-fatal mistakes in calling out the giant once he escaped his cave, which almost cost his and his crew's lives, nor does he mention his "Nobody" ploy. One wonders to what degree Odysseus embellished his stories to the Phaeacians, since the material the narrator omits depicts Odysseus' most hubristic moments. The narrator makes no reference to Aeolus' banishing Odysseus on his second return to the floating island for his carelessness with the bag of winds. He mentions the large losses of men in Laestrygonia and Thrinacia that he alone escaped. His Hades trip evokes memories of Tiresias, his mother's love, and a number of his fallen Trojan War comrades. The narrator basically concludes that Odysseus suffered due to fate, never swayed from his purpose to return home, performed heroic deeds unlike any other (Scylla), and was looked up to by others (Phaeacians). The narrator's summation of Odysseus' adventures differs greatly from Odysseus' own recitation to his audience. To what extent, then, is Odysseus justifying his actions and using his tales to captivate and gain favor from his internal audience?

Penelope's story is summarized in four lines (23.302–305). She suffered at the hands of the suitors, watching her husband's property and wealth squandered because of her. The remainder of the night (23.306–341) is given to Odysseus' adventures. In both summaries the reader is presented with a husband and wife united in a single goal: to reclaim the lives of peace and prosperity they once had. Both suffer equally for twenty years to achieve that goal; neither ever wavers from that purpose. In contrast, the journey of the other family group prominent throughout the epic, the Atridae (Agamemnon and Clytemnestra; Menelaus and Helen), ends in failure. The tales told throughout the *Odyssey* by Agamemnon and by Menelaus and Helen in *Od.* 4 portray a different picture. One surmises that at the end of the epic journey, the Arcesiad line is set next to the Atridae. Why then are the Arcesiads triumphant and the Atridae defeated? The Arcesiads' success is one based on common goals, common values, and a unified family unit. Both Odysseus and Penelope struggle to achieve shared goals—to preserve their family and home. For the Atridae it is the opposite. Agamemnon too wants to return to a wife and son, but Clytemnestra's values are flawed. She is unfaithful, wants power for herself, and gives little thought to her son's inheritance. Menelaus faces a similar situation. He fights a war for an unfaithful wife and lacks a legitimate heir for his immense fortune. Even though he is reunited with his wife, their stories in *Od.* 4 reveal many unresolved issues—they still distrust each other's motives and are reunited in appearance only. The *homophrosunē* that Homer claims is necessary for a successful marriage is possible only for Odysseus and Penelope, whose singular goal is a strong and united home held together by common bonds. Once this unity is achieved, all else can and will follow. Odysseus realizes the new challenges that await him, but together he and Penelope will prevail. His holdings will be replaced through raids and taxation (a picture of Odyssean society in which raids seem to be not only common practice but in fact sanctioned). Penelope is trusted to safeguard their possessions at home, and he will see to the suitors' relatives. Trust, common goals, and common values—the gods can offer nothing better than when a man and his wife keep a well-balanced home (6.183–184).

Selected Bibliography: *Od.* 23

Ahl and Roisman, "*Odyssey*," 247–272.

Clarke, *Art*, 67–85.

Finley, John H., Jr., *Homer's*, 185–208.

Foley, "Reverse."

Fredricksmeyer, "Penelope."

Gonzalez, "Odysseus'."

Heitman, *Taking*, 85–103.

Katz, *Penelope's*, 155–191.

Levine, "Odysseus'."

Martyniuk, "Odysseus'."

Morgan, "*Odyssey*."

Morrison, "Similes."

Reece, *Stranger's*, 165–188.

Roisman, "Penelope's."

Said, *Homer*, 189–222.

Scodel, "Removal."
Segal, "Phaeacians."
Vlahos, "Homer's *Odyssey*, Book 19" (2007).
Zeitlin, "Figuring."
Further commentary on *Od.* 23 in General Bibliography I.

Book 24

Od. 24 brings the *Odyssey* full circle by ending it the way it began—with a council of the gods and an assembly of the Ithacan people. It is not hard to see why the twelfth-century Homeric scholar Eustathius reports that the best Alexandrian critics of Homer, Aristophanes and Aristarchus, end the epic at 23.296. The narrative of *Od.* 24 seems superfluous at times, hurried and not as convincing as the earlier books. Nevertheless, as noted earlier, it serves to tie up important unfinished business. Like the previous two books, *Od.* 24 falls into three sections:

I. The second *Nekyia* (37%)
II. Odysseus and Laertes (38%)
III. The attack by the relatives (25%)

In de Jong's scheme (*Narratological*, 588), *Od.* 23.347–372 through *Od.* 24 covers the forty-first day, while in Stanford's chronology (*Homer*, x–xii), both books cover the fortieth day; the present reading follows the de Jong chronology. Thus, as dawn rises at the end of *Od.* 23 on the forty-first day of the narrative, the hero, his son, and the two herdsmen leave the palace to visit Laertes.

I. The Second Nekyia, 1–204

The relevance of the second descent to the underworld is focused on three episodes:

1. Agamemnon's *kleos*
2. Achilles' funeral
3. Amphimedon's testimony

Homer first crosscuts to follow Hermes of Kyllene (24.1–2)[14] leading the dead suitors to Hades. But why does he lead the suitors' souls to Hades long after their deaths? Why did they not go there on their own immediately after dying as they do in the *Iliad* (16.855–857, 22.361–363)? Odysseus in *Od.* 11.52–54 explains Elpenor's soul cannot rest until his body is buried, whereas the souls of the suitors, who are yet unburied and unwept for, are already entering Hades a day after their deaths. We can infer that since Hermes is leading the souls, they can enter Hades without waiting for burial. Whatever the time of the suitors' descent, rumor of their slaughter does not reach their relatives until Odysseus and company are already at Laertes' estate.

A simile (24.6–10) compares the descending souls arriving in the meadow of asphodel (24.13) to squeaking bats. This meadow, which conjures up a picture of beauty and serenity,[15] is here a dark and gloomy place, which is further implied by the comparison of the suitors' terrified souls to the broken chain of bats, which floats in darkness. The meadow, which they reach after a long descent through moldering paths, is a far cry from the Elysian Field at the limits of the earth, where Menelaus was destined to rest after death (4.561–568).

In Hades, the ghosts encounter the souls of several heroes (Patroclus, Antilochus, and Ajax) gathered around Achilles, the same group that approached Odysseus in 11.467–470. Agamemnon's soul, along with those of his companions who died at the hands of Aegisthus, approaches Achilles, who acknowledges that before the commander in chief's death, Agamemnon was favored above all heroes because he ruled over many (24.24–26). However, Agamemnon's position as commander did not earn him the *kleos* he sought. Had he died fighting as a warrior rather than being murdered, unsung by his wife, he could have won fame for both himself and his son through his prowess and been rewarded with a mound as a reminder of his heroic stature. Achilles' sentiment is a bit ironic, since his wrath in the *Iliad* was due to his interpretation of "the best of the Achaeans." Agamemnon laid claim to being "the best of the Achaeans" precisely for the reason just stated—he had the largest contingent in Troy. Achilles argued the title should be bestowed on the warrior who proved himself in battle (himself) and not on one who often shied away from fighting by relying on his rank (Agamemnon). Is Achilles getting back at Agamemnon for their unresolved argument in the *Iliad*? Even his parting words, that it was his fate to die a pitiful death, contain a taunting tone (24.34).

One reason, then, for the appearance of Achilles' funeral in the final book of the *Odyssey* is that it provides closure for the Achilles-Agamemnon conflict in the *Iliad*. Agamemnon's fifty-nine-line (24.36–94) exposition of the funeral seems to acknowledge Achilles' conclusion that fame is earned on the battlefield. But the commander's gratification in describing the grandeur of the funeral seems to evoke what he hoped for himself. He is clearly envious of the attention given to Achilles when he describes the immortal tears shed by Thetis and her divine maids. Even in death, Achilles' name remains immortal and his glory is forever unlike Agamemnon's, which was cut short by his cursed wife. But throughout Agamemnon's extolling, Achilles remains silent, for regardless of his honors and Agamemnon's lack of them, both remain dead and equal in Hades, perhaps the point Homer wants to underscore in a post-Trojan world.

There are also other reasons for placing Achilles' funeral in *Od.* 24. It provides the aftermath of Achilles' own *nostos*, which ends in Troy. Most of the major warriors (Odysseus, Agamemnon, Nestor, Menelaus, Ajax, and Diomedes) are given their due in the epic except Achilles. Here "the best of the Achaeans" is given closure. The *Iliad* closed with the funeral of Hector, who was mourned for nine days, buried on the tenth, and honored with a mound on the eleventh. Homer in the *Odyssey* now honors the supreme warrior, mourned for seventeen days, cremated on the eighteenth, and buried on the nineteenth. The *Iliad* ended with Hector's death and burial (*Il.* 24.804), and the *Odyssey* ends Achilles' life in a similar way—with his burial. Earlier in the underworld (*Od.* 11), Achilles expressed a view that his silence here confirms: it is better to be an alive nobody on Earth than a dead somebody in Hades. One wonders whether the magnificence of the funeral described is not merely Homer's way of pointing out the same sentiment.

Argeiphontes (see chapter 2, note 2) now draws close, leading the suitors' souls. Struck by the sight, both Achilles and Agamemnon approach them. Agamemnon recognizes Amphimedon, the suitor who injured Telemachus' wrist just before he was fatally wounded by the prince (22.276–284) and who once played host to the Atridae when they came to Ithaca to recruit Odysseus.[16] Agamemnon wonders what brought all these men in their prime to Hades: a shipwreck or defeat in battle while attempting to raid cattle and sheep, an assumption common in a society where travel was mostly by sea and raids commonplace.

Amphimedon's soul summarizes the suitors' deaths in the next seventy-eight lines (125–204). Although much of what he discloses repeats earlier material, he does offer a fresh insight on Penelope's recognition of Odysseus. He cites three events leading to Penelope's recognition of her husband:

1. Her cleverness exposed in her weaving trick
2. Odysseus at Eumaeus' hut, where plans for the suitors' deaths were contrived
3. The beggar/Odysseus at the palace, persevering through suitor abuses until the moment when he and Telemachus stow the weapons in the storeroom

At the palace, Penelope recognizes the beggar and together they secretly plot the suitors' deaths. It is Odysseus who, using the craftiness of his mind, agrees to the bow contest his lady proposes and urges her not to postpone it. If Penelope recognizes her husband when she questions him in *Od.* 19 and contrives the contest, which Odysseus approves, Amphimedon's story supports this early recognition. Both stratagems (the weaving trick and the bow contest) mentioned by the suitor had the same purpose, to eliminate the suitors (24.127). Amphimedon is merely summarizing events as they occurred, all of which the reader is aware happened as narrated by him except for three lines (24.167–169) out of the episode's seventy (24.121–190), in which Odysseus advises his wife to hold the bow contest. Why then not accept these three at face value also? If, on the other hand, these three lines are from a different version of the bow contest episode that found its way into Homer's present version, the three lines still lend support to Penelope's early recognition. Penelope was reluctant to accept a positive outcome for her second strategy, since her first failed, but agreed to the contest at Odysseus' urging. Assisted by a god, Odysseus strung the bow and cut down the suitors, whose bodies still lie unburied, their relatives unaware of their slaughter.

Agamemnon's reaction to Amphimedon's admission shows little concern for the suitors' plight but focuses again on his own situation. Odysseus' victory was achieved with the assistance of Penelope, whom Agamemnon contrasts with his own wife: a wife endowed with virtue versus one who killed her own husband. Clytemnestra's song, unlike Penelope's, will be one of loathing, and her actions will stain the reputation of all womankind, even those unborn.

II. Odysseus and Laertes, 205–411

In true cinematic style, the scene crosscuts again to Odysseus and his company arriving at Laertes' estate. The estate is cared for by an old, nameless Sicilian woman, the wife of the estate's manager, Dolius, and the mother of their six sons. Dolius is also the father of the goatherd Melanthius and the maid Melantho, both of whom outraged the beggar/Odysseus, who killed them. These two servants, having served their purpose in the *Odyssey*, are not mentioned again. Dolius seems ignorant of their activities, and the Sicilian woman is not mentioned as their mother. Sending his son and the two herdsmen to the lodge, Odysseus alone goes to find his father. It is not clear why he feels he must test his father or why his father fails to recognize his undisguised son, whom Athena transformed and made elegant in *Od.* 23.156–157. Approaching him with a heavy heart, Odysseus debates whether to embrace and kiss him or test him first. Weighing his options, he stands apart, using words rather than physical contact to address his father, as is his usual practice (see the Nausicaa episode in 6.145–147). It is not clear why Odysseus uses mocking words (24.240) to test a sad old man. Homer provides no explanation, unless Odysseus is afraid Laertes cannot withstand the shock of an immediate revelation. Since Laertes is tilling his garden with head lowered when Odysseus speaks, a gradual awakening is safer for a man who has given up on life. Odysseus praises his father's expert gardening but reprimands him on his appearance: he is ill cared for, squalid, and wearing foul clothing. His rebuke serves as an awakening, a way of bringing Laertes out of his stupor, since his appearance cannot be a function of laziness, given his meticulous gardening, and his face has the air of a leader, not a slave. In Homer, one's true nature cannot be hidden. Even Odysseus, disguised as a beggar, cannot completely hide his true character, which at times reveals itself through his physique and good manners. Another explanation for Odysseus' need to use yet another lying tale before revealing himself to his father is his character. All through his wandering, lying has been his primary tactic for hiding his identity to preserve his life. By the time he comes in contact with his father, lying has become a habit, a part of who he is. He can no longer approach anyone without exercising caution. In this respect his lies serve to put him more at ease than those he is questioning.

Odysseus asks his father three questions: (1) Who is your master? (2) In whose orchard are you laboring? and (3) Is this place Ithaca? Without waiting for a response, he launches into his final lie. He is searching for a long-lost Ithacan friend, the best he ever entertained, who claimed Ithaca was his home and Laertes his father. The friend was given a hero's welcome, entertained, and offered the hospitality of his host's abundance. The stranger makes a point to let Laertes know he is wealthy, proof of his nobility and good breeding. Good fortune comes only to those who come from noble stock and honor the gods, as we see throughout the *Odyssey*. The stranger lists the many gifts showered on his guest, underscoring not only his wealth but also the high esteem in which Laertes' son is held by the persona Odysseus adopts. Catching the reference to his son, Laertes weeps softly and tells the speaker he is in Ithaca, a land in the grip of violence and lawlessness. Although absent from Ithaca since his son left for Troy, Laertes seems aware of conditions at the palace. His removal from the city's affairs is testament to the closeness of his nuclear family, whose fracture drove him away, incapable of ruling. His condition, then, is the result not just of age but also of depression at the loss of his son, which affected the entire family. Unlike in the Atridae, in a united family each member is responsible for the others, as exemplified by Alcinous' family (*Od.* 7 and 8).

Laertes implies that since cruel men now rule Ithaca, all moral standards have been abandoned. Were his son alive, he would match the stranger's gifts, for kindness deserves recompense. In Ithaca's present situation, he will receive nothing. Laertes is curious to know how long ago the stranger hosted his son, who by now lies dead at the bottom of the sea. Emphasizing family obligations again, he regrets he and Penelope did not have the opportunity to perform the rites due the deceased. Throughout this exchange between father and son, Laertes is preoccupied with an individual's obligation to right behavior, which is not met in Odysseus' absence but is essential to peace and civic order.

Laertes asks the stranger's name and background (parents and city) and his means of transportation in order to determine his motive for travel. Lying, Odysseus gives his name as Eperitos (man of strife; similar etymologically to the word from which his real name is derived, *odussamenos*, one who inflicts or causes pain [*Od.* 19.405–409]), the son of Apheidas, son of Polypemon from Alybas, a prosperous household.[17] He was driven to Ithaca by a storm from Sicania (Sicily), and his ship lies moored not far from town. He last saw Odysseus five years ago when he hosted him. The bird signs at the time Odysseus left Eperitos were in his favor (on his right). Laertes, overcome with grief, claws at the ground and pours dirt over his head, sobbing in spasms. Seeing his father in distress, Eperitos/Odysseus relents and identifies himself (24.321–322). Fearing the old man might hurt himself, Odysseus abandons his lie and begs him to end his grief. He killed the suitors for their vicious crimes but needs Laertes to deal with the relatives, who will soon pursue him. Laertes requires proof that Eperitos is truly his son. Odysseus points to his scar, but as it is an external sign that even Odysseus' casual acquaintances knew, he also decides to reference the trees his father gave him as a boy—thirteen pear trees, ten apple trees, and forty fig trees; he also remembers being promised fifty vine rows. As in his previous lies, Odysseus connects his lie to what he already knows about the person being addressed. In Eumaeus' case, he matches his tale to incidents in the swineherd's past. In the present tale, Odysseus emphasizes the bond he and his father shared through the development of their land, their mutual interest in their orchard.

As Odysseus names the trees and specifies their number, Laertes recognizes the clear proofs only his son can provide. Embracing his son, he thanks Zeus's justice for the suitors' demise. Laertes' greatest anguish has been the thought that the gods allowed the suitors to eradicate the Arcesiad dynasty. Fearing Olympus abandoned him, Laertes retreated into the oblivion of his country estate. Now his son's return and the news of the suitors' deaths renew his sense of order and justice, and he is concerned an attack will come from the surrounding cities. Both Laertes and Odysseus realize that a struggle between the deceased's relatives and his family is unavoidable, since it is the way such disputes are handled in Homeric society. At the lodge, the Sicilian woman bathes Laertes, and Athena rejuvenates the old king, striking wonder in Odysseus. Laertes' own personal journey of sorrow and heartache ends. Reinvigorated with courage and renewed life, Laertes is ready to meet the suitors' relatives. Dolius, who trudges into the lodge with his sons, recognizes Odysseus and rushes to welcome him. Dolius' ability to recognize Odysseus when his own father does not is due mostly to Dolius' intuition, although with Telemachus and the rejuvenated Laertes present at the table, he must sense something celebratory is in progress. Before the twelve men[18] sit to dinner, Dolius is anxious to deliver the good news to Penelope, but Odysseus assures him that she already knows. Based on his concern to inform Penelope, it would seem Dolius is unaware of what has transpired since Odysseus' return to Ithaca, which would explain his ignorance of his son and daughter's fate.

III. The Attack by the Relatives, 412–548

In Ithaca rumor of the suitors' deaths has spread, and relatives of the dead gather before Odysseus' palace, anxious to retrieve the bodies of their sons and fathers. As soon as the local dead are removed and buried, and the foreign dead returned to their countries, the people meet in assembly. Eupithes, father of Antinous, is first to address those present. Weeping for his son, he accuses Odysseus of perpetrating great evils on all Cephalonians.[19] In addition to acknowledging the loss of the 108 suitors killed, Eupithes inquires about the loss of the men who accompanied Odysseus to Troy, a loss that impacted nearly every household in the kingdom. It is no wonder that Odysseus conceals the suitors' slaughter as long as possible while preparing to face his subjects. Eupithes tries to solicit support for his cause in the assembly by reminding the suitors' relatives that they too lost loved ones under Odysseus' command. He urges quick action before Odysseus escapes to Pylos or Elis, arguing that failure to avenge their dead will bring everlasting shame and disgrace.

While Eupithes agitates the crowd, Medon and Phemius, who both served the suitors under compulsion, arrive. Medon informs the assembly that Odysseus did not act alone against the suitors but in fact had the gods' consent. Medon saw a god in the form of Mentor standing beside Odysseus, although Homer does not say how Medon could tell Mentor was a god, but his words grip many of those present with terror. Halitherses, an old warrior gifted in prophecy, blames the crowd for allowing the suitors' evil acts. He warns them against retribution unless they want to incur the gods' wrath, but his words stir less than half the crowd. Most present rise with a great cry to arm themselves. Eupithes takes command to avenge his son's death, and the narrator intercedes to forecast his death. The present assembly, which parallels the assembly in *Od.* 2, now brings the *Odyssey* narrative full circle. In the first assembly, it was Aegyptius who, like Eupithes, stood to mourn his own son, Antiphus, who accompanied Odysseus to Troy and was the first devoured by the Cyclops. After Aegyptius roused the crowd against Telemachus, the same Halitherses tried to warn those gathered of disaster (2.163). The narrative again crosscuts to an assembly on Olympus (24.472–488), where Athena confronts her father, Zeus, to learn how he intends to handle Eupithes and his followers: incite fighting or establish friendship between the two factions. Zeus declares she can do as she pleases but offers what he feels to be proper: friendship, prosperity, and peace (24.485–486).

The narrative again crosscuts to Odysseus' estate, where one of Dolius' sons spots the suitors' relatives nearing the farm. The reader is not told how the relatives know Odysseus is at his country estate, since he went there under cover. Nor is it clear how the relatives appear at the moment Dolius' son is asked to look outside. Poetic license, perhaps? Odysseus leads the assembled men; even Dolius and Laertes, old and gray, strap on armor. Outside, Athena, disguised as Mentor, meets them, but Odysseus recognizes the goddess and is pleased. Turning to Telemachus, he encourages him to be brave, and Telemachus swears not to disgrace his heritage. Laertes is exhilarated as three generations of Arcesiads prepare to win *kleos* in battle. But Odysseus in the *Odyssey*, unlike in the *Iliad*, is armed not to win fame and honor but rather to preserve law and order and bring peace and prosperity to Ithaca. His momentary turn to the *Iliad*'s warrior ethic is short lived, for Zeus abruptly ends it. Athena encourages Laertes to cast his spear, and he prays to both the goddess and Zeus as he throws his spear through Eupithes' bronze helmet. With Eupithes dead, Odysseus and his son charge, but Athena stops them and implores them to settle their differences without bloodshed. Terror and fear grip the relatives at her words; they drop their weapons and take flight. Odysseus lets loose a savage war cry and rushes after them, but Zeus hurls a bolt of lightning at Athena's feet. Athena orders Odysseus to stop for fear he may anger Zeus. Odysseus obeys her, and Mentor/Athena has both warring sides pledge solemn oaths of peace. The *Odyssey* ends with three Arcesiad generations, past, present, and future, fighting side by side to reestablish Themis, the personification of divine order, natural law, and custom, as the rule in Ithaca. Directly behind them stands the goddess Athena, who throughout the *Odyssey* controlled their actions like a puppeteer.

Selected Bibliography: *Od.* 24

Clarke, *Art*, 67–85.
Currie, "Genitive."
Erbse, "Ending."
Finley, John H., Jr., *Homer's*, 185–208, 221–223, 224–234.
Henderson, "Name."
Lowenstam, "Shroud."
Marks, *Zeus*, 62–82, 83–111.
Moulton, "End."
Reese, "Homer's."
Said, *Homer*, 189–222.
Segal, "Phaeacians."
Sels, "Untold."
Tsagalis, "*Odyssey*."
Wender, "In Hades."
Wender, *Last Scenes*.
Whitehead, "Funeral."
Further commentary on *Od.* 24 in General Bibliography I.

AFTERWORD

Likely reasons for the *Odyssey*'s longevity, which has kept the epic on the best-seller list for over 2,500 years, are its modernity, its atypicality, and its emphasis on Themis.

Modernity

The *Odyssey* reads like a modern narrative with all the trappings of a contemporary work—ambiguity, realism, irony, and psychological insights. To begin with, Homer is suggestive more often than not. As we have seen, one encounters an uncertainty in the narrative that makes plausible multiple interpretations. In the second half of the epic (*Od.* 13–24), Odysseus adopts lying as a strategy to accomplish his goal of eliminating the suitors. Is he then also strategizing by manipulating the truth when reciting his wanderings (*Od.* 9–12) to the Phaeacians? How early in the narrative does Penelope suspect her husband is the beggar? What does she mean by asking the beggar to interpret her self-explanatory dream (if it truly is a dream) of the geese and the eagle? What are we to make of Menelaus and Helen's puzzling relationship? These questions, among many others, are left unanswered.

Even the *Odyssey*'s structure is not only more complex than its predecessor, the *Iliad*, composed in the same century, but more realistic and contemporary. Although full of fairytales and folktales, it begins and ends in a real geographical locale, Ithaca, and much of its story is presented in flashbacks and crosscuts, as in a modern film. Digressions and asides often interrupt the narrative flow to create tension and suspense before the poet returns to pick up the narrative where he previously abandoned it (see 4.847 and 15.495, 4.498 and 4.551–555; 15.300 and 15.495; and 19.392 and 19.467). The contemporary appeal of the *Odyssey*'s mythic material (Cyclopes, Laestrygonians, Lotus-Eaters, etc. [*Od.* 9–12]) is often minimized to create a more naturalistic picture. Homer is interested in describing everyday domesticity equally among the aristocracy and ordinary people, including herdsmen and domestics. Even dogs in the *Odyssey* are given a more favorable role (see 14.30–37, 16.4–10, 16.161–162, and 17.291–327) than in the *Iliad*, where the deceased become "the delicate feasting / of dogs" (1.4–5). People throughout the epic are exposed to the realities of nature that are missing in the *Iliad* (see *Od.* 4.441–446, 5.321, 421, 5.466–469, 5.473, 14.457–458, 17.24–25, 17.181, and 17.195–196), and the *Odyssey*'s characters tend to act and speak in a natural way. Take, for instance, Nausicaa's companions' frolicking and squealing when one of them fails to catch the ball (6.111) or blushingly running away from a naked Odysseus (6.138). Recall the touching scene of Pontonous guiding the blind bard among the feasters, carefully hanging his lyre on a peg above his head, showing him how to retrieve it, and setting beside him a table with food and drink (8.65–70). Recall the terrified Eurylochus' refusing to return to Circe's palace when threatened by Odysseus but reluctantly tagging along rather than remain alone (10.429–448), or Alcinous' verifying that Odysseus' treasure stowed on the ship that will carry him home will not interfere with the sailors' rowing (13.20–22). As C. H. Whitman observes, "The *Odyssey* is not an epic in the same sense as the *Iliad*, but, with its openness to all detail, however homely, and its concern with social types and forms, something verging toward the novel" (Whitman, "Odyssey," 87).

Realism in the *Odyssey* takes a variety of forms: Odysseus' changing his mind on how to handle the weapons in the *megaron* or asking

Eurycleia not to reveal the names of the immoral maids but later seeking her advice. Recall the detailed descriptive passages (not to be found in the *Iliad*) of the islands of Calypso and the Cyclopes and Alcinous' garden or Homer's handling of simultaneous events concurrently, such as Athena's leaving to visit Telemachus in *Od.* 1 while Hermes is sent at the same time to release Odysseus from Calypso's embrace in *Od.* 5. A similar blurring of timescale occurs when Odysseus and Telemachus return to Ithaca for their reunion. Odysseus leaves for Ithaca and arrives in *Od.* 13, while Telemachus leaves at the same time at the end of *Od.* 4 but arrives in *Od.* 15.

The *Odyssey*'s emphasis on home and family, on accentuating human feelings, both masculine and feminine, and its celebration of ordinary life (see Eumaeus, 20.149–154) go beyond what one finds in the *Iliad*, another reason why this epic might be considered a distant ancestor of the modern novel. In *Od.* 6 Odysseus finds no greater blessing to bestow on Nausicaa than marital harmony (180–185). In *Od.* 4 Menelaus praises Nestor for a marriage that gave him more sons than any other Greek hero in either epic (208). Odysseus' Cretan persona in his lying tale to Eumaeus returns home after ten years of fighting in Troy to take "pleasure in [his] children and [his] wedded wife and [his] possessions" (14.244). Throughout the epic, Homer presents family members and ordinary people trying to assert themselves as they struggle to understand their place in the world, to justify their actions, and to deal with life—growing up, recognition, love, marriage, and death. Odysseus passes from a world dominated by the heroic code to a world of family and community life whose values are represented in the actions of women like Penelope and Arete.

The *Odyssey*'s modernity and realism are further expressed in the epic's treatment of women, as they enjoy a status and dignity equal to their husbands', in contrast to the women in the *Iliad*, whose voices are muted (with the exception of Andromache, Hecuba, and Helen, who receive some attention, though their influence is negligible). Women in the *Odyssey* are portrayed not only as men's equals but at times as being more perceptive: Penelope is equal to Odysseus (23.177–180, 24.125–141); Arete is often more influential than Alcinous (6.303–315, 7.53–77); Helen seems shrewder than Menelaus; Clytemnestra is presented as more keen-witted than Agamemnon; Anticleia's stalwartness causes Laertes to think twice before approaching Eurycleia, whom he desires (1.432–433). Even minor female characters like Melantho and Eurynome and divine figures like Circe, Calypso, Leucothea, and Eidothea have a strong influence over men.

Irene J. F. de Jong compares the *Odyssey* to the modern novels of James Joyce and Virginia Woolf for its capacity to portray the unspoken thoughts, feelings, and perceptions of characters, a device of unspoken thought that she terms "embedded focalization" (de Jong, "Between," 62). Nausicaa dreams of her neglected laundry and her reputation as a future bride and worries of gossip that might taint her family's good name (6.25–30). In the same book, Odysseus ruminates about how to approach a young princess in his naked and battered state (141–147). While Eumaeus describes Odysseus' assets, the disguised hero eats quietly, devising evils for the suitors (*Od.* 14), or silently weighs whether to kill Melanthius for threatening him and kicking him in the hip (17.233–238). Similar thoughts plague his mind when Antinous throws a stool at him (17.462–465), when he is about to fight Irus (18.91–94), when he considers the fate of the immoral maids on their way to lie with the insolent suitors (20.10–13), and when Ctesippus hurls an ox foot at him (20.299–302). Likewise, Penelope debates how to approach the beggar/Odysseus (23.85–87), and Telemachus patiently waits for the moment of attack while the suitors tease his guests (20.384–386). Even Eurymachus secretly calculates Telemachus' murder at the same time he assures Penelope of his safety (16.444–449), just as the suitors externally praise him while internally contriving his death (17.65–66). Thinking in the *Odyssey* is often preferable to talking, in contrast to Achilles' view in the *Iliad*: "For as I detest the doorways of Death, I detest the man, who hides one thing in the depths of his heart, and speaks forth another" (*Il.* 9.312–313). Scenes like these are full of deep psychological undercurrents, but Homer refuses to explain them. One might easily assume that there is some latent father-son antagonism between Odysseus and Laertes to explain their strange reunion or wonder at the causes of the rocky son-mother relationship between Telemachus and Penelope.

Atypicality

When considering Odysseus' characterization in the *Odyssey*, which W. B. Stanford (*Ulysses*) called untypical, his dissimilarities to the heroes of the *Iliad* become apparent. When Hector demands a challenger to end the Greek-Trojan conflict (*Il.* 7.96–180), Achilles' absence obligates an embarrassed Menelaus to challenge him, but after he is quickly discouraged by his brother Agamemnon, nine other Greek warriors step forward to defy the Trojan.[1] Among those named, Odysseus is the lowest in priority, even lower than Menelaus. However, it is Odysseus' hoax, the Trojan horse, that conquers Troy; it is his *mētis*, not *biē*, that causes Troy's demise and distinguishes him from his fellow warriors. The new world he enters after Troy no longer requires military prowess alone but rather calls for a hero who is *polytropos* (one who can change with the situations at hand, clever and cunning), *polytlas* (much enduring), *polymetis* (one with great intelligence), and *polymechanos* (one rich in devices to gain an end)—a hero unlike the Iliadic warriors.

1. Odysseus' atypicality is seen in his prudent resourcefulness, his patience, and his endurance. Trapped in the Cyclops' cave and aware that the giant is too powerful to be overcome by force, he uses his intellect to find a solution to his dilemma—he intoxicates him, blinds him, and finds an escape route from the cave. Such resourcefulness is a hallmark of his character. When necessary, he resorts to well-thought-out lies and disguises either to gain support for his goal or to cause his enemies to submit. Nor is it beneath his heroic dignity to spy on the Trojans, disguised as a beggar (*Od.* 4.244–250), or to promise Dolon's safety only to have him killed once he obtains the

information he seeks (*Il.* 10). Keep in mind that it is his counsel that prevents mutiny among the Greek troops after Agamemnon's dream (*Il.* 2).

2. Odysseus' atypicality is evident in his agility with the bow, whose use in the *Iliad* is considered unheroic when compared to hand-to-hand combat with swords and spears. Its use is limited to Paris, whose cowardice is often alluded to by his brother Hector, and to Pandarus, whose skill as an archer breaks the truce between the two warring sides and condemns the Trojans to their fate (*Il.* 4).
3. Unlike the Iliadic heroes, Odysseus is inquisitive, constantly seeking new knowledge. In the Sirens episode (*Od.* 12), he alone is privy to their enticing and deadly songs, although he has nothing to gain by hearing them. Warned by his companions not to linger in the Cyclops' cave, he is compelled by his curiosity and thirst for knowledge to explore not only the cave but also the giant's island to "find out about these people and learn what they are" (*Od.* 9.174), endangering his life and that of his crew (9.229). Warned by Eurylochus against pursuing the antidote for those companions turned into pigs by Circe, Odysseus' curiosity prevails: "I shall go. For there is strong compulsion upon me" (*Od.* 10.273).
4. Odysseus exhibits great self-control, best seen in the Nausicaa episode (*Od.* 6). Arriving on Scheria naked, exhausted, and hungry, he exercises great resilience in concealing his basic instincts before approaching Nausicaa and the young maidens who greet him. Only after careful reflection on an approach to win the princess's confidence does he gain her trust. The same self-control is exhibited throughout the *Odyssey*'s final twelve books, where, disguised as a beggar, he endures the suitors' physical and mental abuse until he has the resources to eliminate them.
5. Odysseus' emphasis on hunger, experienced during his ten-year-long wanderings, further sets him apart from his Iliadic compatriots (see chapter 2, notes 13 and 14). When Alcinous questions his identity, the

hero requests that he first be allowed to finish his dinner, "for there is no other thing so shameless as to be set over / the belly" (*Od.* 7.216–217), and he continues to comment on the power hunger holds over him, forcing "forgetfulness / of all [he has] suffered" (7.220–221). Odysseus' preoccupation with hunger is not limited, however, to the *Odyssey*. When Achilles in the *Iliad* refuses to delay avenging Patroclus' death, Odysseus urges him to first consider feeding the army. Achilles' refusal to listen ("food and drink mean nothing to my heart / but blood does" [*Il.* 19.213–214]) hastens Odysseus' practical and well-reasoned response on the need for food (*Il.* 19.216–234), convincing Achilles to postpone his attack until the army is fed.

6. Odysseus' eloquence further adds to his atypicality. Although Nestor and Diomedes in the *Iliad* are also celebrated public speakers, Odysseus' speeches are functional, used to achieve his objectives—to stem a mutiny (*Il.* 2) and to feed an army before returning to battle (*Il.* 19). Perhaps one of the best examples of the functionality of his speeches is when he forcefully quells the insolent Phaeacian Euryalus. Angered at his insults, Odysseus reprimands him, but unlike Achilles, who holds a grudge throughout the *Iliad*, Odysseus accepts Euryalus' apology and graciously thanks him: "Farewell . . . dear friend, and may the gods grant you / prosperity" (*Od.* 8.413–414).
7. Odysseus fights not just for glory but to restore order and peace in Ithaca. The few lapses that revert him to his Iliadic past (his attack on the suitors' relatives) are quickly repelled by Zeus and Athena (*Od.* 24.542–544), nor does he boast at his successes as do the heroes of the *Iliad*. When Eurycleia begins to raise a triumphal cry at the dead suitors' pools of blood on the *megaron* floor, Odysseus checks her, warning, "It is not piety to glory so over slain men" (*Od.* 22.412). Along with resilience, concentration, and intuitive intelligence Odysseus exhibits a civilized gentleness throughout the Phaeacian books (*Od.* 6–8) and particularly in the Amphinomus episode (*Od.* 18), where he tries to save the suitor's life. In the underworld,

Odysseus' mother explains her death as a result of her longing for her son's cleverness and gentle ways (*Od.* 11.202–203). Even Athena, at the council of the gods expresses anger that the gods are not facilitating the homecoming of Odysseus, a gentle and kind man whose thought is schooled in justice (Od. 5.8–9).

8. Finally, Odysseus is an artist as much as he is a hero. In his *apologoi* (*Od.* 9–12), he himself becomes a bard whose powers of delivery are compared to Homer's own. His audience is stricken to silence, enthralled by his recitation (Od. 11.334, 13.2). Overcome by sleep while recounting his Hades adventure, he is nevertheless urged by Alcinous to continue telling his "wonderful story" (11.374). Even Eumaeus alerts Penelope that the beggar he has been hosting enchanted him with his stories like a singer whose skill comes from the gods (17.518–521). Odysseus, throughout the *Odyssey*, remains an eccentric figure but with a good share of heroic qualities to hide his eccentricity.

Themis

Themis, a Titaness, personifies divine order, fairness, natural law, and custom, themes central to the *Odyssey* and its gods, who endorse a world governed by an ethical code (*Od.* 22.413–417). The young suitors become indignant at Antinous' abuse of the beggar/Odysseus and fear retribution should he turn out to be one of the gods, who are ever watchful to see which men keep the laws and which are violent (*Od.* 17.487). Odysseus justifies the suitors' deaths by blaming their own recklessness in respecting neither the base nor the noble. In requesting an end to Odysseus' exile, Athena reminds the gods of his piety and sacrifices, and Zeus agrees that beyond any other, Odysseus gave the gods their due (*Od.* 1.60–62). Only those who knowingly do wrong after being warned by the gods must pay for their reckless behavior, like Aegisthus, who pays for marrying his cousin's wife and having his cousin killed upon his return, even though he was warned by the gods of the illegality of such an act. Similarly, the suitors, warned through omens and prophecies of what is unlawful and wrong, must pay for the paths they chose to follow. In Hades, Odysseus expresses his humanity, attempting to befriend Ajax, who stands at a distance, seething at Odysseus for being granted the arms of Achilles. Feeling partly responsible for Ajax's suicide, Odysseus grieves for a warrior who, in beauty and achievement, surpassed all but Achilles (*Od.* 11.548–551). At the end of the epic, Zeus opts for law and peace and orders a stop to warfare, which Odysseus obeys with a happy heart. The *Odyssey* respects a world of cooperation, kindness, and understanding, a world that honors the gods and the natural forces that rule it. Unlike the *Iliad*, it celebrates ordinary life, home, family, and the triumph of life over death. Perhaps the *Odyssey*'s greatness is best revealed in the moral revolution that occurs both in the epic itself and in Odysseus' character—the shift from power to the principle of justice.

ACKNOWLEDGMENTS

I would like to express my gratitude to the anonymous reader for reading this manuscript with meticulousness and for providing insightful comments, which I am sure resulted in a better text.

I also thank my wife, Linda, and my colleague of many years John W. Ward for their comments and suggestions, which were much appreciated. I owe a special thank you to the Interlibrary Loan Department of West Chester University whose efficient staff has provided me with fifty years of outstanding service.

NOTES

PREFACE

1. Metis was Zeus's first wife. He swallowed her to give birth to Athena, who popped out of his head, the center of intelligence (*mētis*).

CHAPTER 1 — TELEMACHUS' JOURNEY (*OD.* 1–4)

1. Later tradition identifies this muse as Calliope, a goddess and daughter of Zeus and Mnemosyne (memory).

2. The divisions of the *Odyssey* books are my own.

3. This is the percentage of the total book devoted to this section.

4. The *Iliad*'s theme is its first word, *mēnin* (wrath), the wrath of Achilles.

5. All references to the *Odyssey* are from Lattimore, *"Odyssey,"* unless otherwise noted.

6. Helius is the sun god; Apollo is later associated with the sun.

7. Atreus was the father of Agamemnon and Menelaus, and his name is used to refer to the entire myth. This myth is made famous in the fifth century B.C.E. by Aeschylus in his trilogy *The Oresteia*.

8. *Od.* 1.35–43, 46–47, 298–300; *Od.* 3.193–198, 234–235, 255–275, 303–312; *Od.* 4.90–92, 512–537, 546–547; *Od.* 11.387–389, 409–434, 451–453; *Od.* 13.383–385; *Od.* 24.19–22, 96–97, 199–202.

9. Zeus Xenios (from *xenia*, hospitality) is the god of strangers and hospitality.

10. Little else is mentioned or known about this myth recounted by Athena, which is not cited again in the epic.

11. Telemachus is described as "thoughtful" sixteen times in the *Telemachia* (1.345, 1.367, 1.388, 1.412, 2.128, 2.208, 2.309, 2.371, 3.21, 3.75, 3.201, 3.225, 3.239, 4.290, 4.315, and 4.593).

12. The speakers are Aegyptius, Telemachus, Antinous, Halitherses, Eurymachus, Mentor (the man, not Athena in disguise), and Leocritus.

13. A *skeptron* is a wooden staff symbolizing the authority to speak for the one who wields it.

14. Themis refers to divine law, those rules of conduct established by custom. Themis was the Titan goddess of divine law and order.

15. Tyro, daughter of Salmoneus and wife of Cretheus, was in love with the river Enipeus. Poseidon, taking the river's likeness, seduced her and, after his lovemaking, informed her that she would bear glorious children to the god Poseidon (11.235–252).

16. Alcmene, wife of Amphitryon, was secretly seduced by Zeus and thereafter gave birth to Herakles (11.266–268).

17. Mycene, whose name was given to Agamemnon's city, is not mentioned elsewhere in the *Odyssey*, and little is known about her other than that she is the daughter of one Inachos and wife of Arestor.

18. The patronymic for Odysseus' line is taken from Odysseus' grandfather Arcesius (see *Od.* 16.118–120).

19. Amphitrite stands for the sea (3.91). In later Greek mythology, this name is given to the sea goddess and wife of Poseidon.

20. All references to the *Iliad* are from Lattimore, "*Iliad.*"

21. Later tradition attributes the returning heroes' hardships to Athena's anger at Locrian Aias' (Ajax the Lesser's) rape of Cassandra in her temple. A more traditional version, which Homer sidesteps, has Athena punishing and prolonging the Achaeans' homecomings for their transgressions after Troy's fall. Odysseus' desertion and his years of wandering were Athena's punishment for his role (along with Diomedes) in the Palladium's theft. The Palladium was a wooden statue of Athena that Odysseus and Diomedes stole from the citadel of Troy. It was revealed by Helenus (Priam's prophetic son) that Troy would not fall while the Palladium remained within Troy's walls.

22. Atrides (pl. Atridae) refers to Agamemnon and Menelaus, whose father was Atreus. Their patronymic is thus Atrides, son of Atreus.

23. It will take almost another three hundred years (fifth century B.C.E.) before Orestes' deeds are questioned in Aeschylus' *Oresteia*; Orestes is hounded by his mother's furies before being acquitted of murder in a court of law.

24. Tritogeneia is a term explained in different ways: (1) derived from Lake Tritonis in Libya, near where she was born; (2) derived from the stream Triton in Boeotia, where she was worshiped and, for some, where she was also born; (3) derived from the word *trito*, which for some signifies "head," since the goddess was born out of Zeus's head.

25. Nestor's six living sons are Echephron, Stratius, Perseus, Aretus, Thrasymedes, and Pisistratus.

26. Deiphobus was Helen's lover and husband after Paris' death.

27. Philomelides, king of Lesbos, whom Odysseus defeated, challenged anyone sailing past his kingdom to a wrestling match in which those who lost forfeited their lives.

28. *Cyclopeia* is the name given to the Cyclops episode.

29. Athena's hatred, mentioned in line 502, is not pursued by Homer. Later tradition attributes this hatred to Ajax's (Aias the Lesser's) rape of Cassandra, Priam's daughter, in the goddess's temple.

30. This event is elaborated on in Aeschylus' fifth-century B.C.E. tragedy *Agamemnon*.

31. This is his first of five appearances in the *Odyssey*: 4.677–715, 16.411–412, 17.172–176, 22.357–380, and 24.439–450.

CHAPTER 2 — ODYSSEUS FROM CALYPSO TO THE PHAEACIANS (*OD.* 5–8)

1. In myth, Tithonus (not covered in the *Odyssey*), the son of Laomedon, Priam's brother, was snatched up by Dawn (Eos) and at her request made immortal but not ageless by Zeus. When Tithonus aged, Dawn shunned him.

2. Hermes earned this epithet (Argeiphontes = slayer of Argos) for having slain the one-hundred-eyed giant Argos, whom Hera put in charge of Io. Io, a priestess of Hera, was desired by Zeus, but his jealous wife, Hera, forced him to turn her into a cow in order to save her.

3. This is the reader's first face to face with Odysseus.

4. "*Alati o thanatos kai ti zoi polu ti nostimizei*" (18.912; my translation).

5. Scheria is also known as Phaeacia.

6. Homer identifies Ino as "a winged gannet" (5.337), but in Greek mythology she was one of Cadmus' daughters who nursed her sister's (Semele's) infant son, the god Dionysos. Hera became jealous that Ino consented to nurse a son from Zeus's adulterous affair and drove her insane. In her madness, Ino leapt into the sea with her own baby Melicertes and was transformed into a benevolent sea goddess, Leucothea (white goddess or goddess of spray). From that moment on, she and her son, who became the god Palaemon, guided storm-tossed sailors to safety.

7. Artemis was seen bathing naked in the woods by the hunter Actaeon, and for this transgression the goddess transformed him into a stag, which his hounds tore apart.

8. Delos is an island sacred to Apollo, the god of prophecy, visited by believers as today pilgrims visit the Vatican or Mecca.

9. E.g., Persephone is raped by Hades while gathering flowers; Helen is abducted by Theseus while dancing.

10. Eurymedon led his people (Gigantes) to their slaughter in a war against the gods. The Cyclopes are another race of giants.

11. Erechtheus is a mythical king of Athens, born from the earth and tended by Athena, who places him in her own temple (*Il.* 2.547–551).

12. The Spinners are Clotho, who spins the thread of life; Lachesis, who allots the length of the string of life; and Atropos, who snips the string of life.

13. *Od.* 6.132–134, 7.216–221, 17.226–228, 17.286, 17.473, 17.558–559, 18.1–3, 18.53–54, 18.363–364, 18.379–380.

14. *Od.* 4.368–369, 5.95, 5.165–166, 10.176–177, 12.332, 12.342–343, 15.407, 16.478–479, 19.425, 20.137.

15. The athletes' names are Topsail, Riptide, Rowhard, Seaman, Sternman, Surf-at-the-Beach, Stroke-Oar, Breaker, Bowsprit, Racing-the-Wind, Swing-Aboard, Seagirt, Shipwrightson, Broadsea (Fagles, *Odyssey*, 195).

16. See chapter 1, note 25.

17. *Aristeia* means "excellence"; a scene in Homer's epics in which a hero in battle has his finest moments.

CHAPTER 3 — ODYSSEUS' WANDERINGS (*OD.* 9–12)

1. *Apologoi* refers to Odysseus' narration of his wanderings (Od. 9-12) to the Phaeacians (*Od.* 6–8), his twelfth episode. Odysseus' eleventh episode (Calypso) is narrated in *Od.* 5, which Odysseus recounts in *Od.* 7.

2. Ismarus was once a city on the Aegean coast of Thrace.

3. From "Ulysses" by Alfred, Lord Tennyson.

4. "*Onom' echapátesen emōn kai mētis amumōn.*"

5. Homer does not say how long Odysseus and his men remain under the sheep waiting for dawn. If the blinding takes place in the evening, they are suspended all night long.

6. Aeolus is the son of Hippotes and is frequently conflated with Aeolus, the son of Poseidon. In the *Odyssey* he is a mortal keeper of the winds. Post-Homeric authors perceived him as a god.

7. Artakiē is a spring whose name seems to originate from an older epic, *Argonautica*.

8. Aeetes was king of Colchis, a barbarian kingdom, Helius' son, and the father of Medea and Jason's taskmaster.

9. This is reminiscent of Dante's *Inferno* (1303): "Midway on our life's journey, I found myself / In dark woods, the right road lost" (Pinsky, Canto 1.1–2).

10. In the epic cycle's *Telegony*, written by Eugammon of Cyrene in the sixth century B.C.E., Circe does give birth to a son, Telegonus, who eventually slays Odysseus and marries Penelope, while Circe weds Telemachus.

11. Circe refers to these two rivers as offshoots of the Styx; an oath sworn by the river Styx was considered by the gods the most solemn of oaths (*Il.*15.37–38).

12. Acheron is the river of woe, one of the five rivers of the underworld (Cocytus, Styx, Acheron, Pyriphlegethon, and Lethe). In Homer, Acheron is described as a river of Hades into which Cocytus and Pyriphlegethon both flow.

13. The other two, discussed earlier, are Eurylochus and Polites.

14. Ezra Pound reworked this famous passage (11.1–22) to open his *Cantos*. The ship, which in Aeaea was dragged on land and its gear stowed (10.402–403), is here miraculously ready to sail.

15. The Cimmerians are a mythical people inhabiting a land of perpetual darkness.

16. Such unheroic behavior in an age of heroes will in the twentieth century become a symbol of modern man, as in Nobel Prize–winning poet (1963) George Seferis' "Thrush" (1947).

17. This second journey foretold by Tiresias inspired later generations to continue Odysseus' adventures from the point the *Odyssey* ends. Chief among the works that extend the *Odyssey* beyond Homer's version is Dante's *Inferno* (1303) and Nikos Kazantzakis' *Odyssey: A Modern Sequel* (1939), in which Odysseus' journey continues through the twentieth century, tripling the size of Homer's epic to 33,333 verses.

18. This is a reference to Artemis' poisonous but painless arrows, which were presumed to bring relief to those who sorrowed.

19. If the Aeolus mentioned here is the same as the keeper of winds, it is hard to reconcile the two versions of Aeolus presented in *Od.* 10 and 11. In *Od.* 10, Aeolus lives on a floating island with a family of six sons and six daughters married to each other (Tyro is her brother's wife). But in *Od.* 11 Tyro is the daughter of Salmoneus, who, according to legend, lived in Thessaly before migrating to Elis, where he founded the city of Salmone.

20. Her three sons by her mortal husband, Cretheus, are also distinguished: Aison is the father of Jason, the hero of the epic *Argonautica*; Pheres is a Thessalian king who bore a distinguished line; and Amythaon is the father of the prophet Melampous and thus a distant relative of Theoclymenus, the young prophet who befriends Telemachus in *Od.* 15.223–258.

21. The son referred to in this case, Heracles, is probably obvious to Homer's audience and thus needs no further exposition. Heracles, the son of Zeus, is also

called the son of Amphitryon, his mortal father. After his death, Heracles becomes a god himself, residing on Olympus as the husband of Hera's daughter Hebe. Having Megara follow Heracles' mother, Alcmene, serves to transition to the second set of four women who speak to Odysseus. It is noteworthy that there is no mention of Megara's murder by Heracles, a version perhaps not familiar to Homer or, if familiar, irrelevant to his theme that the greatest *kleos* women attain is through union with a god.

22. Epikaste was better known as Jocasta in post-Homeric times, as in Sophocles' fifth-century B.C.E. tragedy *Oedipus the King*.

23. *Oedipus the King* (aka *Oedipus Tyrannus*), 429 B.C.E.

24. As she is the wife of Neleus, her story has ties to Tyro (Neleus is her son by Poseidon). Chloris, the daughter of Iasos' son Amphion, is tied to Antiope (the second woman to approach Odysseus), Amphion's mother. Neleus' myth also has ties to Heracles, who once led an expedition against him in which Neleus lost eleven of his twelve sons; Nestor (*Od.* 3) was the sole survivor. Although Homer does not mention Heracles in Chloris' story, it nevertheless ties her story to the last two women of the first group (1a)—Alcmene (Heracles' mother) and Megara (Heracles' wife).

25. Pero is the daughter of Neleus and Chloris and wife of her cousin Bias. Pero's beauty attracts many suitors, but Neleus refuses to give his daughter to any man unless he can raid the cattle of Iphicles from Phylake. Melampous, a seer fleeing Neleus, who holds his possessions by force for one year, finds himself a prisoner of Phylakos (father of Iphicles), who eventually releases him, drives the stolen cattle to Neleus, and returns Pero to his brother Bias (*Od.* 15).

26. In the best-known version of this myth, Leda is seduced by Zeus in the form of a swan, a union that gives birth to Helen, Clytemnestra, and the two sons. Most versions of the myth have Zeus seducing Leda on the same night as she lies with her mortal husband, Tyndareos; the two pairs of twins born are attributed as follows: Polydeuces and Helen to Zeus, and Castor and Clytemnestra to Tyndareos.

27. It is difficult to decipher Homer's purpose in linking these three women together, although all three are connected to Minos. Phaedra and Ariadne are Minos' daughters, and Procris is a woman he tries to seduce when she seeks his protection.

28. Eriphyle is the wife of Amphiaraus and mother of two heroic sons, Alcmaeon and Amphilochus. Knowing that her husband is destined not to survive the war against Thebes, she persuades him to join the battle, bribed by Polyneices, Oedipus' son, who promises her Harmonia's golden necklace.

29. Cassandra is the daughter of Priam (king of Troy). Agamemnon takes her as a mistress at the end of the Trojan War and returns with her to Mycenae. Her story is told in Aeschylus' fifth-century B.C.E. drama *Agamemnon*.

30. Atreus is the father of Agamemnon and Menelaus. When his brother Thyestes seduced his wife, Atreus murdered his brother's two sons in retaliation. Thyestes then cursed the House of Atreus before he died. Thyestes' remaining son, Aegisthus, avenged his father by murdering Agamemnon, whose son, Orestes, later killed him.

31. Patroclus is Achilles' best friend; Antilochus (also a close friend of Achilles) is Nestor' son; Ajax the Greater is second to Achilles in battle.

32. Telephus is the son of Heracles (Hercules) and Auge.

33. Memnon is the son of the goddess Eos (Dawn). Memnon had fought Ajax to a draw, had killed Antilochus (Nestor's son), and was himself killed by Achilles, only to be granted immortality by Zeus at his mother's entreaties.

34. Aeacides is a patronymic given to the descendants of Aeacus, Achilles' grandfather.

35. Ajax the Greater's suicide is told in Sophocles' tragedy *Ajax*.

36. In Greek mythology, Minos was the first king of Crete, son of Zeus and Europa. After his death, he became a judge of the dead.

37. Orion was a giant hunter, the son of Poseidon and Euryale, daughter of Minos. He wanted to kill every animal in the world, but Gaea, the goddess of the earth, got angry and sent a giant scorpion to kill him.

38. The meadow of asphodel is a section of the underworld where ordinary souls are sent to live after death.

39. Tityos is the son of Zeus and Elara. Zeus buried the pregnant Elara in the earth to hide her from his wife. Tityos burst through the earth, who carried him to term. In adulthood Tityos attempted to rape Leto at Hera's behest but was later slain by Artemis and Apollo (Leto's children). As punishment, he is tortured in the underworld by two vultures who feed on his liver, which grows back every night.

40. Tantalus is the son of Zeus and the nymph Plouto. Tantalus boiled his son Pelops and served him in a banquet for the gods. The gods punished him in the underworld by placing him in the lake described.

41. Sisyphus was the king of Ephyra (present-day Corinth) and is punished by the gods for hubris, craftiness, and the many tricks he played on them (see also the mention in chapter 1).

42. This is a reference to his cousin Eurystheus, who subjected him to twelve impossible labors.

43. Cerberus, the fierce, three-headed, monstrous dog that guards the entrance to Hades.

44. Perithous was king of the Lapiths. At his wedding to Hippodamia, the Battle of Lapiths and Centaurs occurred. He was Theseus' best friend. Theseus was king of Athens, a national hero of Athens and slayer of the Minotaur.

45. See de Jong, *Narratological*, appendix A.

46. The Planctae are referred to also as the Rovers, Clashing Rocks, or Wandering Rocks.

47. The *Argo* is the ship on which Jason and the Argonauts sail to Colchis to retrieve the Golden Fleece. The best source for the myth is the *Argonautica*, a Greek epic poem written by Apollonius Rhodius in the third century B.C.E.

48. Charybdis is a female sea monster later rationalized as a whirlpool.

49. Helius is a Titan, the son of Hyperion (son of Uranus and Gaea), who marries his sister Theia and fathers the moon (Selene) and the dawn (Eos). Helius is to be distinguished from Apollo, later associated with the sun. Helius' father, Hyperion, is often used interchangeably with Helius to indicate the sun.

50. Helius, not yet associated with the god Apollo, seeks the gods' assistance.

51. *Alkinou apologoi* refers to his tales to King Alcinous.

CHAPTER 4 — ODYSSEUS AND TELEMACHUS AT EUMAEUS' HUT (*OD.* 13–16)

1. Lies to Athena, 13.327–365; to Eumaeus, 14.229–417; to the suitors, 17.552–582; to Penelope, 19.195–362; and to Laertes, 24.270–345.

2. Phorkys is named after the ancient sea god Phorkys (13.96; Old Man of the Sea), who once probably had his home on this site.

3. The Naiads are female nymphs or spirits presiding over bodies of fresh water.

4. Since ancient times, scholars have argued that *mega* (great) is a misprint for *me* (not). In other words, Zeus agrees on turning the ship to stone but does not approve a mountain surrounding the city. English translations support one or the other of these possibilities: Lattimore ("*Odyssey*") translates the phrase, "But do not hide their city under a mountain"; Fagles (*Homer*) translates, "Then pile your huge mountain round about their port."

5. *Demos* = district, community.

6. Idomeneus was the Cretan commander who fought in Troy with an armada of eighty ships (*Il.* 2.652), as well as the grandson of King Minos of Crete.

7. Orsilochus only appears in this lie made up by Odysseus.

8. In the *Odyssey*, slaves can own slaves if they have enough money to afford them.

9. Sparta was a city-state in ancient Greece known as Lacedaemon in antiquity.

10. In Greek mythology, Icarius, Penelope's father, had five sons and two daughters by his wife, Periboea. In the *Odyssey*, only Penelope's sister, Iphthime (4.797), is mentioned by name. The brothers referred to here (no number is given) are neither named nor mentioned again.

11. Either Athena is lying to Telemachus to prompt him to action or, as the goddess of wisdom, she is voicing what he himself has deduced.

12. In the *Iliad*, Diocles has two sons, Crethon and Orsilochus, who fall in Troy at the hands of Aeneas (*Il.* 5.541–49). Diocles' father, Ortilochus, king of Messinian Phera, is mentioned in *Il.* 5.545–549 and three times in the *Odyssey* (3.488–489, 15.186–187, and 21.15–16) as the father of Diocles. Diocles' grandfather Alpheus, mentioned both in the *Iliad* (2.592, 5.545, and 11.712–728) and in the *Odyssey* (3.489 and 15.187), is identified as the father of Ortilochus. In myth, Alpheus was the god of the largest river in the Peloponnese, the river that Heracles rerouted through Augeias' stables in one of his twelve labors.

13. Well-known fugitives are Phoenix and Patroclus from the *Iliad*.

14. These two lines refer to Amphiaraus' quarrel with Adrastus, the king of Argos. A reconciliation reached between these two men sealed Amphiaraus' marriage to Adrastus' sister Eriphyle. Oedipus' son, Polyneices, later bribed Eriphyle to compel her husband to join the Seven against Thebes, which leads to his death (a prophecy Amphiaraus predicts). Amphiaraus' son Alcmaeon later avenges his father's death by murdering his mother.

15. Oral epics like Homer's are full of digressions—similes, descriptions, catalogs, genealogies, etc. These digressions interrupt the flow of the main narrative to provide background information (see Finkelberg, *Homer*, 1:205–207).

16. In the standard version of this myth (variations exist), which Homer abridges, Melampus and his brother Bias leave their home in Thessaly for Neleus' (their uncle's) home in Pylos. Established in Pylos, Bias falls in love with Pero, Neleus' daughter. When Bias asks for her hand in marriage, her father demands completion of a task: Bias can marry Pero only if he drives Phylacus' cattle in Phylace (guarded by a vicious dog) to Pylos. Bias seeks help from his brother Melampus, who consents to perform the task. Unfortunately, Melampus is caught stealing the cattle and is imprisoned by Phylacus for one year. While in prison, Melampus has a vision that a beam is about to fall on him but saves himself. Recognizing his prophetic powers, Phylacus promises to release him from prison if he cures his son, Iphiclus, from impotence. Melampus succeeds and is granted the herd of cattle. The required labor completed, Neleus allows Bias to marry Pero, but Melampus by this time desires Pero himself. Subsequently, Melampus is called on by Proetus, the king of Argos, to cure his three daughters (the Proetides) from madness. In return, Melampus receives a third of the kingdom for himself and

another third for his brother. Although he cures the three women of their madness, the oldest daughter, Iphinoe, dies. The remaining two, Iphianassa and Lysippe, marry Bias and Melampus, respectively. Eventually, Melampus becomes king of Argos and produces the line Homer recites.

17. The vocative (used sixteen times) shows the narrator's interest in and affection for Eumaeus.

18. Although attempts have been made by both ancient and modern scholars to identify these places as real locales, they are more likely fantasy lands.

19. Here Odysseus is younger but also has a darker complexion and hair (16.176; *kuaneai d'egenonto*), whereas in his earlier transformation, Athena changes his fair skin and his blond hair (13.399; *xanthas d'ek kephalēs oleso trichas*).

20. The pun is a play on the words *theos* (god) and *teos* (thy, thine).

21. There are 52 suitors from Doulichion with 6 servants; 24 from Same; 20 from Zacynthos; and 12 from Ithaca, along with Medon, the herald Phemius, the divine singer, and two henchmen, a total of 118 men.

22. Odysseus does not add the six servants, two henchmen, Medon, and Phemius to the 108 suitors, although at the end we are told only Medon and Phemius are saved.

CHAPTER 5 — ODYSSEUS AND TELEMACHUS STRATEGIZE AT THE PALACE (*OD.* 17–20)

1. A three-part division in which a middle section is framed by two halves of another is popular in the *Odyssey*. Besides the present book, it is also encountered in *Od.* 15 (Telemachus' return to Ithaca framing Eumaeus' story to Odysseus); in *Od.* 16 (the suitors and Penelope at the palace framing Telemachus at Eumaeus' hut); and in *Od.* 18 (Penelope occupying the center, framed by Odysseus' dealings with the beggar Arnaeus and the suitors and maids at the palace).

2. Iris, a goddess, is messenger of the gods, along with Hermes. Irus is the masculine form of the feminine Iris.

3. This is the first of four laughs in this book: 18.40, 100, 111, and 350.

4. This is a play on Irus' name: *iros aïros*—Irus unhappy Irus.

5. The reference to King Echetus (holder) is most likely to the folktale of the wicked king who put all strangers who came his way to death by mutilating them. Not much is known about him other than what Homer says in *Od.* 18.85, 18.116, and 21.307.

6. The sentiment expressed here is not unlike the one Achilles expresses in *Il.* 24.525–533 when he speaks of the two urns that stand at Zeus's side: one contains evils and the other blessings. Zeus bestows to each human either a portion from

the urn of evils or a mixture of the two urns; no one, however, receives a portion from the urn of blessings alone (*Il.* 24.525–526).

7. The other three from longest to shortest are *Od.* 4, 11, and 17.

8. Either this omission is an oversight on Odysseus' part, or he is now considering a different course of action.

9. The lines in 19.7–13 are identical to those used in 16.288–294.

10. In *Il.* 18 Homer devotes 147 lines (468–614) to the armor Achilles wears to defeat Hector.

11. Autolycus is associated with trickery and fraud—gifts bestowed on him by Hermes, god of thieves, in return for his devotion.

12. The story to which Penelope alludes in this simile could be a variant of the tale of Procne, daughter of Pandion and wife to Tereus. Procne kills her son Itys in revenge against her husband, who raped her sister Philomela and severed her tongue.

13. The line is always translated in reverse to put the words in logical order (invoking the rhetorical device of *hysteron proteron*, in which the first key word of the idea refers to something that happens temporally later than the second key word).

14. Among the most common interpretations for the meaning of the gates of horn and ivory are the following:

1. The gate of ivory is associated with deception because the word for "ivory" (*elephas*) is similar to the word for "to deceive" (*elephairomai*). On the other hand, the word for "horn" (*keras*) is similar to both the word for "to fulfill" (*kraino*) and the word for "real" (*akranta*; see Eustathius, *(Parekbolai)*).
2. The word *horn* can be associated with the eye (the outermost covering of the eye is horny)—that is, the cornea, with which one sees—whereas ivory is associated with teeth, with which one speaks. Because what is seen is more reliable than what is said, the gates of horn are more reliable than the gates of ivory (see Eustathius, *(Parekbolai)*).
3. Horn is more transparent than ivory, so the gates of horn can be associated with truth and the gates of ivory with deceit (see Eustathius, *(Parekbolai)*).
4. Because Odysseus' eyes in 19.211 are referred to "as if they were made of horn or iron," and since he knows what will occur, horn is regarded as truth. Penelope, who sat in a chair "inlaid with ivory and silver" (19.56), does not know what will happen or whether the beggar deceives her by leading her to believe he is her husband (see Amory, "Gates").

5. Since ivory is more impressive in appearance, it can be deceptive. Horn frequently goes unnoticed and is less impressive. Though unremarkable, dreams from the gates of horn are nevertheless more likely to be fulfilled (see Rozokoki, "Penelope's").

15. "*Epei ouk ephamēn onar emmenai, all' hupar ēdē.*"

16. "*Dokēse de hoi kata thumon / ēdē gignōskousa parestamenai kephalēphi.*"

17. These unnamed daughters of Pandareus were orphaned when the gods inexplicably destroyed their parents. The orphaned girls were raised by Aphrodite, Hera, Artemis, and Athena, each goddess contributing attributes: Aphrodite nurtured them on cheese, honey, and wine; Hera gave them beauty and good sense; Artemis made them tall; and Athena honed their homemaking skills. In time, Aphrodite approached Zeus to arrange marriages for the girls, but Zeus knew the storm winds would snatch them away to become servants of the Furies.

18. "*Idion, hōs enoēsa, dedakruntai de moi osse mnēsamenōi oduseōs*" (20.204–205; I started sweating when I saw you and my eyes filled with tears thinking of Odysseus [my translation]).

19. "*Megan orkon omoumai*" (20.229; I swear a great oath [my translation]).

20. Either Penelope's earlier comment (19.321) that the beggar was to sit beside Telemachus is forgotten or Telemachus was not informed.

21. Amphinomus, Telemachus, Antinous, Athena, Ctesippus, Agelaus, Theoclymenus, Eurymachus, Odysseus, Penelope, and assorted suitors.

22. "*Loetrochoōoi dōēi geras.*"

CHAPTER 6 — REVENGE, REUNION, AND RECONCILIATION (*OD.* 21–24)

1. Messenia and Lacedaemon are regions in the southern Peloponnese, home of Menelaus and Helen; Ortilochus was king of Messenian Phera, where in *Od.* 4 Telemachus and Pisistratus spent the night on their way from Pylos to Sparta and again on their return trip as guests of Diocles, son of Ortilochus (4.487–489).

2. Homer does not say why Iphitus was a guest of Heracles (Hercules). The myths concerning Heracles, including his dealings with Iphitus, were well known in ancient Greece. Homer possibly feels it unnecessary to elaborate on such popular myths.

3. Homer does not say how Eurytus acquired the bow.

4. There are at least three different versions of why Heracles kills Iphitus, by Homer, Apollodorus, and Sophocles. In Apollodorus, Iphitus asks Heracles' help in searching for missing cattle. During the search, Heracles goes mad and kills Iphitus by throwing him off a wall. In Sophocles, Heracles, while a guest of Eurytus, gets drunk, is kicked out of Eurytus' house, and in revenge kills Iphitus by throwing him off a tower. Homer merely says Heracles killed Iphitus.

5. Some versions of this myth claim Eurytus taught Heracles how to use the bow.

6. "*Endon men de od' autos egō.*"

7. The bow of horn provides a further meaning for Penelope's dream in 19.562–567, where she explains that dreams entering through the gate of ivory are deceptive, whereas those that enter through the gate of horn bring the truth when any mortal sees them (19.567). Can she be signaling to the beggar/Odysseus that the bow of horn is the way to make her dream come true?

8. Why a swallow and not a nightingale, which seems a more appropriate image for the slaughter to come? The nightingale's song in the Philomela and Procne myth is interpreted as a lament and thus could reference the suitors' deaths here, but since swallows return home every year, it acts as a symbol of homecoming and return and places the emphasis on Odysseus.

9. The *mnēstērophonia* uses the same type of battle scenes found in the *Iliad*:

1. Arming: Odysseus, 22:122–125
2. Challenges: Odysseus vs. Eurymachus, 22.60–67
3. *Parainesis* (advice, council): Eurymachus and Odysseus, 22.69–78; Athena and Odysseus, 22.226–235; Agelaus and the suitors, 22.247–254; Odysseus and his supporters, 22.262–64
4. Divine interventions: Athena assists Odysseus, 22.126–380
5. Supplications: Leodes and Odysseus, 22.310–315; Phemius and Medon, 22.340–343, 364–370
6. Vauntings: Eumaeus jeering at Melanthius, 22.194–199; Philoetius jeering at Ctesippus, 22.287–291

10. Margaret Atwood, in *The Penelopiad* (New York: Canongate, 2006), a work of fiction, gives a more sympathetic view of these twelve maids.

11. Homer offers no further information concerning this structure.

12. The modern Greek poet Yannis Ritsos has Penelope thinking these very thoughts in his poem "Penelope's Despair":

> Not that she didn't recognize him in the fireside light; nor was it
> the beggar's rags, the disguise; no: transparent signs—
> the scarred knee, the sturdiness, the craftiness in the eye. Startled,
> leaning her back against the wall, she sought some justification,
> a short reprieve from having to respond,
> to be betrayed. Were twenty years wasted for him then?
> Twenty years of dreams and anticipation, for this wretch,
> these white whiskers soaked in blood? She sank mute onto a chair,
> slowly she gazed at the slaughtered suitors on the floor, as if seeing

her own muffled aspirations. And she uttered, "Welcome,"
heeding her own strange and distant voice. In the corner her loom
veiled the ceiling in trelliswork shadows; and those birds, woven
against green foliage in striking red yarn, suddenly
turned black and gray on this homecoming night,
hovering in the unbroken sky of her final perseverance.

("Penelope's Despair," trans. Kostas Myrsiades, in *Yannis Ritsos: Selected Poems, 1938–1988*, ed. Kimon Friar and Kostas Myrsiades [Brockport, NY: Boa Editions, 1989]).

13. "*Mēter emē dusmēter.*"

14. The epithet "of Kyllene" refers to Mount Kyllene, located in Arcadia in southern Greece, on which the god was born.

15. Homer's meadow of asphodel has been seen throughout Western literary history as a desirable place (see Reece, "Homer's").

16. Homer does not mention the story of Odysseus' recruitment—he feigned insanity by plowing the beach; the recruits called his bluff by setting Telemachus before the plow; Odysseus swerved to avoid killing his son, thus proving his sanity. Homer merely mentions that after a monthlong trip to Ithaca, Agamemnon and Menelaus hardly won over Odysseus (24.119).

17. Fagles translates these names into their English equivalents: "I come from Roamer-Town . . . my father's Unsparing, son of King Pain, and my name's Man of Strife." Fagles, *Homer*, 477–478.

18. The swineherd, the cowherd, Dolius and his six sons, Laertes, Odysseus, and Telemachus.

19. In the late Bronze Age, Cephalonia was a separate island, perhaps the one Homer refers to when describing Ithaca; the present Ithaca was perhaps a part of Cephalonia before splitting off. It is also possible that both islands existed and Odysseus ruled both.

AFTERWORD

1. Agamemnon, Diomedes, the two Aiantes, Idomeneus, Meriones, Eurypyos, Thoas, and Odysseus.

GENERAL BIBLIOGRAPHY

JOURNAL ABBREVIATIONS

AJP	*American Journal of Philology*
CA	*Classical Antiquity*
CJ	*Classical Journal*
CL	*College Literature*
CML	*Classical and Modern Literature*
CP	*Classical Philology*
CQ	*Classical Quarterly*
CR	*Classical Review*
CW	*Classical World*
G&R	*Greece and Rome*
GRBS	*Greek, Roman and Byzantine Studies*
HSCP	*Harvard Studies in Classical Philology*
ICS	*Illinois Classical Studies*
JCS	*Journal of Classical Studies*
JHS	*Journal of Hellenic Studies*
JIES	*Journal of Indo-European Studies*
PQ	*Psychoanalytic Quarterly*
QUCC	*Quaderni urbinati di cultura classica*
SA	*Studies in Antiquity*

SIFC	*Studi italiani di filologia classica*
SO	*Symbolae Osloenses*
TAPA	*Transactions of the American Philological Association*

I. BOOK-BY-BOOK COMMENTARY ON THE *ODYSSEY*

Barker, Elton, and Joel Christenson. *Homer: A Beginner's Guide.* London: Oneworld, 2013.

Bowie, A. M. *Homer: "Odyssey" XIII and XIV.* Cambridge: Cambridge University Press, 2013.

de Jong, Irene. *A Narratological Commentary on the "Odyssey."* Cambridge: Cambridge University Press, 2001.

Dimock, George E. *The Unity of the "Odyssey."* Amherst: University of Massachusetts Press, 1989.

Garvie, A. F. *Homer: "Odyssey" VI–VIII.* Cambridge: Cambridge University Press, 1994.

Gaunt, D. M. *Surge and Thunder: Critical Readings in Homer's "Odyssey."* Oxford: Oxford University Press, 1971.

Heubeck, Alfred, and Arie Hoekstra. *A Commentary on Homer's "Odyssey."* Vol. 2, *Books IX–XVI.* Oxford: Clarendon, 1989.

Heubeck, Alfred, Stephanie West, and J. B. Hainsworth. *A Commentary on Homer's "Odyssey."* Vol. 1, *Introduction and Books I–VIII.* Oxford: Clarendon, 1988.

Hexter, Ralph. *A Guide to the "Odyssey": A Commentary on the English Translation of Robert Fitzgerald.* New York: Random House, 1993.

Jones, Peter V. *Homer's "Odyssey": A Companion to the Translation of Richmond Lattimore.* Carbondale: Southern Illinois University Press, 1988.

Kahana, Ahuvia. *Homer: A Guide for the Perplexed.* London: Bloomsbury, 2012.

Merry, W. W. *"Odyssey," Books XIII–XXIV.* 1878. Reprint, Oxford: Clarendon, 1964.

Monro, D. B., ed. *Homer's "Odyssey," Books XIII–XXIV.* Oxford: Oxford University Press, 1901.

Russo, Joseph, Manuel Fernandez-Galiano, and Alfred Heubeck. *A Commentary on Homer's "Odyssey."* Vol. 3, *Books XVII–XXIV.* Oxford: Clarendon, 1992.

Rutherford, R. B. *Homer: "Odyssey" XIX and XX.* Cambridge: Cambridge University Press, 1992.

Stanford, W. B. *Homer: "Odyssey."* 2 vols. Bristol: Bristol Classical, 1998.

Steiner, D. *Homer: "Odyssey" XVII and XVIII.* Cambridge: Cambridge University Press, 2010.

Tracy, Stephen V. *The Story of the "Odyssey."* Princeton, NJ: Princeton University Press, 1990.

Weiss, Charles. *Homer's "Odyssey."* Greece and Rome: Texts and Contexts. Cambridge: Cambridge University Press, 2012.

II. BOOKS AND ESSAYS ON HOMER AND THE *ODYSSEY*

Aasved, Mikal J. "The Sirens and Cargo Cults." *CW* 89, no. 5 (1996): 383–392.

Adkins, A.W.H. *From the Many to the One*. Ithaca, NY: Cornell University Press, 1970.

Adorno, Theodor W., and Max Horkheimer. "Odysseus or Myth and Enlightenment." *New German Critique* 56 (1992): 109–141.

Ahl, Frederick. "Wordplay and Apparent Fiction in the *Odyssey*." *Arethusa* 35, no. 1 (2002): 117–132.

Ahl, Frederick, and H. Roisman. *The "Odyssey" Re-formed*. Ithaca, NY: Cornell University Press, 1996.

Alden, M. J. "Lions in Paradise." *CQ* 55, no. 2 (2005): 335–342.

———. "The Resonances of the Song of Ares and Aphrodite." *Mnemosyne*, 4th ser., 50, no. 5 (1997): 513–529.

———. "The Role of Telemachus in the *Odyssey*." *Hermes* 115 (1987): 129–137.

Alexander, Caroline. "A Note on the Stag: *Odyssey* 10.156–72." *CQ* 41, no. 2 (1991): 520–524.

Allen, W., Jr. "The Theme of the Suitors in the *Odyssey*." *TAPA* 70 (1939): 104–124.

Amory, Anne. *Blameless Aegisthus*. *Arion* 5, no. 2 (1997): 166.

———. "The Reunion of Odysseus and Penelope." In *Essays on the "Odyssey": Selected Modern Criticism*, edited by C.H. Taylor, Jr., 100–121. Bloomington: Indiana University Press, 1963.

———. "The Gates of Horn and Ivory." *Yale Classical Studies* 20 (1966): 1–58.

———. "Omens and Dreams in the Odyssey." *HSCP* 63 (1958): 517–519.

Andersen, Oivind. "Agamemnon's Singer (*Od*. 3.262–272)." *SO* 67 (1992): 5–26.

———. "Odysseus and the Wooden Horse." *SO* 52 (1977): 5–18.

Anderson, W. S. "Calypso and Elysium." *CJ* 54, no. 1 (1963): 2–11.

Anhalt, Emily K. "A Bull for Poseidon: The Bull's Bellow in *Odyssey* 21.46–50." *CQ* 47, no. 1 (1997): 15–25.

———. "A Matter of Perspective: Penelope and the Nightingale in *Odyssey* 19.512–534." *CJ* 97, no. 2 (2001): 145–159.

Apthorp, M. J. "The Language of the *Odyssey* 5.7–20." *CQ* 27, no. 1 (1977): 1–9.

———. "Nochmals the Authenticity of *Odyssey* 10.475–9." *CQ* 42, no. 1 (1992): 270–271.

———. "The Obstacles to Telemachus' Return." *CQ* 30, no. 1 (1980): 1–22.

Arans, Olga R., and Christine R. Shea. "The Fall of Elpenor: Homeric Kirke and the Folklore of the Caucasus." *JIES* 22, nos. 3–4 (1994): 371.

Arbeitman, Yoël L. "Odysseus by Any Other." *Emerita* 63, no. 2 (1995): 225–244.

Armitage, S. *Homer's "Odyssey."* London: Faber and Faber, 2006.

Armstrong, Richard H. "Penelope's Challenge to Her . . . Translators." *CML* 20, no. 1 (1999): 37–76.

———. "A Picture Waiting to Happen: Penelope's Agency and Illustrations to the *Odyssey*." *CML* 20, no. 4 (2000–2001): 19–57.

Aronen, J. "Genealogy as a Form of Mythic Discourse: The Case of the Phaeacians." In *Myth and Symbol I: Symbolic Phenomena in Ancient Greek Culture*, edited by Synnove des Bouvrie, 89–111. Bergen, Norway: Norwegian Institute at Athens, 2002.

Atchity, Kenneth. *Critical Essays on Homer.* Critical Essays on World Literature. Boston: G. K. Hall, 1987.

Athanassakis, Apostolos N. "The Eagle of Penelope's Dream." *Ancient World* 25, no. 1 (1994): 121–134.

———. "Proteus, the Old Man of the Sea: Homeric Merman or Shaman?" *Mélanges G. Germain* (n.d.): 45–56.

Auerbach, Eric. "Odysseus' Scar." In *Homer: A Collection of Critical Essays*, edited by George Steiner and Robert Fagles, 19–37. Twentieth Century Views. Englewood Cliffs, NJ: Prentice Hall, 1962.

———. *Mimesis: The Representation of Reality in Western Literature.* Translated by W. Trask. Princeton, NJ: Princeton University Press, 1953.

Austin, Norman. *Archery at the Dark of the Moon: Poetic Problems in Homer's "Odyssey."* Berkeley: University of California Press, 1975.

———. "Homeric Nostalgia." *Yale Review* 98, no. 2 (2010): 37–64.

———. "Nausikaa and the Word That Must Not Be Spoken: A Reading of Homer's *Odyssey*, Book Six." *Arion* 25, no. 1(2017): 5–36.

———. "Odysseus and the Cyclops: Who Is Who." In *Approaches to Home*, edited by C. A. Rubino, and C. W. Shelmerdine, 3–37. Austin: University of Texas Press, 1983.

———. "Telemachos Polymechanos." *California Studies in Classical Antiquity* 2 (1969): 45–63.

———. "The Wedding Text in Homer's *Odyssey*." *Arion* 1, no. 2 (1991): 227–243.

Awine, Andrew T. "The Non-Homeric Cyclops in the Homeric *Odyssey*." *GRBS* 49, no. 3 (2009): 323–333.

Bakker, Egbert J. *The Meaning of Meat and the Structure of the "Odyssey."* Cambridge: Cambridge University Press, 2013.

———. "Polyphemos." *CQ* 38, no. 2 (2002): 135–150.

Balot, Ryan. Review of *The Swineherd and the Bow: Representations of Class in the "Odyssey,"* by William G. Thalmann. *CP* 96, no. 1 (2001): 82–86.

Barker, Elton, and Joel Christensen. *Homer: A Beginner's Guide*. London: Oneworld, 2013.

Barnouw, Jeffrey. *Odysseus, Hero of Practical Intelligence: Deliberation and Signs in Homer's "Odyssey."* Lanham, MD: University Press of America, 2004.

Barrett, D. S. "Homer *Odyssey* 21.406–9." *CP* 65, no. 1 (1970): 38–39.

Bassett, Samuel E. "Hysteron Proteron homerikos (Cicero, Att. 1, 16, 1)." *HSCP* 31 (1920): 39–62.

———. "The Proems of the *Iliad* and the *Odyssey*." *AJP* 44, no. 4 (1923): 339–348.

———. "The Suitors of Penelope." *TAPA* 49 (1910): 41–52.

Beck, Deborah. "Ecphrasis, Interpretation, and Audience in *Aeneid* 1 and *Odyssey* 8." *AJP* 128, no. 4 (2007): 533–549.

———. "Odysseus: Narrator, Storyteller, Poet?" *CP* 100, no. 3 (2005): 213–227.

———. "Speech Introductions and the Character Development of Telemachus." *CJ* 94, no. 2 (1998–1999): 121–141.

Beck, William. "Dogs, Dwellings, and Masters: Ensemble and Symbol in the *Odyssey*." *Hermes* 119, no. 2 (1991): 158–167.

Belmont, David E. "Athena and Telemachus." *CJ* 65, no. 3 (1969): 109–116.

———. "Menelaus and Proteus." *CW* 60 (1969–1970): 104–116.

———. "Telemachus and Nausicaa: A Study of Youth." *CJ* 63, no. 1 (1967): 1–9.

Benardete, Seth. *The Bow and the Lyre: A Platonic Reading of the "Odyssey."* Lanham, MD: Rowman and Littlefield, 1997.

Bergren, Ann. "Helen's 'Good Drug': *Odyssey* IV.1.305." In *Contemporary Literary Hermeneutics and Interpretation of Classical Texts*, edited by S. Kresic, 210–214. Ottawa: Ottawa University Press, 1981.

Bertolín, Reyes. "The Mast and the Loom: Signifiers of Separation and Authority." *Phoenix* 62, nos. 1–2 (2008): 92–108, 240.

Beye, Charles Rowan. *The "Iliad," the "Odyssey," and the Epic Tradition*. New York: Doubleday, 1966.

———. *Odysseus: A Life*. New York: Hyperion, 2004.

Bierl, Anton. "'Turn on the Light!': Epiphany, the God-Like Hero Odysseus, and the Golden Lamp of Athena in Homer's *Odyssey* (Especially 19.1–43)." *ICS* 29 (2004): 43–61.

Biles, Zachary. "Perils of Song in Homer's *Odyssey*." *Phoenix* 57, nos. 3–4 (2003): 191–208.

Birge, Darice. "Ambiguity and the Stage Hunt in *Odyssey* 10." *Helios* 20 (1993): 17–28.

Blanchot, Maurice. "The Song of the Sirens: Encountering the Imaginary." In *Homer*, edited by Harold Bloom, 39–45. Modern Critical Views. New York: Chelsea House, 1986.

Bliss, F. R. "Homer and the Critics: The Structural Unity of *Odyssey* 8." *Bucknell Review* 16, no. 3 (1968): 53–73.

Block, Elizabeth. "Clothing Makes the Man: A Pattern in the *Odyssey*." *TAPA* 115 (1985): 1–11.

Bloom, Harold, ed. *Homer.* Modern Critical Views. New York: Chelsea House, 1986.

———, ed. *Homer's "The Odyssey."* Updated ed. Bloom's Modern Critical Interpretations. New York: Bloom's Literary Criticism, 2007.

———, ed. *Odysseus/Ulysses.* Modern Literary Characters. New York: Chelsea House Publishers, 1991.

Bolmarcich, Sarah. "Homophrosune in the *Odyssey*." *CP* 96, no. 3 (2001): 205–213.

Bonifazi, Anna. "Inquiring into *Nostos* and Its Cognates." *AJP* 130, no. 4 (2009): 481–510.

Borthwick, E. K. "Odysseus and the Return of the Swallow." *G&R* 35, no. 1 (1988): 14–22.

Bowman, Curtis. "Odysseus and the Siren Call of Reason: The Frankfurt School Critique of Enlightenment." *Other Voices: A Journal of Critical Thought* 1, no. 1 (1997). http://www.othervoices.org/1.1/cubowman/siren.php.

Bowra, C. M. *Homer.* London: Duckworth, 1972

Bradley, Edward M. "'The Greatness of His Nature': Fire and Justice in the *Odyssey*." *Ramus* 5 (1976): 137–148.

Brain, Peter, and D. D. Skinner. "Odysseus and the Axes: Homeric Ballistics Reconstructed." *G&R* 25, no. 1 (1978): 55–58.

Brann, Eva. *Homeric Moments: Clues to Delight in Reading the Odyssey.* Philadelphia: Paul Dry Books, 2002.

Braswell, Bruce K. "*Odyssey* 8.166–77 and *Theogony* 79–93." *CQ* 31, no. 2 (1981): 237–239.

———. "The Song of Ares and Aphrodite: Theme and Relevance to *Odyssey* 8." *Hermes* 110 (1982): 129–137.

Bremer, J. M., I.J.F. de Jong, and J. Kalff, eds. *Homer: Beyond Oral Poetry.* Amsterdam: B. R. Gruner, 1987.

Bremer, J. M. "A Homeric Goat Island (*Od.* 9.116–41)." *CQ* 36, no. 1 (1986): 256–257.

———. "Odysseus versus the Cyclops." In *Myth and Symbol I: Symbolic Phenomena in Ancient Greek Culture,* edited by Synnove des Bouvrie, 135–152. Bergen, Norway: Norwegian Institute at Athens, 2002.

Brennan, T. Corey. "An Ethnic Joke in Homer?" *HSCP* 91 (1987): 1–3.

Brilliant, Richard. "Kirke's Men: Swine and Sweethearts." In *The Distaff Side: Representing the Female in Homer's "Odyssey,"* edited by Beth Cohen, 165–174. Oxford: Oxford University Press, 1995.

Broeniman, Clifford. "Demodocus, Odysseus, and the Trojan War in *Odyssey* 8." *CW* 90, no. 1 (1996–1997): 3–14.

Brown, Calvin S. "Odysseus and Polyphemus: The Name and the Curse." *Comparative Literature* 18 (1966): 193–202.

Brown, Christopher G. "Ares, Aphrodite, and the Laughter of the Gods." *Phoenix* 43 (1989): 283–293.

———. "In the Cyclops' Cave: Revenge and Justice in *Odyssey* 9." *Mnemosyne*, 4th ser., 49, no. 1 (1996): 1–29.

Brown, Edwin L. "Eumaeus' Native Isle." *CJ* 80, no. 4 (1985): 292–296.

Buchan, Mark. *The Limits of Heroism: Homer and the Ethics of Reading.* Ann Arbor: University of Michigan Press, 2004.

———. "Looking to the Feet: The Riddles of the Scylla." *Helios* 31, nos. 1–2 (2004): 21 49.

Buckley, Theodore Alois. *The Odyssey of Homer, with Hymns, Epigrams, and the Battle of the Frogs and Mice.* London: Henry G. Bohn, 1851.

Buitron, D., and B. Cohen, eds. *The Odyssey and Ancient Art: An Epic in Word and Image.* New York: Edith C. Blum Art Institute, 1992.

Burgess, Jonathan S. "Framing Odysseus: The Death of the Suitors." In *Crime and Punishment in Homeric and Archaic Epic: Proceedings of the 12th International Symposium on the "Odyssey," Ithaca, September 3–7, 2013*, edited by Menelaos Christopoulos and Machi Païzi-Apostolopoulou, 337–354. Ithaca, Greece: Kentro Odysseiakōn Spudōn, 2014.

———. *Homer.* Understanding Classics. London: I. B. Tauris, 2015.

———. *The Tradition of the Trojan War in Homer and the Epic Cycle.* Baltimore: Johns Hopkins University Press, 2001.

Burkert, Walter. "The Song of Ares and Aphrodite: On the Relationship between the *Odyssey* and the *Iliad*." In *Homer: German Scholarship in Translation*, edited and translated by G. M. Wright and P. V. Jones, 249–262. Oxford: Clarendon, 1997.

Burrows, Reynold Z. "Deception Used for Comic Effect in the 'Odyssey'." In *Readings on Homer*, edited by Don Nardo, 158–164. Literary Companions to World Authors. San Diego, CA: Greenhaven, 1998

Bushnell, Rebecca W. "Reading 'Winged Words': Homeric Bird Signs, Similes, and Epiphanies." *Helios* 9 (1982): 1–13.

Byre, Calvin S. "On the Description of the Harbor of Phorkys and the Cave of the Nymphs, *Odyssey* 13.96–112." *AJP* 115, no. 1 (1994): 1–13.

———. "Penelope and the Suitors before Odysseus: *Odyssey* 18.158–303." *AJP* 109, no. 2 (1988): 159–173.

———. "The Rhetoric of Description in *Odyssey* 9.116–41: Odysseus and Goat Island." *CJ* 89, no. 4 (1994): 357–367.

Cairns, Douglas L. "Mixing with Men and Nausicaa's Nemesis." *CQ* 40, no. 1 (1990): 263–266.

Calame, Claude. "Myth and Tale: The Legend of the Cyclops and Its Narrative Transformations." In *The Craft of Poetic Speech in Ancient Greece*, translated by Janice Orion, 139–173. Ithaca, NY: Cornell University Press, 1995.

Callaway, Cathy. "Odysseus' Three Unsworn Oaths." *AJP* 119, no. 2 (1998): 159–170.

Camps, W. A. *An Introduction to Homer.* Oxford: Clarendon Press, 1980.

Carlisle, Miriam, and Olga Levaniouk, eds. *Nine Essays on Homer.* Lanham, MD: Rowman and Littlefield, 1999.

Carnes, Jeffrey S. "With Friends like These: Understanding the Mythic Background of Homer's Phaiakians." *Ramus* 22, no. 2 (1993): 103–115.

Carpenter, Rhys. *Folklore, Fiction and Saga in the Homeric Epics.* Berkeley: University of California Press, 1946.

Carter, Jane Burr, and Sarah P. Morris. *The Ages of Homer: A Tribute to Emily Townsend Vermeule.* Austin: University of Texas Press, 1995.

Casson, Lionel. "Odysseus' Boat (Od.5.244–5)." *International Journal of Nautical Archaeology* 21 (1992): 73–74.

Chaston, Colleen. "Three Models of Authority in the *Odyssey.*" *CW* 96, no. 1 (2002–2003): 3–19.

Clark, Matthew. "Was Telemachus Rude to His Mother? *Odyssey* 1.356–59." *CP* 96, no. 4 (2001): 335–354.

Clarke, Howard W. *The Art of the "Odyssey."* Englewood Cliffs, NJ: Prentice-Hall, 1967.

———, ed. *Twentieth Century Interpretations of the "Odyssey."* Englewood Cliffs, NJ: Prentice-Hall, 1983.

Clay, Jenny Strauss. "Aeolia, or under the Sign of the Circle." *CJ* 80, no. 4 (1985): 289–291.

———. "The Beginning of the *Odyssey.*" *AJP* 97, no. 4 (1976): 313–326.

———. "Goat Island: *Od.* 9.116–141." *CQ* 30, no. 2 (1980): 261–264.

———. "Homeric AXREION." *AJP* 105, no. 1 (1984): 73–76.

———. "Sex, Drugs, and . . . Poetry." In *Epic and Epoch: Essays on the Interpretation and History of Genre*, edited by Steven M. Oberhelman, Van Kelly, and Richard J. Goslan, 40–48. Lubbock: Texas Tech University Press, 1994.

———. *The Wrath of Athena: Gods and Men in the "Odyssey."* Princeton, NJ: Princeton University Press, 1983.

Clayton, Barbara. *A Penelopean Poetics: Reweaving the Feminine in Homer's "Odyssey."* Lanham, MD: Lexington Books, 2004.

———. "Polyphemus and Odysseus in the Nursery: Mother's Milk in the Cyclopeia." *Arethusa* 44, no. 3 (2011): 255–277.

Coffey, M. "The Function of the Homeric Simile." *AJP* 78, no. 2 (1957): 113–132.

Cohen, Beth, ed. *The Distaff Side: Representing the Female in Homer's "Odyssey."* Oxford: Oxford University Press, 1995.

Colakis, Marianthe. "The Laughter of the Suitors in *Odyssey*." *CW* 79, no. 3 (1986): 137–141.

Combellack, Frederic. "Three Odyssean Problems." *California Studies in Classical Antiquity* 6 (1973): 17–46.

———. "Wise Peneope and the Contest of the Bow." In *Twentieth Century Interpretations of the "Odyssey,"* edited by Howard W. Clarke, 103–111. Englewood Cliffs, NJ: Prentice-Hall, 1983.

———. "Why Does Wise Penelope Act So Rashly." In *Readings on Homer*, edited by Don Nardo, 150–157. Literary Companions to World Authors. San Diego, CA: Greenhaven, 1998.

———. "Two Blameless Homeric Characters." *AJP* 103, no. 4 (1982): 361–372.

Cook, Erwin F. "'Active' and 'Passive' Heroics in the *Odyssey*." *CW* 93 (1999): 149–167.

———. "Ferrymen of Elysium and the Homeric Phaeacians." *JIES* 20, nos. 3–4 (1992): 239–267.

———. "A Note on *Odyssey* 3.216–38." *CP* 89, no. 2 (1994): 140–147.

———. *The "Odyssey" in Athens: Myths of Cultural Origins*. Ithaca, NY: Cornell University Press, 1995.

———. "The Raft of Odysseus: The Ethnographic Imagination of Homer's *Odyssey*." *CP* 98, no. 2 (2003): 184–189.

———. *Worlds in Apposition: Towards a Synoptic Interpretation of the Homeric Odyssey*. Berkeley: University of California Press, 1990.

Coughanowr, E. "The Meaning of *Molobros* in Homer." *CQ* 29, no. 2 (1979): 229–230.

Crane, Gregory. *Calypso: Background and Conventions of the "Odyssey."* Athenaum Monografien 191. Frankfurt am Main: Athenaum, 1988.

Crayola, Robert. *The "Odyssey": A Reader's Guide to the Homer Epic*. New York: CreateSpace, 2014.

Crissy, Katherine. "Herakles, Odysseus, and the Bow: *Odyssey* 21.11–41." *CJ* 93, no. 1 (1997): 41–53.

Crooke, W. "The Wooing of Penelope." *Folklore* 9, no. 2 (1898): 121–133.

Crotty, Kevin. *The Poetics of Supplication: Homer's "Iliad" and "Odyssey."* Ithaca, NY: Cornell University Press, 1994.

Currie, Bruno. "The Genitive *Odyseus* (*Od.* 24.398) and Homer's 'Awkward' Parentheses." *JHS* 133 (2013): 21.

Damon, Philip. "Dilation and Displacement in the *Odyssey*." *Pacific Coast Philology* 5 (1970): 19–23.

D'Arms, E. F., and Karl K. Hulley. "The Oresteia-Story in the *Odyssey*." *TAPA* 77 (1946): 207–213.

Davidson, John F. "Arrival at the Cave: The *Odyssey* and Greek Drama." *Wiener Studien* 115 (2002): 45–57.

———. "Tragic Daughter of Atlas?" *Mnemosyne*, 4th ser., 45, no. 3 (1992): 367–371.

Davies, Malcolm. "Anticipation and Foreshadowing: A Use of Myth." *Studi italiani di filologia classica* 7 (1989): 7–11.

———. "The Boar-Hunt in Greek Myth." *Prometheus* 27 (2001): 1–8.

———. "Climax and Structure in *Odyssey* 8.492–520: Further Reflections on Odysseus and the Wooden Horse." *SO* 75, no. 1 (2000): 56–61.

———. "Homer and the Fable: *Odyssey* 21.293–306." *Prometheus* 27, no. 3 (2001): 193–210.

———. "*Odyssey* 22.474–7: Murder or Mutilation?" *CQ* 44, no. 2 (1994): 534–536.

———. "The Sirens at Mid-day." *Prometheus* 31, no. 3 (2005): 225–228.

Dawe, R. D. *The Odyssey: Translation and Analysis.* Sussex, England: Book Guild, 1993.

de Jong, Irene J. F. "Aristotle on the Homeric Narrator." *CQ* 55, no. 2 (2005): 616–621.

———. "Between Word and Deed. Hidden Thoughts in the *Odyssey*." In *Oxford Readings in Classical Studies: Homer's "Odyssey,"* edited by Lillian E. Doherty, 62–90. Oxford: Oxford University Press, 2009.

———. "Developments in Narrative Technique in the *Odyssey*." In *Epea Pteroenta: Beiträge zur Homerforschung—Festschrift Wolfgang Kullmann*, edited by Michael Reichel and Antonios Rengakos, 77–91. Stuttgart, Germany: Franz Steiner, 2002.

———. "Eurykleia and Odysseus' Scar: *Odyssey* 19:393–466." *CQ* 35, no. 2 (1985): 517–518.

———, ed. *Homer: Critical Assessments.* 4 vols. New York: Routledge, 1999.

———. "The Homeric Narrator and His Own *Kleos*." *Mnemosyne*, 4th ser., 59, no. 2 (2006): 188–207.

———. Review of *Homeric Conversation*, by D. Beck. *Mnemosyne*, 4th ser., 61, no. 3 (2008): 482–484.

———. "The Subjective Style in Odysseus' Wanderings." *CQ* 42, no. 1 (1992): 1–11.

Delcomminette, Sylvain. "Odysseus and the Home of the Stranger from Elea." *CQ* 64, no. 2 (2014): 533–541.

DeSmidt, D. Ben. "Horn and Ivory, Bow and Scar: *Odyssey* 19.559–81." *CQ* 56, no. 1 (2006): 284–289.

Detienne, Marcel, and Jean-Pierre Vernant. *Cunning Intelligence in Greek Culture and Society.* Translated by Janet Lloyd. Chicago: University of Chicago Press, 1978.

Devereux, George. "Penelope's Character." *Psychoanalytic Quarterly* 26 (1957): 378–386.

De Vries, G. J. "Difficulties in *Odyssey* VI." *Mnemosyne*, 4th ser., 43, no. 3/4 (1990): 424–426.

———. "Phaeacian Manners." *Mnemosyne*, 4th ser., 30, no. 2 (1977): 113–121.

Dilworth, Thomas. "The Fall of Troy and the Slaughter of the Suitors: Ultimate Symbolic Correspondence in the *Odyssey*." *Mosaic* 27, no. 2 (1994): 1–14.

Dimock, George. "Crime and Punishment in the *Odyssey*." In *Readings on Homer*, edited by Don Nardo, 143–149. Literary Companions to World Authors. San Diego, CA: Greenhaven, 1998

———. "The Name of Odysseus." *Hudson Review* 9 (1956): 52–70.

Dodds, E. R. *The Greek and the Irrational.* Sather Classical Lectures 25. Berkeley: University of California Press, 1951.

Doherty, Lillian E. "Athena and Penelope as Foils for Odysseus in the *Odyssey*." *QUCC* 39 (1991): 31–44.

———. "Gender and Internal Audiences in the *Odyssey*." *AJP* 113, no. 2 (1992): 161–177.

———. "The Internal and Implied Audiences of *Odyssey* 11." *Arethusa* 24, no. 2 (1991): 145–176.

———. "The Narrative 'Openings' in the *Odyssey*." *Arethusa* 35, no. 1 (2002): 51–62.

———. "Nausikaa and Tyro: Idylls of Courtship in the Phaiakian Episode of the *Odyssey* and the Hesiodic Catalogue of Women." *Phoenix* 62, nos. 1–2 (2008): 63–76, 239.

———, ed. *Oxford Readings in Classical Studies: Homer's "Odyssey."* Oxford: Oxford University Press, 2009.

———. *Siren Songs: Gender, Audiences, and Narrators in the "Odyssey."* Ann Arbor: University of Michigan Press, 1995.

———. "Tyro in *Odyssey* 11: Closed and Open Readings." *Helios* 20 (1993): 3–15.

Dolin, E. "Odysseus in Phaeacia." *Grazer Beitrage* 1 (1973): 274–282.

Donlan, Walter. "Homer's Agamemnon." *CW* 65 (1971): 109–15.

———. "Political Reciprocity in Dark Age Greece: Odysseus and His Hetairoi." In *Reciprocity in Ancient Greece*, edited by Christopher Gill, Norman Postlethwaite, and Richard Seaford, 51–71. Oxford: Oxford University Press, 1998.

Dougherty, Carol. *The Raft of Odysseus: The Ethnographic Imagination of Homer's "Odyssey."* Oxford: Oxford University Press, 2001.

Dyson, M. "The Second Assembly of the Gods in the *Odyssey.*" *Antichthon* 4 (1970): 1–12.

Eckert, Charles, W. "Initiatory Motifs in the Story of Telemachus." *CJ* 59, no. 2 (1963): 49–57.

Edinger, Harry G. "The Lay of Demodocus in Context." *Humanities Association Review* 31 (1980): 45–52.

Edwards, Anthony T. "Homer's Ethical Geography: Country and City in the *Odyssey.*" *TAPA* 123 (1993): 27–78.

Edwards, Mark W. "Homer and Oral Tradition: The Type-Scene." *Oral Tradition* 7 (1992): 285–330.

———. "Type-Scenes and Homeric Hospitality." *TAPA* 105 (1975): 51–72.

Edwards, M. J "Scenes from the Later Wanderings of Odysseus." *CQ* 38, no. 2 (1988): 509–521.

Emlyn-Jones, Chris. "The Reunion of Odysseus and Penelope." *Homer.* Greece and Rome Studies 4, edited by Ian McAuslan and Peter Walcot, 126–143. Oxford: Oxford University Press, 1998.

———. "True and Lying Tales in the *Odyssey.*" *G&R* 33, no. 1 (1986): 1–10.

———. "The Reunion of Penelope and Odysseus." *G&R* 31, no. 1 (1984): 1–10.

Emlyn-Jones, Chris, L. Hardwick, and J. Pukis, eds. *Homer: Readings and Images.* Bemidji, MN: Focus, 1992.

Erbse, Hartmut. "The Ending of the *Odyssey*: Linguistic Problems." In *Homer: German Scholarship in Translation*, edited and translated by G. M. Wright and P. V. Jones, 263–320. Oxford: Clarendon, 1997.

Eustathius. *(Parekbolai) Eustathii Archiepiscopi Thessalonicensis Commentarii ad Homeri Odysseam.* 2 vols. Edited by J. G. Stallbaum. Leipzig: Weigel, 1825–1829.

Fagles, Robert, trans. *Homer: The Odyssey.* Introduction by Bernard Knox. New York: Penguin, 1996.

Faraone, Christopher A. 1987. "Hephaestus the Magician and Near Easter Parallels for Alcinous' Watchdogs." *GRBS* 28, no. 3 (1987): 281–306.

Farron, S. G. "The *Odyssey* as an Anti-aristocratic Statement." *Studies in Antiquity* 1 (1979–1980): 59–101.

Felson-Rubin, Nancy. "Penelope's Perspective: Character from Plot." In *Reading the "Odyssey,"* edited by Seth L. Schein, 163–184. Princeton, NJ: Princeton University Press, 1995.

———. *Regarding Penelope: From Character to Poetics.* Princeton, NJ: Princeton University Press, 1994.

Felson-Rubin, Nancy, and William Merritt Sale. "Meleager and Odysseus: A Structural and Cultural Study of the Greek Hunting-Maturation Myth." *Arethusa* 16 (1983): 137–171.

Fenik, Bernard, ed. *Homer: Tradition and Invention.* Cincinnati Classical Studies, n.s., 2. Leiden: E. J. Brill, 1978.

———. *Studies in the "Odyssey."* Hermes Einzelschriften 30. Wiesbaden, Germany: Franz Steiner Verlag, 1974.

Finkelberg, Margalit. "The First Song of Demodocus." *Mnemosyne*, 4th ser., 40, no. 1/2 (1987): 128–132.

———. *The Homer Encyclopedia.* 3 vols. Oxford: Wiley-Blackwell, 2011.

———. "Odysseus and the Genus 'Hero.'" *G&R* 42, no. 1 (1995): 1–13.

———. "Time and Arête in Homer." *CQ* 48, no. 1 (1998): 14–28.

Finley, John H., Jr. *Homer's "Odyssey."* Cambridge, MA: Harvard University Press, 1978.

Finley, M. I. *The World of Odysseus.* 2nd ed. New York: New York Review Books, 1982.

Flaumenhaft, M. "The Undercover Hero: Odysseus from Dark to Daylight." *Interpretation: A Journal of Political Philosophy* 10 (1982): 9–41.

Fletcher, Judith. "Women's Space and Wingless Words in the *Odyssey.*" *Phoenix* 62, nos. 1–2 (2008): 77–91, 240.

Floyd, Edwin D. "Homer's *Odyssey* Book 1, Line 1." *Explicator* 49, no. 2 (1991): 70–72.

———. "Linguistic, Mycenaean, and Iliadic Traditions behind Penelope's Recognition of Odysseus." *CL* 38, no. 2 (2011): 131–158.

Foley, Helene P. "Penelope as Moral Agent." In *Homer's "The Odyssey,"* updated ed., edited by Harold Bloom, 87–108. Bloom's Modern Critical Interpretations. New York: Bloom's Literary Criticism, 2007.

———. "Reverse Similes and Sex-Roles in the *Odyssey.*" *Arethusa* 11 (1978): 7–26.

———. "Virgins, Wives, and Mothers: Penelope as Paradigm." In *Female Acts in Greek Tragedy*, 109–144. Princeton, NJ: Princeton University Press, 2001.

Ford, Andrew. *Homer: The Poetry of the Past.* Ithaca, NY: Cornell University Press, 1992.

———. "Odysseus after Dinner: *Odyssey* 9.2–11 and the Traditions of Sympotic Song." In *Euphrosyne: Studies in Ancient Epic and Its Legacy in Honor of Dimitris N. Maronitis*, edited by John N. Kazasis and Antonios Rengakos, 109–123. Stuttgart, Germany: Franz Steiner, 1999.

Fowler, Robert, ed. *The Cambridge Companion to Homer.* Cambridge: Cambridge University Press, 2004.

Frame, D. *The Myth of Return in Early Greek Epic*. New Haven, CT: Yale University Press, 1978.

Frank, Bernhard. "Homer's *Odyssey*." *Explicator* 58, no. 4 (2000): 179–180.

———. "Homer's *Odyssey*, Book 17, Lines 291–327." *Explicator* 51, no. 4 (1993): 202–203.

Frazer, R. M. "Eurymachus' Question at *Odyssey* 1. 409." *CP* 68, no. 4 (1973): 259–267.

Fredricksmeyer, Hardy C. "Penelope Polutropos: The Crux at *Odyssey* 23.218–24." *AJP* 118, no. 4 (1997): 487–497.

Freidman, J., and S. Gassel. "Odysseus: The Return of the Primal Father." *Psychoanalytic Quarterly* 21 (1952): 215–223.

Friedrich, Rainer. "Heroic Man and Polymetis Odysseus in the Cyclopeia." *GRBS* 28, no. 2 (1987): 121–133.

———. "The Hybris of Odysseus." *JHS* 111 (1991): 16–28.

———. "On the Compositional Use of Similes in the *Odyssey*." *AJP* 102, no. 2 (1981): 120–137.

———. "Thrinakia and Zeus' Ways to Men in the *Odyssey*." *GRBS* 28, no. 4 (1987): 375–400.

———. "Zeus and the Phaeacians: *Odyssey* 13.158." *AJP* 110, no. 3 (1989): 395–399.

Fulkerson, Laurel. "Epic Ways of Killing a Woman: Gender and Transgression in *Odyssey* 22.465–72." *CJ* 97, no. 4 (2002): 335–350.

Fuqua, Charles. "Proper Behavior in the *Odyssey*." *ICS* 16 (1991): 49–58.

Garrison, Daniel H. "The Great Wanderingss of Odysseus: Theme and Structure." In *Daidalikon: Studies in Memory of Raymond V. Schoder, S.J.*, edited by Robert F. Sutton, 117–123. Wauconda, IL: Bolchazy-Carducci, 1988.

Germain, Gabriel. "The Sirens and the Temptations of Knowledge." In *Homer: A Collection of Critical Essays*, edited by George Steiner and Robert Fagles, 91–97. Twentieth Century Views. Englewood Cliffs, NJ: Prentice Hall, 1962.

Glenn, Justin M. "Mezentius and Polyphemus." *AJP* 92, no. 2 (1971): 129–155.

———. "Odysseus Confronts Nausicaa: The Lion Simile of *Odyssey* 6.13–36." *CW* 92, no. 2 (1998): 107–116.

———. "The Polyphemus Folktale and Homer's *Kyklopeia*." *TAPA* 102 (1971): 133–181.

———. "The Polyphemus Myth: Its Origin and Interpretation." *G&R* 25, no. 2 (1978): 141–155.

Goff, Barbara E. "The Sign of the Fall: The Scars of Orestes and Odysseus." *CA* 10, no. 2 (1991): 259–267.

Goldhill, Silmon. "Reading Differences: Juxtaposition and the *Odyssey*." *Ramus* 17 (1988): 1–31.

Gonzalez, Eduardo. "Odysseus' Bed and Cleopatra's Mattress." In *Comparative Literature*, special issue, *MLN* 119, no. 5 (2004): 930–948.

Gottesman, Alex. "The Pragmatics of Homeri *Kertomia*." *CQ* 58, no. 1 (2008): 1–12.

Graver, Margaret. "Dog-Helen and Homeric Insult." *CA* 14, no. 1 (1995): 41–61.

Graziosi, Barbara. *Homer*. Oxford: Oxford University Press, 2016.

Graziosi, Barbara, and J. Haubold. *Homer: The Resonance of Epic*. London: Duckworth, 2005.

Green, Peter, trans. *The Odyssey: Homer*. Berkeley: University of California Press, 2018.

Greene, Elizabeth S. "The Critical Element in the Embarkation Scenes of the *Odyssey*." *GRBS* 36, no. 3 (1995): 217–230.

Gregory, Elizabeth S. "Unravelling Penelope: The Construction of the Faithful Wife in Homer's Heroines." *Helios* 23, no. 1 (1996): 3–20.

Gresseth, Gerald K. "The Homeric Sirens." *TAPA* 101, no. 2 (1970): 3–18.

Grethlein, Jonas. "How Old Is Nestor?" *Eikasmos* 17 (2006): 11–16.

Griffin, Jasper. *Homer*. Past Masters. New York: Hill and Wang, 1980.

———. *Homer on Life and Death*. Oxford: Clarendon, 1980.

———. *Homer: The Odyssey*. 2nd ed. Cambridge: Cambridge University Press, 2004.

Griffith, R. Drew. "Community and Its Ritual Orders in *Odyssey* 21." *Res Publica Litterarum* 12 (1989): 69–76.

———. "Homer's Black Earth and the Land of Egypt." *Athenaeum* 84, no. 1 (1996): 251–254.

———. *Mummy Wheat: Egyptian Influence on the Homeric View of the Afterlife and the Eleusinian Mysteries*. Lanham, MD: University Press of America, 2008.

———. "Sailing to Elysium: Menelaus' Afterlife (*Odyssey* 4.561–569) and Egyptian Religion." *Phoenix* 55, nos. 3–4 (2001): 213–243.

———. "Temple as Ship in *Odyssey* 6.10." *AJP* 123, no. 4 (2002): 541–547.

———. "The Voice of the Dead in Homer's *Odyssey* and in Egyptian Funerary Texts." *Studi micenei ed egeo-anatolici* 39 (1997): 219–240.

Gross, N. "Nausikaa: A Female Threat." *CW* 69 (1976): 311–317.

Guidorizzi, Giulio. "The Laughter of the Suitors: A Case of Collective Madness in the *Odyssey*." In *Poet, Public, and Performance in Ancient Greece*, edited by Lowell Edmunds and Robert W. Wallace, 1–7. Baltimore: Johns Hopkins University Press, 2000.

Gutglueck, John. "A Detestable Encounter in *Odyssey* VI." *CJ* 83, no. 2 (1987–1988): 97–102.

Gutting, Edward. "An Emendation to the Scholia on Homer's *Nekuia*." *CQ* 50, no. 1 (2000): 290–292.

Haft, Adele. "Odysseus, Idomeneus, and Meriones: The Cretan Lies of *Odyssey* 13–19." *CJ* 79, no. 4 (1983–1984): 289–306.

———. "*Ta de nun panta teleitai*: Prophecy and Recollection in the Assemblies of *Iliad* 2 and *Odyssey* 2." *Arethusa* 25, no. 2 (1992): 223–240.

Hainsworth, J. B. *Homer*. Greece and Rome: New Surveys in the Classics 3. Oxford: Clarendon, 1979.

———. *The Idea of Epic*. Berkeley: University of California Press, 1991.

Hall, Edith. "No Man's Lands: Modern Myth of the Cyclops." *Times Literary Supplement*, May 26, 2006, 14–15.

Haller, Benjamin. "The Gates of Horn and Ivory in *Odyssey* 19: Penelope's Call for Deeds, Not Words." *CP* 104, no. 4 (2009): 397–417.

Halverson, John. "Social Order in the *Odyssey*." *Hermes* 113 (1985): 129–145.

———. "The Succession Issue in the *Odyssey*." *G&R* 33, no. 2 (1986): 119–128.

Hammond, Martin, trans. *Homer: The Odyssey*. London: Duckworth, 2000.

Hankey, Robin, and Douglas Little, eds. *Essays in Honour of Agathe Thornton*. Dunedin, New Zealand: University of Otago Press, 1985.

Hansen, William F. "Odysseus and the Oar: A Folkloric Approach." In *Approaches to Greek Myth*, edited by Lowell Edmunds, 239–274. Baltimore: Johns Hopkins University Press, 1990.

Harris, John. "Proteus Surrenders: The Life and Death of Death-and-Rebirth." *Renascence* 49, no. 2 (1997): 121–139.

Harrison, E. L. "Odysseus and Demodocus: Homer, *Odyssey* 8.492f." *Hermes* 99 (1971): 378–379.

Harsh, Philip Whaley. "Penelope and Odysseus in *Odyssey* XIX." *AJP* 71, no. 1 (1950): 1–21.

Hart, Walter Morris. "High Comedy in the *Odyssey*." *California Publications in Classical Philology* 13, no. 4 (1942): 263–278.

Hartog, Francois. *Memories of Odysseus: Frontier Tales from Ancient Greece*. Translated by Janet Lloyd. The University of Chicago Press, 2001.

Haubold, Johannes. *Homer's People: Epic Poetry and Social Formation*. Cambridge: Cambridge University Press, 2000.

Havelock, Christine Mitchell. "The Intimate Act of Footwashing: *Odyssey* 19." In *The Distaff Side: Representing the Female in Homer's "Odyssey,"* edited by Beth Cohen, 185–199. Oxford: Oxford University Press, 1995.

Heath, John. "Telemachus *Pepnymenos*: Growing into an Epithet." *Mnemosyne*, 4th ser., 54, no. 2 (2001): 129–157.

Heatherington, M. E. "Chaos, Order, and Cunning in the *Odyssey*." *Studies in Philology* 73 (1976): 225–38.

Heiden, Bruce. "The Placement of 'Book Divisions' in the *Odyssey*." *CP* 95, no. 3 (2000): 247–259.

Heitman, Richard. "The Stakes of the Plot." In *Homer's "The Odyssey,"* updated ed., edited by Harold Bloom, 223–244. Bloom's Modern Critical Interpretations. New York: Bloom's Literary Criticism, 2007.

———. *Taking Her Seriously: Penelope and the Plot of Homer's "Odyssey."* Ann Arbor: University of Michigan Press, 2005.

Hellelman, Wendy. "Homer's Penelope: A Tale of Feminine Arete." *Echos du Monde Classique* 39, no. 14 (1995): 227–250.

———. "Penelope as Lady Philosophy." *Phoenix* 49 (1995): 283–302.

Henderson, John. "The Name of the Tree: Recounting *Odyssey* XXIV 340–2." *JHS* 117 (1997): 87–116.

Hershbell, Jackson P. "Parmenides and Outis in *Odyssey* 9." *CJ* 68, no. 2 (1972): 178–180.

Highbarger, E. L. *The Gates of Dreams*. Baltimore: Johns Hopkins University Press, 1940.

Hoffer, Stanley E. "Telemachus' 'Laugh' (*Odyssey* 21.105): Deceit, Authority, and Communication in the Bow Contest." *AJP* 116, no. 4 (1995): 515–529.

Hogan, James. "The Temptation of Odysseus." *TAPA* 106 (1976): 187–210.

Holmberg, Ingrid E. "Hephaistos and Spiders' Webs." *Phoenix* 57, nos. 1–2 (2003): 1–17.

———. "The *Odyssey* and Female Subjectivity." *Helios* 22, no. 2 (1995): 103–122.

———. "The Sign of Metis." *Arethusa* 30, no. 1 (1997): 1–33.

Hölscher, Uvo. "Penelope and the Suitors." In *Reading the "Odyssey,"* edited by Seth L. Schein, 133–140. Princeton, NJ: Princeton University Press, 1995.

Holtsmark, Erling B. "Spiritual Rebirth of the Hero: *Odyssey* 5." *CJ* 61, no. 5 (1966): 206–210.

Hopman, Marianne. "Narrative and Rhetoric in Odysseus' Tales to the Phaeacians." *AJP* 133, no. 1 (2012): 1–30.

Houston, George W. "*Thronos, Dhifros*, and Odysseus' Change from Beggar to Avenger." *CP* 70, no. 3 (1975): 212–214.

Howell, Emily Nicole. "Odysseus Deconstructed: Crossing the Threshold into Critical Thinking." *English Journal* 102, no. 1 (2012): 61–66.

Hunter, Richard. *The Measure of Homer: The Ancient Reception of the "Iliad" and "Odyssey."* Cambridge: Cambridge University Press, 2018.

Ingalls, W. B. "Nausikaa, Penelope, and Initiation." *Echos du monde classique* 19 (2000): 1–18.

Irwin, Eleanor M. "Odysseus' 'Hyacinthine Hair' in *Odyssey* 6.231." *Phoenix* 44, no. 3 (1990): 205–218.

Jacobson, Howard. "Cacus and the Cyclops." *Mnemosyne*, 4th ser., 42, no. 1/2 (1989): 101–102.

———. "Homer, *Odyssey* 1.132–3." *CQ* 50, no. 1 (2000): 290.

———. "Homer, *Odyssey* 17.221." *CQ* 49, no. 1 (1999): 315.

Jamison, Stephanie. "Penelope and the Pigs: Indic Perspectives on the *Odyssey*." *CA* 18, no. 2 (1999): 227–272.

Johnson, Claudia Durst, and Vernon Johnson. *Understanding "The Odyssey."* Literature in Context. Westport, CT: Greenwood, 2003.

Johnston, S. I. "Penelope and the Erinyes: *Odyssey* 20.61–82." *Helios* 21 (1994): 137–159.

Jones, Peter V, Homer's "Odyssey": A Companion to the Translation of Richmond Lattimore. Southern Illinois University Press, 1988.

———. "The KLEOS of Telemachus: *Odyssey* 1.95." *AJP* 109, no. 4 (1988): 496–506.

———, trans. *"Odyssey" Books 1 & 2*. Introduction by Peter V. Jones. Warminster, England: Aris and Phillips, 1991.

———. "*Odyssey* 6.209–223: The Instructions to Bathe." *Mnemosyne*, 4th ser., 42, nos. 3–4 (1989): 349–364.

———. "The Past in Homer's *Odyssey*." *JHS* 112 (1992): 74–90.

Kadletz, E. "The Sacrifice of Eumaios the Pig Herder." *GRBS* 25, no. 2 (1984): 99–105.

Kafka, Franz. "The Silence of the Sirens." In *Homer: A Collection of Critical Essays*, edited by George Steiner and Robert Fagles, 98–99. Twentieth Century Views. Englewood Cliffs, NJ: Prentice Hall, 1962.

Kahane, Ahuvia. "The First Word of the *Odyssey*." *TAPA* 122 (1992): 115–131.

Kakridis, J. "The Recognition of Odysseus." In *Homer Revisited*, 151–163. Publications of the New Society of Letters at Lund 64. Lund, Sweden: Gleerup, 1971.

Karakantza, E. D. "Odysseia or Penelopeia?: An Assessment of Penelope's Character and Position in the *Odyssey*." *Mètis* 12 (1997): 161–79.

Karanika, Andromache. "The End of the Nekyia: Odysseus, Heracles, and the Gorgon in the Underworld." *Arethusa* 44, no. 1 (2011): 1–27.

Kardulias, Dianna Rhyan. "Odysseus in Ino's Veil: Feminine Headdress and the Hero in *Odyssey* 5." *TAPA* 131 (2001): 23–51.

Karp, A. "The Need for Boundaries: Homer's Critique of the Phaeakian Utopia in the *Odyssey*." *Utopian Studies* 6, no. 2 (1995): 25–34.

Katsouris, Andreas G. "Euripides' *Cyclops* and Homer's *Odyssey*: An Interpretative Comparison." *Prometheus* 23, no. 1 (1997): 1–24.

Katz, Marilyn A. "Homecoming and Hospitality: Recognition and the Construction of Identity in the *Odyssey*." In *Epic and Epoch: Essays on the Interpretation and History of Genre*, edited by Steven M. Oberhelman, Van Kelly, and Richard J. Goslan, 49–75. Lubbock: Texas Tech University Press, 1994.

———. *Penelope's Renown: Meaning and Indeterminacy in the "Odyssey."* Princeton, NJ: Princeton University Press, 1991.

———. "Review: Commentaries on the *Odyssey*." *CJ* 91, no. 1 (1995): 95–99.

Kearns, E. "The Return of Odysseus: A Homeric Theoxeny." *CQ* 32, no. 1 (1982): 2–8.

King, B. "The Rhetoric of the Victim: Odysseus in the Swineherd's Hut." *CA* 18, no. 1 (1999): 74–93.

Kirk, G. S. *Homer and the Oral Tradition*. Cambridge: Cambridge University Press, 1978.

———. *The Language and Background of Homer*. Cambridge: Cambridge University Press, 1964.

———. *The Songs of Homer*. Cambridge: Cambridge University Press, 1962.

Kirk, G. S., and Adam Parry. *Yale Classical Studies*. Vol. 20, *Homeric Studies*. New Haven, CT: Yale University Press, 1966.

Klingner, Friedrich. "The Fight for Justice and Departure of Telemachus." In *Homer: German Scholarship in Translation*, edited and translated by G. M. Wright and P. V. Jones, 192–216. Oxford: Clarendon, 1997.

Knox, Bernard M. W. *The Heroic Temper*. Berkeley: University of California Press, 1964.

———. Introduction to *Homer: The Odyssey*, translated by Robert Fagles, 3–64. New York: Penguin, 1996.

Kohl, John C., Jr. "The Fabric of the Longer Repeated Passages in the *Odyssey*." *Interpretation: A Journal of Political Philosophy* 23, no. 1 (1995): 3–39.

Köhnken, Adolf. "Odysseus' Scar: An Essay on Homeric Epic Narrative Technique." In *Oxford Readings in Classical Studies: Homer's "Odyssey,"* edited by Lillian E. Doherty, 44–61. Oxford: Oxford University Press, 2009.

Krischer, Tilman. "Odysseus und Telemachus." *Hermes* 116 (1988): 1–12.

Kurtz, J. G. "The Mind and Heart of Penelope." *New England Classical Newsletter and Journal* 17 (1989): 11–25.

Larson, Stephanie. "Boiotia, Athens, the Peisistratids, and the *Odyssey*'s Catalogue of Heroines." *GRBS* 41, no. 3 (2000): 193–222.

Latacz, Joachim. *Homer: His Art and His World*. Translated by James P. Holoka. Ann Arbor: University of Michigan Press, 1996.

Lateiner, Donald. "Heroic Proxemics: Social Space and Distance in the *Odyssey*." *TAPA* 122 (1992): 133–163.

———. *Sardonic Smile: Nonverbal Behavior in Homeric Epic*. Ann Arbor: University of Michigan Press, 1995.

———. "The Suitors' Take: Manners and Power in Ithaka." In "Essays on Homeric Epic," edited by Hanna M. Roisman and Joseph Roisman, special issue, *Colby Quarterly* 29, no. 3 (1993): 173–196.

———. "Telemakhos' One Sneeze and Penelope's Two Laughs." In *Approaches to Homer: Ancient and Modern*, edited by Robert Rabel, 91–104. Swansea: Classical Press of Wales, 2005.

Lattimore, Richmond, trans. *The "Iliad" of Homer*. Chicago: University of Chicago Press, 1951.

———. "Nausikaa's Suitors." *Illinois Studies in Language and Literature* 58 (1969): 88–102.

———, trans. *The "Odyssey" of Homer*. New York: Harper Perennial Modern Classics, 1967.

Lee, D.J.N. *The Similes of the "Iliad" and the "Odyssey" Compared*. Melbourne: Melbourne University Press, 1964.

Levaniouk, Olga A. "Aithon, Aithon, and Odysseus." *HSCP* 100 (2000): 25–51.

———. *Eve of the Festival: Making Myth in "Odyssey" 19*. Washington, DC: Center for Hellenic Studies, 2011.

———. "Penelope and the Pandareids." *Phoenix* 62, nos. 1–2 (2008): 5–38.

———. "Penelope and the *Pênelops*." In *Nine Essays on Homer*, edited by Miriam Carlisle and Olga Levaniouk, 95–136. Lanham, MD: Rowman and Littlefield, 1999.

Levine, Daniel B. "*Flens Matrona et Meretrices Gaudentes*: Penelope and Her Maids." *CW* 81 (1987): 23–27.

———. "Homeric Laughter and the Unsmiling Suitors." *CJ* 78, no. 2 (1982–1983): 97–104.

———. "Odysseus' Smiles: *Odyssey* 20.301, 22.371, 23.111." *TAPA* 114 (1984): 1–9.

———. "*Odyssey* 18: Iros as Paradigm for the Suitors." *CJ* 77, no. 3 (1982): 200–204.

———. "Penelope's Laugh: *Odyssey* 18.163." *AJP* 104, no. 2 (1983): 172–178.

———. "Sophocles' *Philoctetes* and *Odyssey* 9: Odysseus versus the Cave Man." *Scholia* 12 (2003): 3–26.

———. "Theoklymenos and the Apocalypse." *CJ* 79, no. 1 (1983): 1–7.

Levy, Harry L. "The Odyssean Suitors and the Host-Guest Relationship." *TAPA* 94 (1963): 145–153.

Lind, L. R., and Shirley Clay Scott. "Man, Mind, and Monster: Polyphemus from Homer through Joyce." *CML* 16, no. 1 (1995): 19–75.

Lombardo, Stanley, trans. *Odyssey: Homer*. Introduction by Sheila Murnaghan. Indianapolis: Hackett, 2000.

Long, A. A. "Morals and Values in Homer." *JHS* 90 (1970): 121–139.

Lonsdale, Steven. "Protean Forms and Disguise in *Odyssey* 4." *Lexis* 2 (1989): 165–178.

Lord, Albert Bates. *The Singer of Tales*. Cambridge, MA: Harvard University Press, 1960.

Losada, Luis A. "*Odyssey* 21.411: The Swallow's Call." *CP* 80, no. 1 (1985): 33–34.

Louden, Bruce. "Epeios, Odysseus, and the Indo-European Metaphor for Poet." *JIES* 24, nos. 3–4 (1996): 277–304.

———. "Eumaios and Alkinoos: The Audience and the *Odyssey*." *Phoenix* 51, no. 2 (1997): 95–114.

———. "An Extended Narrative Pattern in the *Odyssey*." *GRBS* 34, no. 1 (1993): 5–33.

———. *Homer's "Odyssey" and the Near East*. Cambridge: Cambridge University Press, 2011.

———. "Is There Early Recognition between Penelope and Odysseus? Book 19 in the Larger Context of the *Odyssey*." *CL* 38, no. 2 (2011): 76–100.

———. *The "Odyssey": Structure, Narration, and Meaning*. Baltimore: Johns Hopkins University Press, 1999.

Lowenstam, Steven. "The Shroud of Laertes and Penelope's Guile." *CJ* 95, no. 4 (2000): 333–348.

MacDonald, Dennis R. "Luke's Eutychus and Homer's Elpenor: Acts 20:7–12 and *Odyssey* 10–12." *Journal of Higher Criticism* 1 (1994): 5–24.

Mackail, J. W. "Penelope in the *Odyssey*." *CS* (1925): 54–75.

Mackie, Hilary Susan. "Song and Storytelling: An Odyssean Perspective." *TAPA* 127 (1997): 77–95.

MacLachlan, Bonnie. "Feasting with Ethiopians: Life on the Fringe." *QUCC* 40, no. 69 (1992): 15–33.

Marinatos, Nanno. "Circe and Liminality: Ritual Background and Narrative Structure." In *Homer's World*, edited by Oivind Anderson and Matthew Dickie, 133–140. Athens, Greece: Norwegian Institute, 1995.

———. "The Cosmic Journey of Odysseus." *Numen* 48, no. 4 (2001): 381–416.

Marincola, J. "Odysseus and the Historians." *Syllecta Classica* 18 (2007): 1–79.

Mark, Samuel E. "*Odyssey* (5.234–53) and Homeric Ship Construction: A Clarification." *International Journal of Nautical Archaeology* 25, no. 1 (1996): 46–48.

———. "*Odyssey* 5.234–53 and Homeric Ship Construction: A Reappraisal." *American Journal of Archaeology* 95 (1991): 441–445.

Marks, James R. "Alternative Odysseys: The Case of Thoas and Odysseus." *TAPA* 133, no. 2 (2003): 209–226.

———. "The Ongoing Neikos: Thersites, Odysseus and Achilleus." *AJP* 126, no. 1 (2005): 1–31.

———. *Zeus in the "Odyssey."* Cambridge, MA: Harvard University Press, 2008.

Maronites, D. N. *Homeric Megathemes: War-Homilia-Homecoming.* Translated by David Connolly. Lanham, MD: Lexington Books, 2004.

Marquardt, Patricia. "Penelope *Polutropos.*" *AJP* 106, no. 1 (1985): 32–48.

Martin, Bridget. "Blood, Honour and Status in *Odyssey* 11." *CQ* 64, no. 1 (2014): 1–12.

Martin, Richard M. "Telemachus and the Last Hero Song." *Colby Quarterly* 29 (1993): 222–240.

Martin, Ruth. "Love at a Distance: Kafka and the Sirens." In *Sexual Politics of Desire and Belonging*, 81–99. Amsterdam: Rodopi, 2007.

Martyniuk, Irene. "Odysseus' Bed and Cleopatra's Mattress." *MLN* 119, no. 5 (2004): 930–948.

Matsumoto, Nisuke. "From Folktale to Epic: In Relation to the Matter of Penelope's Remarriage." *JCS* 45 (1997): 1–15.

McAuslan, I., and P. Walcot, eds. *Homer.* Greece and Rome Studies 4. Oxford: Oxford University Press, 1998.

McClymont, J. D. "The Character of Circe in the *Odyssey.*" *Akroterion* 53 (2008): 21–29.

McDonald, W. E. "On Hearing the Silent Voice: Penelope and the Daughters of Pandareus." *Helios* 24, no. 1 (1997): 3–22.

McGrath, William T. "Progression of the Lion Simile in the *Odyssey.*" *CJ* 77, no. 3 (1982): 205–212.

McInerney, J. *The Cattle of the Sun: Cows and Culture in the World of the Ancient Greeks.* Princeton, NJ: Princeton University Press, 2010.

McKay, K. J. "Studies in Aithon." *Mnemosyne*, 4th ser., 12, no. 3 (1959): 12–13.

McLeod, Wallace. "The Bow and the Axes." In *Studies Presented to Sterling Dow on His Eightieth Birthday*, edited by Kent J. Rigsby, 203–210. Durham, NC: Duke University Press, 1984.

Mendelsohn, D. *An Odyssey: A Father, a Son, and an Epic.* New York: Knopf, 2017.

Millar, C.M.H., and J.W.S. Carmichael. "The Growth of Telemachus." *G&R* 1, no. 2 (1954): 58–64.

Minchin, Elizabeth. "The Expression of Sarcasm in the Odyssey." *Mnemosyne*, 4th ser., 63, no. 4 (2010): 533.

———. "Homer on Autobiographical Memory: The Case of Nestor." In *Approaches to Homer: Ancient and Modern*, edited by Robert Rabel, 55–72. Swansea: Classical Press of Wales, 2005.

———. *Homeric Voices: Discourse, Memory, Gender.* Oxford: Oxford University Press, 2007.

———. "Homer Springs a Surprise: Eumaios' Tale at *Od.*15.403–484." *Hermes* 120 (1992): 259–266.

———. "How Homeric Is *Hysteron Proteron*?" *Mnemosyne*, 4th ser., 54, no. 6 (2001): 635–645.

———. "The Poet Appeals to His Muse: Homeric Invocations in the Context of Epic Performance." *CJ* 91, no. 1 (1995): 25–33.

———. "Ring-Patterns and Ring-Composition: Some Observations on the Framing of Stories in Homer." *Helios* 22, no. 1 (1995): 23–35.

———. "Verbal Behavior in Its Social Context: Three Question Strategies in Homer's *Odyssey*." *CQ* 52, no. 1 (2002): 15–32.

Mitchell, Lynette G. "Euboean Io." *CQ* 51, no. 2 (2001): 339–352.

Mondi, R. "The Homeric Cyclopes: Folktale, Tradition, and Theme." *TAPA* 113 (1983): 17–38.

Monro, David B., and Thomas W. Allen, eds. *Homeri Opera.* Vols. 3 and 4. 2nd ed. Oxford: Oxford University Press, 1917.

Morgan, Kathleen. "*Odyssey* 23.218–24: Adultery, Shame, and Marriage." *AJP* 112, no. 1 (1991): 1–3.

Morris, Ian, and Barry Powell, eds. *A New Companion to Homer.* Leiden: Brill, 1998.

Morris, J. F. "'Dream Scenes' in Homer: A Study in Variation." *TAPA* 113 (1983): 39–54.

Morrison, James. "Similes for Odysseus and Penelope: Mortality, Divinity, Identity." In *Approaches to Homer: Ancient and Modern*, edited by Robert Rabel, 73–89. Swansea: Classical Press of Wales, 2005.

———. *A Companion to Homer's "Odyssey."* Westport, CT: Greenwood, 2003.

Most, Glenn. "The Structure and Function of Odysseus' Apologoi." *TAPA* 119 (1989): 15–30.

Moulton, Carroll. "The End of the *Odyssey*." *GRBS* 15, no. 2 (1974): 153–169.

———. "Homeric Metaphor." *CP* 74, no. 4 (1979): 279–293.

———. *Similes in the Homeric Poems.* Göttingen, Germany: Vandenhoeck and Ruprecht, 1977

Mueller, Melissa. "Penelope and the Poetics of Remembering." *Arethusa* 40, no. 3 (2007): 337–362.

Murnaghan, Sheila. "Desire in the Odyssey." *CR* 57, no. 1 (2007): 3–4.

———. *Disguise and Recognition in the "Odyssey."* Princeton, NJ: Princeton University Press, 1987.

———. "Maternity and Mortality in Homeric Poetry." *CA* 11, no. 2 (1992): 242–264.

———. "Odysseus and the Suitors." In *Odysseus/Ulysses*, edited by Harold Bloom, 273–288. Modern Literary Characters. New York: Chelsea House Publishers, 1991.

———. "Penelope's *Agnoia*: Knowledge, Power, and Gender in the *Odyssey*." *Helios* 13 (1986): 103–115.

———. "The Plan of Athena." In *The Distaff Side: Representing the Female in Homer's "Odyssey,"* edited by Beth Cohen, 61–80. Oxford: Oxford University Press, 1995.

———. "Reading Penelope." In *Epic and Epoch: Essays on the Interpretation and History of Genre*, edited by Steven M. Oberhelman, Van Kelly, and Richard J. Goslan, 76–96. Lubbock: Texas Tech University Press, 1994.

———. "The Trials of Telemachus: Who Was the *Odyssey* Meant For?" *Arethusa* 35, no. 1 (2002): 133–153.

Murnaghan, Sheila, and D. H. Roberts. "Penelope's Song: The Lyric Odysseys of Linda Pastan and Louise Gluck." *CML* 22, no. 1 (2002): 1–33.

Murray, A. T. *Homer: The Odyssey*. Vols. 1 and 2. 1919. Reprint, Cambridge, MA: Harvard University Press, 1972.

Muse, Kevin. "'Don't Dally in This Valley': Wordplay in *Odyssey* 15.10 and *Aeneid* 4.271." *CQ* 55, no. 2 (2005): 646–649.

Myres, J. L. "The Pattern of the *Odyssey*." *JHS* 72 (1952): 1–11.

Myrsiades, Kostas, ed. *Approaches to Homer's "Iliad" and "Odyssey."* American University Studies 38. New York: Peter Lang, 2010.

———, ed. *Approaches to Teaching Homer's "Iliad" and "Odyssey."* New York: MLA, 1987.

———, ed. "Early Recognition in Homer's 'Odyssey.'" Special issue, *CL* 38, no. 2 (2011).

———, ed. "Homer: Analysis and Influence." Special issue, *CL* 35, no. 4 (2008).

———, ed. "The Homeric Epic." Special issue, *CL* 3, no. 3 (1976).

———, ed. *Reading Homer: Film and Text*. Madison, NJ: Fairleigh Dickinson University Press, 2009.

———, ed. "Reading Homer in the 21st Century." Special issue, *CL* 34, no. 2 (2007).

Nagler, Michael N. "Dread Goddess Revisited." In *Reading the "Odyssey,"* edited by Seth L. Schein, 140–161. Princeton, NJ: Princeton University Press, 1995.

———. "Odysseus: The Proem and the Problem." *CA* 9, no. 2 (1990): 335–356.

———. "Penelope's Male Hand: Gender and Violence in the *Odyssey*." In "Essays on Homeric Epic," edited by Hanna M. Roisman and Joseph Roisman, special issue, *Colby Quarterly* 29, no. 3 (1993): 241–257.

———. *Spontaneity and Tradition: A Study in the Oral Art of Homer.* Berkeley: University of California Press, 1974.

Nagy, Gregory. *The Ancient Greek Hero in 24 Hours.* Cambridge, MA: Belknap Press of Harvard University Press, 2013.

———. *Homer's Text and Language.* Champaign: University of Illinois Press, 2004.

Nardo, Don, ed. *Readings on Homer.* Literary Companions to World Authors. San Diego, CA: Greenhaven, 1998.

Neils, Jenifer. "Les Femmes Fatales: Skylla and the Sirens in Greek Art." In *The Distaff Side: Representing the Female in Homer's "Odyssey,"* edited by Beth Cohen, 175–184. Oxford: Oxford University Press, 1995.

Nelis, Damien P. "Demodocus and the Song of Orpheus (Ap. Rhod. Arg. I, 496–511)." *Museum Helveticum* 49 (1992): 153–170.

Nelson, Conny, ed. *Homer's "Odyssey": A Critical Handbook.* Belmont, CA: Wadsworth, 1969.

Newton, Rick M. "The Aristotelian Unity of Odysseus' Wanderings." *Approaches to Teaching Homer's "Iliad" and "Odyssey,"* edited by Kostas Myrsiades, 137–142. New York: MLA, 1987.

———. "Assembly and Hospitality in the *Cyclôpeia.*" In "Homer: Analysis and Influence," edited by Kostas Myrsiades, special issue, *CL* 35, no. 4 (2008): 1–44.

———. "The Ciconians, Revisited (Homer, 'Odyssey' 9.39–66)." In *Approaches to Homer: Ancient and Modern,* edited by Robert Rabel, 135–146. Swansea: Classical Press of Wales, 2005.

———. "Cloak and Shield in *Odyssey* 14." *CJ* 93, no. 2 (1997–1998): 143–156.

———. "Odysseus and Hephaestus in the *Odyssey.*" *CJ* 83, no. 1 (1987): 12–20.

———. "Odysseus and Melanthius." *GRBS* 38, no. 1 (1997): 5–18.

———. "Poor Polyphemus: Emotional Ambivalence in *Odyssey* 9 and 17." *CW* 76 (1983): 137–142.

———. "The Rebirth of Odysseus." *GRBS* 25, no. 1 (1984): 5–20.

Nickel, Roberto. "Homer's *Odyssey.*" *CR* 61, no. 1 (2011): 16–19.

Nieto Hernández, Pura. "Back in the Cave of the Cyclops." *AJP* 121, no. 3 (2000): 345–366.

———. "Odysseus, Agamemnon and Apollo." *CJ* 97, no. 4 (2002): 319–334.

———. "*Odyssey, Agamemnon,* and Apollo." *CJ* 97, no. 2 (1992): 145–159.

———. "Penelope's Absent Song." *Phoenix* 62 (2008): 39–62.

———. "Reading Homer in the 21st Century." *CL* 34, no. 2 (2007): 29–54.

Niles, John D. "Patterning in the Wanderings of Odysseus." *Ramus* 7 (1978): 46–60.

Nimis, Stephen A. "Ring Composition and Linearity in Homer." In *Signs of Orality: The Oral Tradition and Its Influence in the Greek and Roman World*, edited by E. Anne Mackay, 65–78. Leiden: Brill, 1998.

Nishimura, Yoshiko T. "The Circe-Episodes in the *Odyssey*." *JCS* 45 (1997): 40–49.

Nobus, Dany. "*Polymetis* Freud: Some Reflections on the Psychoanalytic Significance of Homer's *Odyssey*." *Comparative Literature Studies* 43, no. 3 (2006): 252–268.

Nugent, Pauline. "The Sounds of Sirens: *Odyssey* 12. 184–91." In "Homer: Analysis and Influence," edited by Kostas Myrsiades, special issue, *CL* 35, no. 4 (2008): 45–54.

Oberhelman, Steven M., Van Kelly, and Richard J. Goslan, eds. *Epic and Epoch: Essays on the Interpretation and History of Genre*. Lubbock: Texas Tech University Press, 1994.

O'Brien, Joan. "Homer's Savage Hera." *CJ* 86, no. 2 (1990–1991): 105–125.

Olson, S. Douglas. *Blood and Iron: Stories and Storytelling in Homer's "Odyssey."* Mnemosyne Supplement 148. Leiden: Brill, 1995.

———. "Name-Magic and the Threat of Lying Stranger's in Homer's *Odyssey*." *ICS* 17, no. 1 (1992): 1–7.

———. "*Odyssey* 8: Guile, Force, and the Subversive Poetics of Desire." *Arethusa* 22 (1989): 135–145.

———. "Servants' Suggestions in Homer's *Odyssey*." *CJ* 87, no. 3 (1992): 219–227.

———. "The Stories of Agamemnon in Homer's *Odyssey*." *TAPA* 120 (1990): 57–71.

———. "The Stories of Helen and Menelaus (*Odyssey* 4.240–89) and the Return of Odysseus." *AJP* 110, no. 3 (1989): 387–394.

———. "Telemachos' Laugh (*Od.* 21.101–105)." *CJ* 89, no. 4 (1994): 369–372.

———. "Women's Names and the Reception of Odysseus on Scheria." *Echos du monde classique/Classical Views* 36, no. 11 (1991): 1–6.

O'Sullivan, James N. "Nature and Culture in *Odyssey* 9." *SO* 65 (1990): 7–17.

———. "Observations on the Kyklopeia." *SO* 62 (1987): 5–24.

O'Sullivan, Luke. Review of *The Odyssey of Political Theory: The Politics of Departure and Return*, by Patrick J. Deneen. *Political Studies* 49, no. 2 (2001): 349.

Pache, Corinne Ondine. "Mourning Lions and Penelope's Revenge." *Arethusa* 49, no. 1 (2016): 1–24.

———. "Odysseus and the Phaeacians." In *Nine Essays on Homer*, edited by Miriam Carlisle and Olga Levaniouk, 21–34. Lanham, MD: Rowman and Littlefield, 1999.

———. "War Games: Odysseus at Troy." *HSCP* 100 (2000): 15–23.

Page, Denys L. *Folktales in Homer's "Odyssey."* Cambridge, MA: Harvard University Press, 1973.

———. *The Homeric "Odyssey."* Oxford: Oxford University Press, 1955.

Panchenko, Dmitri V. "Aoidos Aner, Aegisthus and Clytemnestra (the *Odyssey* 3.263–272)." *Hyperboreus* 2, no. 2 (1996): 178–182.

Pantelia, M. C. "Spinning and Weaving: Ideas of Domestic Order in Homer." *AJP* 114, no. 4 (1993): 493–501.

Parry, Adam. *The Homeric "Odyssey."* Oxford: Clarendon, 1955.

———, ed. *The Making of Homeric Verse: The Collected Papers of Milman Parry.* Oxford: Clarendon, 1971.

Parry, Hugh. "The *Apologos* of Odysseus: Lies, All Lies?" *Phoenix* 48, no. 1 (1994): 1–22.

Paton, W. R. "Book VIII of the *Odyssey.*" *CR* 26 (1912): 215–116.

Pazdernik, Charles F. "Odysseus and His Audience: *Odyssey* 9.39–40 and Its Formulaic Resonances." *AJP* 116, no. 3 (1995): 347–369.

Pedrick, Victoria. "Eurycleia and Eurynome as Penelope's Confidantes." In In *Epic and Epoch: Essays on the Interpretation and History of Genre,* edited by Steven M. Oberhelman, Van Kelly, and Richard J. Goslan, 97–116. Lubbock: Texas Tech University Press, 1994.

———. "The Hospitality of Noble Women in the *Odyssey.*" *Helios* 15 (1988): 85–101.

———. "The Muse Corrects the Opening of the *Odyssey.*" *Yale Classical Studies* 29 (1992): 39–62.

———. "Supplication in the *Iliad* and the *Odyssey.*" *TAPA* 112 (1982): 125–140.

Peek, Philip Sheffield. "Propriety, Impropriety, and the Gaining of *Kleos* in the Phaiakian Episode." *GRBS* 43, no. 4 (2002–2003): 309–339.

Peradotto, John. *Man in the Middle Voice: Name and Narration in the "Odyssey."* Martin Classical Lectures, n.s., vol. 1. Princeton, NJ: Princeton University Press, 1990.

———. "Prophecy and Persons: Reading Character in the *Odyssey.*" *Arethusa* 35, no. 1 (2002): 3–15.

———. "The Social Control of Sexuality: Odyssean Dialogics." *Arethusa* 26, no. 2 (1993): 173–182.

Perry, C., and A. A. Perry. "The Archery Trial in the *Odyssey.*" *Ancient World* 34, no. 2 (2003): 169–196.

Perysinakis, I. N. "Penelope's *Eedna* Again." *CQ* 41, no. 2 (1991): 297–302.

Petropoulos, A. "The Sacrifice of Eumaeus Reconsidered." *GRBS* 28, no. 2 (1987): 135–149.

Petropoulos, J.C.B. *Kleos in a Minor Key: The Homeric Education of a Little Prince.* Cambridge, MA: Harvard University Press, 2011.

Pinsky, Robert, trans. *The Inferno of Dante.* New York: Farrar Straus and Giroux, 1996.

Plass, Paul. "Menelaus and Proteus." *CJ* 65, no. 3 (1969): 104–108.

Platt, Arthur. "Notes on the *Odyssey*." *CR* 13 (1899): 382–384.

Pocock, L. G. "A Note on *Odyssey* 10.86." *CQ* 18, no. 1 (1968): 1–3.

Podlecki, A. J. "Guest-Gifts and Nobodies in '*Odyssey* 9.'" *Phoenix* 15, no. 3 (1961): 125–133.

———. "Omens in the *Odyssey*." *G&R* 14, no. 1 (1967): 12–23.

———. "Some Odyssean Similes." *G&R* 18, no. 1 (1971): 81–90.

Powell, Barry B. *Homer*. Blackwell Introductions to the Classical World. Malden, MA: Blackwell, 2004.

———. "Narrative Pattern in the Homeric Tale of Menelaus." *TAPA* 101 (1970): 419–431.

———, trans. *The Odyssey: Homer*. Oxford: Oxford University Press, 2015.

Power, Henry. *Homer's "Odyssey": A Reading Guide*. Edinburgh: Edinburgh University Press, 2011.

Pratt, Louise. "*Odyssey* 19.535–50: On the Interpretation of Dreams and Signs in Homer." *CP* 89, no. 2 (1994): 147–152.

Psyrouki-Tombrou, M. "Three Homeric Passages" *Habis* 24 (1993): 7–9.

Pucci, Pietro. *Odysseus Polytropos: Intertextual Readings in the "Odyssey" and the "Iliad."* Ithaca, NY: Cornell University Press, 1987.

———. "The Proem of the *Odyssey*." *Arethusa* 15 (1982): 39–62.

———. "The Song of the Sirens." In *Reading the "Odyssey": Selected Interpretive Essays*, edited by Seth L. Schein, 191–200. Princeton, NJ: Princeton University Press, 1996.

———. *The Song of the Sirens: Essays on Homer*. Lanham, MD: Rowman and Littlefield, 1998.

Purves, Alex C. "Homer and the Art of Overtaking." *AJP* 132, no. 4 (2011): 523–551.

———. "Unmarked Space: Odysseus and the Inland Journey." *Arethusa* 39, no. 1 (2006): 1–20.

Rabel, Robert J., ed. *Approaches to Homer: Ancient and Modern*. Swansea: Classical Press of Wales, 2005.

———. "Impersonation and Representation in the *Odyssey*." *CW* 93, no. 2 (1999): 169–183.

———. "Interruption in the *Odyssey*." *Colby Quarterly* 38, no. 1 (2002): 77–93.

Race, William H. "First Appearances in the *Odyssey*." *TAPA* 123 (1993): 79–107.

Rankin, Anne. "Penelope's Dreams in Books XIX and XX of the *Odyssey*." *Helikon* 2 (1962): 617–624.

Ready, Jonathan L. "ATU 974 *The Homecoming Husband*, the Returns of Odysseus, and the End of *Odyssey* 21." *Arethusa* 47, no. 3 (2014): 265–285.

Reece, Steve. "The Cretan *Odyssey*: A Lie Truer than Truth." *AJP* 115, no. 2 (1994): 157–173.

———. "Homer's Asphodel Meadow." *GRBS* 47, no. 4 (2007): 389–400.

———. "Penelope's 'Early Recognition' of Odysseus from a Neoanalytic and Oral Perspective." *CL* 38, no. 2 (2011): 101–117.

———. "The Phaeacians (*Od.* 5.388–13.187)." In *The Stranger's Welcome: Oral Theory and the Aesthetics of the Homeric Hospitality Scene*, by Steve Reece, 101–122. Ann Arbor: University of Michigan Press, 1993.

———. "Polyphemus (*Od.* 9.105–564)." In *The Stranger's Welcome: Oral Theory and the Aesthetics of the Homeric Hospitality Scene*, by Steve Reece, 123–144. Ann Arbor: University of Michigan Press, 1993.

———. *The Stranger's Welcome: Oral Theory and the Aesthetics of the Homeric Hospitality Scene*. Ann Arbor: University of Michigan Press, 1993.

Reinhardt, Karl. "The Adventures in the *Odyssey*." In *Reading the "Odyssey": Selected Interpretive Essays*, edited by Seth L. Schein, 63–132. Princeton, NJ: Princeton University Press, 1996.

———. "Homer and the *Telemachy*, Circe and Calypso, the Phaeacians." In *Homer: German Scholarship in Translation*, edited and translated by G. M. Wright and P. V. Jones, 217–248. Oxford: Clarendon, 1997.

Renehan, Robert. "The Staunching of Odysseus' Blood: The Healing Power of Magic." *AJP* 113, no. 1 (1992): 1–4.

Richardson, N. J. "Recognition Scenes in the *Odyssey* and Ancient Literary Criticism." *Papers of the Liverpool Latin Seminar* 4 (1983): 219–235.

Richardson, Scott. "The Case for the Defense." *CL* 38, no. 2 (2011): 118–121.

———. "Conversation in the *Odyssey*." *CL* 34, no. 2 (2007): 132–149.

———. "The Devious Narrator of the *Odyssey*." *CJ* 101, no. 4 (2006): 337–358.

———. *The Homeric Narrator*. Nashville, TN: Vanderbilt University Press, 1990.

———. Review of *The "Odyssey": Structure, Narration, and Meaning*, by Bruce Louden. *JHS* 122 (2002): 158.

———. "Truth in the Tales of the *Odyssey*." *Mnemosyne*, 4th ser., 49, no. 4 (1996): 393–402.

Rijksbaron, A. "Why Is the Incident on Thrinacia Mentioned in *Od.*1.7–9?" *Mnemosyne*, 4th ser., 46 (1993): 528–529.

Rinon, Yoav. "*Mise en abyme* and Tragic Signification in the *Odyssey*: The Three Songs of Demodocus." *Mnemosyne*, 4th ser., 59, no. 2 (2006): 208–225.

———. "The Pivotal Scene: Narration, Colonial Focalization, and Transition in *Odyssey* 9." *AJP* 128, no. 3 (2007): 301–334.

———. "Tragic Hephaestus: The Humanized God in the *Iliad* and the *Odyssey*." *Phoenix* 60, nos. 1–2 (2006): 1–20.

Ritoók, Zsigmond. "Homeric Moral Values and the Language of the Suitors." *Eirene* 35 (1999): 7–13.

Roessel, D. "The Stag on Circe's Island: An Exegesis of a Homeric Digression." *TAPA* 119 (1989): 31–36.

Roisman, Hanna M. "Eumaeus and Odysseus—Covert Recognition and Self-Revelation." *ICS* 15 (1990): 215–38.

———. "Like Father like Son: Telemachus' *Kerdea*." *Rheilnisches Museum fur Philologie* 137, no. 1 (1994): 1–22.

———. "Nestor the Good Counsellor." *CQ* 55, no. 1 (2005): 17–38.

———. "Penelope's Indignation." *TAPA* 117 (1987): 59–68.

Roisman, Hanna M., and Joseph Roisman, eds. "Essays on Homeric Epic." Special issue, *Colby Quarterly* 29, no. 3 (1993).

———, eds. "Essays on Homeric Epic." Special issue, *Colby Quarterly* 38, no. 1 (2002).

———, eds. "Essays on Homeric Epic." Special issue, *Colby Quarterly* 38, no. 2 (2002).

Roller, Duane W., and Letitia K. Roller. "Penelope's Thick Hand (*Odyssey* 21.6)." *CJ* 90, no. 1 (1994): 9–19.

Rood, Naomi. "Implied Vengeance in the Simile of Grieving Vultures (*Odyssey* 16.216–19)." *CQ* 56, no. 1 (2006): 1–11.

Rose, Gilbert P. "Odysseus' Barking Heart." *TAPA* 109 (1979): 215–230.

———. "*Odyssey* 15.143–82: A Narrative Inconsistency?" *TAPA* 102 (1971): 509–514.

———. "The Quest of Telemachus." *TAPA* 98 (1967): 391–98.

———. "The Swineherd and the Beggar." *Phoenix* 34, no. 4 (1980): 285–297.

———. "The Unfriendly Phaeacians." *TAPA* 100 (1969): 387–406.

Rose, P. W. "Class Ambivalence in the *Odyssey*." *Hermes* 24 (2009): 129–147.

Rosen, Ralph M. "Hipponax and the Homeric Odysseus." *Eikasmos* 1 (1990): 11–25.

Roth, John W. *Speech Acts and the Poetics of Manhood: The "Lies" of Odysseus.* New York: New York University Press, 1991.

Rozokoki, Alexandra. "Penelope's Dream in Book 19 of the *Odyssey*." *CQ* 51, no. 1 (2001): 1–6.

Rubino, C. A., and C. W. Shelmerdine, eds. *Approaches to Homer.* Austin: University of Texas Press, 1983.

Russo, Joseph. "Homer against His Tradition." *Arion* 7 (1968): 275–295.

———. "Interview and Aftermath: Dream, Fantasy, and Intuition in *Odyssey* 19 and 20." *AJP* 103, no. 1 (1982): 4–18.

Rutherford, R. B. "At Home and Abroad: Aspects of the Structure of the *Odyssey*." *Proceedings of the Cambridge Philological Society* 31 (1985): 133–150.

———. *Homer.* Greece and Rome: New Surveys in the Classics 26. Cambridge: Cambridge University Press, 1996.

———. *Homer.* 2nd ed. Cambridge: Cambridge University Press, 2013.

———, ed. Homer, "Odyssey," Books XIX and XX. Cambridge: Cambridge University Press, 1992.

Said, Suzanne. *Homer and the "Odyssey."* Translated by Ruth Webb. Oxford: Oxford University Press, 2011.

Sally, David. "I, Too, Sail Past: Odysseus and the Logic of Self-Control." *Kyklos* 53, no. 2 (2000): 173–200.

Sammons, Benjamin. "The Quarrel of Agamemnon & Menelaus." *Mnemosyne*, 4th ser., 67, no. 1 (2014): 1–27.

Sano, Yoshinori. "The Story of the Wooden Horse in the *Odyssey*." *JCS* 47 (1999): 1–11.

Saussy, Haun. "Writing in the *Odyssey*: Eurykleia, Parry, Jousse, and the Opening of a Letter from Homer." *Arethusa* 29, no. 3 (1996): 299–338.

Schachter, A. "The Seer Tisamenos and the Klytiadai." *CQ* 50, no. 1 (2000): 292–295.

Scheid, John, and Jesper Svenbro. *The Craft of Zeus: Myths of Weaving and Fabric*. Translated by Carol Volk. Cambridge, MA: Harvard University Press, 1996.

Schein, Seth L. "Female Representation and Interpreting the *Odyssey*." In *The Distaff Side: Representing the Female in Homer's "Odyssey,"* edited by Beth Cohen, 17–27. Oxford: Oxford University Press, 1995.

———. "Odysseus and Polyphemus in the *Odyssey*." *GRBS* 11, no. 22 (1970): 74–83.

———, ed. *Reading the "Odyssey": Selected Interpretive Essays*. Princeton, NJ: Princeton University Press, 1996.

Schmiel, Robert. "Telemachus in Sparta." *TAPA* 103 (1972): 463–472.

Schmoll, E. A. "The First Cretan Lie of Odysseus." *Classical Bulletin* 66 (1990): 67–71.

———. "Odysseus and the Stag: The Parander." *Helios* 14 (1987): 22–28.

Schroeder, Frederic M. "Cyclopean Superlatives." *Dionysius* 20 (2002): 9–22.

Schur, David. "The Silence of Homer's Sirens." *Arethusa* 47, no. 1 (2014): 1–17.

Scodel, Ruth. *Listening to Homer: Tradition, Narrative, and Audience*. Ann Arbor: University of Michigan Press, 2002.

———. "Odysseus and the Stag." *CQ* 44, no. 2 (1994): 530–534.

———. "Odysseus' Dog and the Productive Household." *Hermes* 133, no. 4 (2005): 401–408.

———. "The Paths of Day and Night." *Ordia prima* 2 (2003): 83–86.

———. "The Removal of the Arms, the Recognition with Laertes, and Narrative Tension in the *Odyssey*." *CP* 93, no. 1 (1998): 1–17.

———. "Stupid, Pointless Wars." *TAPA* 138, no. 2 (2008): 219–235.

———. "The Suitors' Games." *AJP* 122, no. 3 (2001): 307–327.

———. "Zielinski's Law Reconsidered." *TAPA* 138, no. 1 (2008): 107–125.

Scott, John A. "Eurynome and Eurycleia in the *Odyssey.*" *CQ* 12, no. 2 (1918): 75–79.

———. "The First Book of the *Odyssey. TAPA* 67 (1936): 1–6.

———. "The Journey Made by Telemachus and Its Influence on the Action of the *Odyssey.*" *CP* 13, no. 6 (1917): 420–428.

———. "Odysseus Disguised as an Aged Beggar." *CJ* 13, no. 3 (1917–1918): 214–215.

Scott, William C. *The Artistry of the Homeric Simile.* Hanover, NH: University Press of New England, 2009.

———. "A Repeated Episode at *Odyssey* 1.125–48." *TAPA* 102 (1971): 541–551.

———. "Teaching Homer from the Top Down: The Telemachy." In *Approaches to Teaching Homer's "Iliad" and "Odyssey,"* edited by, Kostas Myrsiades, 132–136. New York: MLA, 1987.

Scully, Stephen. "The Bard as the Custodian of Homeric Society: *Odyssey* 3.263–272." *QUCC* 8 (1981): 67–83.

———. "Doubling in the Tale of Odysseus." *CW* 80 (1987): 401–417.

Segal, Charles P. "Circean Temptations: Homer, Vergil, Ovid." *TAPA* 99 (1968): 419–42.

———. "Divine Justice in the *Odyssey*: Poseidon, Cyclops, and Helios." *AJP* 113, no. 4 (1992): 489–518.

———. "*Kleos* and Its Ironies in the *Odyssey.*" *L'Antiquité Classique* 52 (1983): 2–47.

———. "The Phaeacians and the Symbolism of Odysseus' Return." *Arion* 1, no. 4 (1962): 17–64.

———. *Singers, Heroes, and Gods in the "Odyssey."* Myth and Poetics. Ithaca, NY: Cornell University Press, 1994.

———. "Transition and Ritual in Odysseus' Return." *La Parola del Passato* 40 (1967): 331–342.

———. "The Wanderer's Truth: Punning and Lying in *Odyssey* XIV." In *Studia classica Johanni Tarditi oblata*, edited by Luigi Belloni, Guido Milanese, and Antoinetta Porro, 103–109. Milan: Vita e Pensiero, 1995.

Sels, Nadia. "The Untold Death of Laertes. Revaluating Odysseus's Meeting with His Father." *Mnemosyne*, 4th ser., 66, no. 2 (2013): 181–205.

Shapiro, Harold Alan. "Coming of Age in Phaiakia: The Meeting of Odysseus and Nausikaa." In *The Distaff Side: Representing the Female in Homer's "Odyssey,"* edited by Beth Cohen, 155–164. Oxford: Oxford University Press, 1995.

———. "*Odyssey* 2.40–79: Telemachus as Rhetorician." *Classical Bulletin* 48 (1972): 57–58.

Sherratt, E. Susan. "Feasting in Homeric Epic." *Hesperia* 73, no. 2 (2004): 301–337.

Shewan, A. "Does the *Odyssey* Imitate the *Iliad*?" *CQ* (1934): 234–242.

———. "Telemachus at Sparta." *CJ* 22, no. 1 (1926): 31–37.

Silvermintz, Daniel. "Unravelling the Shroud for Laertes and Weaving the Fabric of the City: Kingship and Politics in Homer's *Odyssey.*" *Polis: The Journal of the Society for the Study of Greek Political Thought* 21, nos. 1–2 (2004): 26–42.

Simon, Bennett. "The Hero as an Only Child: An Unconscious Fantasy Structuring Homer's *Odyssey.*" *International Journal of Psycho-analysis* 55 (1974): 555–562.

Simpson, Michael. "*Odyssey* 9: Symmetry and Paradox in Outis." *CJ* 68, no. 1 (1972): 22–25.

Slater, William J. "Sympotic Ethics in the *Odyssey.*" In *Sympotica: A Symposium on the Symposion*, edited by Oswyn Murray, 213–220. Oxford: Clarendon, 1990.

Slatkin, Laura M. "Genre and Generation in the *Odyssey.*" *Mètis* 2, no. 2 (1987): 259–268.

———. *The Power of Thetis and Selected Essays.* Washington, DC: Center for Hellenic Studies, 2011.

Sluiter, Ineke. "Fish Similes and Converging Story Lines in the *Odyssey.*" *CQ* 64, no. 2 (2014): 821–824.

Snell, Bruno. *The Discovery of the Mind.* Translated by T. G. Rosenmeyer. Cambridge, MA: Harvard University Press, 1953.

Snider, Denton J. *Homer's "Odyssey."* Saint Louis: Sigma, 1895.

Stanford, W. B. "The Homeric Etymology of the Name Odysseus." *CP* 47, no. 4 (1952): 209–213.

———. "The Lies of Odysseus." *Hermathena* 75 (1950): 35–48.

———. *The Ulysses Theme: A Study in Adaptability of the Homeric Hero.* Oxford: Oxford University Press, 1954.

Starobinski, Jean. "The Inside and the Outside." *Hudson Review* 28 (1975): 333–351.

Steiner, Deborah. "Diverting Demons: Ritual, Poetic Mockery and the Odysseus-Iros Encounter." *CA* 28, no. 1 (2009): 71–100.

Steiner, George, and Robert Fagles, eds. *Homer: A Collection of Critical Essays.* Twentieth Century Views. Englewood Cliffs, NJ: Prentice Hall, 1962.

Stephens, J. Ceri. "Thoughts on a Vanishing Distinction: A Discussion of Teiresias' and Circe's Warnings about the Cattle of Helios in *Odyssey* 11 and 12." *CJ* 71, no. 2 (1975): 169–176.

Sternruck, Martin. *The Suitors in the "Odyssey."* New York: Peter Lang, 2008.

Stewart, Douglas J. *The Disguised Guest: Rank, Role, and Identity in the "Odyssey."* Lewisburg, PA: Bucknell University Press, 1976.

———. "Odysseus and the Cyclops: The Heroic Code Reviewd . . . and Rejected." In *The Disguised Guest: Rank, Role, and Identity in the "Odyssey,"* by Douglas J. Stewart, 31–74. Lewisburg, PA: Bucknell University Press, 1976.

Strong, David. "The Possibility of a Homecoming for Us: A Reflection on *The Odyssey.*" *Philosophy Today* 35, no. 4 (1991): 325–338.

Sutton, Robert F., ed. *Daidalikon: Studies in Memory of Raymond V. Schoder, S.J.* Wauconda, IL: Bolchazy-Carducci, 1988.

Taaffe, Lauren K. "There's No Place like Home: *Aspasios* and Related Words in the *Odyssey*." *CJ* 86, no. 2 (1990–1991): 131–138.

Taylor, C. H., Jr., ed. *Essays on the "Odyssey": Selected Modern Criticism*. Bloomington: Indiana University Press, 1963.

Tebben, Joseph R. "Alkinoös and Phaiakian Security." *SO* 66 (1991): 27–45.

Teffeteller, Annette. "Homeric Conversation." *Phoenix* 62, nos. 1–2 (2008): 197–199.

———. "Homeric Excuses." *CQ* 53, no. 1 (2003): 15–31.

Thalmann, W. G. *The "Odyssey": An Epic of Return*. Twayne's Masterwork Studies. New York: Twayne, 1992.

———. *The Swineherd and the Bow: Representations of Class in the Odyssey*. Ithaca, NY: Cornell University Press, 1998.

Thomas, C. G. "Penelope's Worth: Looming Larger in Early Greece." *Hermes* 116 (1988): 257–264.

Thomson, J.A.K. *Studies in the "Odyssey."* Oxford: Clarendon, 1914.

Thorton, Agathe. *People and Themes in Homer's "Odyssey."* London: Methuen, 1970.

Trahman, C. "Odysseus' Lies (*Odyssey*, Bks. 13–19)." *Phoenix* 6 (1952): 31–43.

Tsagalis, Christos. "*Odyssey* 24, 191–200: A Reconsideration." *Wiener Studien* 116 (2003): 43–56.

Tsagarakis, Odysseus. "*Odyssey* 11: The Question of the Sources." In *Homer's World*, edited by Oivind Anderson and Matthew Dickie, 123–131. Athens, Greece: Norwegian Institute, 2000.

———. *Studies in "Odyssey" 11*. Stuttgart, Germany: Franz Steiner, 2000.

Vallillee, G. "The Nausicaa Episode." *Phoenix* 9 (1955): 175–179.

Van der Valk, M.H.A.L.H. *Textual Criticism of the "Odyssey."* Leiden: Brill, 1949.

Van Nortwick, Thomas. "Penelope and Nausicaa." *TAPA* 109 (1979): 269–276.

———. "Penelope as Double Agent: *Odyssey* 21.1–60." *CW* 77 (1983): 24–25.

———. *The Unknown Odysseus: Alternate Worlds in Homer's "Odyssey."* Ann Arbor: University of Michigan Press, 2011.

Verdenius, W. J. "NOSTOS." *Mnemosyne*, 4th ser., 22, no. 2 (1969): 195.

Verity, Anthony, trans. *Homer: The Odyssey*. Oxford: Oxford University Press, 2016.

Vernant, Jean-Pierre. "Death with Two Faces." In *Reading the "Odyssey": Selected Interpretive Essays*, edited by Seth L. Schein, 55–62. Princeton, NJ: Princeton University Press, 1996.

———. "The Refusal of Odysseus." In *Reading the "Odyssey": Selected Interpretive Essays*, edited by Seth L. Schein, 185–190. Princeton, NJ: Princeton University Press, 1996.

Vivante, Paolo. *The Epithets of Homer: A Study in Poetic Values.* New Haven, CT: Yale University Press, 1982.

———. *Homer.* Hermes Books, edited by John Herington. New Haven, CT: Yale University Press, 1985.

Vlahos, John B. "Homer's *Odyssey*, Books 19 and 23: Early Recognition; A Solution to the Enigmas of Ivory and Horns, and the Test of the Bed." *CL* 34, no. 2 (2007): 107–131.

———. "Homer's *Odyssey*, Books 19 and 23: Early Recognition; A Solution to the Enigmas of Ivory and Horns, and the Test of the Bed." In *Reading Homer: Film and Text*, edited by Kostas Myrsiades, 89–116. Madison, NJ: Fairleigh Dickinson University Press, 2009.

———. "Homer's *Odyssey*: Penelope and the Case for Early Recognition." *CL* 38, no. 2 (2011): 1–75.

Volk, K. "*Kleos Aphthiton* Revisited." *CP* 97, no. 1 (2002): 61–68.

Wace, Alan J. B., and Frank H. Stubbings, eds. *A Companion to Homer.* New York: Macmillan, 1962.

Walcot, P. "Odysseus and the Art of Lying." *Ancient Society* 8 (1977): 1–19.

———. "Odysseus' Lies." *Phoenix* 6 (1977): 31–43.

Walsh, Thomas R. "*Odyssey* 1.6–9: A Little More than Kine." *Mnemosyne*, 4th ser., 48, no. 4 (1995): 385–410.

Warner, Marina. "The Enchantments of Circe: The Refusal of Odysseus, the Choice of Gryllus." *Pegasus* 42 (1999): 3–14.

Waterhouse, Helen. "From Ithaca to the *Odyssey*." *Annual of the British School at Athens* 91 (1996): 301–317.

Watrous, John. "Artemis and the Lion: Two Similes in *Odyssey* 6." In *Nine Essays on Homer*, edited by Miriam Carlisle and Olga Levaniouk, 165–176. Lanham, MD: Rowman and Littlefield, 1999.

Webber, A. "The Hero Tells His Name: Formula and Variation in the Phaeacian Episode of the *Odyssey*." *TAPA* 119 (1989): 1–13.

Wehrli, F. "Penelope and Telemachus." *Museum Helveticum* 16 (1959): 228–237.

Wender, Dorothea. "In Hades' Halls." In *Twentieth Century Interpretations of the "Odyssey,"* edited by Howard W. Clarke, 112–129. Englewood Cliffs, NJ: Prentice-Hall, 1983.

———. *The Last Scenes of the "Odyssey."* Mnemosyne Supplement 52. Leiden: Brill, 1978.

West, M. L. "Aristophanes of Byzantium's Text of Homer." *CP* 112, no. 1 (2017): 20–44.

———. *The Making of the "Odyssey."* Oxford: Oxford University Press, 2014.

———. "Odyssey and Argonautica." *CQ* 55, no. 1 (2005): 39–64.

West, Stephanie. "An Alternative Nostos for Odysseus." *Liverpool Classical Monthly* 6 (1981): 169–175.

———. "Laertes Revisited." *Proceedings of the Cambridge Philological Society* 35 (1989): 113–143.

———. "Odyssean Stratigraphy." In *Relative Chronology in Early Greek Epic Poetry*, edited by Oivind Anderson and Dag T. T. Haug, 122–137. Cambridge: Cambridge University Press, 2012.

Whallon, William. "How the Shroud for Laertes Became the Robe of Odysseus." *CQ* 50, no. 2 (2000): 331–337.

———. "The Name of Penelope." *GRBS* 3, no. 2/3 (1960): 57–64.

Whitehead, Oliver. "The Funeral of Achilles: An Epilogue to the *Iliad* in Book 24 of the *Odyssey*." *G&R* 31, no. 2 (1984): 119–125.

Whitman, Cedric H. *Homer and the Heroic Tradition*. Cambridge, MA: Harvard University Press, 1958.

———. "The Odyssey and Change." In *Twentieth Century Interpretations of the "Odyssey,"* edited by Howard W. Clarke, 72–91. Englewood Cliffs, NJ: Prentice-Hall, 1983.

Whittaker, Helene. "The Status of Arete in the Phaeacian Episode of the *Odyssey*." *SO* 74 (1999): 140–150.

Willett, Steven J. "Homer: The *Odyssey*." *CJ* 93, no. 2 (1998): 203–206.

Williams, B. 1993. *Shame and Necessity*. Berkeley: University of California Press, 1993.

Williams, Frederick. "Odysseus' Homecoming as a Parody of Homeric Formal Welcomes." *CW* 79 (1986): 395–397.

Wilson, Donna Faye. "Demodokos' *Iliad* and Homer's." In *Approaches to Homer: Ancient and Modern*, edited by Robert J. Rabel, 1–20. Swansea: Classical Press of Wales, 2005.

———. "Lion Kings: Heroes in the Epic Mirror." *Colby Quarterly* 35, no. 2 (2002): 231–254.

Wilson, Emily, trans. *Homer: The Odyssey*. New York: W. W. Norton, 2018.

Wilson, Joe. "Homer and the Will of Zeus." *CL* 32, no. 4 (2007): 150–173.

Winkler, John J. "Penelope's Cunning and Homer's." In *The Constraints of Desire: The Anthropology of Sex and Gender in Ancient Greece*, 129–161. New York: Routledge, 1990.

Wissmann, Jessica. "Athena's 'Unreasonable Advice': The Education of Telemachus in Ancient Interpretations of Homer." *GRBS* 49, no. 3 (2009): 413–452.

Wohl, V. "Standing by the *Stathmos*: The Creation of Sexual Ideology in the *Odyssey*." *Arethusa* 26 (1993): 19–50.

Wong, Siu-ling, Ka-wai Cecilia Chun, and Se-yuen Mak. "Odysseus's Sailboat Dilemma." *Physics Education* 42, no. 2 (2007): 180–184.

Woodhouse, W. J. *The Composition of Homer's "Odyssey."* 1930. Reprint, Oxford: Clarendon, 1969.

Worman, Nancy. "Odysseus, Ingestive Rhetoric, and Euripides' *Cyclops*." *Helios* 29, no. 2 (2002): 101–125.

Wright, G. M., and P. V. Jones, eds. and trans. *Homer: German Scholarship in Translation*. Oxford: Clarendon, 1997.

Wyatt, William F. "Homeric Hiatus." *Glotta* 70 (1992): 20–30.

———. "Penelope's Fat Hand (*Od.* 21. 6–7)." *CP* 73, no. 4 (1978): 343–344.

Yamagata, Naoko. "Clothing and Identity in Homer: The Case of Penelope's Web." *Mnemosyne*, 4th ser., 58, no. 4 (2005): 539–546.

———. "Penelope and Early Recognition: Vlahos, Harsh, and Eustathius." *CL* 38, no. 2 (2011): 122–130.

Zeitlin, Froma. "Figuring Fidelity in Homer's *Odyssey*." In *Playing the Other: Gender and Society in Classical Greek Literature*, 19–52. Chicago: University of Chicago Press, 1996.

Zerba, Michelle. "Odyssean Charisma and the Uses of Persuasion." *AJP* 130, no. 3 (2009): 314–340.

———. "What Penelope Knew: Doubt and Scepticism in the *Odyssey*." *CQ* 59, no. 2 (2009): 295–316.

Zoidis, Evangelos. "Odusseus Outis: Odysseus Nobody." *Arcadia* 39, no. 2 (2004): 382–389.

INDEX

ABOUT THE AUTHOR

Dr. Kostas Myrsiades, professor emeritus of comparative and Greek literature at West Chester University, is a distinguished translator and Neohellenist and the first American to receive the Gold Medallion (1995) for his translations from the Hellenic Society of Translators of Literature, given annually by the Greek government to a scholar from any country. His work in Greek letters is not only demonstrated in his 20 published books and numerous articles on modern and ancient Greek literature but also in the many invited lectures he has delivered for such groups as the Jane Globus Seminar Series Lecture at Baruch College, the Elytis Chair Lecture Series of Poetry and Neohellenic Studies at Rutgers, and the Embassy of Greece/National Library of Canada Lecture at Ottawa. He was the editor of *College Literature*, a quarterly of literary criticism, theory, and pedagogy (1990–2011), which since 1990 has been the recipient of seven awards from the Council of Editors of Learned Journals, including the Phoenix Award for distinguished editorial achievement. Professor Myrsiades was also coeditor of the *Journal of the Hellenic Diaspora* (1991–2010), one of the leading journals in Neohellenic studies.

Printed in the United States
By Bookmasters